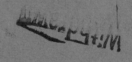

Options For a New Canada

The sharp and overwhelming reaction in Quebec to the failure of the Meech Lake Accord has been unprecedented public support for sovereignty and practically no support for the current form of Canadian federalism. This has led to renewed demands for a major constitutional restructuring which, if unsuccessful, is likely this time around to result in the separation of Quebec from Canada. At the same time there is considerable pressure from many other quarters in Canada for other sorts of constitutional change, such as Senate reform and aboriginal self-government. There are also calls for Canadian federalism to be modernized to provide a more effective political response to the global challenges of the contemporary world.

Recognizing that Canada is facing a renewed and potentially disastrous constitutional impasse, the Business Council on National Issues has commissioned the papers in this book to provide a fresh analysis of our difficult constitutional problems. The contributors include some of Canada's leading academic commentators in the fields of political science, economics, philosophy and law.

These papers do not provide a single blueprint for Canada's future; rather they present a range of possible solutions and arrangements, each with attendant opportunities and risks. Among the alternatives explored are a restructured federalism, a looser federal union with stronger provinces, and an arrangement called "asymmetrical federalism" which would treat Quebec differently than the other nine provinces. Other options include looser forms of confederal economic union, and the possible separation of Canada into two or more independent successor-states.

Choosing among the alternatives will not be easy, but the message of these papers is that if Canadians do not now weigh the alternatives carefully and decide what they want, the options will narrow and could produce unintended and undesired results. The choice is up to Canadians.

Ronald L. Watts and Douglas M. Brown are Director and Associate Director, respectively, of the Institute of Intergovernmental Relations at Queen's University.

The Business Council on National Issues is the senior voice of Canadian business on public policy issues in Canada and abroad.

Options for a New Canada

Edited by
Ronald L. Watts and
Douglas M. Brown

Published in Association with the
Institute of Intergovernmental Relations,
Queen's University and the
Business Council on National Issues,
Ottawa

University of Toronto Press
Toronto Buffalo London

© University of Toronto Press 1991
Toronto Buffalo London
Printed in Canada

ISBN 0-8020-5921-X (cloth)
ISBN 0-8020-6901-0 (paper)

∞

Printed on acid-free paper

Canadian Cataloguing in Publication Data

Main entry under title:

Options for a new Canada

"Published in association with the Institute of Intergovernmental
Relations, Queen's University and the Business Council on National
Issues, Ottawa."
ISBN 0-8020-5921-X (bound)   ISBN 0-8020-6901-0 (pbk.)

1. Canada - Constitutional law - Amendments.
2. Federal government - Canada. 3. Federal-provincial relations -
Canada.* I. Watts, Ronald L. II. Brown, Douglas Mitchell, 1954 - .
III. Queen's University (Kingston, Ont.). Institute of Intergovernmental Relations. IV. Business Council on National Issues.

JL65 1991.077 1991   342.71'03   C91-093812-1

CONTENTS

FOREWORD

Canada is one of the world's most successful countries. By any measurement — economic prosperity, social justice, quality of life — Canadians enjoy a range of advantages among the most generous in the world. Little understood or appreciated by many Canadians is how important a role our political system and government institutions have been in the realization of these achievements. In consistently delivering a high degree of "peace, order and good government," they have provided the stability and the confidence upon which so much has been built. Much of the credit for this success is due to federalism which has allowed for flexibility and diversity in a country marked by its great size, and significant differences in its regions and peoples.

Today, status quo federalism is under attack. In western Canada, the demands for change are growing stronger. And in Quebec, the failure of the Meech Lake Accord has sparked a powerful movement among some for greater autonomy, and among others, for full political sovereignty. These rising expectations for change to Canada's political system come at a time when the country is engaged in a profound economic adjustment, to a large extent imposed by global economic forces.

Recognizing that a sound and workable political system is the prerequisite of progress and success in the economic and social domains, the Business Council on National Issues decided in July 1990, to launch a number of initiatives aimed at achieving a better understanding of the strengths and weaknesses of Canadian federalism as we know it now and to examine ways of making federalism work better in the future. A key part of this initiative was to assemble a group of Canada's leading authorities on constitutional reform to consider options for the country's future constitutional development. Under the leadership of Professor Ronald Watts, Director of the Institute of Intergovernmental Relations at Queen's University, a team of political scientists, economists, lawyers, and constitutional scholars drawn from all parts of Canada worked on the project. The papers in this volume reflect the views of the individual members of the team as they were presented at an all-day symposium sponsored by the Business Council on National Issues in Toronto on 16 January 1991. It is with pride that the Council has agreed to sponsor the work of the project team and to make possible this publication.

As the debate about Canada's future in the coming months intensifies, it is vital that the discussion be based on a sound understanding of the problems and opportunities that face us as a people. The Business Council looks forward to playing a constructive role in the debate and to being guided in part by the excellent insights offered by the papers in this volume.

Thomas P. d'Aquino
President and Chief Executive
Business Council on National Issues

INTRODUCTORY STATEMENT

I would like to offer some thoughts about why this volume has been put together. The Business Council on National Issues has as one of its principal goals the commitment of senior business leaders to the building of strong political institutions in Canada. In the past, this commitment led the Council and its task forces to undertake research, consultation, and advocacy in areas such as the reform of parliament — including the House of Commons and the Senate; ways of improving intergovernmental relations and the operation of the federal system; the reform of the federal public service; and both in the early 1980s and more recently, the reform of the Canadian constitution.

Our work in these areas has been consistent with our mandate as a nonpartisan, nonprofit, organization devoted to resolving national issues — both economic and noneconomic in nature. Our work on governmental matters also is consistent with the belief of every chief executive in the Business Council that a healthy political system is a vital underpinning of a strong economy.

Following the failure of the Meech Lake Accord which, as an organization, we greatly regretted, we immediately faced up to the fact that vital constitutional questions facing Canada remained unresolved and that the debate about Canada's political future would intensify. Accordingly, we were determined that the next and perhaps decisive chapter of this debate should be conducted on the basis of fresh and rational thinking, and that Canadian business leaders should contribute to the debate in a most responsible way. We sought out some of Canada's leading thinkers and practitioners on constitutional matters and launched a major study on Canada's constitutional options under the leadership of Professor Ronald Watts, the Director of the Institute of Intergovernmental Relations, Queen's University. At the Symposium on 16 January 1991, the research team led by Professor Watts tabled their findings and we are pleased to share them with a wider public.

William W. Stinson
Co-chairman, Symposium on
Canada's Constitutional Options

INTRODUCTORY STATEMENT

I am pleased to be associated with this initiative because it deals with a subject of great importance to all of us as Canadians. Bill Stinson has stressed that the business community must get involved. He has pointed to the critical linkage between economic strength and political stability. I would add another perspective. Reform of the constitution and deciding on how to govern ourselves is too important to be left only to politicians and officials. It is the responsibility of all citizens to understand what the issues are and what is at stake. This requires an open mind and access to carefully developed points of view.

Professor Watts and his team who have been working on this project for some six months, were asked at the outset to examine a variety of options for shaping Canada's constitutional future. In the presentations in this volume a number of options are discussed and diverse perspectives are offered on a wide range of issues that cover politics, economics, social dimensions, and culture. The objective of the symposium was not to reach any definitive conclusions but rather to inform and to stimulate thought and debate.

In the coming months, whether we like it or not, the debate about Canada's political future will intensify. It is critical that the debate be constructive and that it lead to change that will be welcomed by the vast majority of Canadians. Canada is a remarkable country. It has a record of success with few parallels in the world. But it is apparent now that some changes to how we govern ourselves will be necessary to ensure that we enter the twenty-first century with the political, economic, and social cohesion that befits a leading industrial power.

I am delighted that so many members of the Business Council demonstrated their interest in this vital subject by being at the symposium on 16 January 1991, and that so many of the special guests we invited accepted our invitation. The presentations throughout the day were stimulating and rewarding.

Guy Saint-Pierre
Co-chairman, Symposium on
Canada's Constitutional Options

ACKNOWLEDGEMENTS

On behalf of the Institute of Intergovernmental Relations at Queen's University and the authors in this volume, we would like to acknowledge our appreciation to the Business Council on National Issues for the support required to pursue the ideas expressed in this volume. The Council funded the independent studies, organized a one-day symposium which provided an opportunity for comment and discussion prior to their revision for publication, and provided resources for the revision and editing of the papers in this volume. The views expressed by the authors are their own and do not necessarily reflect the views of the Business Council on National Issues or the Institute of Intergovernmental Relations.

The publication of a volume of papers so soon after their first delivery at the symposium sponsored by the Business Council on 16 January 1991 has required the cooperation of many people. The editors would like to thank in particular each and every one of the authors for their cheerful acceptance of our very tight publication deadlines. Thanks are also due to Tom D'Aquino and the staff at the Business Council, and to Virgil Duff and the staff at the University of Toronto Press for ensuring the arrangements for timely publication.

We would like to express our appreciation to the staff of the Institute of Intergovernmental Relations for a superb effort in preparing this text under the pressure of a very constrained schedule. We would especially thank Valerie Jarus who with the help of Patti Candido, Darrel Reid and Lita San Pedro prepared the text for publication, and Marilyn Banting for proofreading.

Ronald L. Watts
Douglas M. Brown
Kingston
February 1991

NOTES ABOUT THE AUTHORS

Robin Boadway is the Sir Edward Peacock Professor of Economics at Queen's University. He has been at Queen's University since 1973 and served as Head of the Department of Economics from 1981-86. He is editor of the *Canadian Journal of Economics*. His research interests are in tax policy and fiscal federalism. He is author or co-author of the following books or monographs in the area: *Public Sector Economics* (1984); *Welfare Economics* (1984); *Canadian Tax Policy* (1984); *Intergovernmental Transfers in Canada* (1980); *Equalization in a Federal State* (1982); *Taxes on Capital Income in Canada* (1987), and *Taxation and Savings in Canada* (1988).

Alan C. Cairns is Professor of Political Science at the University of British Columbia and, from 1983-85 was a Research Director for the Royal Commission on the Economic Union and Development Prospects for Canada. He is the author of numerous articles, some of which have been collected in the volume edited by Douglas Williams, *Constitution, Government and Society in Canada* (1988). He is also the author of *Constitutional Change in Contemporary Canada: Interpretive Essays* (forthcoming, McGill-Queen's Press).

Thomas J. Courchene is the Director of the School of Policy Studies at Queen's University, where he holds the Stauffer-Dunning Chair and is a member of the Department of Economics, the School of Public Administration and the Faculty of Law. He is the author of well over a hundred books and articles on Canadian policy issues, including *Social Policy in the 1990s: Agenda for Reform* (1987); *Equalization Payments: Past, Present and Future* (1984); *Economic Management and the Division of Powers* (1986); and *What Does Ontario Want?*(1988 Robarts Lecture, York University) (1988).

Alain-G. Gagnon is Associate Professor in the Department of Political Science at McGill University, and is a member of the International Political Science Association Research Committee on Comparative Federalism and Federations. In 1983-84, he worked for the Federal-Provincial Relations Office, of the Government of Canada. His publications include *Quebec: State and Society* (1984); *Social Scientists and Politics in Canada* (1988); *Canadian Parties in*

Transition (1989); *Canadian Politics: An Introduction to the Discipline* (1990); and *Quebec: Beyond the Quiet Revolution* (1990).

David C. Hawkes is Adjunct Professor in the School of Public Administration at Carleton University. From 1975 to 1982 he held senior posts with the Government of Saskatchewan, including Deputy Minister of Intergovernmental Affairs. As the former Associate Director of the Institute of Intergovernmental Relations, Queen's University he was both manager and principal researcher for the major project on "Aboriginal Peoples and Constitutional Reform." His recent works include *Aboriginal Peoples and Government Responsibility: Exploring Federal and Provincial Roles* (1989).

Guy Laforest is Assistant Professor, Department of Political Science, Université Laval. He received his Ph.D. from McGill in 1987, and taught for two years at the University of Calgary. He is currently working on a book-length manuscript on the fate of political duality in Canada. His articles have been published in journals such as *Government and Opposition; Les Cahiers de Droit; Canadian Journal of Political Science; Recherches sociographiques*; and *Politique*. He serves as French book-review editor for the *Canadian Journal of Political Science.*

Peter M. Leslie is Professor of Political Studies and former director of the Institute of Intergovernmental Relations at Queen's University. He received his M.Sc. (Economics) from the University of London School of Economics and his Ph.D. from Queen's University. From 1988 to 1990, he was Assistant Secretary to the Cabinet (Policy Development) in the Federal-Provincial Relations Office, Government of Canada. His interests have focused on Canadian politics and political economy, federalism and public policy. Among his publications are: *Canadian Universities: 1980 and Beyond* (1980); *Federal State, National Economy* (1987); and, as editor, *Canada: The State of the Federation, 1985, 1986,* and *1987-88.*

John N. McDougall is Associate Professor of Political Science at the University of Western Ontario and a Visiting Professor at the School of Policy Studies, Queen's University, for the 1990-91 academic year. He received a Ph.D. in political science from the University of Alberta in 1975. He is the author of *Fuels and the National Policy* (1982), a history of Canadian energy policy, and several articles on Canadian resource policies. His recently-completed book on Eric Kierans' ideas on political economy is being reviewed for publication.

Peter Meekison is Professor of Political Science and Vice President (Academic) at the University of Alberta. During the period 1974-84 he served for ten years with the Alberta Department of Federal and Intergovernmental Affairs, the latter seven years as Deputy Minister. He was involved in constitutional discussions during that period. He has served as an advisor on constitutional matters to the Alberta Government since 1986. He received his Ph.D. from Duke University and has published in the area of Canadian federalism.

David Milne is Professor of Political Studies at the University of Prince Edward Island. A graduate of the University of Toronto and of Queen's University, he is a well-known analyst of Canadian federalism and constitutional law. His books include *The Canadian Constitution* (1989), soon to be issued in a third edition, and *Tug of War: Ottawa and the Provinces Under Trudeau and Mulroney* (1986).

Patrick Monahan is Associate Professor at Osgoode Hall Law School of York University and Director of the York University Centre for Public Law and Public Policy. He served as Senior Policy Advisor in the Office of Ontario Premier David Peterson during the Meech Lake negotiations. He is the author of *Meech Lake: The Inside Story* (forthcoming), and *Politics and the Constitution: The Charter, Federalism and the Supreme Court of Canada* (1987).

Bradford W. Morse is Professor of Law and Director of Graduate Studies in Law at the University of Ottawa. He has been involved in many facets of aboriginal legal issues over the past 17 years including serving as legal counsel to a number of First Nations and aboriginal organizations, as well as currently serving as Director of Research to the Aboriginal Justice Inquiry of Manitoba. His recent works include *Aboriginal Peoples and the Law: Indian, Metis and Inuit Rights in Canada* (1989).

Peter H. Russell is Professor of Political Science and Director of Graduate Studies in the Department of Political Science at the University of Toronto. He was educated at the University of Toronto and Oxford University. He has written several books and articles on constitutional and judicial politics including *Leading Constitutional Decisions* (1982); and (with R. Knopff and T. Morton) *Federalism and the Charter* (rev. ed. 1989). Currently he is President of the Canadian Political Science Association.

Dan Soberman received his B.A. and LL.B. from Dalhousie University and his LL.M. from Harvard University. He taught at Dalhousie, 1955-57, and has been at Queen's University since 1957, where he was Dean of the Faculty of Law, 1968-77. His main areas of research have been business law and federalism. In addition to a number of articles in these fields, he is co-author of *The Law and Business Administration in Canada* (1987). He also chairs federal and provincial human rights tribunals.

Katherine Swinton is a Professor at the Faculty of Law, University of Toronto. She has a B.A. from the University of Alberta, an LL.B. from Osgoode Hall Law School of York University, and an LL.M. from Yale University. She has numerous publications in constitutional and labour law, including a recent book on the *Supreme Court and Canadian Federalism: The Laskin-Dickson Years*(1990).

Charles Taylor is Professor of Philosophy and Political Science at McGill University. He took his B.A. at McGill, and his D.Phil at Oxford, where he also taught for a number of years. He was the Chichele Professor of Social and Political Theory at the University of Oxford and Fellow of All Souls College from 1976 to 1981. He is the author of numerous articles, and his books include *Pattern of Politics* (1970), *Hegel* (1975), *Social Theory as Practice* (1983) and *Source of the Self* (1989).

Ronald L. Watts is Director of the Institute of Intergovernmental Relations and Professor of Political Studies at Queen's University where he was Principal and Vice-Chancellor from 1974-84. He served as a commissioner on the Task Force on Canadian Unity and as a consultant to the Government of Canada during the constitutional negotiations in 1980. He specializes in the creation, operation, and disintegration of old and new federations. His publications include *Federalism in Multicultural Societies* (1970); (with D. Smiley) *Intra-state Federalism in Canada* (1986) and (edited with P.M. Leslie or D.M. Brown) *Canada: The State of the Federation, 1987-88, 1989,* and *1990.*

I

Introduction

1

An Overview

Ronald L. Watts

INTRODUCTION

This book contains the papers prepared for a two-stage project sponsored by the Business Council on National Issues to examine possible options for Canada's constitutional future following the demise of the Meech Lake Accord. The first phase was the preparation of a paper by the Institute of Intergovernmental Relations at Queen's University, originally released in September 1990, identifying in broad terms the strategic options. That paper in revised and updated form is now included as Chapter 2 in this collection. In the second phase of the project 13 additional studies were prepared analyzing these options and various aspects and issues relating to them. These were written by a team of political scientists, economists, lawyers and constitutional scholars drawn from Queen's University and other parts of Canada coordinated by the Institute of Intergovernmental Relations at Queen's University. It must be emphasized that these are independent studies prepared at the request of the Business Council on National Issues, and that the views expressed are those of their authors and do not represent the official views of the Council or of the Institute. The original papers were presented at a one-day symposium sponsored by the Business Council on National Issues held in Toronto on 16 January 1991 which provided an opportunity for comment and reactions to this research prior to its formal publication. These papers together with two formal commentaries on them have been revised in the light of that discussion for inclusion in this volume.

Two preliminary points should be made about the papers in this collection. First, the authors were asked not simply to diagnose the current problems, but to seek solutions or at least possible directions for solutions. Second, the papers were not produced to advocate a single blueprint for future constitutional reform but rather to examine the implications of various possible alternatives.

Thus, they present a considerable range of views, although there are many points of interconnection among them.

THE CHAPTERS AND AUTHORS

Part II contains a single chapter "Canada's Constitutional Options: An Outline," which identifies in summary form the issues and options for Canada's future without trying to choose among them. It was prepared by the Institute of Intergovernmental Relations under the direction of Ronald Watts. It provided a starting point for the discussions in the subsequent chapters in this volume. The paper deals with three sets of questions: (a) strategic factors affecting the consideration of constitutional options, i.e., the main driving forces that will shape or constrain the outcome; (b) options for the constitutional review process, since negotiating the processes employed will themselves be a critical element in determining the outcome; and (c) options for future institutional structures. The latter are of three types. In the first category are federal systems where sovereignty is constitutionally divided between central and provincial governments. Five federal variants are identified. These range from the status quo to a variety of forms of restructured federalism. The second category consists of confederal arrangements. These are structures where sovereignty ultimately resides with the constituent political units but a superstructure is established to deal with common policies subject to the assent of the constituent units. Three variants of this type are identified. Among these is sovereignty-association. The third category relates to the establishment of two or more politically and economically independent successor-states.

Part III contains three chapters dealing with the context for future constitutional options. Thomas Courchene of Queen's University and John N. McDougall of the University of Western Ontario, deal in Chapter 3 with the global and domestic economic context as well as some other factors that will affect the character of any constitutional development. Charles Taylor of McGill University, examines in Chapter 4 the shared and divergent values between Quebec and the rest-of-Canada and the possibilities of reconciling different levels of diversity. In Chapter 5 Alan Cairns of the University of British Columbia, identifies three conflicting concepts of equality — equality of citizens, equality of provinces, and equality of the two communities represented by Quebec and the rest-of-Canada — and suggests that these can be reconciled only through the adoption of a radically asymmetric federalism, difficult as such an arrangement may be to work out.

Part IV contains five chapters examining the basic options for future constitutional structures and the processes for arriving at them. These are analyzed with particular attention to their feasibility and desirability. Guy Laforest of Laval University, describes in a compelling way in Chapter 6 the emerging consensus within Quebec in favour of abandoning federalism for a looser confederal structure, as expressed in the public presentations before the Bélanger-Campeau Commission. In Chapter 7 Peter Leslie of Queen's University emphasizes that the feasibility of different options for future structures is closely related to the processes by which they might be achieved. After examining the alternative scenarios he concludes that the only realistic alternatives are a reconstituted federalism or two or more independent successor-states. In Chapter 8 Peter Russell of the University of Toronto examines ways in which the process of constitutional development in Canada might be made more open and more effective, and he proposes the use of a particular form of constituent assembly. Patrick Monahan of York University provides in Chapter 9 a commentary on some of the issues raised in the three preceding chapters. Bradford Morse of the University of Ottawa and David Hawkes of Carleton University review in Chapter 10 possible alternatives for participation of the aboriginal peoples in the general process of constitutional revision.

In Part V two papers assess the relevance of external models. Daniel Soberman of Queen's University looks in Chapter 11 at the relevance of the European Community as a model for Canada and offers some important cautions. In Chapter 12 Alain Gagnon of McGill University seeks lessons that might be learned by Canadians from the operations of other federations elsewhere.

Part VI contains chapters examining possible areas of constitutional adjustment. The first two chapters examine possible adjustments to the distribution of powers: one from the point of view of an economist, the other from the point of view of a political scientist. In Chapter 13 Robin Boadway of Queen's University analyzes the economic criteria that might be applied to an adjustment in the distribution of powers between federal and provincial governments. In Chapter 14 Peter Meekison of the University of Alberta writes on possible modifications to the federal-provincial distribution of powers as a political scientist who has had practical experience in constitutional deliberations. He looks in particular at the mechanisms that might contribute to flexibility and pragmatic adjustment. In Chapter 15 David Milne of the University of Prince Edward Island explores the history of pressures for provincial asymmetry and for provincial equality in the Canadian federation. He advocates concurrent jurisdiction with provincial paramountcy as a practical device for reconciling the two principles. In Chapter 16 Ronald Watts of Queen's University examines possible revisions to the common federative institutions to determine which are likely to be both desirable and feasible. Finally, in Chapter 17 Katherine Swinton of the University of Toronto provides a commentary on the preceding chapters in this part.

CONCLUSIONS

The papers in this collection do not present a single view. As already noted, the intention was not to advocate a single position. The intention was rather to examine the various possible options and the related issues in more depth and to draw out their implications. It was hoped that this approach would contribute to the consideration and evaluation of these options and reduce the dangers of miscalculation by those involved in the constitutional deliberations.

The range of analyses in these papers and the discussion at the symposium held to review the original papers made clear the complexity and difficulty of the issues that will have to be resolved. Nevertheless, despite the apparent variety of views expressed in the papers and at the symposium it is possible to determine some points of convergence and some tentative conclusions. For example, some approaches and options were clearly identified as unlikely to be fruitful when measured by the tests of desirability or feasibility. In my view seven conclusions emerge from the papers and the discussion at the symposium.

First, a common theme in all the papers, although with differing degrees of emphasis, is a recognition of the extreme seriousness of the current political and constitutional polarization in Canada. Laforest makes the point by suggesting that the federal regime created in 1867 is now, following the demise of the Meech Lake Accord, clinically dead as far as Quebec is concerned. Virtually all the authors agree that the status quo unmodified will be untenable for more than an interim negotiating period of a year or two. Courchene, Taylor and Cairns analyze why this is the case. And as Leslie suggests, if we fail to reach agreement on substantial constitutional change, the result is likely in the end to be not the status quo but two or more successor-states. Authors in this collection have not limited themselves to diagnosis, however. Each, while recognizing the difficulties, has attempted to suggest possible directions for resolution. There are variations among the authors in the degree to which they call for comprehensive change or pragmatic incremental adaptation, but all agree on the seriousness of the situation and the need to address these problems immediately.

Second, implicit in these chapters, and certainly made explicit in the discussion at the symposium, is the recognition that any constitutional revision must embrace the concerns of western Canada, of the Atlantic provinces, of Ontario, of the aboriginal peoples, and of the Territories. The next stage of constitutional revision cannot be limited to just a Quebec round. Any effort at constitutional revision that does not include an accommodation of the wider deeply felt concerns and interests across Canada, difficult as that may be, is virtually doomed to failure because the procedures required for constitutional amendment require broad support across the whole country.

Third, it is clear that account will have to be taken both of economic issues and of the values and the vision of the country that is to be embodied in any resolution of the current problems. Courchene and Boadway examine the former and Taylor and Cairns emphasize the latter. On the economic front important objectives will be to achieve a more effective and internationally competitive economic union, to accommodate the economic interests of all the regions of Canada in that union and to take account of issues of equity. But differing values and visions of the country will also have to be reconciled. A common theme running through many of the chapters including those of Taylor, Cairns, Courchene, Laforest, Gagnon and Swinton concerns the different views of the Charter of Rights and Freedoms and the related different implicit conceptions of the country held in Quebec and in the rest-of-Canada. Taylor and Cairns suggest that a resolution might require a different application of the Charter in Quebec. Many Canadians outside Quebec who see the Charter as a pillar of the constitution embodying a statement of the rights of all citizens across Canada, will be extremely reluctant to accept that. But the choice for them may come down to one of two ways of limiting the application of the Charter: either limiting its application within a Canada containing Quebec, or having a uniform application of the Charter in a Canada-without-Quebec.

Fourth, a number of the authors point to the dangers of resorting to the "legal discontinuity" route for constitutional revision. Such a route would be one going outside the existing constitutional amendment procedure. An example would be a unilateral declaration of independence by Quebec prior to further negotiation, thus breaking the legal continuity with the existing constitution. Laforest emphasizes Quebec's *de facto* sovereignty if it chooses to exercise it. He is correct. But others especially Leslie, and also Russell, Courchene, Milne and Watts point to the likely results of Quebec exercising its *de facto* sovereignty by separating first and then attempting to negotiate a new association. Strong emotions are likely to be aroused in the rest-of-Canada by such an action.

Furthermore, there are complications arising from the lack of institutions to negotiate on behalf of the rest-of-Canada as a corporate entity. These factors are likely to make remote the prospects for agreement upon a future reassociation following such a scenario. Thus, breaking up as the first step to reformulating federalism or a new form of association is likely in the end to lead to a permanent breakup. But if the "legal discontinuity" route is to be avoided, the "legal continuity" route employing the current constitutional amendment procedures must be made sufficiently effective to produce substantial change. Failure to do so would simply lead Quebec in frustration to turn to the legal discontinuity scenario. The choice appears to be stark: make the existing constitutional amendment process productive or risk fragmentation into two or more successor-states. Russell analyzes and suggests possible prenegotiation and negotiating processes for developing sufficient consensus prior to employing the current formal constitutional amendment processes. In addition, Leslie, Milne and Meekison suggest some pragmatic devices that might help in arriving at a flexible accommodation. While the authors point to the difficulties and present a variety of suggestions, there is general agreement that to avoid the dangers of the legal discontinuity scenario, arrangements must be developed to ensure that the current procedures for constitutional change are able to produce significant results.

Fifth, a common theme running through the discussion at the symposium was the critical importance of giving careful attention to the processes by which constitutional revision is to be negotiated. These processes are important because they will shape and determine the outcome. Russell's chapter focuses particularly on this issue but a number of other papers also draw attention to its importance. Both Russell and Leslie emphasize the need to work out processes of public discussion and negotiation that will then enable the current constitutional amendment procedures to produce significant results in the end. It is generally recognized that processes of elite accommodation based solely on negotiations among first ministers will no longer be acceptable and that, both in the prenegotiation and post-negotiation ratification stages, the public will have to play an important part. Furthermore, as Taylor, Courchene, Morse and Hawkes, and Russell point out, the deliberations will have to be broader in scope than just a consideration of Quebec's concerns. Any substantial constitutional amendment will require widespread support for ratification under the existing requirements for constitutional amendment. It will, therefore, have to take into account the concerns and interests of other parts of Canada and of the aboriginal peoples. Attention is also drawn by some authors to two complicating factors affecting the processes of deliberation and negotiation. Cairns, Leslie and Russell point to the difficulty of articulating the "voice" of Canada-outside-Quebec. Russell goes on to suggest that it may be necessary to institutionalize this voice as the first stage in a two-stage process involving a constituent assembly. A second complication to which Cairns draws attention arises from the intertwining of two concurrent sets of negotiations. He describes these as first, the "renewing federalism" game and second, the "negotiating independence arrangements" game. Because governments outside Quebec have no mandate to negotiate the latter, Cairns suggests that it will be important for nongovernmental organizations to play a leading role in articulating the views of a potentially independent Canada without Quebec.

Sixth, many of the authors suggest that the confederal alternatives are neither desirable nor feasible. Laforest makes a good case for a confederal solution as providing in ideal terms an innovative solution that would accommodate an apparently emerging consensus within Quebec and provide a model for other countries. But many of the other authors pour cold water on confederal solutions in terms of their practicality. Cairns and Leslie point to the difficulties in negotiating a bicommunal confederal structure because of the institutional incapacity of Canada-outside-Quebec to negotiate as a single unit. Soberman points out that the European Community which began as a confederal structure is in fact moving to correct the economic deficiencies of its confederal structure by evolving towards a more federal structure. Watts, on the basis of historical and comparative evidence, notes the weaknesses and instability of confederal central institutions where these have been established. Thus, a common theme running through a number of papers is that confederal structures, of which sovereignty-association is one variant, have some attractiveness in theory, but are not promising in practical terms as a long-term solution. At best such arrangements have elsewhere only provided a transitional solution.

Seventh, the preferred option for the future constitutional structure of Canada advanced by most of the authors is some form of restructured or reconstituted federalism. In terms of feasibility most of them take the position that, since the status quo unamended cannot survive and since confederal solutions are unlikely to be practicable, the only realistic alternatives come down to either a substantially modified federal structure or two or more politically and economically independent successor states. Faced with this choice most of the authors see the preferred option as the former. Most also recognize that any restructuring will have to involve two major aspects: adjustments to the distribution of powers between the federal and provincial governments; and alterations to the common federative institutions to improve their representativeness and effectiveness. While the primary focus of Quebec appears to be on the former (i.e., powers) and of western Canada and the Atlantic provinces on the latter (i.e., central institutions), both aspects will be important to improving the effective functioning of the Canadian federal system.

While there is a general consensus among the authors (with the emphatic exception of Laforest) on the desirability of a restructured federalism, there is considerable variation among them concerning the form which such a restructured federation might take. Courchene and Monahan favour a general decentralization. Cairns and Taylor suggest a radically asymmetric relationship for Quebec within the federation. Milne and Meekison emphasize a variety of arrangements enabling pragmatic adjustments in the distribution of powers. Leslie and Boadway point to the need for a rebalancing in the distribution of powers. Leslie suggests, furthermore, that there might have to be a blend of these different elements, some achieved through formal constitutional amendments and others through pragmatic political arrangements. Clearly the papers taken together do not provide a single common proposal for a restructured federation. Instead, what they do is identify a variety of arrangements worthy of consideration in the expectation that the ultimate resolution will have to arise out of negotiation over each element. Above all, we must be wary of allowing simplistic labels for different possible structures to constrain the possibility of negotiating pragmatic solutions.

Despite this broad consensus that some form of reconstituted federation is the most desirable and feasible option, in many of the chapters there is a recognition of the difficulties of achieving such a resolution. These difficulties relate to getting Quebec's agreement to a restructured federalism, given the strong pressure for some form of confederal relationship being urged upon the Bélanger-Campeau Commission. And they relate to finding a solution that will both satisfy Quebec and at the same time accommodate the interests of other parts of Canada.

There are clearly differences among the authors in terms of the strategy advocated for reconciling within a restructured federation the pressures from Quebec for greater autonomy and distinctiveness and the pressures from the rest-of-Canada for a continued substantial role for the federal government and for equality among the provinces. One path, advocated by Courchene and Monahan, is to adopt a considerable transfer of powers to all the provinces. This approach is based on two premises: the aversion of Canada-outside-Quebec to any "special status" and the economic desirability in any case of greater decentralization. A second path advocated especially by Cairns but discussed by a number of other authors, is to accept a substantial measure of asymmetry between Quebec and the other provinces. This would enable Quebec to achieve a larger measure of autonomy in certain fields in order to maintain its distinctiveness but enable the citizens of the other nine provinces to continue to obtain the benefits of federal common action in those fields. To those who argue that special status is a nonstarter, it may be worth pointing out that greater autonomy for one province does not mean that the citizens of other provinces would benefit less. Indeed the citizens of these other provinces would continue to get the real benefits of common federal action which the more autonomous province gives up. A third path, advocated by Leslie and Boadway, would involve a rebalancing in the distribution of powers including elements of the first two approaches. Given the general acceptance, even in Quebec, of the need for a stronger economic union, the federal role in this area might be enhanced. At the same time, greater economic efficiency might require decentralization in some other areas. In some specific areas Quebec's special concerns might be met by introducing elements of asymmetry.

Among those who see a solution through some form of federal asymmetry there are also two distinct strategies advocated by the authors of these papers. Meekison and Milne, recognizing the emphasis upon equality of provinces and the aversion to special status in Canada-outside-Quebec, advocate a piecemeal approach. Formal equality of provinces would be retained, but Quebec's needs would be achieved by a variety of constitutional devices enabling considerable *de facto* asymmetry. In the symposium there was considerable interest in these proposals, but there was some doubt whether such arrangements would by themselves be sufficient to meet the symbolic change that Quebec seeks, a point which Katherine Swinton raises in her commentary.

An alternative and more daring strategy is implicit in Taylor's appeal that we recognize in the constitution the deeper level of diversity represented by Quebec and by the aboriginal peoples. In relation to Quebec the implications are spelled out by Cairns when he argues that the only solution to Quebec-Canada tensions within a federal arrangement is one that openly recognizes Quebec's asymmetrical status. This he suggests be done through a differential distribution of powers assigned to Quebec, a more limited role of federal MPs from Quebec in voting in the areas where Quebec has greater autonomy, and some limits on the application of the Charter of Rights and Freedoms in Quebec. Cairns acknowledges that critics will point to the reluctance of Canadians outside Quebec to accept the formal recognition of Quebec's distinctiveness in the Meech Lake Accord. He argues, however, that the large and explicit move to full asymmetric status together with its implications for the more limited role of federal MPs from Quebec, may prove more widely acceptable than the relatively modest move to a distinct society proposed in the Meech Lake Accord. Cairns clearly recognizes that agreement on such a revision would at the very least be difficult, but he suggests that it may be, nevertheless, the only way to resolve Quebec-Canada differences within a single federal framework.

It is perhaps a recognition of the difficulties of each of these strategies that leads Leslie to suggest that any resolution may have to encompass a pragmatic blend of both the daring and the incremental approaches. He suggests, therefore, a combination of practical adjustments and some fundamental constitutional amendments. The basic issue, however, will be whether in any future negotiations we will be able to find the right balance to satisfy the variety of concerns that will be brought into play.

Readers of this collection of papers will no doubt be dismayed by the bewildering complexity and difficulty of the problems identified and of the challenge that lies ahead. But the issues are not simple, nor are the solutions. An understanding of their complexity is a prerequisite to reaching an effective resolution.

In the negotiations of the next year or two, the continuity of Canada as we have known it will be seriously at risk, but the current situation may also provide us with the opportunity to create a new constitutional structure that will deal more satisfactorily with the changing concerns of Canadians all across the country. The clear choice seems to be between a radical redesign of the federation or a number of separate successor-states. Mere resistance to change and efforts to maintain the status quo unaltered do not appear to any of the authors in this volume, nor of the participants of the symposium, to be feasible alternatives. But none of the authors is under the illusion that the task will be easy. It will call for a careful rational calculation of both the desirability and feasibility of the likely alternative scenarios and their outcomes. Above all we must minimize the possibility of taking irrevocable steps without recognizing the ultimate consequences and the constraints that will result from them. We should also avoid assuming that a constitution's task is to embody and impose one single vision upon the country; the true task of any federal constitution is to provide a framework that can embrace and encompass the diversity of visions existing within a country. Emotion and imagination will play an important role in influencing public choices. Any resolution will require, therefore, more than just mechanical fixes. It will require a renewed vision, a tolerance of Canada's diversity, and a will to resolve differences.

Once before, in 1864-67, Canadians responded to a constitutional impasse by overcoming their differences and agreeing upon an imaginative and creative solution — the Confederation of 1867. Now, after a century and a quarter during which conditions have changed so much, it is time for us to rise again to the challenge by creating a new and imaginative constitutional resolution.

II

An Outline of the Options

2

Canada's Constitutional Options:
An Outline

Ronald L. Watts

INTRODUCTION

With the demise of the Meech Lake Accord, Canada as a federation enters a critical phase. The relatively tranquil immediate aftermath during the latter half of 1990 may suggest that current constitutional arrangements will continue, requiring only minor incremental adjustments. But it is more likely that the next two or three years will be a period of tension and uncertainty with the future of Canada as a whole being questioned and constitutional issues dominating the political agenda. The debate over the Accord and its demise has introduced new political dynamics: a growing French-English polarization over the status of Quebec; preparation by Quebec to bring forward more radical demands in the spring of 1991; challenges by western Canada to the dominance of central Canada; and a weakened ability of the national political parties to aggregate and integrate regional interests. Canada is about to embark on a discussion about its constitutional future more critical than any in its history. The continuity of Canada may be threatened but this may also be an opportunity to negotiate a new constitutional structure that will deal more satisfactorily with the changing concerns of Canadians across the country.

Three sets of questions are outlined in this paper:

- strategic factors affecting the consideration of constitutional options, i.e., the main driving forces that will shape or constrain the outcome;
- options for the constitutional review process, since the processes employed will themselves be a critical element in determining the outcome; and
- options for future institutional structures.

STRATEGIC FACTORS

The Global Context

Global interdependence. Increasing global interdependence in economic and security matters has perforated the reality of political sovereignty and made the concept of the nation-state as the ultimate political entity increasingly obsolescent. The nation-state is proving both too small and too large to meet the full needs of citizens.

Consequent concurrent pressures for integration and disintegration. Canada is not alone in facing political pressures both for integration and for decentralization. This is a global phenomenon of the late twentieth century. There have been potent concurrent pressures: for larger political units capable of fostering economic unity and enhancing security and, at the same time, for smaller political units more sensitive to their electorates and capable of expressing regional distinctiveness and ethnic, linguistic or historically derived diversity. The result has been a variety of forms of federalism (many of them varying considerably from the older traditional models) each attempting to reconcile the apparently contradictory dual pressures. In dealing with our own contemporary Canadian problems we may benefit from an understanding of these dual pressures and the variety of political institutional forms that have been developed in response elsewhere.

The impact of the global information society. The rapidity of information dissemination and the role of the electronic media now makes elite accommodation and brokerage politics as the major means for achieving political accommodation more difficult.

The Canadian Context

Economic factors. Regional and interprovincial trade patterns in goods, services, investment and migration will provide the incentives and disincentives for the positions taken by different provinces and groups (e.g., Premier Peterson's statement, 10 August 1990, that Ontario in 1989 exported $35 billion worth of goods to other provinces, including $16 billion to Quebec, and imported $13 billion from Quebec). A significant aspect of the economic context is where the control and ownership of businesses is concentrated.

International pressures and constraints upon trade elsewhere will also have a bearing upon the perceived benefits and requirements for economic integration. Particularly important is the orientation of the regional economies to southern markets enhancing north-south pulls sometimes at the expense of east-west ones, and the impact of the operation of the Free Trade Agreement with the United States.

Another important economic factor leading to pressures for decentralization is the perception in certain sectors of the business community, not only in Quebec but elsewhere, that the current deficit problems of Canada have been produced by the overextended activities of the federal government and by the inefficiency of the large overlaps in the activities of the federal and provincial governments.

Social and demographic factors. The predominantly English-French duality of nineteenth century Canada, is now cut across, as a result of more recent immigration, by regional and ethnic diversity and hence by a much greater variety of interests and values within the Canadian mosaic of the 1990s.

The erosion of uniting beliefs. Traditionally Canadians have emphasized the importance of compromise and the recognition of diversity as essential elements in continued federal unity. The past decade, however, has seen the emphasis instead on issues of rights and equality. The Charter has placed an emphasis upon the predominance of individual rights at the expense of collective ones (although it does contain collective rights). Provincial equality has been stressed at the expense of asymmetry (of which there were elements in the original 1867 constitution, e.g., sections 93(2), 94 and 133 relating to Quebec). For its part Quebec has been preoccupied with asserting its own rights and equality as a province in relation to the rest-of-Canada. Thus, of the traditional political ideals of "Liberalism, Equality and Fraternity," preoccupation with the first two has led to a neglect of the compromises necessary for achieving the third.

The impact of the Charter. Since 1982 there has been an insistence by a host of new constitutional actors — women, aboriginals, visible minorities, official language minorities, the disabled and others — upon their participation in constitutional reform processes in order to protect their constitutional identities. This "constitutional minoritarianism" complicates the processes for constitutional change.

Immediate Conditions

Growing polarization between Quebec and the rest-of-Canada since June 1990. Since 1980 Quebec has expected a new constitutional deal. The rejection of the Meech Lake Accord in June 1990 has changed many attitudes there, arousing an emotional sense of rejection. Previous supporters of federalism are disillusioned and opinion surveys indicate a growing majority in Quebec favouring political independence. While a consensus on what *sovereignty* might mean in practice has not yet solidified, it is clear that there will be pressure for a radical change from the status quo. The public deliberations of the Commission on the Political and Constitutional Future of Quebec (Bélanger-Campeau) and the

release of the report of the Constitutional Committee of the Quebec Liberal
Party (Allaire) provide evidence of this.

Opinion surveys indicate that the rest-of-Canada has at the same time become
increasingly less supportive of Quebec's aspirations. There is growing opposition to demands for the recognition of its distinct society interpreted as a
"special status," a feeling that Quebec has had more than its fair share of
influence in Ottawa and is the spoiled child of the Canadian federation, and
increasing acceptance of the idea that Quebec will eventually separate anyway.
Some of this opposition in the rest-of-Canada comes from centralists who see
devolution in Quebec as undermining central jurisdiction, and some comes from
decentralists who insist that devolution should apply not just to Quebec but
equally to all provinces. The hardening of attitudes on both sides of the divide
between Quebec and the rest-of-Canada will make a resolution even more
difficult than in the 1987-90 period.

Regional attitudes. The post-Meech Lake attitudes in the various regions,
provinces and territories will affect what is achievable. Some recent surveys
have suggested an increasingly centrifugal character of attitudes across Canada
in terms of increased regional identification, decline in the importance Canadians attach to various symbols of Canadian identity, general preference for
reduction in areas of federal government jurisdiction, and widespread dissatisfaction of citizens in most provinces with their share of the national pie. How
much this is derived from hostility to the federal government of the day and
how much from changes in fundamental attitudes to the federal regime is
difficult to determine. Countering this evidence of centrifugal attitudes is the
fact that much of the opposition to the Meech Lake Accord was expressed in
terms of opposition to any weakening of the central government. In any case,
the particular constitutional concerns of western Canada, the Atlantic provinces, Ontario and the Territories will have to be taken into account to get
agreement on any constitutional revision.

Aboriginal land claims and self-government. As events during the summer of
1990 have made amply clear, the issues of aboriginal land claims and self-
government can no longer be left out of consideration in any major constitutional deliberations. This will make more complex any efforts to resolve the
shape of Canada's constitutional future, and will have important implications
for the appropriate processes by which constitutional revision is to be carried
out.

The decline in the aggregative capacity of national parties. The increasing
difficulties which all three national parties, the Progressive Conservatives, the
Liberals, and the New Democratic Party, are currently having in embracing
regional views across Canada, and the rise of new parties and groups such as

the Reform Party and the Bloc Québécois are likely to undermine the ability of Parliament to achieve a resolution.

Short-run economic conditions. The fiscal difficulties and the deficit of the federal government will limit its ability to use financial incentives to induce intergovernmental agreement on constitutional revision. A further major economic slow down or negative signals from the international business community might temper the drive for independence in Quebec or the willingness of other Canadians to contemplate weakening the central government.

The Gulf War. Given Quebec's traditional isolationist outlook to international conflicts, this war may help to widen the gap between Quebec and the rest-of-Canada. Furthermore, preoccupation with the Gulf War may reduce the attention that Canadians outside Quebec are willing to give to the urgent issues of constitutional revision.

Strategic Objectives

The primary task for Canadians will be to devise a constitutional framework that balances the desires for effective economic and political association on the one hand and for adequate expression of cultural, economic and political diversity across Canada on the other. A basic choice that will have to be made is whether the primary objectives are to be solely economic, i.e., continuing and strengthening the common market and internal trade within the space that is currently Canada, or whether they are to be more widely-based embracing shared political and cultural values while recognizing diversity. The debates over the Free Trade Agreement and the Meech Lake Accord indicate that broader values are important to many Canadians. The choice of objectives will have an important bearing on the selection of appropriate processes for constitutional change since these processes will play a critical role in determining the likely outcome.

In evaluating constitutional alternatives two kinds of questions will need to be considered. The first is a normative question: what is the desirability of each alternative in the light of broad conceptions of the Canadian economy and society. The second is a practical question: what is the feasibility of each of the alternatives under consideration.

PROCESSES FOR CONSTITUTIONAL CHANGE

Issues

The processes adopted will be critical in determining the outcome. It will be important, therefore, to seek processes and scenarios that are likely to produce positive rather than negative results. It will also be important to minimize the possibility of irrevocable steps being taken without recognition of the irreversible consequences that may follow from those steps. Consideration must be given to the appropriate prenegotiation, negotiation and ratification stages and to such issues as forum, nature of consultation, public discussion, consensus-building, the dynamics of discussion within Quebec and within the rest-of-Canada, and timing.

Incremental versus comprehensive negotiations. Should constitutional revision address specific issues that cry out for change, item by item, or be an omnibus reordering of constitutional arrangements? There is a better chance under the former of retaining Canada's corporate entity, and less risk of losing the whole relationship in zero-sum confrontations. Furthermore, recent Swiss experience suggests that by comparison with piecemeal resolutions of constitutional issues, comprehensive revision is much more difficult. The debate over the Meech Lake Accord showed, however, how difficult it is to isolate specific constitutional issues from other concerns. Comprehensive bargaining may enable creative trade-offs between issues. For example, it might prove possible to obtain more effective arrangements for the economic union and central institutions in return for devolution to Quebec of powers over matters of most concern to it, such as some of those outlined in the Allaire report of the Quebec Liberal Party.

Arrangements for public participation. The discrediting of politicians and intergovernmental executive negotiations following Meech Lake means that pressures for more extensive public participation earlier in the process will be unavoidable. This will make the process more complex, and make it vulnerable to interest group and media manipulation affecting outcomes. An important issue to be addressed is how the public participation process should relate to the political decision-making process.

Dynamics of discussion in Quebec. The demise of the Meech Lake Accord has produced an apparent public consensus favouring some form of sovereignty, but there are a variety of views about how this is to be implemented. The Commission on the Political and Constitutional Future of Quebec (Bélanger-Campeau) and the Quebec government will have to resolve these differences, taking into account the probable impact of various institutional options upon the economic and social welfare of Quebec, and the possibilities of securing agreement with the rest-of-Canada.

Dynamics of discussion in "English Canada." Quebec spokespersons have declared that future negotiations should be bilateral between Quebec and English Canada. But "English Canada" has no corporate existence as such. Moreover, it is not simply English. This raises a number of questions: Who speaks for the rest-of-Canada? Can the federal government, composed of representatives from both Quebec and the other nine provinces? Can national party leaders, who are themselves rooted in Quebec? Can individual premiers in the other nine provinces given the differences among them? Will an institutional framework need to be established for this purpose?

Processes for involving the particular interests of the aboriginal peoples and the Territories. Consideration will have to be given to how the aboriginal peoples and the territorial governments are to be involved in the constitutional negotiations in order that due account may be taken of their aspirations.

The role of the federal government. The federal government will have to play a dual role: (a) as broker of the different interests within Canada, and (b) as fighter for its own survival and power. This will complicate its role.

The role of national parties and Parliament. The weakened capacity of each of the national parties to aggregate interests across regions will affect the ability of Parliament to serve as a major forum for resolving constitutional issues.

The role of commissions. In what way do provincial, federal, federal-provincial or nongovernmental commissions help or hinder the process? Should such commissions be composed of legislators, prominent citizens, or experts?

Timing of federal and provincial elections. The timing of federal and provincial elections will affect the governmental players on the scene and provincial positions. In the case of the federal government and of Quebec, there will be pressures for a definitive resolution before the next elections due by 1993 and 1994. Indeed the Allaire report of the Quebec Liberal Party has set late 1992 as the deadline for a referendum on whether a revised federalism or separation should be the path Quebec chooses.

Legal requirements for constitutional revision. Unless the constitutional amendment procedure is itself first revised, any constitutional revision will have to meet the legal requirements of the *Constitution Act, 1982*, sections 38-48. These leave only limited room for major constitutional revisions through bilateral negotiations between Ottawa and Quebec under section 43.

Most major constitutional amendments inevitably affect other provinces and will require their assent through the 7 provinces plus 50 percent rule or through unanimity. A role for the premiers and legislatures of the other provinces will be unavoidable if comprehensive, rather than more limited, revisions are sought. As the Meech Lake debate has shown, comprehensive change and acceptance of Quebec sovereignty is likely to have difficulty under these requirements. Problems with the current procedures might encourage Quebec to declare its independence unilaterally as the first step of negotiating a new arrangement. That in turn might produce a negative emotional reaction in the rest-of-Canada, and hence failure to agree on any subsequent association.

Adjudication processes. If the federal structure is radically altered or Quebec unilaterally declares independence and a negotiated settlement is not reached, what sort of processes will there be for the adjudication of conflicts over assets, liabilities, boundaries, interests of aboriginal peoples, and transportation and communications?

Basic Options for Constitutional Revision Processes

The general considerations above thus lead to the following options for proceeding with constitutional revision:

The status quo. First Ministers' Conferences can facilitate the prior multilateral negotiation of agreed proposals for subsequent ratification by Parliament and provincial legislatures as required by the *Constitution Act, 1982*, sections 38-49. In the aftermath of Meech Lake the process has become publicly discredited. Furthermore, it has been rejected by Quebec.

Bilateral Quebec-Ottawa negotiations. Following the failure of the Meech Lake process Premier Bourassa has insisted that Quebec will deal only with Ottawa. Formal constitutional amendments can be achieved under the *Constitution Act, 1982*, section 43, in this bilateral manner, and some adjustments to meet Quebec concerns could be made in this way. The scope for achieving the major restructuring desired by Quebec would be limited under this procedure, however.

Parallel negotiations. The federal government might attempt to conduct simultaneous negotiations with Quebec on the one hand and collectively or individually with the other nine provincial governments on the other. The complexity of such a process would probably make an ultimate resolution difficult, especially within a restricted time frame.

Commissions. Any of the processes above might be supplemented by the establishment of commissions to facilitate the input of public views prior to intergovernmental negotiations. Commissions might take the form of:

- provincial commissions. Commissions or legislative committees to study constitutional revision have already been established in Alberta, Manitoba, New Brunswick, Ontario and Quebec. Will the results of all these commissions solidify provincial positions and so make subsequent willingness to compromise more constrained?
- a federal commission. The Rowell-Sirois, Pepin-Robarts, and Macdonald Commissions provide precedents. The federal government has chosen not to follow these precedents. It has, however, already taken two

initiatives. The first was establishing the Citizens' Forum led by Keith Spicer to draw out public opinion on views of the country. The second was the appointment of a joint parliamentary committee to review the constitutional amendment procedures.

- a federal-provincial commission of legislators (as proposed for Senate reform in the First Ministers' Agreement of 9 June 1990).

- a nongovernmental commission composed of prominent Canadians of such distinction and balance that some provincial governments and even the federal government might choose to support it rather than create their own (proposed by John Godfrey, *The Financial Post*, 30 July 1990). This would require a neutral third party or parties to set up the organization, nominate members and solicit funds. Though advocated by some, no such body has yet been formed.

A two-stage process. Given the difficulties of achieving substantial constitutional reform using the existing apparently "unworkable" procedures for constitutional amendment adopted in 1982, a two-stage process might be established. The first stage would concentrate upon changing the way in which the constitution is amended, and then the second would deal with making changes to the institutional structure using the revised procedures. The appointment of a joint parliamentary committee to review the constitutional amendment procedures appears to be an attempt by Ottawa to follow such a strategy. Past experience indicates, however, how difficult it is to get the required unanimous agreement of the federal and all provincial governments on any change to the amendment procedure itself.

A constitutional convention. This might be modelled somewhat on the 1787 Philadelphia Convention in the United States or precedents in the establishment of other federations. A convention composed of delegates selected by the provincial legislatures and Parliament would have the responsibility for drafting a new constitution. The recommendations would then have to be ratified by the formal process for constitutional amendments provided by the existing *Constitution Act, 1982.* Issues of composition and voting procedure for the convention would have to be decided in advance and would be contentious. At Philadelphia each state had one vote, but different arrangements might be devised. One variant of the convention process would be for convention recommendations to be ratified by a Canada-wide referendum requiring special regional majorities. This would broaden the sense of popular participation.

Unilateral declarations followed by bilateral or multilateral negotiations. Quebec or another government might declare independence unilaterally in order to force the negotiation of a new political structure or association. This would involve risks both for Quebec and the rest-of-Canada. Such unilateral

actions often provoke sharp emotional responses and unpredicted consequences. Moreover, if subsequent agreement upon a new structure were not
reached, there would remain no ongoing federation or association. This pattern
has occurred in the disintegration of several federations, even where the
seceding unit expressed strong desires for a continued association.

FUTURE INSTITUTIONAL STRUCTURES

Basic Structural Options

One may identify in broad terms a continuum of alternative structural models.
These fall into three broad categories. The first are various *federal forms*.
Common to them all is the distinguishing mark of federations as political
systems in which sovereignty is constitutionally divided between central and
provincial governments. The second are various *confederal forms* where the
definitive characteristic is that sovereignty ultimately resides with the constituent political units but a superstructure is established to deal with common
policies subject to the assent of the constituent units. The third is the *separation*
of the current federation into two or more independent successor states.

A fundamental choice to be made is which of these basic forms of political
organization is to provide the future framework for political institutions within
the geographic space that is now Canada. The strategies of political negotiators
will vary according to whether they are seeking some form of revised federalism, some form of confederalism, or complete economic and political independence.

Of the nine options listed below, the first five represent different forms of
federalism, options six to eight different forms of confederalism, and the last,
complete separation into two or more independent states.

1. Status quo federalism. The Canadian federal structure devised in 1867 has
for nearly a century and a quarter proved remarkably effective and flexible
through many changing conditions. Nevertheless, the post-Meech Lake conditions and the strategic factors outlined previously suggest that the existing
federal structure is unlikely to be tenable for more than an interim period of a
few years. At the very least it is no longer acceptable to a majority in Quebec.
Furthermore, it is the source of much dissatisfaction not only in western Canada
but also in the Atlantic provinces and the Territories, and among the aboriginal
peoples.

2. A rebalanced federation. The distribution of jurisdiction and the structure of
central institutions might be modernized to make the Canadian federal system
more effective in contemporary conditions. Central powers might be increased
in some areas and decreased in others. For example, federal jurisdiction might

be enhanced to ensure the freer movement of people, goods and services. The European Community is often cited, even in Quebec, as a superior example to Canada in this respect. Indeed, the Allaire report of the Quebec Liberal Party advocates "a stronger economic union" although it specifies few specific federal instruments to achieve this. At the same time jurisdiction over some other areas where centralization is not a prerequisite for effectiveness might be devolved to the provinces. This would go a significant distance towards meeting the concerns of Quebec and of some other provinces while also improving efficiency. Central institutions and structures (e.g., the Senate) might also be modernized.

3. A more decentralized federation. This solution would involve a devolution of some programs and responsibilities (e.g., industrial development, training and communications) and of some taxing powers (in place of shared-cost programs). This alternative would accord with the apparent centrifugal trends in Quebec and in Canadian opinion elsewhere. Dissatisfaction within the business community with the current inefficiency of the deficit-ridden federal government and with the excessive overlaps in the operations of the federal and provincial governments provides a strong impetus for greater decentralization. It is unlikely, however, to be supported by centralists outside Quebec or by those in the Atlantic provinces and Manitoba concerned that a weaker central government would be unable to undertake effective redistribution of resources through regional development and equalization programs. Nevertheless, the western premiers at their post-Meech Lake meeting in July 1990 did appear to give some support to this alternative. If there were sufficient devolution, such a model might be acceptable to Quebec. The Allaire report of the Quebec Liberal Party has advanced an extreme example of this variant of federalism. A critical issue in designing a more decentralized federation would be identifying the degree of central jurisdiction still required to maintain an effective federal system including an effective economic union.

4. A more radically asymmetrical federation. The 1867 constitution included some elements of asymmetry. A more radical asymmetry would enable concerns of centralists outside Quebec to be reconciled with the desires in Quebec for greater devolution. Efforts to increase moderately the degree of asymmetry within the Canadian federation as proposed in the Meech Lake Accord failed, however, to receive the support required for ratification. Nevertheless, faced with the realization of a potential breakup of the federation as the only alternative, a more radically asymmetrical federation might be accepted. The clearest example of such an arrangement is the Malaysian federation where there is a marked greater autonomy for the two Borneo states. The experience of that federation indicates both that such an arrangement is feasible but that there may be limits to how far such arrangements can go (e.g., in Malaysia the conditions which led to Singapore's departure). A more asymmetrical federal structure in Canada might take the form of "opt-out federalism," (through a more extensive variant of section 7 of the Meech Lake Accord allowing provinces to opt-out of certain federal programs). Or it might take the form of "opt-in federalism," starting with greater devolution but providing arrangements for individual provinces to delegate powers back to the federal government. The Allaire report of the Quebec Liberal Party has proposed leaving room for such a possibility. This could be done by a more extensive variant of section 94 of the *Constitution Act, 1867*. An alternative device enabling *de facto* asymmetry would be to specify areas of concurrent jurisdiction with provincial paramountcy as has already been done under section 94A of the *Constitution Act, 1867* relating to jurisdiction over pensions. In any alternative involving substantial asymmetry there would be serious questions about the appropriate role to be played by the representatives of those constituent units having greater jurisdictional autonomy when federal policy in those areas is being deliberated within the central institutions.

5. A binational federation. This would be a federation in which the two constituent units would be Quebec and the rest-of-Canada, the latter taking either a unitary form or more likely existing as a federation within a federation. There have been examples elsewhere of a federation within a federation. Experience elsewhere suggests, however, that bipolar political unions have been notoriously unstable. Furthermore, the population ratio of 3:1 between the two units would raise major problems in arriving at agreement on appropriate representation within the central institutions. Any Quebec proposal of parity with the other nine provinces in a binational federation is likely to be strongly resisted by the rest-of-Canada.

6. A confederalism of regions. In this model there would be a loose confederation of four or five regional units with the prairies and the Atlantic provinces (or at least the Maritimes) each constituting a single unit. The grouping of the smaller provinces into larger units would enable the new units to match the capacity of Ontario, Quebec and British Columbia to exercise extended powers. A very real difficulty with this solution is that it would require the willingness of the smaller provinces to coalesce. In this option the central superstructure would have responsibility for coordinating policy relating to economic, monetary and a number of other agreed policy areas. It would be necessary to assess at what point devolution hinders effective economic and monetary union to the detriment of all the constituent units. It would be ironic, just at a time when Europe is evolving from confederalism, because of its inadequacies, towards its own unique form of federalism, for Canada to go in the opposite direction.

7. Sovereignty-association confederalism. This solution, advocated by the Parti Québécois and others in Quebec, would take the form of a loose economic confederation in a binational form. It would combine Quebec as one unit and a federation of the other nine provinces as the other unit. The bipolar superstructure would be responsible mainly for the common market and a common currency, and for common armed forces and a few other programs. Such proposals have often suggested that the two components should have parity within the central superstructure (e.g., Parti Québécois proposals in 1979-80). It will probably be difficult, however, to convince the majority in the rest-of-Canada, representing 75 percent of the total population in the confederal association, to accept a veto by Quebec on all policies dealt with by the common superstructure. A further possible problem is that the operation of such a superstructure with only two constituent units is almost certain to produce repeated deadlocks, thus hampering international competitiveness.

8. *A common market.* This might consist of five to ten constituent units with only the minimal central structures and powers necessary for a common market and possibly a monetary union. While avoiding the problems of a bipolar superstructure, such an arrangement is unlikely, even with the increasingly centrifugal attitudes throughout Canada, to meet the desires among most Canadians outside Quebec for effective coordinated national action in a range of policy areas.

9. *Two or more economically and politically independent successor-states.* Quebec's complete economic and political separation may be seen by some as a cleaner and neater solution than many of the complex alternatives listed above. It does raise questions, however, of the need to deal with such issues as the allocation of assets and liabilities, the adjustment of boundaries (by referendum?) to meet the wishes of minorities otherwise left on each side, and of transportation arrangements between Ontario and the Atlantic provinces. For a Canada-without-Quebec it raises not only the spectre of "Pakistanization" but also the prospect of the permanent dominance of Ontario. How radically would the structure of the rest-of-Canada have to be revised? Would the rest-of-Canada remain as one or become a number of economically and politically independent successor-states?

Variations Within the Basic Options

While one may identify in broad terms basic alternative models for future institutional structures, it is worth noting that within each basic approach outlined above there are infinite possible variations in the elements composing them. There are no pure ideal models. Such variable elements include the following:

The appropriate constituent units. This issue in turn depends upon various institutional and other factors, including:

- A binational federation or confederation: There have been examples elsewhere of bipolar (e.g., Belgium and Pakistan) and tripolar (e.g., Nigeria, East Africa and Central Africa) unions, federations or economic associations. Balancing representation of different-sized units in their central institutions has usually proved contentious, and most examples have proved unstable.
- Federations within federations: Germany within the European Community and Russia within the USSR are examples. Spain within the European Community is moving in the same direction as internal regional autonomy is developed.
- Equality or asymmetry of provincial autonomy: In most but not all federations the states have equal constitutional status. Malaysia provides an example, however, of radical asymmetry in terms of the degree of state autonomy possessed by Sabah and Sarawak.
- Relative size of units: Disparities of size and wealth of constituent units in federations have generally contributed to instability. The most extreme examples of disproportionately large units have been Prussia in prewar Germany, Ontario, and Northern Nigeria prior to restructuring. In a federation of nine provinces without Quebec, Ontario would represent 49 percent of the population and 54 percent of the Gross National Product (GNP).
- Smaller, more numerous units: Two of the more stable federations contain 50 states (United States) and 26 cantons (Switzerland). Restructuring to create a larger number of provinces might recognize the political role of major metropolitan centres (e.g., Toronto, Montreal and Vancouver) which are already economically, financially and politically more influential than some provinces. Restructuring of existing units has occurred in some federations (e.g., Germany, India and Nigeria), but no doubt there would be strong resistance within existing Canadian provinces.
- Units of aboriginal self-government: The establishment and status of political units appropriate for aboriginal self-government will need to be considered, including their status relative to the provinces.

The distribution of jurisdiction. There are many variations among federations, and also among different confederal structures, in the allocation of legislative, executive, fiscal and monetary jurisdiction to central institutions. In some cases (e.g., Germany) there is a higher degree of legislative centralization combined with a larger degree of administrative decentralization than in the current Canadian structure. There are also a variety of devices that might be considered such as concurrent jurisdiction with federal or with provincial paramountcy and provisions for intergovernmental delegation that would provide pragmatic flexibility to meet the varied needs of different provinces.

A key issue is where the minimum thresholds for effective central jurisdiction lie in federations, in confederations, in economic unions, in monetary unions and in common markets. Depending on basic decisions about the appropriate role of the central government, some areas of jurisdiction might be transferred in one direction or the other for greater effectiveness and to accommodate political concerns. There is no reason to assume that sections 91 and 92 adopted in 1867 represent the optimum solution in contemporary modern circumstances.

Central institutional structures. Should Canada continue with its parliamentary institutions? There are variations among federations between those employing parliamentary cabinets (e.g., Canada, Australia and Germany) and those with separate fixed-term executive bodies (e.g., U.S. Presidency and Swiss Federal Council). The latter provide more checks and balances and are less majoritarian in their operation. Do legislative institutions need strengthening? The dominance of the executive and bureaucratic branches has produced concerns in a number of countries and particularly in the European Community about "the democratic deficit" and the need for reforms to ensure more political accountability.

What is the appropriate role of the Senate (inevitably limited within parliamentary institutions) in representing regional and minority interests ?

If an asymmetrical assignment of jurisdiction to provinces is adopted, what is to be the role in the central institutions of the representatives of the more autonomous provinces? Will special decision-making rules (e.g., special or concurrent majorities) be required for specified subjects?

Intergovernmental machinery. This may take the form of predominantly executive intergovernmental negotiation (e.g., Canada, Australia, European Community), or accommodation through deliberations in the central legislative institutions (e.g., United States), or both (Germany). The Germans have succeeded in building integration by establishing bridging institutional structures. Intergovernmental institutions may be informal (e.g., Canada) or formal (e.g., the European Community and Germany). Confederal models often require formal voting rules (e.g., European Community).

Umpiring institutions. These may take the form of supreme courts (e.g., United States, Canada and Australia), constitutional courts (e.g., Germany), or of referenda (e.g., Switzerland).

Constitutional revision procedures. Ratification of constitutional amendments in federations has usually required either special majorities of the state or provincial legislatures (e.g., United States and Canada) or special regional majorities in federation-wide referenda (e.g., Switzerland and Australia). No federation other than Canada has required unanimity, although confederacies often have.

Protection of individual and collective rights. A number of federations have included constitutional provisions or charters for protecting and advancing rights of individuals and minorities. A closely related issue is whether language policies are to be determined federally or, as advocated by Quebec, territorially. Switzerland is an example of the latter alternative.

CONCLUSIONS

The increasing polarization within Canada in the post-Meech Lake era will require substantial constitutional change. The direction of this change will be significantly affected by the particular form of negotiating processes used, and this must be clearly borne in mind in establishing them. There are a variety of options for future institutional structures that might be considered. Fuller analysis of these options and their implications including their desirability and feasibility is the subject of the subsequent chapters.

III

The Context

3

The Context for Future Constitutional Options

Thomas J. Courchene and John N. McDougall

INTRODUCTION

Our assigned role in this conference volume is to focus on the context for Canada's constitutional future. We define context rather broadly to include those forces or factors, whether global or domestic, that must be taken as immutable or at least given over the period during which we Canadians must decide on our collective future. Specifically, included among these forces will be geographic determinism (both physical and socio-economic), demolinguistics (the interaction among language, culture and population), globalization and its impact on nation-states, Canada-U.S. free trade, debt- and deficit-driven fiscal decentralization and aspects of the institutional/political malaise across the land. Since almost all of these factors or forces are seen to undermine the viability of the status quo, this paper will likely leave the reader (as it has left the writers) rather dispirited about the future of Canada.

Accordingly, a few brief interpretive comments are warranted at the outset. The first is that, depressing as it may be, it is absolutely essential to confront all these conditions squarely. This is particularly the case because many of these forces, while running counter to the traditional conception of Canada, do nonetheless point in a common direction. For example, globalization, the Free Trade Agreement (FTA), the burden of the public debt and the underlying geoeconomics appear to be driving Canada towards greater decentralization in selected areas. Transferred to the political or constitutional domain, this suggests that it may make little sense to oppose a potential request from Quebec for a much more decentralized Canada if this is where these underlying forces are driving the country in any event. In other words, while the context, as elaborated below, may challenge the status quo, it may also embrace key aspects of the solution.

Second, most of these forces are operative in all developed nations. For example, the internal economic challenges facing the Americans, particularly in light of their erstwhile hegemony on the economic front, are arguably much worse than ours: their entire banking system, not just the high-profile Savings and Loan debacle, is in dire straits. Not so here. The critical difference is, of course, that their internal political integrity is not threatened. However, the general point is that one could sketch out a fairly pessimistic scenario, at least over the near term, for *all* of the Group of Seven (G-7) nations.

Third, there are shared Canadian values and common societal goals that remain powerfully integrative for citizens in *all* provinces. Moreover, perhaps moreso than was the case as recently as a decade ago, Canadians are virtually unanimous in terms of not wanting to become Americans. However, the focus on values and goals is the subject of Charles Taylor's contribution to this volume, thereby leaving us with the task of dealing largely with forces that, if not actually *disintegrative*, are at least inimical to the wholesale reconstitution of the Canadian union.

Finally, and perhaps most importantly, we are effectively doomed as a nation if we attempt to find formal *constitutional* solutions to all aspects of our current impasse. This has never been the Canadian way. Historically, we have lived collectively through waves of centralization and decentralization. Focusing only on the post-1930s, World War II and its immediate aftermath represented an apex of centralization in terms of taxing powers. The pendulum then swung sharply the other way, with the 1977 block-funding of the Established Programs Financing probably representing the high-point in terms of fiscal decentralization. More recently, Pierre Trudeau's "second coming" was again a highly centralizing period, much of which has been reversed under Brian Mulroney. The point is that, setting the Charter aside for the moment, all of this was accomplished under the *same* formal constitution.

Indeed, our constitution has proved to be remarkably flexible. As one of us[1] has pointed out, changes in the nature of, and incentives embodied within, federal-provincial transfers are tantamount to changes in the formal division of powers themselves (essentially conditional grants centralize, unconditional grants decentralize). The formal constitution is silent on these intergovernmental transfers. Nonetheless, in 1957 Canada embarked on a system of equalization payments which has become an essential part of the glue that binds us together as a nation. For 25 years (until 1982) equalization payments had no formal constitutional underpinning. While the process of executive federalism (the apex of which is the First Ministers' Conference) has fallen on hard times recently, it did and still does represent an alternative solution to the lack of

---

1   Thomas J. Courchene, *Refinancing the Canadian Federation: A Survey of the 1977 Fiscal Arrangements Act* (Toronto: C.D. Howe Research Institute, 1979), pp. 47-48.

effective regional representation in central institutions. The most prominent example of the latter is the lack of a Triple E (Elected, Equal and Effective) Senate. Likewise, opting-out is now increasingly viewed as a problem, although one can argue, as does Bird,[2] that over the years opting-out has been an integral part of the solution and may well be Canada's key contribution to the "art" of federalism. To these mechanisms one can add transfers of tax points, bilateral agreements and ordinary legislation.

The central message here is that there has always existed a whole range of instruments other than formal amendments to the constitution that allowed our federation to adjust to differing needs and differing challenges. This same range of instruments must be brought to bear in addressing the issues dealt with below and, more generally, our current political-constitutional impasse.

With these caveats, we now turn to a brief survey of selected factors that will impinge on the nature of the Canadian federation as we approach the millenium.

GEOGRAPHICAL DETERMINISM

Economic

All Canadians learn at an early age that Canada is an economic artifact: physically geography would dictate north-south, not east-west economic integration.[3] At the time of Confederation, however, there was an important offset to this pull of geography. In addition to the obvious political rationale for Canadian nationhood emanating from events south of the border, there were also powerful economic elites interested in forging an east-west nation in the upper half of North America — thus preserving and extending what Donald Creighton has called the "Commercial Empire of the St. Lawrence." The continued viability of this "empire" required, at the very least, the completion of the western link of the transcontinental railroad, which in turn was facilitated by the National Policy. Arguably, the railroad was not built because a national deal had been struck but, rather, a national deal was struck so that the railway could be built. Thus, a new political structure was necessary to sustain what was essentially an *economic* project or strategy.

Moreover, from the standpoint of Canadian unity, the key contribution to Canadian nationhood made by the Commercial Empire of the St. Lawrence was

---

2   Richard Bird, "Federal Finance in Comparative Perspective" in Thomas J. Courchene, David W. Conklin and Gail C.A. Cook (eds.), *Ottawa and the Provinces: The Distribution of Money and Power* (Toronto: Ontario Economic Council, 1985).

3   John N. McDougall, "Canadian Constitutional Reform: The Socio-Economic Context," background paper prepared for C.D. Howe Roundtable on "Imagining Constitutional Futures," Toronto, 17-19 November 1990.

that it was built around the economic enterprise of exporting Canadian staples to *transatlantic* markets. The sequence of staple exports — furs, then square timber, then grains — had the virtue, from a nation-building perspective, of unifying Canada in a west-to-east direction as a necessary adjunct to moving those same goods to their ultimate, European markets (with various "backhauls" moving people and goods from east to west over the same transportation systems).

From this vantage point, the problem for Canada throughout the twentieth century has been that the mix of Canada's exportable staples has changed dramatically. All that is left of the original transatlantic pattern is a reduced European grain trade, while the exploitation of the modern staples — metals, hydrocarbons, and forest products — has been predicated predominantly on exports to the American market. They have, hence, contributed to a north-south, not an east-west, axis of trade and, if anything, have accentuated Canadian regional fragmentation by integrating parts of Canada with their respective adjacent regions of the United States while disassociating them (relatively speaking) from one another. Moreover, the political-economic effects of these shifting trade patterns were amplified by a major reorientation of investment patterns over the past 80 years: foreign investment shifted decisively from being predominantly portfolio and British to being predominantly direct and American.[4]

In addition, a new version of the staples model is emerging that is driving an even wider wedge between western and central Canada: Alberta and British Columbia are increasingly exporting resources such as coal, lumber, foodstuffs and wood pulp to Japan and the Japanese-dominated Pacific Rim, and reciprocating by importing from there capital, manufactures and people. From the point

---

4   All of this means, incidentally, that contrary to the claims of its opponents, the FTA represents not the cause but the culmination of North American economic integration. Moreover, without adopting a conspiratorial view of history, it could well be that an important ingredient of national unity for all countries is a common objective or shared purpose among its dominant economic actors, which then serves to define the *national interest* of the country and provide it with a sense of national direction. It could then be said that Canadian unity is threatened because Canada is no longer anybody's economic project.

This problem is reflected in studies of the structure of Canadian society, which repeatedly stumble over the issue of whether, given the high incidence of American ownership of Canada's largest corporations, Canadian economic elites should be categorized as Canadian or North American. For a classical statement of the problem, see John Porter, *The Vertical Mosaic: An Analysis of Social Class and Power in Canada* (Toronto: University of Toronto Press, 1965), pp. 263-73, and especially p. 266. For a brief overview of updates of Porter's work on this score, see John Goyder, *Essentials of Canadian Society* (Toronto: McClelland and Stewart, 1990), pp. 149-53.

of view of the westernmost provinces, the "Commercial Empire of the St. Lawrence" is being converted into the "commercial empire of the Pacific." Thus, the staples model, in both its economic and communications dimensions, would predict an increasing alienation of these provinces from central Canada as a direct consequence of this new geoeconomic or trading pattern.

Montreal was hardest hit by all of this. Progressively its traditional role as the supplier of a wide range of nationally distributed goods shifted westward, largely to Toronto. With the advent of Quebec's market nationalism, its emerging entrepreneurial class faced the choice of: (a) attempting to reclaim aspects of this former role and to leap-frog Toronto to supply the west; or (b) to look towards the market to the south which was both larger and closer. Small wonder that Quebec became the most ardent advocate of Canada-U.S. free trade.

Socio-cultural

Progressive north-south integration on the economic front has been characterized in part by direct investment and the resulting high incidence of parent-subsidiary relations. It has, not surprisingly, also come to affect profoundly the nature of Canada's socio-cultural and professional subsystems. The important structural characteristics of most of these subsystems (to be sure, there are some exceptions) is that, rather like subsidiary firms, they are typically a marginal extension of the particular U.S. subsystem. This is true not only of a wide range of private service and trade associations, but also of numerous branches of the entertainment industry, the arts, professional sports and the media.[5]

If horizonal integration is defined as the integration of various cultural and social subsystems across a given country, and if vertical integration is defined

---

5 The extent to which Canadian professionals are integrated with their American counterparts is a seriously understudied subject. No doubt, we all possess directly personal and/or anecdotal evidence of active Canadian participation in American-centred professional associations. Charles Pentland observed almost 20 years ago (but without references or documentation) that "Canadians and Americans have traditionally contributed to each other's specialized publications and belonged to each other's professional associations to a far greater extent than is the case among Europeans." See Charles Pentland, *The Canadian Dilemma* (Paris: Atlantic Institute for International Affairs, 1973), p. 47.

As for the arts, entertainment and sports, a conference at the University of Western Ontario, "American Popular Culture in Canada: Mass Communication and Public Performance," 4-6 May 1988, heard papers that described numerous popular-cultural subsystems conforming to the described model to various degrees: turn-of-the-century vaudeville; professional and minor-league football and baseball; movie making and distribution; music production and distribution; "televangelism"; news production and distribution; advertising; television program production; and, believe it or not, the design and construction of international exhibitions.

as the integration of each such subsystem to its central core, then we can say that, for Canada, vertical integration of these subsystems tends to frustrate their horizontal integration across Canada. The same is not true for the United States. This is so because it is easy, or at least possible, to integrate subsystems horizontally near their centres, but it is impossible or very difficult to integrate them horizontally on their peripheries.

Moreover, for all of these subsystems, whether in the Canadian or the American segment of them, to "make it" is to rise to the "top" of the subsystem's hierarchy (where "rising to the top" actually means "getting nearer the centre" of the system). The problem is that for Canadians, but not for Americans, at some point on the "way to the top," rising stars must leave the country because the centre of their respective subsystem is located in the United States. The Canadian "bests" in various fields are infrequently in touch with one another in their own country and often do not work together in Canada while at the top of their form.[6] Thus, on the Canadian peripheries of these subsystems, vertical integration frustrates horizontal integration: While American subsystems are cumulative and socially integrative, in Canada they are typically disintegrative and fragmentary. And where they are integrative in Canada at all, they tend to be integrative continentally rather than nationally.

What does one make of this geoeconomic and socio-cultural determinism? At one level, it need not erode our *desire* to be Canadian. For example, the fact that Ontario is by far the most north-south integrated province, did not prevent it from being the most vocal anti-free-trade (or pro-Canadian-values) advocate in the FTA election. At a deeper level, however, there appears to be no mobilizing strategy on the horizon with the unifying force of the original transcontinental railway project that would integrate these desires into an all-embracing political-economic rationale for nationhood. (Perhaps the last stab at this was the turning inward, and anti-Americanism, in the early 1980s centred around the $260 billion or so of potential "major projects," which largely evaporated when the price of energy collapsed.)

---

6   This is a counterpart to the familiar Canadian artists' complaint that they cannot attain full recognition in Canada until they have "made it big" in the United States. Of course, we are more concerned with the implications of this for the cohesiveness of the Canadian socio-cultural fabric. These are that Canadians in a wide variety of professional and cultural pursuits rarely look "across" at what their Canadian counterparts are doing in other parts of the country, but rather look "up" to what is going on at the peak of their field in the United States. The essential cross-fertilization among such Canadian artists and professionals thus happens, if at all, only by virtue of their coincidental sojourns in the American centres of their fields or possibly through indirect exposure (recordings and other media) which, characteristically, are also distributed through American-centred systems of production and distribution.

There is an incredible irony in all of this. The policies associated with the Commercial Empire of the St. Lawrence effectively bestowed on Canadians their existing value structure, including a benevolent approach towards government and a genuine concern for the well-being of their fellow Canadians as reflected, for example, in our comprehensive system of social programs and our system of equalization payments to the "have-less" provinces. Now that we have come to cherish these values, we cannot seem to find an integrative political-economic rationale or strategy within which to sustain them.

Of and by itself, this set of factors is unlikely to rend the Canadian nation. If, however, other forces tear at our fabric then these aspects of geography — physical, economic and socio-cultural may come powerfully into play insomuch as they may inhibit attempts at any reconciliation or reintegration.

We now turn to a series of forces that *do* have the potential to unwind the federation. This is the potent combination of population and language, which we refer to as "demolinguistics."

DEMOLINGUISTICS

As Mario Polèse points out, somewhere in the 1950s the "fragile internal balance between anglophones and francophones in Canada broke down."[7] After hovering in the vicinity of 30 percent for roughly eight decades, the proportion of francophones has, at last count, (1986 census) fallen to 24 percent (based on "home language") and the trend is clearly down. At what point will this decline lead not only to a substantially diminished influence for Quebec and Quebecers in Canadian governance, but perhaps more importantly, to a substantial undermining of the enshrined equality of English and French?

Demolinguistics are also rapidly transforming the face of anglophone Canada. Harvey Lazar reflects on this as follows:

> A large and growing proportion of Canadians is now from non-European cultures and backgrounds. Our largest cities are increasingly inhabited by people whose origins are in Asia, Latin America, the Caribbean and Middle East. Canadian myth celebrates the cultural diversity these new Canadians provide to our mosaic. But diversity, in and of itself, cannot build the shared values that will enable Canadians to continue to live in harmony in a single political community. Insufficient attention is being given to the articulation of a higher sense of shared purpose which transcends cultural differences (without eliminating them).[8]

---

7   Mario Polèse, "Misplaced Priorities: A Review of Demolinguistic Trends and the Evolution of Canadian Institutions" *Canadian Public Policy/Analyse de politique* volume XVI, no.4 (December 1990): 466.

8   Harvey Lazar, "Life After Meech," mimeo, (Ottawa: Economic Council of Canada, 1990), pp. 13-14.

These developments have now begun to interact with each other in ways that are, perhaps, predictable. As multiculturalism gains strength (both by sheer dint of numbers and by constitutional enshrinement) it challenges, at least implicitly, the concept of the two founding nations and linguistic duality. Sally Weaver has noted that the notion of two founding peoples or nations is not only increasingly intellectually hostile to the emerging ethnic plurality of Canada, let alone to the first nations, but as well stands in the way of conceptualizing Canadian society accurately and realistically as a first step towards rethinking our future.[9] At the other end of the spectrum, the rising popularity of the Reform Party indicates that a growing number of Canadians may be taking a rather dim view of these developments since among the key tenets of the party is the elimination of both official bilingualism *and* official multiculturalism.

All of this reverberates back on Quebec and Quebecers. They may or may not agree with the view prevalent in the rest-of-Canada that it is the existing constitutional structure and processes that have allowed the French language to flourish in Quebec and in selected other parts of Canada. Their concerns are riveted on the future, not the past. Full sovereignty becomes progressively more appealing to Quebecers as the *only way* to preserve their language and culture in the face of a variety of threats. These threats include declining birth rates, ambiguity and controversy concerning the net contribution of immigration to the problem, expectations of declining influence in the federation based on reduced numbers of everything from MPs to seats on national commissions, and attitudes outside Quebec that are perceived to be increasingly intolerant. One can, of course, question whether sovereignty is a bulwark against an erosion of language and culture, but the relevant issue is that it is perceived to be.

In our view, the only way to counter this perception or reality and, therefore, the only way to maintain the political integrity of Canada is to transfer (*à la* Switzerland) more control over language, culture and important aspects of immigration to the provinces (or at least to Quebec). This is hardly a new theme in Canadian federalism: the Pepin-Robarts Task Force recommended that "each provincial legislature should have the right to determine an official language or languages for that province, within its sphere of jurisdiction."[10] However, such a recommendation may now be more difficult for English Canada to accept in light of the 1982 constitutional amendments. Specifically, English-speaking Canadians may not want to be this accommodating, particularly since it would

---

9   Sally Weaver, "Speaking Notes," prepared for the C.D. Howe Roundtable on "Imagining Constitutional Futures," Toronto, 17-19 November 1990.

10 The Task Force on Canadian Unity, *A Future Together: Observations and Recommendations.* This is generally referred to as the Pepin-Robarts Report, after its co-chairs. (Ottawa: Minister of Supply and Services Canada, 1979), p.121.

likely represent a watering down of aspects of the Charter. However, they should at least be fully aware of the consequences of nonaccommodation.

GLOBALIZATION

A third force that is exerting, and will continue to exert, enormous influence on peoples and nations is the sweep of globalization.[11] At one level this is captured by the internationalization of production. Globalization in this sense decouples firms from the factor endowments of a single nation since raw materials, components, machinery, services and, increasingly, human capital are available globally and can be realigned, geographically, relatively quickly. Boundaries on a political map may be as clear as ever, but boundaries on a competitive map have vanished.[12]

But globalization is more than this. Spurred on by the telecomputational revolution of the 1980s, we can now speak meaningfully of an integrated global capital market. Partly as a result, firms have restructured themselves to become much less hierarchical with respect to their internal organization and far more flexible with respect to production. Moreover, the information explosion has empowered citizens to such an extent that Kenichi Ohmae's preferred definition of globalization is "consumer sovereignty": "performance standards are now set in the global marketplace by those who buy the products, not those who make or regulate them."[13] For present purposes what matters is not the precise definition or definitions of globalization, but rather the implications that flow from it. Drawing from earlier work, it seems apparent that the major loser in this process is the traditional role and conception of the nation-state. It is at one and the same time too small to cope with the inherent mobility that attends globalization and in many instances too large to address aspects of community that are rising to the fore.[14] Hence, the powers of the nation-state are passing both upwards and downwards as it were.

Concerning the former, the geographically fixed nation-state is proving increasingly unable to counter the ability of the international private sector to organize and manoeuvre globally. In a sense, more and more nation-states are the authors of their own misfortune. They are negotiating international trade

---

11 Thomas J. Courchene, "Global Competitiveness and the Canadian Federation," a paper prepared for the International Business and Trade Law Programme Conference "Global Competition and Canadian Federalism," University of Toronto, September 1990.

12 Kenichi Ohmae, *The Borderless Economy: Power and Strategy in the Interlinked Economy* (New York: Harper & Row, 1990), pp.18-19.

13 Ibid., dustjacket.

14 Courchene, "Global Competitiveness and the Canadian Federation."

rules that increasingly endorse the principle of national treatment, which means that each country's domestic rules must cease to discriminate against foreign-based firms, goods or services. This facilitates the capacity of multinational enterprises to operate on a par with local firms, which in turn fosters the internationalization of production and investment.

Of necessity, this drive towards global production efficiency requires a countervailing move towards supranational forms of governance — free trade agreements, international environmental pacts, and international regulatory standards such as the Bank for International Settlement's capital-adequacy rules for monitoring global banking, as well as more formal supranational structures such as Europe 1992 and, soon perhaps, a federal Europe. The message here appears clear: as nations become increasingly integrated, little will be left that is the domain of domestic agendas alone.[15] While this process can also impinge on the provinces (e.g., the operations of the International Organization of Securities Commissions impinges on the provincial securities commissions) the major impacts are felt at the national level.

Perhaps more important for purposes of this paper is the influence of globalization in terms of passing power downward from the national level. There are several aspects to this. One has already been alluded to — the information revolution is privileging citizens who, as a result, are garnering enormous power and complicating old-style governance for unitary and federal states alike. Indeed, citizen power is itself flexing its muscle internationally! Multinational or global organizations of like-minded citizens or citizen groups are becoming increasingly common in the areas of the environment and civil rights. This was brought home to Quebec recently in the Vermont hydro sale which effectively contained a rider to the effect that the power was not to come from newly-constructed dams. Presumably this reflected the cross-border inter-play of concerns relating to human rights and to the environment.

More intriguing still, globalization is for the present at least spreading across the world through a network of "international cities." Nothing much has changed over the last decade in the relationship between Ottawa and Bonn, except that now it may be Berlin. But much has altered in the relationship between Toronto and Frankfurt. Yet, despite their growing importance econom-ically and culturally, our international cities (Toronto, Montreal and Vancouver) are not recognized in the constitution. They are creatures of their respective provincial governments. This poses governance concerns under the existing constitution let alone under any future constitutional options because, for

---

15 Harvey Lazar, "The Changing International Context," background paper prepared for the C.D. Howe Roundtable on "Imagining Constitutional Futures," Toronto, 17-19 November 1990, p.6.

example, Saskatchewan's international city is not in the province and the Maritimes' international city (Boston/New York) is not even in the country.

The implications of all of this are far from straightforward. First, in the face of a diminished role for national governments in the economic and regulatory sphere, citizens will, we believe, increasingly come to view sovereignty as the ability to exercise control over their immediate environment, meaning principally the local and regional circumstances in which they live and work and play. This may produce a version of McLuhan's "global village."[16]

For homogeneous societies, the integrating unit may well be the existing nation-state. For the culturally and economically diverse Canadian federation, it is less clear that citizens would look to Ottawa to play this role, particularly since the critical functions (education, health, welfare, work-place standards, etc.) largely fall under provincial, not federal, jurisdiction. It would appear, therefore, that the forces of globalization are inherently decentralizing in those nation-states where there exist distinct societies (and where the definition of a distinct society includes an international city).

Second, and again drawing from Lazar, it is likely the case that there are benefits from small relatively homogeneous polities relative to large heterogeneous ones from the perspective of the changing international context: "one advantage of a small homogeneous polity is that it can mobilize domestic consensus relatively quickly to respond to a rapidly changing international setting and rapid change is bound to be a constant in coming decades."[17] Both of these would seem to point in the direction of a much more autonomous or, perhaps, sovereign Quebec, particularly since, as noted above, Montreal provides its own "link" to the international community. Indeed, were Quebec in Europe, rather than in North America, there is probably little doubt that it would attempt to link itself directly to Brussels, as the Scots and Catalans will be tempted to do. But there is no North American equivalent of a pluralistic or multinational Brussels, so that sovereignty on this side of the Atlantic becomes more complicated.

---

16 Of course, McLuhan's "global village" was a world that had been so closely integrated by means of modern communications and transportation technologies that individuals everywhere became the modern equivalent of the inhabitants of primitive villages, with their almost instantaneous dissemination of information and pervasive, homogeneous culture. Here, Courchene considers the "global village" to be evolving in the form of a number of major "internationalized metropoli" across the world, integrated among themselves and integrating their respective hinterlands with the global economy. McDougall does not entirely buy this conception, but sees a possible synthesis of the Courchene and McLuhan viewpoints: for now, the inhabitants (constituent units) of McLuhan's global village (global villagers?) are not individuals, but major cities.

17 Lazar, "The Changing International Context," p.12.

Counteracting much or all of this potential for or thrust towards sovereignty is the fact that there is not all that much to sovereignty beyond what can be gained via distinct-society status or a very decentralized federation. As *The Economist* puts it:

> Tribes [e.g., the Scots or Catalans or South Tyroleans] resisted nation-states that tried to run everything. In states that defer to some higher order, who really cares?[18]

To this one might add that there probably is some advantage to the existing Canadian polity rather than a series of Canadian states: given that much of the old domestic agenda will be on the international bargaining table, a single Canadian polity would have more claim to be at the table.[19] In more concrete terms, our membership in the G-7 is obviously at stake if some or all of us go our separate ways.

By way of summary, the message we draw from the impact of globalization in terms of Canada's constitutional options is that it is fully consistent with the accrual of greater powers to subnational governments. For Quebec at least, this interacts powerfully with similar pressures arising on the socio-cultural front (e.g., demolinguistics).

FISCAL-DRIVEN DECENTRALIZATION

Thus far the analysis has focused on forces that are best described as exogenous to the ongoing constitutional impasse — geography is immutable, the two founding nations will comprise an ever-decreasing share of our overall population, and there is precious little that Canada can do about the pace of globalization. There are, however, some powerful endogenous or policy forces that are also playing a major role of late. Foremost among these is fiscal-driven decentralization.[20]

Despite the fact that many non-Quebec Canadians tend to look to Ottawa to play a greater role, the reality of the last few years is that the federal deficit and debt burden are driving Canada into unprecedented decentralization. Leading the way here is the current two-year freeze in Established Programs Financing (EPF), after which the EPF growth will be equal to Gross National Product (GNP) growth minus 3 percent. Since the financing of EPF is a combination of tax-point transfers and cash transfers and since the tax-point transfer tends to grow roughly at the rate of growth of GNP, what this means is that as a result

---

18 "My Tribe, right or wrong," *The Economist,* 8 December 1990, p.16.
19 Lazar, "The Changing International Context," p.12.
20 Thomas J. Courchene, *Forever Amber,* Reflections/Reflexions no. 6 (Kingston: Institute of Intergovernmental Relations, Queen's University, 1990).

of the overall EPF "freeze" the tax-point transfer component will progressively account for more of the total transfer. Indeed, some analysts have suggested that, under this new regime, cash transfers to Quebec will fall to zero before the year 2000 and those for the rest of the provinces sometime before 2010.[21] Thus the roughly $12 billion of federal cash transfers may eventually fall to zero.

If this occurs, or even if there is a significant decrease in these cash transfers, this can be viewed as decentralizing on three counts. First, if the provinces maintain service levels by increasing their taxes, the share of provincial to federal taxes will increase. This is one definition of decentralization. Second, if the provinces react by cutting back these programs or redesigning them, this is also decentralizing in the sense that these so-called national programs will progressively be designed provincially. The third reason is closely related to the second: when the federal cash transfer falls to zero, how does or can Ottawa enforce any standards at all?

Less dramatic, but nonetheless very significant, are the selected freezes in the Canada Assistance Plan (for the "have" provinces) and the unemployment insurance (UI) strictures which, for the poorer provinces, will transfer unfortunate citizens from federally financed UI to jointly-financed welfare.

All of this focuses on expenditure-shifting, as it were. However, the revenue side also comes into the picture. Specifically, the Goods and Services Tax (GST) invades the sales tax area traditionally viewed by the provinces as their home turf. In an intriguing way, there have been two polar responses to this. On the one hand, Quebec will integrate its sales tax with the GST (and will collect it for Ottawa and presumably will, at Ottawa's expense, employ Quebecers rather than "feds") and thus will take advantage of the broader base to lower its sales tax rate. By its very nature, this is decentralizing since Quebec will in affect be the tax collector (and will be transferring some portion to Ottawa) and will, therefore, eventually have considerable say about the nature of the tax base, the timing of the transfers to Ottawa, the auditing of delinquent firms, and so on.

On the other hand, the western premiers, meeting in Lloydminster in July 1990 argued that since the GST invades a traditional provincial tax base, the cuts in anticipated transfers combined with GST-related revenue constraints may force them to develop, *à la* Quebec, their own, separate, persona- income-

---

21 Quebec has long received extra personal-income-tax points in lieu of the cash transfers aspects of EPF funding. This equals 16.5 percent of federal basic tax. Thus, its cash transfers fall to zero before cash transfers for other provinces. But this raises what will surely be a most contentious issue. When Quebec's tax transfers push through the EPF ceiling it will be in receipt of more overall "transfers" than other provinces for EPF. Eventually, this extra transfer will, as noted, equal 16.5 percent of federal basic tax. This is an enormous amount of money and other provinces will obviously want equal treatment.

tax system.[22] While this initiative may be viewed as a flexing of western muscle in the post-Meech era, it is significant to note that the 20 page document espousing a separate PIT made no mention at all of Meech. Rather it was driven by the issues and concerns raised above. As this paper is being completed, British Columbia has announced that it will release a position paper on a separate personal-income-tax system early in 1991. Again, these developments point clearly in the direction of decentralization.

To this point in the analysis, the various forces are *cumulatively* bearing a rather similar message. East-west economic linkages are coming to be dominated by north-south linkages, admittedly enhanced by the FTA but rather inevitable in any event. This suggests to us that Canada's regions probably should have a larger say in the whole range of policies that affect their north-south viability. Likewise, globalization appears to foster decentralization or at the very least undermines the traditional role of the nation-state. Were we to have focused in more detail on the FTA, this too would have pointed in much the same direction since the FTA's emphasis on market prices and "national treatment" is inherently decentralizing. Demolinguistics also appears to argue for some disentanglement in the area of language and culture. Thus, the solution appears rather straightforward (although not necessarily achievable), namely a much more decentralized Canada particularly for Quebec but possibly for other provinces and/or regions as well. For those Canadians that want a stronger Ottawa, the challenge is to find an appropriate role for the federal government in this emerging global reality. It cannot be the old role. Elsewhere, one of us has suggested that an emphasis on human capital issues may be the most appropriate policy focus in an increasingly integrated and integrating world.[23]

However, things are not so straightforward. There are a series of other forces that are either integrative in their own right or at least severely complicate potential redesign based on the analysis thus far. Foremost among these is the Canadian Charter of Rights and Freedoms, to which we now turn.

THE CHARTER AND CANADIAN FEDERALISM

The Charter is easily the most significant amendment to our constitution and far and away the most complex. At one level, its impact is "republicanizing" since it introduces a checks-and-balances feature (the Courts) into our former Parliament-is-supreme approach to government. At another level, it is highly

---

22 Western Finance Ministers, *Economic and Fiscal Developments and Federal-Provincial Fiscal Relations in Canada*. A report submitted to the Western Premiers' Conference, Lloydminster, 26-27 July 1990.
23 Courchene, "Global Competitiveness and the Canadian Federation."

"Americanizing" since, despite some collective rights provisions, the emphasis on individual rights and the reliance on U.S. jurisprudence to determine Charter cases conjures up visions in the eyes of some Canadians of importing the essence of the "American Creed."

From a further perspective, the Charter is decentralizing since it empowers citizens (via the Courts) with rights that *no* government can take away from them, except via the Notwithstanding Clause. Yet, at the same time the Charter is "centralizing" in the important sense that the "resultant rights and freedoms [are] country-wide in scope, enforced by a national supreme court, and entrenched in a national constitution beyond the reach of fleeting majorities at either level of government."[24] Moreover, "the language of rights is a Canadian language, not a provincial language" and as "the Charter takes root over time the psyche of the citizenry will be progressively Canadianized."[25]

However, the Charter is much more than this. Not only has it taken root among Canadians, particularly English-speaking Canadians, it is also beginning to redefine Canada.[26] Essentially the new vision is that of a nonterritorial conception of the federation, a vision that has little to do with the traditional federal-provincial cleavages but rather one that focuses on cleavages that are pan-Canadian, e.g., Charter-enshrined interests on the one hand and all manner of vested interests or elites on the other. In effect, by enshrining citizens (whether individually or in groups) the Charter has "democratized" the constitution and this directly or indirectly challenges the existing amending formula which remains in the domain of executive federalism.

In sum, there are at least two concerns associated with redefining Canadianism along Charter lines. The first is that, as S.M. Lipset argues, over time individual rights will dominate collective rights so that the Charter will

---

24 Alan Cairns, "Recent Federalist Constitutional Proposals: A Review Essay," *Canadian Public Policy/Analyse de Politique* volume V, 1979, p. 354.

25 Alan Cairns, "The Politics of Constitution Making: The Canadian Experience," in K. Banting and R. Simeon (eds.), *Redesigning the State: Constitutional Change in Comparative Perspective* (London: Macmillan, 1984), p. 130.

26 Our ambivalence on the unifying force of the Charter can be simply stated: while there are unmistakable signs that the Charter is (as we are about to argue) serving to divide English Canada and Quebec, it is possible that (as we have just suggested) it is simultaneously serving to provide a common legal/political frame of reference and focal-point for English Canadians. McDougall dissents from even the latter view to some extent because he is not persuaded that homogenization necessarily equals (or produces) unity. The fact that Canadians (or even just English Canadians) all have similar links with a national core (the Charter and decisions of the Supreme Court) does not necessarily say anything about their links with one another, and social cohesion probably has more to do with the latter than the former.

eventually make us more "American."[27] The second is that the Charter runs counter to the collective aspirations of Quebecers. In Andrew Petter's words:

> The 1982 amendment [essentially the Charter] undermined the constitution's stabilizing and unifying influence by formalizing and thereby privileging political values that were acceptable to elites in English Canada, but were inimical to elites in Quebec. The commitments made in 1982 to pan-Canadian identity over regional identity, to individual bilingualism over territorial bilingualism and to provincial equality over special status for Quebec have contributed to a deepening sense of anger and alienation among Quebec nationalists (including moderate nationalists), fueling demands for further constitutional reform. At the same time, the political values that were formalized in 1982 have attracted growing support from other Canadians, making it increasingly difficult to dislodge or counterbalance those values in order to satisfy the concerns of Quebec nationalists.[28]

This poses problems or challenges in its own right, but it is magnified by the two final forces that we shall highlight briefly — institutional crisis and First Nations' concerns.

INSTITUTIONAL CRISIS

In the interests of brevity (but probably at the cost of some degree of misrepresentation), we simply assert that Canadians appear to have had their fill of party or parliamentary government and desire a greater degree of representative government, i.e., where MPs reflect constituents' rather than party interests. This has been brought to the fore by the GST debate, but the general concern has been mounting throughout the 1980s. Since the issue cannot be addressed directly (via abandoning the party system of government), it has surfaced under various guises. Two of these merit highlighting. The first is the momentum towards a Triple E Senate. Setting aside the critical issue of whether this is indeed a solution, the perceived role of this reconstructed Senate would be to bring provincial input, on an equal basis by province, *directly* into national decision-making, thereby providing an offset to party government. The second is more direct in the sense that it attempts to get at the root of the problem: if one cannot change party government, then the next best thing is to destroy the "national" parties. Hence the rise of the Reform Party in the west, the *Bloc Québécois* in Quebec and the Confederation of Regions (COR) party in provinces like New Brunswick.

---

27 S.M. Lipset, *Continental Divide: The Values and Institutions of the United States and Canada* (Toronto: C.D. Howe Institute, 1989), pp. 101-109.

28 Andrew Petter, "Comments on the *Constitution Act, 1867*," background paper prepared for C.D. Howe Roundtable on "Imagining Constitutional Futures," Toronto, 17-19 November 1990.

In terms of the subject matter of this paper, there are two significant implications that derive from these developments. The first is that underlying the conception of the Triple E Senate is an implicit, if not explicit, suggestion that all provinces must be equal in terms of their powers. This recent emphasis on equality of provinces or symmetry, as it has come to be known, is the subject matter of David Milne's paper in this volume. The only point we wish to make here is that this notion of symmetry (which is enhanced substantially by the Charter) is quite revisionist in terms of the practice of Canadian federalism: the original British North America (BNA) Act contained major elements of asymmetry and mechanisms such as "opting-out" have led to important asymmetries in Canadian federalism. If symmetry is the way of the future (and it likely is since the lightening rod in Meech Lake was the asymmetric "distinct society" clause), then this severely complicates the search for viable future options.

The second implication is equally problematic. As we interpret the thrust of the Reform Party phenomenon, it is a "the west wants in" movement, replete with a Triple E Senate and a strong central government and, therefore, quite removed from the "Quebec wants out" scenario that is playing so well before Quebec's Bélanger-Campeau Commission. What this means is that the so-called Quebec-west axis is really a broadside against the status quo, with little if any, agreement on possible solutions. This too, is complicating.

THE CONSTITUTION AS "ORGANIC"

The final element in our selective review of the context of future constitutional options relates more to process. Even if Canadians were able to come up with acceptable options to some of the outstanding concerns, it is not clear that the way is open any longer to amend the constitution in piecemeal fashion. As Donna Greschner notes: "The more Quebec uses the rhetoric of distinctiveness and self-determination, the more the First Nations gain credibility and legitimacy for their struggle."[29] And the more likely it is that they will press for their own demands. In other words, constitutional reform is progressively being viewed as organic. What this means is that in spite of the crisis that we will likely find ourselves in this spring (after the Quebec commissions issue their reports), there is growing and deep-seated disenchantment with the prospect of another Quebec round. This time around, other groups' long-standing concerns will have to be part of any package. While this will make the exercise far more daunting, it may also open up options that were heretofore assumed to be closed. In any event, we probably have no choice.

---

29 Donna Greschner, "Aboriginal Peoples and Constitutional Futures," background paper prepared for the C.D. Howe Roundtable "Imagining Constitutional Futures," p. 3.

CONCLUSION

This, then, is our overview of the context underlying Canada's constitutional options. As noted earlier, our treatment of the forces at play has been quite selective. For example, complicating all of the above is the fact that Ottawa's role in the process is quite different this time around. First, the fiscal cupboard is empty so that there is little in the way of federal largesse that can be spread around to finesse a deal. Second, and more important, Ottawa is much more than a mere umpire. Given that a much-more-decentralized federation is one of the viable options, Ottawa is now a full player with its own interests and positions to defend.

As noted in the introduction, it is not difficult to become rather dispirited in terms of Canada's future. However, it is also the case that some of the above factors are mutually reinforcing. For example, without addressing the issue of whose concerns should be dealt with first, the prospect of somehow recognizing Quebec as a distinct society in a reconstructed federation is surely good news to the First Nations who also want to be "distinct." Nor is there much point to denying Quebec's distinctiveness if, upon reflection, it is evident that British Columbia will demand the same in a decade or two when it becomes fully Pacific-Rim oriented and, perhaps, Pacific-Rim peopled. Similarly, there is not much point over the next year or so in opposing greater powers for Quebec (and others) if this is where globalization and our fiscal position is going to drive us in any event. Meanwhile, it is likely that an overall decentralization can only come about with political units larger than some of the existing provinces.

Unfortunately, other parts of the analysis stand out in isolation and hold little promise of reconciliation. Foremost among these is Quebec's desire for greater control over language and culture. In our view, Quebec *will* get substantially enhanced powers here. The only question for the rest of Canadians is whether they want Quebec to exercise these powers within Canada or outside it. But even here there may be scope for bargaining — a more territorial, rather than a pan-Canadian, approach to linguistic duality, with some side-contracting for areas where either French or English is an important minority language, may well find many adherents.

A final word: a major lesson from the Meech debacle is that "elite accommodation," our traditional trump card, has failed. And in our view it failed in part because the provisions of Meech did not come to grips with the full range of challenges elaborated above. The current notion that the failure was triggered by the process (e.g., the amending procedure) and that the principal challenge now is to reform the amending process (e.g., the Joint House/Senate Committee) is not so much wrong as it is beside the point. Indeed, one might marvel at how such a poorly marketed and unpopular amendment came so close to being enshrined, and perhaps would have been had it not been for the last-minute federal high jinks. For it seems clear to us that the lesson of the failure of the Meech Lake Accord must not be seen independently of the unpopularity, in English Canada, of its *substance*. To stir the constitutional pot in this fragile, disconnected society, and especially to do so in a manner that seems to much of the country to favour one province and class of Canadians above others, is unlikely to survive *any* democratic form of ratification.

Our view is that the impasse now has reached the point where the key to the maintenance of the political integrity of Canada rests with the political will of individual Canadians. We must and will become involved. If the majority of Canadians cannot find within themselves a constitutionally salient image of themselves and their country that transcends the differences among their various groups and regions, then no change in the amending formula is likely to hold us together. But if we Canadians can rethink our country in creative ways that preserve and enhance what we value, and at the same time accommodate the long-standing concerns of the various regions, then no amending formula is likely to thwart us.[30] As Ogopogo might hope to say, "we have met our friends, and they are us."

---

30 Thomas J. Courchene presents one such reworking of the Canadian federation based largely on an attempt to accommodate the various "forces" that have been dealt with above. See "The Community of the Canadas," an invited paper presented to the Bélanger-Campeau Commission (La Commission sur l'avenir politique et constitutionnel du Québec). (Kingston: School of Policy Studies, Queen's University, 1990).

4

Shared and Divergent Values

Charles Taylor

Are there divergences of value between the different regions of Canada? In a sense, these are minimal. There appears to be a remarkable similarity throughout the country, and across the French/English difference, when it comes to the things in life which are important. Even when it comes to the values that specifically relate to political culture, there seems to be broad agreement. About equality, nondiscrimination, the rule of law, the mores of representative democracy, about social provision, about violence and firearms, and a host of issues.

This was not always the case. Half a century ago, it seemed that there were serious differences between the two major groups as far as political culture was concerned. Pierre Trudeau wrote about this.[1] The ravages of Maurice Duplessis on the rule of law, which he seemed to be able to get away with — his treatment of Jehovah's witnesses and Communists — seemed to indicate that Quebec and French Canada had different views about the toleration of dissent. Some people were ready to believe that the two societies gave quite different values to the maintenance of unity around certain cherished truths and standards when these conflicted with the goods of tolerance, freedom, or permitted diversity. Not that the rest-of-Canada was all that liberal in those days. Various minorities and dissidents had a rough time. But the particular grounds for illiberalism were rather strikingly different in Quebec, seemingly organized around the values of a traditional, ultramontane Catholicism. They made the province stand out as exotic and disturbing in the eyes of other Canadians.

This difference has disappeared today. Partly one might say that French Canada has rejoined "English Canada"; more accurately one might say that the forces within Quebec that were always striving for a liberal society have won out. Perhaps it would be more insightful to say that both parts of Canada have been swept up into the liberal consensus that has become established in the

---

1   "La Province de Québec au moment de la grève" in Pierre Trudeau (ed.), *La Grève de l'Amiante* (Montréal: les Éditions Cité Libre, 1956).

whole western world in the wake of World War II. As we shall see below, some English-speaking Canadians seem still to doubt this, to harbour a suspicion of Quebec's liberal credentials, but this is quite unfounded in the 1990s. Or rather, suspicions are in order, but just as they are about any other Atlantic society, for none of these is exempt from racism, chauvinism, and similar ills.

Ironically, at the very moment when we agree upon so much, we are close to breakup. We have never been closer to breakup in our history, although our values have never been so uniform. The road to uniformity goes beyond the ironing out of differences between the two major cultures. There has also been a steady erosion of urban-rural differences in outlook over the last half century. And the prodigious effect of modern communications has probably lessened all the various regional differences as well.

WHY CANADA?

So what is the problem? It emerges when you ask another kind of question, also in the realm of values in some broad sense. Not what do people cherish as good, but what is a country for? That is, what ought to be the basis of unity around which a sovereign political entity can be built? This is a strange question in a way; it is not one that would likely be asked in many countries. But it arises here because there are alternatives, and therefore a felt need for justification. These alternatives exist for us — in our understanding of our situation — even when they are not very likely, when they enjoy minimal support and are hardly in the cards politically. They can still exist as a challenge to self-justification because they existed historically, and we retain the sense that our existing arrangements emerge out of a choice that excluded them.

In Canada-outside-Quebec (COQ)[2] the alternatives are two: the country or bits of it could join, or could have joined the United States; and the bits could also have failed to join together — and indeed, could one day deconfederate again. So there are two existential questions for COQ which we can call the unity and distinctness questions respectively. For Quebec there is one big question, which is too familiar and too much on the agenda today to need much description. It is the issue of whether to be part of Canada or not; and if so, how. I stress that neither of the existential alternatives may be strong options in COQ

---

2   In Quebec we speak blithely of "English Canada," but the people who live there do not identify with this label. We need a handy way of referring to the rest of the country as an entity, even if it lacks for the moment political expression. In order to avoid the clumsy three-word hyphenated expression, I plan to use "COQ" henceforth in this paper. I hope the reader will not take this as a sign of encroaching barbarism, or Québécois self-absorption (although it might partake in small measure of both).

today, but that does not stop them functioning as reference points for self-definition; as ways of defining the question: what do we exist for?

In a sense the existential questions of the two societies are interwoven. Perhaps COQ would not feel the need for self-definition, for an answer to the question, "What is Canada for?" to anything like the same degree if Quebec were not contemplating answering its existential question in a radical form. But once the country's existence is threatened in this way all the suppressed alternatives rise to the surface in the rest-of-Canada as well.

So what are the answers? It will be easier to set out the problem by taking "English Canada" first. The answer here used to be simple. Way back when it really fitted into our official name of "British North America," the distinctness question answered itself; and unity seemed to be the corollary of the drive for distinctness in face of the American colossus. But as the Britishness, even "Englishness" of non-Quebec Canada declines, this becomes less and less viable as an answer. We are all the Queen's subjects, but this seems to mean less to less people; and more awkwardly, it means quite a bit to some still, but nothing at all to others, and thus cannot be the basis of unity.

What binds Canada together outside Quebec is thus no longer a common provenance, and less and less a common history. But people find the bonding elements in political institutions and ways of being. This is not a total break from the old identity, because Britishness also defined itself largely in terms of political institutions: parliamentary government, a certain juridical tradition, and the like. The slide has been continuous and without a sharp break from the old to the new. There are even certain continuing elements, but the package is different.

Canadians feel that they are different from the Americans, because (a) they live in a less violent and conflict-ridden society. This is partly just a matter of luck. We do not have a history that has generated an undeclared, low-level race war continuously feeding itself in our cities. But it is also a matter of political culture. From the very beginning Americans have put a value on energetic, direct defense of rights, and therefore are ready to mitigate their condemnation of violence. There is more understanding of it south of the border, more willingness to make allowances for it. And this has something to do with the actual level of violence being higher there, as well as with a number of strange penchants of American society, such as that expressed in the powerful lobby for personal firearms. Canadians tend to put more value on "peace, order and good government." At least, this is how we see ourselves, which is perhaps what is important for our purposes; but there seems to be some truth in the perception.

As a consequence, there is more tolerance here of rules and restrictions that are justified by the need for order. With it there is more of a favourable prejudice (at least in English Canada), and a free gift of the benefit of the doubt to the police forces. Hence the relative absence of protest when the *War Measures Act* was invoked in 1970; hence also the strange reluctance of the Canadian public to condemn the RCMP, even after all the revelations of its dubious behaviour.

We might add that Americans' tolerance of conflict extends into the domain of law as well. They are more litigious than we are. They think that is a good thing, that it reflects well on them. No one should take any guff from anyone. We tend to deplore it. From an American point of view, we seem to have an endless appetite for guff. But perhaps the long-term effect of the 1982 Charter will be to diminish this difference.

Related to this first point, Canadians (b) see their political society as more committed to collective provision, over against an American society that gives greater weight to individual initiative. Appeals for reduced government can be heard from the right of the political spectrum in both countries, but the idea of what reduced government actually means seems to be very different. There are regional differences in Canada, but generally Canadians are proud of and happy with their social programs, especially health insurance, and find the relative absence of these in the U.S. disturbing. The fact that poverty and destitution have been left to proliferate in American cities as they have during the Reagan years is generally seen here as a black mark against that society. Canadian practice may not be as much better as many of us believe; but the important point is that this is seen as a difference worth preserving.

Thus these two answers, (a) *law and order* and (b) *collective provision*, help to address the distinctness question. They explain why we are and want to remain a distinct political unit. But what answers the unity question? Why be a single country, and what common goals ought to animate this country? In one sense, (a) and (b) can serve here as well, if one thinks (as many Canadians instinctively do) that we need to hang together in order to maintain this alternative political culture as a viable option in North America. And then (b) can be logically extended into one of the principal declared common objectives of the Canadian federation in recent decades: (c) the equalization of life conditions and life chances between the regions. The solidarity of collective provision, which within each regional society generates such programs as Medicare, can be seen as finding its logical expression in a solidarity of mutual help between regions.

And so Canadian federalism has generated the practices of large-scale redistribution of fiscal resources through equalization payments, and attempts have been made at regional development. This too contrasts with recent American practice and provides a further answer to the distinctness question. We perhaps owe the drive to equality to the fact that we have been confronted with existential questions in a way that our neighbours have not since 1865. The Canadian federal union has been induced to justify itself, and greater inter-regional solidarity may be one of the fruits of this underlying angst.

But this bonding principle has also been a worrying source of division, because it is widely seen as a locus of failed aspirations and disappointed expectations. The principles of *regional equality and mutual help* run against a perceived reality of central Canadian domination in the outlying regions, a grievous mismatch of promise and performance. Recently it has become clearer that the disappointment takes two rather different forms, reflecting different ideas of regional equality. In some parts, mainly Atlantic Canada, it is principally the failure of federal programs actually to improve regional economic standards that is the source of disappointment. The failure is one of mutual help. Elsewhere, mainly in western Canada, the sense of grievance is mobilized around neglected interests: the regions are not listened to, their interests are ridden over roughshod by a dominant central Canada. The failure is one of balance of power. In one version, the implicit but undelivered contract calls for redistribution to poorer regions. In the other version, it calls for a redress of power and influence in favour of the regions with less demographic and economic clout. In one case, the implicit promise is of equalized incomes; in the other it points to more equalized power between regional societies.

It is clear that this issue of regional equality is a very troubled one in Canada. That is because it is on one hand an indispensable part of the answer to the unity question; while on the other it seems to many so largely unrealized, and on top of it all, we agree less and less on what it actually means.

But even if things were going swimmingly in this domain, we still would not have a full answer to the unity question. English Canada has been becoming more and more diverse, less and less "English," over the decades. The fact that it has always been an immigrant society, i.e., one which functions through admitting a steady stream of new arrivals, on top of the fact that it could not aspire to make immigrants over to its original mould, has meant that it has *de facto* become more and more multicultural over the years. It could not aspire to assimilate the newcomers to an existing mould, because this was originally British, hence ethnic. In the United States, which has always operated on a strong sense that it incarnates unrivalled political institutions, the drive to make everyone American could proceed apace. It was never as clear what the Canadian identity amounted to in political terms, and insofar as it was conceived as British it could not be considered normative for new arrivals. First, it was only the identity of one part of the country, and second, it could not but come to be seen as one ethnic background among others.

Canadians have seen their society as less of a melting pot than the United States; and there has been some truth in this. In contrast to the neighbour society, people have spoken of a Canadian "mosaic." So this has even become for some a new facet of their answer to the distinctiveness question, under the rubric (d) *multiculturalism*. This is also far from trouble-free. Questions are being posed in both the major cultures about the pace and even goals of integration, or assimilation of immigrants into the larger anglophone or francophone society. This is particularly troubling in Quebec, which has much less historic experience of assimilating immigrants and a much higher proportion of whose francophone population is *pure laine.*

This makes even more acute the need for a further point of unity, a common reference point of identity, which can rally people from many diverse backgrounds and regions. In a quite astonishing way, (e) the *Charter of Rights* has come to fill this role in English Canada in recent years. It is astonishing, because nine years ago it did not exist. Nor was there that much of a groundswell of support demanding its introduction before it became a bone of contention between federal and provincial governments in the run-up to the patriation of 1981-82. But the Meech Lake debate showed how important it has become in COQ not just as an additional bulwark of rights, but as part of the indispensable common ground on which all Canadians ought to stand. For many people, it has come in the space of a few years to define in part the Canadian political identity.[3] And since in COQ the national identity has to be defined in terms of political institutions for reasons rehearsed above, this has been a fateful development.

WHY QUEBEC?

How about Quebec? How can it go about answering its existential question? The terms are very different. In Quebec, there is not a distinctness issue. The language and culture by themselves mark us off from Americans, and also from other Canadians. Much of (a) to (e) is seen as a "Good Thing" in Quebec. Regarding (a) — law and order — people do not compare themselves a lot with the U.S., but there is no doubt that Quebecers are spontaneously on the side of law and order, and are even more horrified by internecine conflict than other Canadians. The FLQ utterly and totally relegated themselves to irrecoverable history as soon as they murdered Pierre Laporte. The present rather half-hearted attempts to romanticize their escapades on the twentieth anniversary of the October crisis should not mislead in this regard. The reaction to the massacre of the women at Ecole Polytechnique is also eloquent on this score. Quebec society reacted more like a wounded family than like a large-scale, impersonal political unit.

---

3   Alan Cairns has written very insightfully on this development. See in particular his "Constitutional Minoritarianism in Canada," in Ronald L. Watts and Douglas M. Brown (eds.), *Canada: The State of the Federation 1990* (Kingston: Institute of Intergovernmental Relations, Queen's University, 1990); and "Ritual, Taboo and Bias in Constitutional Controversies in Canada, or Constitutional Talk Canadian Style," in *The Saskatchewan Law Review,* vol 54, 1990, pp. 121-147.

Regarding (b) — collective provision — it goes without saying that people are proud of their social programs in the province, and want to keep them. Point (d) — multiculturalism — is more problematic. As a federal policy, multiculturalism is sometimes seen as a device to deny French-speaking minorities their full recognition, or even to reduce the importance of the French fact in Canada to that of an outsize ethnic minority. And within Quebec itself, the growing diversity of francophone society is causing much heartburn and anxiety. Point (c) — regional equality and mutual self-help — is generally supported in Quebec, and even (e) — the Charter was favourably seen until it came to be perceived as an instrument for the advancement of the uniformity of language regimes across the country. Even now its other provisions are widely popular.

But these do not go very far to answer the question, what is a country for? There is one obvious answer to this question, which has continued down through the decades for over two centuries: (f) you need a country to defend or promote the nation. The nation here was originally "la nation canadienne-française." Now without entirely abandoning the first formulation, it tends to be put as *la nation québécoise*. This does not betoken any change in ethnic identity, of course. It reflects rather a sense, which presents itself as realistic, but may be too pessimistic, that the really survivable elements of la nation canadienne-française are only to be found in Quebec.

But the real point here is that (f) makes the survival and/or flourishing of this nation/language one of the prime goals of political society. No political entity is worth allegiance that does not contribute to this. The issue: independent Quebec versus remaining in Canada turns simply on different judgements about what does contribute to this.

Put in terms of a possible formula for Canada, this means that from a Quebec perspective, (a) to (e) may be attractive features, but the absolutely crucial one that Canada must have to possess a *raison d'être* is that it contribute to the survival and/or furtherance of *la nation canadienne-française*.

This means in practice some kind of dualism. It was this, of course, that successive Quebec leaders always gave expression to when they described Canada as a pact between "deux nations," or "deux peuples fondateurs."

Dualism in turn has to exist at two levels. (i) First, it meant that French had to be recognized as a language along with English in the federation. That is, French had to be given a status clearly different from that of an ethnic immigrant language, even if it was the most important among these. And (ii) second, it meant that *la nation canadienne-française*, or its major part, had to have some autonomy, some ability to act as a unit. Both these features were built to some degree into the original Confederation pact, but in the case of (i) — bilingualism — in partial and somewhat grudging form. Bilingualism (i) and Quebec autonomy (ii) are separate requirements, but also in a sense related. There is a certain degree of complementarity, in that the more freely and completely (i) is granted, in theory the less the need will be felt for autonomous action. It is perhaps the tragedy of Canada that (i) was eventually granted too late, and too grudgingly, and that this established a high and irreversible pattern of demands on (ii).

Both these requirements have been a source of difficulty. The extension of (i) beyond its original limits raised a problem, because COQ in its developing multiculturalism was naturally led to accord English the status of a common language, and to split language from culture. That English was the main language was not meant to imply that people of English descent had privileges or were somehow superior. The hegemony of English had to be justified in purely utilitarian terms. Within this framework, the case for putting French alongside English was impossible to make. Outside Quebec, a special status for French was rarely justified by numbers, and certainly not by its indispensability as a medium of communication. It seemed like indefensible favouritism.

Second, both (i) and (ii) met with resistance because of a perceived difference of Quebec from the values of the rest-of-Canada. This starts off as a dark prejudice in the mind of Orange Protestants, but it continues on in many another milieux because of the supposed appeal of illiberal modes of thought in Quebec. In particular, this militated against further concessions in the area of (ii).

It has been one of the remarkable achievements of the last 30 years, and particularly of the Trudeau government, to have established bilingualism (i) almost integrally. There has been a certain cost in resentment in some areas, and this may be fateful in the forthcoming negotiations. I want to return to this below. But there is no doubt that a big change has been brought about. On Quebec autonomy (ii) as well, great progress has been made. First, the Canadian federation has proven a very flexible instrument, giving lots of powers to the provinces. And second, where Quebec's needs have been different from the other provinces, a large *de facto* special status has been developed. Quebec has its own Pension Plan, levies its own income tax, has a special immigration regime, and so on.

But it is the formal recognition of Quebec's autonomy that has been blocked. Giving Quebec the autonomy it needs, without disbalancing the Canadian federation, would involve giving Quebec a different kind of relation to the federal government and institutions. Although this has been worked *de facto* to a remarkable extent, there are powerful resistances to according it recognition in principle. This is because there is a deep clash of purpose between the two sides of Canada. Where the old clash of values seems to have disappeared, a new conflict of purposes, of answers to the question, "What is a country for?" has surfaced.

The demands of (ii), of a special status for Quebec, run against those of regional equality (c) as these are conceived by many in COQ, and against a widespread understanding of the Charter (e). Point (c) has come to be defined for some as entailing an equality of the provinces. The great moral force of the principle of equity between regions has been mobilized behind the rather abstract juridical issue of the relative constitutional status of provinces. Now regional equity seems to be flouted if all provinces are not placed on the same footing. A special status can be presented as a breach in this kind of equality.

More grievously, the special status for Quebec is plainly justified on the grounds of the defense and promotion of la nation canadienne-française (f). But this is a collective goal. The aim is to ensure the flourishing and survival of a *community*. Now the new patriotism of the Charter has given an impetus to a philosophy of rights and of nondiscrimination that is highly suspicious of collective goals. It can only countenance them if they are clearly subordinated to individual rights and to provisions of nondiscrimination. But for those who take these goals seriously, this subordination is unacceptable. The Charter and the promotion of the nation, as understood in their respective constituencies, are on a collision course. The reactions to Bill 178 and much of the Meech Lake debate were eloquent on this score.

This difficulty arises with the concept of Quebec autonomy (ii), where it did not for bilingualism (i). The provisions for bilingualism in federal legislation can be justified in terms of individual rights. They concern the guarantee that francophones can be dealt with and obtain government services in their language. Once French is given this status along with English, what is protected are the rights of individuals. The collective goal goes beyond this. The aim is not only that francophones be served in French, but that there still be francophones there in the next generation; this is the objective of (f). It cannot be translated into an assurance of rights for *existing* francophones. Indeed, pursuing it may even involve reducing their individual freedom of choice, as Law 101 does in Quebec, where francophone parents must send their children to French language schools.

So the two halves of Canada have come onto a collision course because of the conflict between their respective answers to the question, "What is a country for?" In particular, a conflict between (c) regional equality, and (e) the Charter, on one hand, and (ii) Quebec autonomy, on the other. Other difficulties have been raised about special status; in particular, the problem of participation of Quebecers in a federal parliament if the matters it deals with for other Canadians come to diverge greatly from the matters it deals with affecting Quebec. But I think this difficulty is exaggerated. The two areas of concern have to come very far apart for this to be a real problem.[4]

---

4   I do not wish to dwell on this point at length here, but our own experience and that of some other countries, seems to reduce our grounds for worry on this score. We have to remember that Quebec already has a special status. In 1964, Quebec members sat in the House of Commons while the Canada Pension Plan was voted, following an agreement with Quebec that the province would have its own plan. The

WHY NOW?

One might ask, why the collision course now? Surely the old "English" Canada, before the legislation about bilingualism and the Trudeau revolution, was even more inhospitable to the demands of Quebec. It balked not only at (ii) Quebec autonomy, but at (i) bilingualism as well. Moreover, it penetrated much more within Quebec. In those days, the English minority, backed often by the federal government or pan-Canadian institutions like the CPR, maintained its own English-only forms of operation, excluding or marginalizing or down-grading the French language. Why did things not fly apart then?

The answer is that separation did not seem a realistic option back then for all sorts of reasons. It started with a clear-sighted appreciation of the relation of forces, and a sense of what the English Canadian majority would tolerate. There was also a greater commitment to the francophone minorities outside the province than there now is. But an extremely important factor was the restricted economic role of French Quebecers. The English still had a preponderant role in the economy. Big business spoke English; anglophones dominated the ranks of management and had more than their share of certain key economic professions like engineering. This was a source of grievance on many levels. In particular, it was what permitted English to arrogate to itself a place in the province that demographics would never justify. To take just one instance, before the Quiet Revolution, again and again, union leaders would have to bargain in English with management on behalf of a work force that was 100 percent francophone. But at the same time, this imbalance contributed to a climate in which Quebec society felt incomplete, in which essential functions were being filled by outsiders. The relation was never articulated in this way at the time, but it helped to keep the option of a total break off the agenda. Separation was not a real option before 1960, even though it seems to have been toyed with as an eventual long-term destination by Abbe Groulx.

Paradoxically, as some of the most crying grievances were resolved, as the insulting and sometimes threatening marginalization of the French language was reversed, as francophone Quebecers began to take their full place in the economy, at first through the public and parapublic sectors (e.g., Hydro-Québec) and then the private sector, precisely in the wake of all these successes, the demand for independence gained strength. And it grew until it became one of two major constitutional options, on a par with its federalist rival, and since

---

fact that there was a separate Quebec plan did not mean that Quebecers had no further interest in the Canadian arrangements. On the contrary, because of the demands of portability, each was vitally interested in the other. Other examples of asymmetrical relations of part to whole come to mind, such as, e.g., the "provincial" government that existed for many years in Ulster. The experiment was terminated for reasons that had nothing to do with any constitutional unworkability.

Meech even ahead. And all this while outside Quebec at the federal level, bilingualism is advancing, and Quebecers wield more power than ever before. These are the years of "French power." Some westerners have the feeling that the federal government is run by Quebecers. Why does breakup loom now? How to explain this paradoxical and even perverse result?

Part of the answer, implicit in the above, is that now for the first time, the option looks conceivable, possible, even safe. In this regard, even the last decade has seen a change. In 1980, most Quebecers still found sovereignty a somewhat frightening prospect. The referendum revealed that clearly. In 1990, this no longer seems to be so. A great deal of the difference seems to stem from the now perceived high-profile place of francophones as big players in our economic life. This is something that has been happening over a number of decades, but as is the way with media-driven public perceptions, the realization has come all in a rush. And with this realization, a great flush of confidence. As often with these media-driven perceptions, we go easily from one exaggeration to another. Quebecers were not as powerless before, and they are not as powerful now, as they think. Separation risks being much more economically costly than they now believe, even as it would have been less catastrophic than many thought in 1980. And we may even be in for another swerve of opinion as the present recession dims expectations. But the basic change is undeniable. Separation is really thinkable.

But that cannot be the whole explanation. To claim this would be to say that Quebecers never really wanted anything else, that they were just waiting for the moment when they could dare to go for it. And nothing could be falser than that. A great deal attached francophone Quebecers to this country: first of all, the sense that the larger entity was the home of la nation canadienne-française, whose whole extent included more than Quebec; then a certain attachment to a constitutional home that had become familiar, and which their leaders had had a hand in building. But what was always missing was a genuine patriotism for Canada. That kind of sentiment was reserved for la nation canadienne-française. It has lately been transposed onto Quebec, as the viable segment of that nation, but never managed to spread from there onto the whole political unit.

That is why people have often spoken of Canada as being for Quebecers a *mariage de raison*. This somewhat understates the case, because it does not take account of the multiform attachment to Canada I have just described, but it is emotionally true in this negative sense, that a genuine patriotism for a bilingual, two-nation Canada never developed.

This by itself still does not explain the strength of the independentist option today. After all, if Canada was a *mariage de raison*, why abandon it when it has never been so reasonable, when the deal seems the most favourable ever? Of course, many federalist Quebecers are pleading the cause of Canada today in just these terms. But why does it not have more success? Why are even those who are making the plea profoundly ambivalent about it?

Here one can easily be misled, because the opponents of these partisans of "profitable federalism" seem to want to engage them on their own ground, and strive to prove that Confederation is a bad deal for us. But in fact, the emotional drive behind independence is elsewhere. It is much more a failure of *recognition*. For decades, Quebec leaders explained that Confederation was a pact between two founding peoples, two nations. This was never the way the matter was understood outside the province. But the claim was not so much to the effect that this was the plain sense of the confederation pact, somehow perversely forgotten by the others — although this is how it was often put. It was much more an expression of the profound sentiment that this was the only form in which Confederation could be ultimately acceptable to French Canadians, in a way that could engage their hearts and respect their dignity.

In fact, in the real world it was necessary to live with compromises, in which the duality principle got a rather limited and grudging expression. It was necessary to operate in a country which for many purposes was run much more as a nation with one hegemonic culture, with more or less generous provision for minorities on a regional basis. Present-day Canadians, some of whom still may want to complain about the number of languages on their corn flakes boxes, have no idea of how exiguous the place of French was in the bad old days. In the 1930s even the money was still unilingual English.

Canada had to be accepted, but never so as to engage the heart, or respect dignity. It could not be accepted "dans l'honneur et l'enthousiasme," to use a phrase which has been so often repeated during the drama of Meech Lake. Below the rational acceptance of the marriage of reason, these denials bite deep. This is easy to lose sight of, because those who are frustrated in their desire for recognition understandably do not want to present their case in those terms. It is only when one is recognized that one is happy to avow the desire. So the phrase "dans l'honneur et l'enthousiasme" emerges when it looked as though that aspiration was at last met. But when it is denied, the opponents of federal Canada will pretend that no one was ever interested in mere symbols, that the calculus of independence is made in the realistic terms of power and prosperity, that the attitudes of the English-Canadian partner mean nothing to us. In all this, they do protest a little too much.

The present strength of independentism is thus due in part to the new confidence of Quebecers, and in part to the fact that Canada never gelled as a nation for them. But in large part it is due to the continued denial of their understanding of Canada, of the only terms on which it could have been fully accepted by them. These were articulated, among other forms, in the "two-nations" view of the country. Of course, this was unacceptable as it stood to the rest of the country, which did not itself feel like a "nation." Here there was an attempt by French Canadians to foist a symmetrical identity on their partners. And this attempt is not yet abandoned, as one can see from much of the discussion in Quebec today, to which I will return below. But there was a basic demand that could be separated from this presumptious definition of the other. This was the demand that *la nation canadienne-française* be recognized as a crucial component of the country, as an entity whose survival and flourishing was one of the main purposes of Canada as a political society. If this had been granted, it would not have mattered how the rest of the country defined itself.

Actually, the country has come to arrange itself not at all badly for this purpose, through federal bilingualism, through advances made by some French-speaking minorities elsewhere, and through a *de facto* administrative special status for Quebec. But what was missing was a clear recognition that this was part of our purpose as a federation. This is why Meech Lake was so important, and why its failure will have such dire consequences. If one just listens to what people say in Quebec, this can seem strange. Lots of Quebecers never even admitted that they were in favour of Meech, or expressed lukewarm support. Basically, all the independentists took this line. Those who were skeptical about English Canada hedged their bets, never wanted to allow that the recognition mattered to them. But the depth of the reaction to its demise shows how little this represented how they felt.

Meech was important because it was the first time that recognition of Canadian duality and the special role of Quebec was being written into a statement of what Canada was about. The fact that the Accord conferred no additional powers largely narrowed its significance to this one clear declaration of intent. The importance of this declaration can be understood only in the light of the years of nonrecognition, of the marriage of reason that failed to engage the heart and reflect dignity. It can be understood in the context of a present generation that is quite free of the timidity of its ancestors before a possible break, which is even a little surprised, sometimes a trifle contemptuous of their predecessors, for having put up with nonrecognition for so long. And its refusal when it was *just* this, a declaration of pure intent, takes on fateful significance. (That is the point of the oft-repeated phrase that Meech constituted our *conditions minimales*).

With the demise of Meech, something snapped. I think it can be rather simply described. Quebecers will no longer live in a structure that does not fully recognize their national goals. In the early 1980s, after the defeat of the "yes" in the referendum, many toyed with the idea of accepting the marriage of reason, and making a go of it with or without recognition. The new confidence could also have been motivated by this rather different stance, which marginalized the issue of recognition. After all, if you know your own worth, why do you need the other? But in a sense, Meech wiped out this possibility, just because it raised the hope of recognition. And now we are irretrievably on another track.

(Not that I think the "reasonable" track could have lasted very long anyway; it was always at the mercy of some new development.)

What remains to be explained is the extraordinary euphoria that all observers noted among the crowds celebrating Quebec's national holiday, the *St-Jean* 1990. Why did Quebecers feel so united, and so relieved at being united, almost as though the demise of Meech had taken a great weight off them? I think it is because the long division and hesitation between the "reasonable" acceptance of a structure that did not recognize them and the insistence on having their national purposes openly accepted had at last been resolved. This was felt as a division between Quebecers, and especially painfully at the time of the 1980 referendum when families were often split. But it also divided many Quebecers within themselves. At last the long conflict, the long hesitation, the long ambivalence was over. Quebecers were clear about what they want to ask of any future political structure on the northern half of this continent. Consensus was recovered, but also a kind of psychic unity. A certain kind of compromise was for ever over.

But what does this mean for the future? It means that demand (ii) for Quebec autonomy has become imperious and virtually nonnegotiable. And this brings a real danger of breach between the two parts of the country. For it follows that Quebecers will not accept any structure in which their collective aspirations are not fully and overtly recognized. Already this is expressing itself in the requirement that negotiation be one-on-one, because this is felt to reflect in itself the acknowledgement of Quebec's status as a distinct society. But all this is happening at the moment that COQ's new found Charter patriotism is making it less capable of acknowledging the legitimacy of collective goals; and as regional alienation is lending further strength to the principle of the equality of provinces. The common ground seems to be shrinking fast.

RIGHTS AND NATIONS

Can these demands be reconciled? Let us take the conflicts one at a time. First, that between the Charter and Quebec's collective goals. Our Charter follows the trend of the last half of the twentieth century, and gives a basis for judicial review on two basic scores. First, it protects the rights of the individual in a variety of ways. And second, it guarantees equal treatment of citizens in a variety of respects; or alternatively put, it defends against discriminatory treatment on a number of irrelevant grounds, such as race or sex. There is a lot else in our Charter, including provisions for linguistic rights and aboriginal rights, that could be understood as according powers to collectivities, but the two themes I singled out dominate in the public consciousness.

This is no accident. These two kinds of provisions are now quite common in entrenched schedules of rights that provide the basis for judicial review. In this sense the Western world, perhaps the world as a whole, is following American precedent. The Americans were the first to write out and entrench a bill of rights, which they did during the ratification process of their Constitution and as a condition of its successful outcome. One might argue that they were not entirely clear on judicial retrieval as a method of securing those rights, but this rapidly became the practice. The first amendments secured individuals, and sometimes state governments,[5] against encroachment by the new federal government. It was after the Civil War, in the period of triumphant Reconstruction, and particularly with the Fourteenth Amendment, which called for "equal protection" for all citizens by the laws, that the theme of nondiscrimination became central to judicial review. But it is by now on a par with the older norm of the defence of individual right, and in public consciousness even perhaps ahead.

Now for a number of people in English Canada, a political society's espousing certain collective goals threatens to run against both of these basic provisions of our Charter, or indeed any acceptable bill of rights. First, the collective goals may require restrictions on the behaviour of individuals that may violate their rights. For many nonfrancophone Canadians, both inside and outside Quebec, this feared outcome had already materialized with Quebec's language legislation. Law 101 prescribes, for instance, the type of school to which parents can send their children; and in the most famous instance, it forbids certain kinds of commercial signage. This later provision was actually struck down by the Supreme Court as contrary to the Quebec Bill of Rights, as well as the Charter, and only reenacted through the invocation of the Notwithstanding Clause (section 33 of the *Constitution Act, 1982*).

But second, even if this were not the case, espousing collective goals on behalf of a national group can be thought to be inherently discriminatory. In the modern world it will always be the case that not all those living as citizens under a certain jurisdiction will belong to the national group thus favoured. This by itself could be thought to involve some discrimination. But beyond this, the pursuit of the collective end will in all likelihood involve treating insiders and outsiders differently. Thus the schooling provisions of Law 101 forbid (roughly speaking) francophones and immigrants sending their children to English-language schools, but allow Canadian anglophones to do so.

---

5 For instance, the First Amendment, which forbade Congress from establishing any religion, was not originally meant to separate state and church as such. It was enacted at a time when many states had established churches, and it was plainly meant to prevent the new federal government from interfering with or over-ruling these local arrangements. It was only later after the Fourteenth Amendment, following the so-called "Incorporation" doctrine, that these restrictions on the federal government were held to have been extended to all governments, at whatever level.

This sense that the Charter clashes with basic Quebec policy was one of the strong grounds of opposition in COQ to the Meech Lake Accord. The worry here concerned the "distinct society" clause, and the common demand for amendment was that the Charter be "protected" against this clause, or take precedence over it. There was undoubtedly in this a certain amount of old-style anti-Quebec prejudice, the continuing echoes of the old image of "priest-ridden Quebec." Thus various women's groups voiced the fear that Quebec governments in pursuit of higher birth rates might adopt Ceaucescu-type policies of forbidding abortions or making birth control more difficult. But even when one factors out the silliness, contempt and ill-will, there remains a serious point here. Indeed, there are two kinds of serious points. First, there is a genuine difference in philosophy concerning the bases of a liberal society. And second, there is a difference in view about the basis for national unity.

Let us take the philosophical difference first. Those who take the view that individual rights must always come first, and along with nondiscrimination provisions, must take precedence over collective goals, are often speaking out of a view of a liberal society that has become more and more widespread in the Anglo-American world. Its source is, of course, the United States and it has recently been elaborated and defended by some of the best philosophical and legal minds in that society, for instance John Rawls, Ronald Dworkin, Bruce Ackerman, and others.[6] There are various formulations of the main idea, but perhaps the one that encapsulates most clearly the point that is relevant to us is Dworkin's way of putting things in his short paper entitled "Liberalism."[7]

Dworkin makes a distinction between two kinds of moral commitment. We all have views about the ends of life, about what constitutes a good life, that we and others ought to strive for. But then we also acknowledge a commitment to deal fairly and equally with each other, regardless of how we conceive our ends. We might call these latter "procedural" commitments, while those that concern the ends of life are "substantive." Now Dworkin claims that a liberal society is one which as a society adopts no particular substantive view about the ends of life. The society is rather united around strong procedural commitments, to treat people with equal respect. The reason why the polity as such can espouse no substantive view, cannot for instance, allow that one of the goals of legislation should be to make people virtuous in one or other meaning of that term, is that

---

6   John Rawls, *A Theory of Justice* (Cambridge, MA: Harvard University Press, 1971); "Justice as Fairness: Political not Metaphysical," *Philosophy and Public Affairs*, vol 14, 1985; Ronald Dworkin, *Taking Rights Seriously* (London: Duckworth, 1977); "Liberalism," in Stuart Hampshire (ed.), *Public and Private Morality* (Cambridge: Cambridge University Press, 1978); Bruce Ackerman, *Social Justice in the Liberal State* (New Haven: Yale University Press, 1980.)
7   Dworkin, "Liberalism," in Hampshire, *Public and Private Morality*.

this would involve a violation of its procedural norm. For, granted the diversity of modern societies, it would unfailingly be the case that some people and not others would be commited to the favoured conception of virtue. They might be in a majority; indeed, it is very likely that they would be, for otherwise a democratic society would probably not espouse their view. But nevertheless, this view would not be everyone's, and in espousing this substantive outlook the society would not be treating the dissident minority with equal respect. It would be saying to them, in effect, "your view is not as valuable, in the eyes of this polity, as that of your more numerous compatriots."

There are very profound philosophical assumptions underlying this view of liberalism, which is influenced by the thought of the late eighteenth century German philosopher, Immanuel Kant. Among other features, this view understands human dignity to consist largely in autonomy, that is, in the ability of each person to determine for him or herself a view of the good life. Dignity, that is, is connected less with any particular understanding of the good life, such that someone's departure from this would be a derogation from his or her own dignity, than it is with the power to consider and espouse for oneself some view or other. We are not respecting this power equally in all subjects, it is claimed, if we raise the outcome of some people's deliberations officially over that of others. A liberal society must remain neutral on the good life, and restrict itself to ensuring that however they see things, citizens deal fairly with each other and the state equally with all.

The popularity of this view of the human agent as primarily a subject of self-determining or self-expressive choice helps to explain why this model of liberalism is so strong. But there is also the fact that it has been urged with great force and intelligence by liberal thinkers in the United States, and precisely in the context of constitutional doctrines of judicial review.[8] And so it is not surprising that the idea becomes accredited, well beyond those who might subscribe to a specific Kant-derived philosophy, that a liberal society cannot accommodate publically-espoused notions of the good. This is the conception, as Michael Sandel has called it, of the "procedural republic,"[9] which has a very strong hold on the political agenda in the United States, and which has helped to place increasing emphasis on judicial review on the basis of constitutional texts at the expense of the ordinary political process of building majorities with a view to legislative action.

But a society with collective goals like Quebec's violates this model. It is axiomatic for Quebec governments that the survival and flourishing of French

---

8   See for instance, the arguments deployed by Lawrence Tribe in his *Abortion: The Clash of Absolutes* (New York: Norton, 1990).

9   Michael Sandel, "The Procedural Republic and the Unencumbered Self," *Political Theory*, vol 12, 1984.

culture in Quebec is a good. Political society is not neutral between those who value remaining true to the culture of our ancestors and those who might want to cut loose in the name of some individual goal of self-development. It might be argued that one could after all capture a goal like *survivance* for a procedural-ist liberal society. One could consider the French language, for instance, as a collective resource that individuals might want to make use of, and act for its preservation, just as one does for clean air or green spaces. But this cannot capture the full thrust of policies designed for cultural survival. It is not just a matter of having the French language available for those who might choose it. This might be seen to be the goal of some of the measures of federal bilingual-ism over the last 20 years. But it is also a matter of making sure that there is a community of people here in the future that will want to avail itself of this opportunity. Policies aimed at survival actively seek to create members of the community, for instance in assuring that the rising generations go on identifying as French-speakers or whatever. There is no way that they could be seen as just providing a facility to already existing people.[10]

Quebecers therefore, and those who give similar importance to this kind of collective goal, tend to opt for a rather different model of a liberal society. On this view, a society can be organized around a definition of the good life, without this being seen as a depreciation of those who do not personally share this definition. Where the nature of the good requires that it be sought in common, this is the reason for its being an object of public policy. According to this conception, a liberal society singles itself out as such by the way in which it treats minorities, including those who do not share public definitions of the good; and above all by the rights it accords to all its members. But in this case, the rights in question are conceived to be the fundamental and crucial ones that have been recognized as such from the very beginning of the liberal tradition: such rights as to life, liberty, due process, free speech, free practise of religion

---

10 An ingenious argument has recently been put forward by Will Kymlicka in his brilliant book, *Liberalism, Community and Culture* (Oxford: Clarendon Press, 1989). He argues that what I have been calling procedural liberalism can be made compatible with the defence of collective rights and cultural survival in certain cases. Kymlicka, unlike the major American authors, writes in full knowledge of the Canadian scene, and with a strong commitment to the defence of aboriginal rights in this country. While espousing a politics of "neutral moral concern," that is, a view of the liberal state as neutral between conceptions of the good life (p. 76), he nevertheless argues that collective cultural rights can be defended on the grounds that the members of certain threatened communities would be deprived of the conditions of intelligent, self-generated decisions about the good life, if the "cultural structures" through which they can grasp the options are undermined (p. 165). If Kymlicka's argument really prevailed, it would close the gap between the two models of Liberalism that I am contrasting in these pages.

and the like. On this model, there is something exaggerated, a dangerous overlooking of an essential boundary, in speaking of fundamental rights to things like commercial signage in the language of one's choice. One has to distinguish the fundamental liberties, those which should never at any time be infringed, and which therefore ought to be unassailably entrenched on the one hand, from privileges and immunities that are important, but which can be revoked or restricted for reasons of public policy — although one needs a strong reason to do so — on the other.

A society with strong collective goals can be liberal, on this view, provided it is also capable of respecting diversity, especially when it concerns those who do not share its goals; and provided it can offer adequate safeguards for fundamental rights. There will undoubtedly be tensions involved, and difficulties, in pursuing these objectives together, but they are not uncombinable, and the problems are not in principle greater than those encountered by any liberal society which has to combine, e.g., liberty and equality, or prosperity and justice.

Here are two incompatible views of liberal society. One of the great sources of our present disunity is that they have come to square off against each other in the last decade. The resistance to the distinct society which called for precedence to be given to the Charter came in part from a spreading procedural outlook in English Canada. From this point of view, attributing the goal of promoting Quebec's distinct society to a government is to acknowledge a collective goal, and this move had to be neutralized by being subordinated to the existing Charter. From the standpoint of Quebec, this attempt to impose a procedural model of liberalism not only would deprive the "distinct society" clause of some of its force as a rule of interpretation, but bespoke a rejection of the model of liberalism on which this society has come to be founded. There was a lot of misperception by each society of the other throughout the Meech Lake debate, as I mentioned above. But here both saw something right about the other — and did not like it. COQ saw that the "distinct society" clause legitimated collective goals. And Quebec saw that the move to give the Charter precedence imposed a form of liberal society that is alien, and to which Quebec could never accommodate itself without surrendering its identity. In this context, the protestations by Charter patriots that they were not "against Quebec" rang hollow.

This was one source of deep disagreement. There was also a second one, which was interwoven with it. The Charter has taken on tremendous importance in COQ not only because of the growing force of procedural liberalism, but also because in the steadily increasing diversity of this multicultural society, people are looking for new bases of unity. COQ has also seen its reason for existence partly in terms of its political institutions, for reasons discussed above. Even though the Charter offers a relatively weak answer to the distinctness question, because it makes us more like the United States, it nevertheless can provide a convincing answer to the unity question. The two motives for Charter patriotism come together here. As the country gets more diverse, we are more and more acutely aware of the divergences in our conceptions of the good life. It then appears that what can and ought to bind us together are precisely the procedural norms that govern our interaction. Procedural liberalism not only begins to look more plausible in itself, but it also seems to be the only unquestionable common ground.

But if the Charter is really serving as common ground, then it is hard to accept that its meaning and application may be modulated in one part of the country by something like the "distinct society" clause, differently from the way it applies in others. The resistance to this clause of the Meech Lake Accord came partly from the sense that the Charter of all things had to apply in the same way to all Canadians. If the procedural bond is the only thing that can hold us together without ranking some above others, then it has to hold without exception.

Can this conflict be arbitrated? In a sense not. One side insists on holding the country together around a model of liberalism which the other cannot accept. If there is to be agreement, this first side has to give way. But in another sense, the possible common ground is obvious. Procedural liberals in English Canada just have to acknowledge first that there are other possible models of liberal society, and second that their francophone compatriots wish to live by one such alternative. That the first is true becomes pretty evident once one looks around at the full gamut of contemporary free societies in Europe and elsewhere, instead of attending only to the United States. The truth of the second should be clear to anyone with a modicum of knowledge of Quebec history and politics.

But once you accept both, then it is clear that the attempt to make procedural liberalism the basis of Canadian unity is both illegitimate and doomed to failure. For it represents an imposition of one society's model on another, and in the circumstances of late-twentieth century Canadian democracy this cannot succeed. The only way we can coexist is by allowing ourselves to differ on this. Does this mean that we can only coexist as two independent societies, perhaps loosely linked by supranational institutions? That is the thesis of Quebec sovereignists. But this has never seemed to me to be self-evident. It becomes true only to the extent that procedural liberals stand so firmly on principle that they cannot stand sharing the same country with people who live by another model. Rigidity of this kind began to be evident during the Meech Lake debate. If this were to be COQ's last word, then indeed, the independentists are right, and there is no solution short of sovereignty-association.

EQUALITY OF WHAT?

The second great area of conflict is between the demands of a special status for Quebec, and those of regional equality, once this is interpreted as requiring equality between the provinces. But whereas over the two models of liberalism there is really a genuine philosophic difference underlying all the misunderstanding, here there is still much mutual misperception and cross purposes.

For in fact, the two demands come out of quite different agendas, as has often been remarked. The demand for special status is usually one for assuming a wider range of responsibilities and hence for greater autonomy. The call for regional equality comes generally from those who feel that their interests have been given insufficient weight in federal policy-making, and hence aims for more clout in this process. One side wants to take a greater distance from the central government and legislature; the other wants a weightier place within these. That is why it has taken the form in recent years of a call for reform in federal institutions, notably the Senate.

So understood, these demands are not logically opposed. Of course, they can at many points get in each other's way. There has been a fear among provinces that look to a more active federal government to equalize conditions across the regions, that excessive powers to Quebec might end up weakening the power of the centre to act. This may indeed be, but it is not fated to do so. It is not the reflection of a logical conflict, such as that between equality of all provinces on one hand, and special powers for one of them on the other. The demands for special status and strong central government can possibly be made compatible. What has made this difficult in practice has been precisely the refusal to depart from uniformity. This has meant that any "concession" to Quebec has had to be offered to all the provinces. Fortunately, these have not always been taken up, and so we have evolved quite a considerable *de facto* special status for Quebec, as I remarked above. But it has never been possible to proceed in that direction openly and explicitly, because of the pressure for uniformity. In the Meech Lake Accord itself, designed to address the difficulties of Quebec, most of what was accorded to Quebec had to be distributed to all the others.

The language of "equality" between provinces has in fact been a source of confusion, screening the reality of what is at stake and making solution more difficult. Equality is a notoriously difficult concept to apply, and depends on the respect one makes salient. It could be argued that Quebec needs powers that other provinces do not, to cope with problems and a vocation that other provinces do not have. Accordingly, this point could be seen as a move towards equality (to each province according to its tasks), not away from it. Moreover, the special status has nothing to do with having more clout at the centre. It involves something quite different.

All of this should encourage us to think that it may not be beyond human wit to discover a way to satisfy these different demands together. There are (a) provinces that want more say in the decisions of the federal government. There are others who, while not disinterested in this first goal are mainly concerned with (b) maintaining an active federal government as a force for economic and social equalization between regions. Then there is Quebec, which (c) wants the powers it thinks essential to the preservation and promotion of its distinct society.

To this we now have to add the aboriginal dimension. That means that our arrangements have to accommodate the need for forms of self-government and self-management appropriate to the different first nations. This may mean in practice allowing for a new form of jurisdiction in Canada, perhaps weaker than the provinces, but, unlike municipalities, not simply the creatures of another level of government.

Putting all this together will be very difficult. It will take much ingenuity and good will. Perhaps more of either than we possess. But the task will be utterly impossible if we persist in describing the problem in the misleading and often demagogic language of equality versus inequality of provinces. Put in these terms, the problem is a false one, and the present importance of this formulation is a sign of our lack of lucidity and the decline of good will. It reflects the deep mutual suspicions that have come to cloud our political scene.

The game of multidimensional constitutional tug-of-war that we have been playing in Canada these past years has made our situation worse, partly by creating or strengthening unhealthy linkages, whereby aspirations that are, as such, perfectly compatible come to be seen as deadly rivals. Examples are the linkages made between linguistic duality and multiculturalism, or those between aboriginals and Québécois, or those between regional equality and the distinct society. It may already be too late to climb out of the skein of resentments and mutual suspicion, and it will take far-sighted and courageous leadership to do so. But it will also require that we see each others' aspirations for what they are, as free as possible from the rhetoric of resentment.

LEVELS OF DIVERSITY

Various solutions can be glimpsed beyond the present stalemate. One set would be based on a dualism in which Quebec would no longer be a federal unit just like the others. The other possible range would have as its basis a four- or five-region federalism decentralized enough to accommodate Quebec as a member on all fours with the rest. Either type of solution would have to accommodate difference in a way we have not yet succeeded in doing — at least openly and admittedly.

Can we do it? It looks bad, but I would like to close by saying a few words about what this might mean.

In a way, accommodating difference is what Canada is all about. Many Canadians would concur in this. That is why the recent bout of mutual suspicion and ill-will in the constitutional debate has been so painful to many of our compatriots. It is not just that the two sources of difference I have been describing are becoming more salient. Old questions may be reopened. To some extent Trudeau's remarkable achievement in extending bilingualism was made possible by a growing sympathy towards the French fact among political and social elites in COQ. The elites pushed the bilingual process at a pace faster than many of their fellow citizens wanted. For many people lower down in the hierarchy, French was being "stuffed down their throats," but granted the elite-run nature of the political accomodation process in this country, they seemed to have no option but to take it.

During the Meech debate the procedures of elite negotiation came under sharp criticism and challenge. Moreover, the COQ elites were themselves split on how to respond to the new package, in a way they had not been on bilingualism. It was therefore not surprising that we began to see a rebellion against the accommodation of French. This might be the harbinger of greater resistance to come. Already one hears westerners saying that Canadian duality is an irrelevancy to them, that their experience of Canada is of a multicultural mosaic. The very bases of a two-language federation are being questioned again. This important axis of difference is under threat.

More fundamentally, we face a challenge to our very conception of diversity. Many of the people who rallied around the Charter and multiculturalism to reject the distinct society are proud of their acceptance of diversity. And in some respects rightly so. What is enshrined here is what one might call first-level diversity. There are great differences in culture and outlook and background in a population that nevertheless shares the same idea of what it is to belong to Canada. Their patriotism or manner of belonging is uniform, whatever their other differences, and this is felt to be a necessity if the country is to hold together.

This is far from accommodating all Canadians. For Quebecers, and for most French Canadians, the way of being a Canadian (for those who still want to be) is by their belonging to a constituent element of Canada, *la nation québécoise*, or *canadienne-française*. Something analogous holds for aboriginal communities in this country. Their way of being Canadian is not accommodated by first-level diversity. And yet many people in COQ are puzzled by the resulting sense of exclusion, because first-level diversity is the only kind to which they are sensitive, and which they feel they fully acknowledge.

To build a country for everyone, Canada would have to allow for second-level or "deep" diversity, where a plurality of ways of belonging would also be acknowledged and accepted. Someone of, say, Italian extraction in Toronto, or Ukrainian extraction in Edmonton, might indeed feel Canadian as a bearer of individual rights in a multicultural mosaic. His or her belonging would not "pass through" some other community, although the ethnic identity might be important to him or her in various ways. But this person might nevertheless accept that a Québécois, or a Cree, or a Déné, might belong in a very different way, that they were Canadian through being members of their national communities. And reciprocally, the Québécois, Cree or Déné would accept the perfect legitimacy of the "mosaic" identity.

Is this utopian? Could people ever come to see their country this way? Could they even find it exciting and an object of pride that they belong to a country that allows deep diversity? Pessimists say no, because they do not see how such a country could have a sense of unity. The model of citizenship has to be uniform, or people would have no sense of belonging to the same polity. Those who say this tend to take the United States as their paradigm, which has indeed been hostile to deep diversity, and has sometimes tried to stamp it out as "un-American."

But these pessimists should bear in mind three things. First, deep diversity is the only formula on which a united federal Canada can be rebuilt, once we recall the reasons why we all need Canada — such as those above, i.e., law and order, collective provision, and regional equality and mutual self-help.

Second, in many parts of the world today, the degree and nature of the differences resemble Canada's rather than the United States. If a uniform model of citizenship fits better the classical image of the western liberal state, it is also true that this is a straitjacket for many political societies. The world needs other models to be legitimated, in order to allow for more humane and less constraining modes of political cohabitation. Instead of pushing ourselves to the point of breakup in the name of the uniform model, we would do our own and some other peoples a favour by exploring the space of deep diversity. To those who believe in according people the freedom to be themselves, this would be counted a gain in civilization.

In this exploration we would not be alone. Europe-watchers have noticed how the development of the Community has gone along with an increased breathing space for regional societies — Breton, Basque, Catalan — which were formerly threatened with the steamroller of the national state.

Finally, after dividing to form two polities with uniform citizenship, both successor-states would find that they had failed after all to banish the challenge of deep diversity; because the only way that they can do justice to their aboriginal populations is by adopting a pluralist mould. Neither Quebec nor COQ could succeed in imitating the United States, or the European national states in their chauvinist prime. Why not recognize this now, and take the road of deep diversity together?

5

Constitutional Change and the Three Equalities

Alan C. Cairns

INTRODUCTION

The impediments to a successful future round of constitutional change are many and varied. The long history of failed reform efforts, most recently Meech Lake, confirms that constitutional reform is not a casual game to be lightheartedly undertaken. While analysis of past failures would be instructive, the contemporary situation is *sui generis* for three fundamental reasons:

- In 1982, Canadians constitutionalized a comprehensive domestic amending formula based on the principle of equality of the provinces.
- Formal constitutional change since 1982 confronts a constitutional culture strongly influenced by the Charter.
- The post-Meech Lake Quebec demands will be couched in the language of nationhood. Quebec, according to Premier Bourassa, will negotiate only with Ottawa, one-on-one.

Whether Canadians emerge as one or more people from their contemporary constitutional malaise will be dictated by how they respond to the three equalities hinted in the title of this chapter — of citizens, of provinces, and of two nations. The first equality, of citizens, is symbolized by the Charter, and addresses the citizen-state dimension of Canadian existence. The second equality, of provinces, articulated most explicitly in the amending formula, is a contemporary response to federalism, one of the historic pillars of the Canadian constitutional order. The third equality of two national peoples is implicit in the possible shattering of Canada into two sovereign states. Each of the three equalities is imperialistic, unwilling to be restricted to a narrow sphere of Canadian's constitutional life. Their coexistence is disharmonious. The constitutional task is to decide on their interrelationships, and on how and where each equality is to be favoured or sacrificed in whole or in part.

Meech Lake is inexplicable if the contribution of the first two equalities to its unravelling is not given analytical pride of place. The equality of provinces dictated that what was given to Quebec, the distinct society excepted, was extended to all provinces, transforming a Quebec round into a provincial round and antagonizing supporters of a strong central government. The equality of citizens norm stimulated by the Charter was the source of much of the opposition to Meech Lake, on the grounds that the "distinct society" clause would or could lead to unacceptable inequalities in citizenship between Québécois and other Canadians.

The constraining effect of these two equalities lies behind this paper's argument that an asymmetrical federalism profoundly sensitive to the particularity of Quebec, and that takes Quebec out of the conventional normative frameworks of equal provinces and equal citizens, is one of the few constitutional stopping points available short of Quebec sovereignty. If this is so, an asymmetrical status for Quebec should also be seen as a vehicle to salvage (an admittedly uneven) country-wide role for the federal government.

The impediment to a two independent nations solution is not the existence of equality norms that need to be bypassed, but the inchoate nature of the rest-of-Canada, one of the two imputed national entities that are to emerge from the debris of a failing federalism to confront each other as coexisting sovereign neighbours. That a Canada-without-Quebec might become a cohesive self-confident country is clear. However, that it does not now enjoy an institutional frame that shapes it and official leaders that speak to it and for it is also clear. As long as the Canadian Confederation continues, Canada-without-Quebec is officially headless and voiceless. One of the parties in the prospective third equality of two nations, therefore, is waiting to be born. In formal terms, it will only emerge after the breakup and thus too late to work out in advance the terms of its coexistence with a sovereign Quebec.

Discussion of if and how we can bypass two symbolically potent equalities is not the stuff of empirical social science. Even less so is a speculative appraisal of some complexities of moving towards a two-nations solution when only one of the two prospective polities now exists in corporeal form. Consequently, this paper is written as a reflective essay. Its purpose is to portray certain big constitutional features sharply, rather than to linger lovingly over a nuanced portrait overflowing with detail.

RENEWED FEDERALISM

Constraining Norms: the Charter

There is general agreement that the Charter contributes to a more participant oriented constitutional culture, and, in particular, that it has fostered constitutional interest groups devoted to the protection and enhancement of "their" constitutional clause, section 28 for women, section 27 for ethnocultural elites, section 23 for official language minorities, and section 15 for the particular groups identified in that clause, and for equality-seekers in general.[1] These orientations, when combined with the constitutional politics of the aboriginal peoples, generate what might be called multiple constitutional particularisms, or, from a different perspective, a constitutional fragmentation, as discrete, self-interested social groups seek to monopolize particular constitutional (mainly Charter) clauses. [2] The multiplication of the cast of would-be actors in the constitutional reform process profoundly complicates the pursuit of formal constitutional change. Meech Lake confirms that governments can no longer control the process of constitutional reform and that Canadians lack agreement on the kind of amending process, including formal and informal aspects, able to accommodate both governments and relevant publics. To end the analysis of the Charter's impact at this point, however, would be to miss the more general constraint it injects into the constitutional process.

For its anglophone supporters, the Charter fosters a conception of citizenship that defines Canadians as equal bearers of rights independent of provincial location. This legitimates a citizen concern for the treatment of fellow Canadians by other than one's own provincial government. By contrast, the working theory of federalism, especially in its classical version, had been that an individual's provincial concerns should be restricted to the fellow residents of his or her own province. Federalism presupposed high fences and uninquisitive neighbours.

Historically, this isolation of provincial domains has always been qualified by various constitutional instruments, often viewed as antifederal devices, — disallowance, the declaratory power, the spending power, etc., — that have been vehicles for federal government intervention in provincial affairs. While these traditional instruments have become weakened or obsolete, the Charter was deliberately designed as a new constraint on federalism; indeed, that was its political purpose. The Charter may be thought of as a floor of rights, subject admittedly to the notwithstanding clause, that politicians are instructed to respect and courts to enforce. The Meech Lake debate, however, indicates that the Charter norm is also sustained by a citizenry that views the possibility of a

---

1 All references to *Constitution Act, 1982*
2 I have discussed these and related issues in "Constitutional Minoritarianism in Canada," in Ronald L. Watts and Douglas M. Brown (eds.), *Canada: The State of the Federation 1990* (Kingston: Institute of Intergovernmental Relations, Queen's University, 1990), and in "Ritual, Taboo and Bias in Constitutional Controversies in Canada, or Constitutional Talk Canadian Style," *Saskatchewan Law Review,* 54 (1990).

distinct and weaker Charter regime in another province as a constitutional affront. It offends the norm of an equal rights possessing citizenry uniformly present in the federal, ten provincial and two territorial arenas.

The Charter generates a roving normative Canadianism oblivious to provincial boundaries, and thus hostile to constitutional stratagems such as the Meech Lake "distinct society" that might vary the Charter's availability in one province. Federalist and even stronger dualist justifications for constitutional recognition of Quebec as a distinct society clashed with a Canadian Charter norm applied to Quebec by those who lived elsewhere. The Quebec rationale for an asymmetrical Charter confronted a homogenizing Charter-derived rights-bearing Canadianism that applied not to Québécois but to Canadians who happened to live in Quebec. The psychological potency of the Charter was a recurrent theme in the New Brunswick Select Committee hearings and the Manitoba Task Force hearings. The former stated that "of all the Constitutional acts, the Charter is undoubtedly the most important for individual Canadians" and recommended including it in the Accord as a fundamental characteristic of Canada.[3] The latter reported that over half of its interveners were apprehensive about the Accord's impact on "Charter rights, particularly sex equality rights."[4] The Charter, in the words of a francophone student of the reactions to Meech Lake, has virtually become an icon in English-speaking Canada, a status that is not duplicated among the Quebec francophone majority, especially among nationalist elites.[5]

Anglophone Charter support makes it difficult for the federal and other provincial governments to respond positively to Quebec demands for a distinctive constitutional recognition that might weaken the relative availability of Charter rights. This constraint is exacerbated by the fact that the Charter, as noted above, generates participant orientations in its anglophone supporters that are hostile to the elitist practices of executive federalism.

The Charter's potency derives from its linkage with citizenship a highly symbolic concept infused with elements of the sacred, and a concept that by its very nature is country-wide in application. Federalists such as Clyde Wells objected to the Meech Lake "distinct society" clause for its violation of the equality of the provinces principle.[6] In marked contrast, women's groups and

---

3   Legislative Assembly of New Brunswick, Select Committee on the 1987 Constitutional Accord, *Final Report on the Constitutional Amendment 1987* (Fredericton, 1989), p. 44.
4   Manitoba Task Force on Meech Lake, *Report on the 1987 Constitutional Accord* (Winnipeg, 1989), p. 25.
5   Denis Robert, "La signification de l'Accord du lac Meech au Canada anglais et au Québec francophone: un tour d'horizon du débat public," in Peter M. Leslie and Ronald L. Watts (eds.), *Canada: The State of the Federation 1987-88* (Kingston: Institute of Intergovernmental Relations, Queen's University 1988), pp. 121, 153.
6   "Clearly .... the Meech Lake Accord creates a special legislative status for one

other Charter supporters objected to the distinct society on the ground that it violated the norms of equal citizenship. To Meech Lake's Charter-supporting opponents, the distinct society suggested an asymmetrical citizenship that was viewed as a self-contradiction. Accordingly, advocates of a Quebec constitutional status going beyond Meech Lake must think through the feasibility of and consequences of an asymmetrical application of the Charter to Quebec, and the asymmetrical citizenship that logically follows.

Constraining Norms: Equality of Provinces

One of the key issues in the long-lasting Canadian debate over a domestic amending formula as a prerequisite to patriation was whether province or region should be the basic unit for determining support for a constitutional amendment. The choice of region, as in the Victoria Charter proposals and in the federal government proposals in the 1980-81 unilateral package, necessarily entailed the inequality of the provinces. In each of the four province regions of western and Atlantic Canada up to two provinces could find themselves on the losing side of a successful amendment. Ontario and Quebec, defined as regions, could not suffer a similar fate.

The provincial equality solution to this "inequity" was to devise an amending formula that repudiated the concept of region for amendment purposes and replaced it by province, as was done in the *Constitution Act, 1982*. The relevant formula, therefore, became two-thirds of the provinces with 50 percent of the population plus the federal government; or for a select list of constitutional provisions, the unanimous approval of all governments. The equality of the provinces in the two-thirds plus 50 percent amending category was additionally supported by the opting-out provisions which allowed up to three provinces in a ten province Canada to opt out of an amendment transferring legislative jurisdiction to the federal government, and in certain circumstances to receive financial compensation. The equality principle was further extended in the Meech Lake Accord which enlarged the subject matters covered by the unanimity amending formula, and also enriched the compensation requirement by extending it to all cases of provincial government opting-out of an amendment transferring jurisdiction to the federal government.

The imperialist diffusion of the equality of the provinces principle to other realms is illustrated by its central status as one of the three principles of the proposed Triple E Senate (Equal, Elected, and Effective). Further, the Meech

---

province. No federation is likely to survive for very long if one of its supposedly equal provinces has a legislative jurisdiction in excess of that of the other provinces." Clyde K. Wells, "The Meech Lake Accord: An Address to the Vancouver Board of Trade," 12 February 1990, mimeo, p. 6.

Lake practice of giving to all ten provinces whatever was needed to respond to Quebec's five demands, with the exception of the distinct society interpretive principle, was justified by the federal government as a response to the "principle of the equality of all the provinces." [7] In this way, the Quebec round became a provincial round. What Quebec asked for, British Columbia received.

For Premier Wells, however, this was an insufficient accommodation to the equality of the provinces principle. He feared that the application of the "distinct society" clause to Quebec alone, in conjunction with the affirmation of the "role of the legislature and Government of Quebec to preserve and promote the distinct identity of Quebec," would give the Quebec government powers unavailable to any other provincial government.[8] Premier Vander Zalm responded to this apparent contradiction by releasing a British Columbia government position paper that proposed recognizing all provinces as distinct societies.[9]

The provincial equality principle is a potent constraint on constitutional responses that recognize Quebec's specificity by an asymmetrical federalism granting Quebec jurisdictional powers not possessed by other provincial governments. The ability of the rest-of-Canada to respond to Quebec is restricted by its reluctance to provincialize itself. Alternatively, the provincialization of the rest-of-Canada is to be driven by Quebec nationalism. In this case, the cost of accommodating Quebec is paid by those anglophone Canadians who have no desire to strengthen their provincial against their Canadian selves. The equality of the provinces principle, like the Charter norm of citizen equality, therefore, greatly impedes a sensitive accommodation to Quebec's specificity by jurisdictional differentiation, as long as Quebec is defined as a normal province.

Finding Room to Maneuver: Escape from the Constraints of Minimum Change

One of the conventional post-Meech Lake wisdoms is that if "English Canada" rejected the limited Meech Lake package, they will be even more resistant to a

---

7   *1987 Constitutional Accord, 3 June 1987* reproduced in Anne F. Bayefsky, *Canada's Constitution Act 1982 and Amendments: A Documentary History,* Vol. II (Toronto;: McGraw-Hill Ryerson, 1990), p. 955.
8   Section 2(3) of the Meech Lake Accord, reproduced in Bayefsky, *Canada's Constitution Act 1982,* p. 955.
9   Premier William N. Vander Zalm to Prime Minister Brian Mulroney, 19 January 1990, attached to a News Release, 23 January 1990, from the Office of Premier Vander Zalm, justified recognizing each province and territory as distinct as this would *"balance recognition of our distinction while clearly upholding the principle of equality... "* (italics in original).

larger package. As the proposals of the Bélanger-Campeau Commission, of the Quebec Liberal Party, and of the Quebec government will certainly go beyond Meech Lake, the possibility of an agreement with "English Canada" is considered minuscule. This logic, however, is not irresistible.

The equality of provinces and Charter constraints derive from the definition of Quebec as a province like the others, and of Quebec citizens as citizens like the others. In each case, the constraint flows from the placing of Quebec and its citizenry in the categories "province" and "citizen" from which certain constitutional consequences, in particular a rough uniformity of treatment, are deemed necessarily to follow. Further, as already noted, both equalities of provinces and of citizens have recently been fleshed out and made concrete by the amending formula and the Charter. They are ascending, not declining constitutional norms. Hence, escape from their constricting assumptions in contexts where they fully apply has become more rather than less difficult in the last decade.

These restraints can most logically be avoided by removing Quebec from the category "province" and Quebec residents from the category of homogeneous, standardized rights-bearing Canadians. This requires devising conceptions of the relationships between Quebec and the rest-of-Canada that ruptures the symmetry rationale flowing from the application of the equality of the provinces principle. Such a conception should simultaneously provide a rationale for the application of a greatly weakened Charter regime to the citizens of a jurisdiction that is not a jurisdiction like the others.

The political logic is straightforward. The Meech Lake lesson is that the flexibility and maneuverability of the rest-of-Canada in responding to Quebec are severely limited by the two equalities. However, a larger change can escape the constraints by redefining the Quebec/rest-of-Canada relationship as being unique, as involving neither a province nor a standardized version of Canadian citizenship. Such a redefinition must make it appear "natural" that the reception and applicability of the Charter changes as it hits the Quebec border, and that the criteria applicable to standardized provincehood are irrelevant to the prospectively unique Quebec situation. From this perspective, the difficulty with Meech Lake was that its accompanying rhetoric of returning Quebec with honour and enthusiasm to the Canadian family of governments and couching the Accord, distinct society excepted, in the language of the equality of the provinces immediately brought to the surface the two sets of equality constraints that contributed to the Accord's downfall. Accordingly, a small change may be less digestible than a larger one if it is subject to constraints from which a larger package escapes.

On the other hand, the larger package might generate other problems no less resistant to resolution. That discussion is taken up later. The limited purpose of this section has been only to suggest that some constraints can be avoided by redefining the situation to facilitate escape from a system of otherwise controlling comparisons. If, for example, constraint "X" is a consequence of being a "Y," it may be avoided by transforming a "Y" into a "Z." Meech Lake did not travel that route. It sought instead to make Quebec a special kind of "Y," but the degree of differentiation sought did not lift it above the constraints that apply to a "Y." While an independent "Z" is the most obvious escape route, an asymmetrical "Z (I)" may have an almost equal capacity, along with the added virtue of limiting disruptive discontinuities. This discussion is not tautological and it does not impute magic to changes in labelling. It suggests the need for a convincing argument that Quebec is a "Z (I)" rather than a "Y," and hence not subject to the constraints of "X."

Finding Room to Maneuver: Charter Groups, Aboriginal Peoples and Québécois

The *Constitution Act, 1982* has greatly increased the cast of constitutional stakeholders; they now extend beyond governments to include a variety of Charter constituencies and the aboriginal peoples of Canada. The Charter gives constitutional recognition to a nonterritorial pluralism of women, "multicultural" Canadians, official language minorities, and section 15 equality-seekers, among others. That their recognition occurs via the Charter tempts them to employ the nonbargaining, noncompromising language of rights. That their constitutional status has only recently been achieved, and after struggles and reversals, makes them suspicious of constitutional change proposals fashioned in their absence. That their constitutional identities and ambitions have come to be bound up with "their" Charter clauses infuses their constitutional language with passion and emotion. The Charter groups are joined by the aboriginal peoples — Indians, Inuit and Métis — attached to a different set of constitutional clauses and driven by a different set of constitutional ambitions that, especially for status Indians, challenge Canadianism with rival nationalisms.

Thus, the constitution is now home for a counter culture, for Canadians with a tendency to see themselves as marginal, as overlooked, or as the Métis are often described, as the "forgotten people." The avid response of these groups to the aboriginal constitutional clauses and to the Charter suggests that federalism and the first ministers who speak for it make only limited contact with the multiple particularistic identities of a modern people. Further, the politics of the 1982 amending formula, with its requirement of legislative ratification, gives these new players access to make their case. Finally, they display little willingness to go to the end of the queue and await their constitutional turn.

From one perspective, Meech Lake was the site of a clash between the territorial pluralism of federalism and the homogenizing, universalizing thrust of the Charter. For its anglophone supporters the Charter postulated a country-wide uniformity of rights-bearing citizens. These rights constituted a Canadian floor protected against provincial transgression, save by resort to the notwith-standing clause, whose use was fraught with political danger for its employers. A similar version of the Charter was held by its Quebec opponents, except they evaluated it negatively as a juggernaut of uniformity crushing justified provincial initiatives, most threateningly language policy, that challenged its writ.[10]

Is there an alternative view of the Charter that might soften its conflict with federalism in general and Québécois specificity in particular? Conceptually yes; politically maybe.

A minority tendency in Charter literature, illustrated by Tom Berger and David Elkins, views the Charter as a vehicle for particular groups to realize their objectives. For Berger, the Charter is an instrument for the recognition of indigenous, ethnic and linguistic pluralism.[11] For Elkins, the Canadian Charter contrasts profoundly with the American Bill of Rights in its pervasive emphasis on collective and community rights.[12] Their view of the Charter as more than an instrument of liberal individualism is empirically, if indirectly supported by the nature of the Charter's contribution to constitutional politics. Quite inde-pendently of how the tension between group and individual rights is adjudicated in courtrooms, the Charter enters the arena of constitutional reform under the banner of organizations speaking on behalf of particular groups — women's organizations on behalf of section 28, ethnic organizations on behalf of section 27, official language minority organizations on behalf of section 23, and various equality-seeking groups on behalf of section 15. They, rather than the various civil liberties associations, were the defenders of the Charter against the Meech Lake Accord. When their numbers are swelled by the many aboriginal organi-zations that press aboriginal claims, it is evident that the new constitutional actors who advocate Charter and aboriginal constitutional concerns are drawn from a handful of social categories defined by language, gender, race, indige-nousness, ethnicity, disability, etc.; they are united by ascriptive or acquired characteristics. The members of each group share a certain fellow-feeling derived from some similarity of social condition and a shared constitutional fate. Whether their constitutional condition can best be described as group or

---

10 See the many negative references in Un Dossier du Devoir, *Le Québec et le Lac Meech* (Montreal, 1987), pp. 109-10, 123, 152-54, 157, 158-61, 180-81, 196, 252, 256. See also, Robert, "La signification de l'Accord du lac Meech," pp. 121, 141-42, 149, 153.

11 Thomas R. Berger, "Towards the Regime of Tolerance," in Stephen Brooks (ed.), *Political Thought in Canada: Contemporary Perspectives* (Toronto: Irwin Pub., 1984).

12 David J. Elkins, "Facing our Destiny: Rights and Canadian Distinctiveness," *Canadian Journal of Political Science*, 22, December 1989, pp. 699-716.

collective rights is not germane to my argument here. What is relevant, however, is that when their constitutional situation, self-perceptions and aspirations are approached sociologically it is evident that they share many traits with nationalist Québécois.

It is not unreasonable to see parallels between the desire of various named groups for affirmative action under section 15(2) and Quebec's desire to gain the constitutional leverage of being recognized as a distinct society. Section 25 of the Charter that protects "aboriginal, treaty or other rights or freedoms" from abrogation or derogation by the Charter is practically a constitutional replica of the Quebec desire to use the Meech Lake "distinct society" clause to mute the Charter's impact. Further, both aboriginal peoples and Québécois share a historic sense of once having been masters of their collective fate in ancient times. Both, of course, fear engulfment, resist assimilation, and are apprehensive about the future of their language(s). The opposition of status Indians to the assimilation objectives of the federal government's 1969 White Paper was analogous to the Quebec nationalist concern that the Charter's language rights will weaken the linguistic measures needed to protect the Quebec francophone community. The status Indian attack on the 1969 White paper was mounted behind the banner of "citizen plus" to describe their unique position in Canada,[13] again a relatively clear functional equivalent of Quebec as not a province *comme les autres*, or as a distinct society. Another supportive example is provided by feminist authors who assert that section 28 is not to be thought of as a simple equalizer of the rights of men and women, but rather as a vehicle for the attainment of substantive equality that it contains an implicit directive to the judiciary to make the clause a vehicle for feminist affirmative action.[14]

Conceptually, therefore, there is considerable symmetry or congruity in the constitutional orientations of aboriginal peoples, many Charter supporters and Québécois. The nonterritorial social pluralism of women, the disabled, and ethnocultural Canadians, the self-government aspirations of aboriginal peoples, especially those with a land base, the private fears and the constitutional objectives of official language minorities and the territorially based desire of francophone Québécois for a constitutional arrangement within which their individuality can flourish are all grounded in the belief that diversity may need special constitutional succouring. In some cases, this may require the support of the Charter; in other cases, escape from it.

---

13 Sally M. Weaver, *Making Canadian Indian Policy: The Hidden Agenda 1968-1970* (Toronto: University of Toronto Press, 1981), chap vii.
14 Gwen Brodsky and Shelagh Day, *Canadian Charter Equality Rights for Women: One Step Forward or Two Steps Back?* (Ottawa: Canadian Advisory Council on the Status of Women, 1989), p. 37.

None of the preceding suggests that the apparent conflict that pitted the Charter and aboriginal constituencies against Quebec in the Meech Lake Accord was based on false consciousness. It does suggest, however, that the conflict can be recast as one in which the contestants are playing the same rather than a different game. The constitutional task, therefore, may be redefined as the need to reconcile coexisting solidarities, the search for a modus vivendi among territorial (Quebec, some aboriginal peoples) and nonterritorial social pluralisms (the many diffuse constituencies of Charter supporters, and those aboriginal peoples who are landless and dispersed.)

While recognition of at least some affinity of group identity and aspiration among the above groups does not eliminate their conflicts, it may support mutual understanding and provide a limited common ground for a rapprochement. That rapprochement, of course, must occur within the Québécois community, which is internally plural, as well as between it and the others. Making constitutional sense of our territorial federalism and our social federalism, much of which is caught up in the Charter, requires a blending of affinities that are already intertwined, not a clash of light and darkness.

Asymmetrical Federalism: Two Quebec Asymmetries — Charter and Jurisdiction

Politically, the Charter was conceived as an instrument of Canadian unity. Its Quebec application, however, has been problematic. Initially it was seen by the nationalists as a central component of the "betrayal" of 1980-82. Conceptually, its claimed individual rights emphasis and its minority official language rights were seen as threatening Quebec's attempt to shape its own linguistic future. Quebec political and scholarly analysis is replete with negative references to the homogenizing, universalizing thrust of the Charter.[15] Intellectually, the passionate Charter activists in anglophone Canada have almost no counterparts in francophone Quebec. In particular, the support of anglophone academics for the political, nation-building purposes of the Charter is not duplicated in Quebec.

The notwithstanding clause was initially employed by the Parti Québécois government across the board to limit the Charter's impact on Quebec, and to symbolize the Quebec government's opposition to the 1982 settlement. Subsequently, Premier Bourassa not only used the notwithstanding clause for Quebec's language of signs legislation, but vigorously defended the clause as an essential instrument of Quebec protection against the Charter.[16] Among its

---

15 See the references in fn 9.
16 Benoit Aubin, "Fight looms over opting-out clause," *The Globe and Mail*, 7 April 1989.

other purposes, the Meech Lake "distinct society" clause was intended to constrain the impact of the Charter on Quebec.

If Quebec's moves toward greater autonomy are contained within a revised federalism, a fully applicable Charter will appear even more alien. It will be seen as an unwelcome tight ideological link contrasting strongly with the generally attenuated links with rest-of-Canada characteristic of asymmetry. Asymmetry will strengthen the already well developed tendency to see the Quebec Charter as the appropriate vehicle for rights protection in Quebec. Perhaps in anticipation, francophone representations before the Bélanger-Campeau Commission have been virtually devoid of positive Charter references.

While there are competing political tendencies in Quebec, including strong Charter support from anglophone and other minority communities, and residual reminders that the Charter was conceived by Pierre Trudeau and Quebec federalists, there is little doubt that the overall tendency of Quebec evaluation is much more negative than elsewhere in Canada. Accordingly, the rest-of-Canada should be prepared to consider seriously an asymmetrical federalism in which the Charter has a more limited or even nonexistent application to the enhanced jurisdictional powers that a future Quebec in Canada will wield.

In one sense, the generation of an asymmetrical Charter regime is an easier goal to achieve than is an asymmetrical jurisdictional status for Quebec. This is because the repercussions of the latter on the overall constitution, requiring an asymmetrical status for Quebec MPs at a minimum, would be much more pervasive and consequential than the impact of the former.

In relative terms, an asymmetrical Charter regime by itself would have limited ramifications for other institutions of government. Since it would not directly affect the division of powers, it would not, of itself, affect the status of Quebec MPs in the House of Commons. Federal legislation would apply to Quebec as to the rest-of-Canada, and would, of course, be subject to the Canadian Charter in Quebec as elsewhere. It is true, of course, that an asymmetrical Charter regime for Quebec's domestic legislation has jurisdictional consequences as it subjects that legislation and administrative behaviour to less onerous restraints than are applied elsewhere. The restriction or nonapplication of the Charter to Quebec jurisdiction might involve a reshuffling of procedures and criteria for appointments to the Supreme Court and to the Quebec superior courts, but these pose a lesser order of complexity than the changes to House of Commons representation and to the practice of responsible government that would follow an asymmetrical enhancement of Quebec jurisdictional powers.

On the other hand, an asymmetrical Charter means an asymmetrical citizenship at a time when the Charter has immensely strengthened citizenship as a constitutional category in the rest-of-Canada. It provides the core constitutional identity for many English-speaking Canadians. It is a potent instrument of constitutional mobilization. The input from Charter groups to the various Meech Lake hearings was rivalled in extent and passion only by aboriginal presentations.

Overt constitutional recognition of an asymmetrical Charter, therefore, is not a trivial constitutional adaptation. It is not tinkering. It may be institutionally straightforward, but it is morally complex. It is a profound admission of our constitutional divisions, a recognition of the fact that we are not now and have despaired of becoming a single people whose dualism is transcended by an allegiance to a common regime of rights.

None of this is to suggest that a significantly different Charter regime in Quebec should be automatically rejected. In the practical and psychological sense a different *de facto* regime already exists. To constitutionalize and build on the difference is to admit that the political purposes of the Charter project have not been met in Quebec and cannot be met in the future.

The second and more important asymmetry for Quebec involves jurisdiction. From the mid-sixties to the *Constitution Act, 1982* the division of powers was a priority item on Quebec's constitutional agenda. The federal government under Trudeau sidetracked the issue by stressing the need to deal first with a Charter, and second with the reform of central institutions before turning to the division of powers. Meech Lake addressed the division of powers only indirectly. In the coming round of constitutional negotiations extensive Quebec-strengthening changes to the division of powers are probably unavoidable.

A response to Quebec, which is controlled by the equality of the provinces principle, will at the extremes display one of the following tendencies: (a) the response to Quebec will be minimal as the rest-of-Canada tries to salvage significant responsibilities for the central government; (b) alternatively, a sensitive accommodation of Quebec will produce an extensive across-the-board decentralization that neither in extent nor possibly in substance would represent an optimum division of federal-provincial responsibilities outside Quebec. However, the latter response would deny Quebec the symbolic good of differentiated treatment that its nationalism seeks.

In sum, the equality of the provinces principle in future Quebec-Canada relations within a revised federalism no longer appears tenable. Accordingly, and at a minimum, there will have to be constitutional recognition that Quebec is not a province like the others; preferably, the status of Quebec should be cast in terminology other than provincehood. The magnitude of this change should not be underestimated; however, its serious consideration is necessary if a constitutional option within federalism and short of independence is to be kept alive.

In evaluating this option, and working out the terms of its implementation, it will be necessary to extend the discussion beyond its most recent focus — consideration of the equality of the provinces norm or its violation from the sole vantage point of equity among provincial governments. Significant jurisdictional inequalities among provincial governments are simultaneously inequalities of citizenship between the residents of those provinces with different jurisdictional powers. It necessarily follows that the significance and application of federal government jurisdiction will vary from province to province. Hence, citizens in different provinces will have structural inducements to differ in their evaluations of the relative importance of federal and provincial arenas. If province "X" is not to be a province like the others in terms of jurisdiction, its citizens will not be citizens like the others. Further, the lesser jurisdiction of the federal government in province "X" necessarily suggests a correspondingly diminished role for MPs from province "X." Otherwise the citizens of that province will wield voting power that violates the norm of equality of the vote, and may even violate the Charter.

In other words, major asymmetries in jurisdictional status lead inexorably to inequalities or proportionate asymmetries in the role and responsibilities of Quebec MPs in the House of Commons, and probably of Senators as well. While minor anomalies are ubiquitous in a functioning constitutional order of some vintage, major anomalies that offend fundamental constitutional principles are unacceptable. The one in four members of the House of Commons from Quebec cannot be full participants when the House deals with matters that are in federal government jurisdiction outside Quebec, but in "provincial" government jurisdiction in Quebec. In the negotiation of an asymmetric federalism, this is the crucial issue. It requires a rethinking of the practice and theory of responsible government — no mean task.

Asymmetrical Federalism: Is Asymmetry Viable?

A system of asymmetrical federalism presupposes that the Quebec government has jurisdictional responsibilities not held by other governments, probably a different set of rights and obligations of Quebec MPs, and possibly a less comprehensive or stringent application of the Charter to an enhanced Quebec jurisdiction. Assuming that asymmetry can be attained, is it likely to endure?

On the one hand, it might be assumed that a particular asymmetrical arrangement more responsive than provincial status to Québécois nationalist pressures would have a greater stability than the standard provincehood left behind. By inference, also, the constitutionalization of asymmetry would clearly indicate a rest-of-Canada recognition of the Quebec difference, and thus facilitate a coexistence based on dignity and respect.

On the other hand, these positive features are countered by the inducements to instability seemingly inherent in the absence of an external reference standard for asymmetrical status as a control. A system in which "a province is a province is a province" provides visible external criteria for the status of provincehood in the form of neighbouring provincial jurisdictions belonging to the same system. By the same token, the virtue of independence is that we know in juridical terms what an independent nation-state is; analytically, it is evident that the evolving meaning of statehood is transmitted by the international state system to its component units. In each case, province and nation-state, behaviour is constrained by a system of norms and statuses that have a certain givenness/naturalness. Definitions and criteria are not idiosyncratic, and hence contingent and subject to constant challenge. They are products of a system of evolving meanings, widely understood, sustained by tradition, and upheld by the other actors.

By constrast, any particular version of asymmetrical federalism lacks the stabilizing influence of controlling external models. On the contrary, the influence of the two most powerful models in its environment province and nation-state — are likely to be destabilizing. As the future attraction and repulsion of these two models waxes and wanes within Quebec and in the rest-of-Canada, Quebec will be alternately pushed and pulled in the direction of one or the other reference point. Within Quebec the attractions of nation-statehood are likely to be stimulated by the dynamics of nationalist competition. In the rest-of-Canada, the provincial equality imperative will be wielded by expansive provincial governments hoping to level-up and by others resistant to anomalies seeking to level down.

Any particular asymmetrical position is likely, therefore, to appear contingent and arbitrary, for its justification does not come from a body of rules that apply to many actors. Thus, in the world of constructed political arrangements, significant asymmetrical status is likely to be highly unstable.

This instability will be exaggerated in Quebec because the dynamics of political competition will continue to be driven by nationalism. Further, the diminished pan-Canadianism that will flow from asymmetrical status with its relative enhancement of the status of Quebec politicians at home and the diminished status of Quebec politicians in Ottawa, along with the aggrandizement of Quebec citizenship at the expense of Canadian, will be a weak counterfoil to Quebec nationalism. The relative decline in the status of the MPs from Quebec, and the truncated political careers they will experience, including barriers to holding at least some cabinet posts, will reduce the relative quality of Quebec representation in Ottawa, and the visibility of the federal government in Quebec.

If the Charter's applicability to Quebec were limited as the Parti Québécois suggested in 1985 to democratic rights (sections 3-5),[17] associational ties

---

17 "Draft Agreement on the Constitution: Proposals by the Government of Quebec," in Peter M. Leslie (ed.), *Canada: The State of the Federation 1985* (Kingston: Institute of Intergovernmental Relations, Queen's University, 1985), pp. 64-68.

crossing the Quebec/rest-of-Canada borders would be weakened. Charter litigation interest groups such as LEAF [18] would retreat to the rest-of-Canada, retaining only a tenuous Quebec connection because of the surviving federalist jurisdiction in Quebec still covered by the Charter. The constitutional discourse of Quebec and the rest-of-Canada would increasingly diverge. Outside Quebec, a Charter-influenced series of constitutional discourses would revolve around issues of gender, multiculturalism, the equality rights of section 15, etc. While Québécois might have analogous discourses directed to their own political existence and focusing on Quebec's own Charter, such rhetoric would develop its own rhythms, would be directed to a different polity, and would reinforce the psychological basis of the constitutional separateness of Quebec. Conceptions of a community in Quebec and the rest-of-Canada would respond to different cues. Each would appear as somewhat of a stranger to the other. Conceptions of a common citizenship, perhaps the most potent constitutional category in democratic polities, would be displaced by coexisting if overlapping civic identities. Obviously, the normative assumptions behind what Pepin-Robarts called "sharing," which included "the equitable distribution of benefits," [19] would be eroded. The sense of mutual obligation that is the moral basis of sharing by means of equalization payments and regional development programs would be weakened. The spirit of calculation, already widespread in federalism's accounting mentality, would be especially pronounced on both sides of the asymmetrical divide.

In such circumstances, would Canada outside Quebec, British Columbia for example, not be resistant to making equalization payments to a Quebec whose Canadianism was gravely attenuated? Conversely, would Quebec agree to be treated as a "have" province whose taxpayers contributed extensively to equalization payments distributed to Atlantic Canada and to one or more western provinces?

For Québécois, an asymmetrical federalism produces an asymmetrical psyche in which the balance of loyalties to and identifications with Quebec and Canada is strongly tilted to the former. The emotional connection to the latter exists, so to speak, on sufferance rather than as the balance appropriate to a federalism in equilibrium, with both orders of government applying significant jurisdictional powers to the Quebec citizenry. From the Quebec perspective, stability in such a situation would derive only from a consistency of will over time, ideally informed by an unvarying self-interest. But such an enduring consistency and unvarying self-interest would be highly problematic in a context riven with the passion of nationalism and the spirit of calculation.

---

18 The acronym for women's Legal Education and Action Fund.
19 The Task Force on Canadian Unity, *A Future Together: Observations and Recommendations* (Ottawa: Minister of Supply and Services, 1979), p. 36.

In the transition period, the instability is likely to be aggravated by the learning and unlearning involved in making the new asymmetrical arrangements work. These new arrangements will clearly be complicated with a Quebec government enjoying powers not possessed by other governments, Quebec MPs presumably wielding lesser powers than other MPs, Quebec citizens relating to the Charter differently than other Canadians, and a host of arrangements particular to Quebec with respect to executive federalism, the Supreme Court, and to various boards and commissions.

Accordingly, the task of managing the settling-in process of asymmetrical federalism will be, to say the least, challenging. The difficulties of the task will be compounded if the rest-of-Canada is simultaneously rearranging the relationships between the central government and the other nine provinces and two territories. Concurrently, those Québécois who previously supported the Charter and other arrangements of a departed federalism from which they gained status and identity are likely to be less than fully allied to the new constitutional regime.

Even in the long run, an above-average degree of instability appears probable, as the disputes that will attend asymmetry will not be resolvable by appeals to general rules, but will be responded to in particularistic terms specific to one relationship only. Such a system of dispute resolution appears uniquely prone to allegations of favouritism or unfairness, because of the relative absence of more general criteria to which appeals can be made.

INDEPENDENCE: THE REST-OF-CANADA IN AN AMBIGUOUS GAME

A central ambiguity of the pending round of constitutional change is the coexistence of two very different constitutional games. The first is the traditional federalism game — the refashioning of the constitutional system to reduce the tensions between dualism, provincialism and Canadianism. This time around this game, if played out to a conclusion, will probably produce a drastically different federalism with Quebec breaking through the constraints of provincialism to attain an asymmetrical relationship to the other provinces and to the central government. Provincialism will no longer constrain the Quebec side of dualism. However, such an outcome will still be federal in some minimum sense. The federal government will retain some independent jurisdiction in Quebec and there will continue to be Quebec members in the federal parliament. Consequently, there is an obvious bargaining role for the federal government in achieving such an outcome. It can speak for the modified pan-Canadian dimension that will survive in the next constitutional regime and for its own future role as a government of all Canadians. Thus, this constitutional game can possibly be handled, admittedly with difficulty, by an

adaptation of the amending process to accommodate Premier Bourassa's assertion that from now on he will only negotiate one-on-one with the federal
government.

The second game is the independence game in which Quebec seeks the status
of an independent nation-state, even if it is one linked to a surviving if shrunken
Canada by various agreements. This outcome necessarily implies the emergence of one or more parallel states alongside an independent Quebec. For the
sake of simplicity I will assume that Canada without Quebec will survive as a
single entity, initially at least as a country of nine provinces, two territories and
a central government.

If that is the direction in which we are headed, the second nation-state has
no official spokesperson to articulate its concerns prior to the actual rupture.
The provincial governments outside Quebec, acting either collectively or individually, are incompetent to speak for an English-speaking rest-of-Canada
waiting eagerly or reluctantly to be born. Their concern is with the provincial
jurisdictional dimension of our existence as a people. Further, each of them
speaks only for a limited territorially restricted segment of a future Canada-
without-Quebec. They are thus doubly incapacitated, by jurisdiction and territory, from assuming a Canadian leadership role. They are conditioned by
tradition to be provincial and by electoral constraints not to deviate from
tradition. At least some of them will be tempted to employ the equality of
provinces principle as a vehicle to ride on the coattails of Quebec demands, and
thus strengthen (what might be) the misperception that Canadians are engaged
in a federalism game. This will delay the recognition that Canadians are
engaged in, if such it is, an independence game.

Occasional exceptions to the contrary, there is little recent evidence to
encourage the belief that the premiers of the rest-of-Canada will rise above their
provincial ambitions to speak for a Canadian constituency. A Canada-without-
Quebec fashioned by provincial hands would not do justice to the Canadian
dimension. In 1980-81 the Gang of Eight provincial governments opposed the
Charter, fought successfully for a notwithstanding clause to weaken its impact
when they realized they could not defeat it, and were the successful sponsors
of an amending formula more sensitive to the provincial than to the Canadian
dimension. Wielding the 1982 rules the provincial governments turned the
Meech Lake Quebec round into a provincial round.

It is futile to deprecate their behaviour. They are simply doing their provincial
job in response to the powerful shaping cues of federalism which make concern
for the whole someone else's responsibility. Accordingly, to look to the provincial governments outside Quebec to speak for and to the national dimension of
a Canada-without-Quebec is to be guilty of a constitutional oxymoron. It is also
to subscribe to a modern version of the compact theory by which what the
rest-of-Canada holds in common is attributed to provincial government

generosity. Unfortunately, however, it is structurally easier for provincial governments to anticipate and prepare for their future in a Canada-without-Quebec than it is for the federal government. They lose only a partner. They continue as political, constitutional entities, with territory, jurisdiction and population intact. In a Canada-without-Quebec, the federal government loses territory, citizens, a historic identity, some of its bureaucracy, and many of the political responsibilities that flowed from its former management of a linguistically dual people. Little preparation by the federal government for such an unsought goal is likely.

The federal government cannot speak or bargain for Canada-without-Quebec, for its mandate is Canada-with-Quebec. It cannot speak for anglophone Canada in the nine provinces and two territories as a potentially separate people. It speaks for them only as they are part of a pan-Canadian people linked to their francophone confreres in a common country. The pressure of institutional self-interest and the weight of the past drive the federal government to speak for a federal solution, for any other solution dismembers it along with the country that is breaking up. Political responsibility drives it in the same direction, for up until the final rupture there will still be Canadians within Quebec who seek a federal solution, and who resist having a Québécois identity totally displace their Canadian identity. At least some Quebec anglophones and members of other minorities will query the legitimacy of a constitutional change that removes them from a country they do not wish to leave. Aboriginal peoples will continue to assert a distinctiveness that is transprovincial and for status Indians is historically linked to the federal government. Some federal and federalist MPs from Quebec will express the surviving Canadian concerns among their Québécois constituents.

For all of these reasons, the federal government of all of Canada lacks the capacity and inclination to speak as the prospective federal government of a Canada bereft of Quebec. In fact, the federal government is inherently incapable of impartially assessing the relative advantages of Canada with and Canada without Quebec. Its self-interest as a government and its traditional identity will drive it to prefer even a slender thread of continuity to a complete rupture and its own dismemberment, even when the balance of advantages more judicially assessed from the perspective of the rest-of-Canada might deliver a verdict in favour of a breakup. In other words, a federal government leadership role treats the rest-of-Canada not as a prospective independent people, but as an integral component of a dualist pan-Canada. This will have deleterious consequences for the rest-of-Canada if the independence game is the real one.

Thus, if constitutional game number two displaces constitutional game number one, the cast of actors has to be reshuffled. The Canadian government speaking for a Canada that has been rejected by Quebec leaves the table to be replaced by what? Canada outside Quebec is headless and voiceless. It has no institutional or corporate existence. At this point, we leave the stage of normal constitutional politics and enter uncharted constitutional territory.

The difficulty is even more serious than has been suggested because the problem is not only who will be available, occupying what legitimate office, to speak for an emergent Canada-without-Quebec, but what preparation, what forethought, what anticipatory socialization of a new people has prepared Canada-without-Quebec for its truncated future.

At this stage, the contrast with Quebec will be chastening. A strain of *indépendantiste* thought has never been absent from Quebec political and intellectual life. Movements and parties seeking independence or sovereignty association have flourished in the last 30 years. An independence-oriented party was in power for a decade, and is now the official opposition. One referendum has already been held in 1980; the Bélanger-Campeau hearings are underway as I write (December 1990); the governing Quebec Liberal party is separately exploring constitutional options; and sometime in the next few months the Quebec government will announce the constitutional goal it seeks for Quebec. The francophone majority in Quebec is further aided in its constitutional exploration by the self-consciousness that attends its historic minority status in Canada and North America.

Canada-without-Quebec lacks a lengthy preparation and conditioning for an independent existence. Anglophone Canada within and without Quebec has been attached to the whole from which it gained many benefits. The anglophone majority in the rest-of-Canada is inevitably poorly prepared for an unchosen future. The expanded sense of identity that independence will produce for many Québécois is unlikely to be duplicated for the other partner, at least initially, painfully adjusting to a shrunken sense of self and identity.

The complexities of the situation are compounded by the fact that the federalism game and the independence game are being played simultaneously, not sequentially. This is much less of a problem for Quebec than for the rest-of-Canada. Although at any given time supporters of both games, and thus opponents of each other, will vie to control the content of Quebec's constitutional demands, the government of Quebec remains the official spokesperson for whatever constitutional objectives Quebec pursues. In fact, the Quebec government, relative to the other actors in federalism or to a prospective rest-of-Canada national partner, can flexibly move from one game to another. The rest-of-Canada is not so fortunate. It is extremely difficult for it to play both games at once, and even more difficult to switch from one game to another for the two games require different actors, and they appeal to competing versions of identity and community. In the federalism game, the rest-of-Canada is submerged in all of Canada that is struggling to survive. Its sociological existence is implicit. Its political existence is imaginary. In the independence game, the rest-of-Canada acquires a potential sense of itself as a political people, but that sense still lacks institutional expression. For Canada outside Quebec the independence game prior to disruption has to be played by an inchoate cast of nongovernmental actors, and they risk being accused of scuttling a historic people. Official Canada has to get ready for a federalism response to Quebec, while the unofficial the rest-of-Canada should simultaneously be preparing for the possibility of its own independence.

The coexistence of two games, one actual and one potential, will be underlined when the next round of official negotiations gets underway. The asymmetrical status that will be Quebec's minimum goal will explicitly define the rest-of-Canada as a discrete community. That definition will be strengthened by the recognition that Quebec independence is a serious viable alternative in Quebec. For the rest-of-Canada this period will be one of intense, rapid learning and a somewhat chaotic exploration of alternative futures. In functional terms, therefore, the negotiation stage should be seen as a crucial forum for educating and preparing the rest-of-Canada for future choices that up until then it will have scarcely considered. Psychologically at least, negotiations will begin the process of separating out the Canadian and the rest-of-Canada dimensions. The former will be redefined to accommodate the weaker presence of Quebec if historic Canada survives, and the latter will commence to reshape itself from a leftover category to a potential people sharing an asymmetrical federalism with Quebec, or sharing as a separate people the northern portions of North America with an independent Quebec.

CONCLUSION

The two most plausible constitutional options confronting Canadians — an asymmetrical federalism according unique status to Quebec, or an independent Quebec coexisting with an independent still federal, but diminished, Canada — both require Canadians in and out of Quebec to maneuver through the minefield of three equalities: of provinces, of citizens, and of two national communities.

The first two equalities, of provinces and citizens, are emergent constitutional principles that have been hammered out and refined in the last two decades. The former dominates the amending formula and illustrates the contemporary tendency to subject the operation of federalism to federal principles. The latter is the powerful message of the Charter. Both equalities reduce flexibility in responding to a Quebec that seeks differential treatment, especially if the latter is highly visible and highly symbolic. They remove the issue of asymmetry, either of government jurisdiction or of citizen rights, from the realm of pragmatism to the stratosphere of high constitutional principle. They are examples of constitutional rationalization, the application of principles to citizen-state relations and to the range of acceptable variations in the cluster of factors that comprise provincehood. The symmetry these principles bring is paid for by a diminished constitutional capacity to provide individualized responses to distinct societies and to distinct situations. They are more sympathetic to uniformity than to diversity in the domains to which they apply.

They obviously do not apply to an independent Quebec, and an asymmetrical Quebec by definition would not be a province like the others, and almost certainly would be subjected, at a minimum, to a lesser Charter regime. The first two equalities, therefore, have to be breached whether Quebec is accommodated inside or outside federalism. Escape from their reach within federalism appears essential if the enhancement of Quebec's powers is to stop short of sovereignty. The equality of provinces principle either constrains Quebec or becomes the vehicle for an unacceptable expansion of the jurisdiction of all provinces driven by Québécois nationalism. A relaxation of the Charter's application to Quebec, especially relating to minority language education, would remove a chafing constraint and would give pride of place to the Quebec Charter.

The Canadian Charter is so clearly linked to conceptions of citizenship outside Quebec that it seems inappropriate to have it apply to the unique status of Quebec citizens in an asymmetrical federalism. Acceptance of this escape from the Charter may be eased by the recognition that the Quebec desire to give constitutional support to a language and a way of life has many similarities with other groups who see the Charter as a vehicle to enhance their objectives as women, the disabled, visible minorities, and others. Such recognition could also extend to aboriginal peoples whose as yet unrealized constitutional ambitions are driven by a nationalist rhetoric little different from that of Quebec nationalists.

Escape from the coverage of these two equalities would be a clear and symbolically potent affirmation of Quebec's specificity. Two of the central components of the Canadian constitutional order would have no or an incomplete application to Quebec. The big change of escape from these two equalities is cleaner and less troublesome than the small change of partial accommodation attempted by the Meech Lake distinct society. The stability of such an arrangement, however, is problematic. The dynamics of an asymmetrical federal relationship may make it only a waystation on the road to a fuller independence.

The difficulty with the third equality if our future is to be two independent peoples coexisting side by side is that the rest-of-Canada partner has a potential rather than a contemporary existence. At the moment, while a federalism that includes Quebec still lingers, the "rest-of-Canada" is a mental construct only. Paradoxically, Québécois speak and write much more confidently of the "rest-of-Canada," than do those who belong to it. To Québécois nationalists, the rest-of-Canada is the "not us" to whom they attribute a collective self-consciousness akin to their own. Unfortunately, to look out from Quebec in the search for the other "nation" whose existence will confirm a pleasing symmetry, and thus facilitate one-on-one bargaining, is a recipe for failure. Outside Quebec are Canadians, Manitobans, aboriginals, Charter supporters and a society that is increasingly multicultural and multiracial. One does not, however, find the rest-of-Canadians. One does not find a community with a distinctive sense of self, with political institutions that shape it, with office holders having a responsibility to educate that community in its needs and options, a community with a long history of trying to make the rest-of-Canada its very own country. On the contrary, the history has not been one of trying to get out, but rather of positive attachment to a coast to coast country built by all Canadians. Rotstein identifies the anglophone attitude to Canada as "mappism";[20] Resnick correctly notes how allegiance to the government of Canada is central to the anglophone political identity.[21] McNaught earlier referred to the increasingly nonnational outlook of anglophone Canadians;[22] more recently, for many Canadians outside Quebec and for anglophones and other minorities within Quebec, the Charter's elevation of the status of a country-wide rights possessing citizenship has stimulated a Canadian, not the rest-of-Canadian, identification with the constitutional order. These all speak to the Canadian, not to the rest-of-Canada dimension.

For Quebec to get its act together has not been easy, and is not yet completed, but blessed with the focus of a single government to channel the politics of self-affirmation the Quebec task is simplicity itself compared to the task confronting rest-of-Canada. The very labels employed — the "rest-of-Canada," "Canada-without-Quebec" or "anglophone Canada" (which awkwardly includes aboriginal peoples and francophone minorities and excludes Quebec anglophones) — attest to the institutional and psychological impediments to a coherent sense of self while traditional Canada remains alive.

The two-nations solution encounters the non- or at best incipient existence of one side of the prospective two-nation equality. This asymmetry of self-consciousness and self-identification is most serious, of course, in the preparatory stages leading to the possible rupture of Canada. As noted elsewhere in this essay, the difficulty is compounded because the rest-of-Canada is being asked to play two games at once, the save-federalism game and the two-nations game. The systemic bias of an existing federal system with a central government fighting for its country-wide survival favours the allocation of political and intellectual resources to the first game, and almost inevitably reduces the

---

20 Abraham Rotstein, "Is there an English-Canadian Nationalism? *Journal of Canadian Studies,* 13, Summer 1978, p.114.
21 Philip Resnick, *Letters to a Québécois Friend, with a reply by Daniel Latouche* (Montreal and Kingston: McGill-Queen's University Press, 1990), p.15.
22 Kenneth McNaught, "The National Outlook of English-speaking Canadians," in Peter Russell (ed.), *Nationalism in Canada* (Toronto: McGraw-Hill Ryerson, 1966).

attention paid and the quality of effort devoted to the second game, which may well be the more important of the two. No such bias applies to the challenging Quebec government.

The likelihood of governments outside Quebec devoting adequate and appropriately directed intellectual, political and bureaucratic resources to this urgent political task for the rest-of-Canada is minimal. The responsibility must be assumed by other than governmental actors, unless the ostrich is to be the emblem of the rest-of-Canada. The tendency of academics and others to line up behind governments must be tempered by the recognition that the rest-of-Canada is an empty chair at the constitutional bargaining table. Of all the constitutional players it is most in need of assistance to address its constitutional concerns.

IV

Basic Options and Processes

6

Quebec Beyond the Federal Regime of 1867-1982: From Distinct Society to National Community

Guy Laforest

No science can offer absolute certainties concerning the evolution of political events in post-Meech Lake Quebec and Canada. As a political philosopher and as a historian of ideas, I wish to recognize clearly from the start that my interpretation of our predicament is guided by two firm convictions. First, I have come to the belief that the Canadian federal regime of 1867, partially renovated in 1982, is now bankrupt in Quebec and that it cannot regenerate itself within its institutional and legal parameters. Second, I also think that the acknowledgment of the nature of this profound impasse by the leading economic, intellectual and political leaders of both Quebec and Canada, would greatly improve the chances of success of a restructuring process that has now become inevitable.

The federalist cause in Quebec has been damaged beyond repair by the failure of the Meech Lake Accord. In this paper on the constitutional and political options of Quebec, as they are currently being examined by the Bélanger-Campeau Commission, I will outline what I see as a common challenge for Quebec and Canada in the twenty-first century. However, I shall not deny that this future in common will have to start by a rupture. The population of Quebec seems poised to disentangle itself from the Canadian federation. This evokes feelings of both sadness and cold resoluteness. For a good number of those who have come to embrace sovereignty, the loss of Canada is the loss of a country.

As economist Pierre Fortin has phrased it, Canada was part of their soul.[1] But this same country, as many perceive it, has refused to recognize Quebec as a distinct society within Canada ten years after the referendum. In the words of

---

1 Pierre Fortin, "Le choix forcé du Québec," *Le Devoir*, 14 December 1990, p. B8.

Charles Taylor, the Meech Lake Accord represented the first official recognition by Canada of the French Canadian nation as the members of this nation define it.[2] Quebec, confident of possessing all the attributes of a national community, offered a symbolic compromise to Canada and its federal regime by presenting itself as a distinct society. The compromise, for various reasons, was rejected. The consequences of this gesture are incalculable. For Quebec, for its leaders and for the majority of its population, the rejection of the Meech Lake Accord meant nothing less than the end of a Canadian dream. Is it possible to reinvent a Canadian dream that would include Quebec in a significant fashion? I think so. Undeniably though, the dream in question would have to be conceptualized beyond federalism, with a clear recognition of Quebec as a politically sovereign national community. Such is the price of Meech Lake.

This paper will be divided into five parts. In the first part, I will summarize the activities of the parliamentary Commission on the Constitutional and Political Future of Quebec, headed by two men who symbolize the achievements of the Quiet Revolution, Michel Bélanger and Jean Campeau. I shall discuss next a number of strategic considerations, borrowing at times from the format of Ronald Watts' preliminary study (chapter 2 in this volume). In the third and fourth parts, I shall examine the various processes and institutional structures that are being contemplated by the Commission. Finally, I will present a new and challenging vision for the common future of Quebec and Canada. I think the Bélanger-Campeau Commission will ultimately formulate proposals more or less along these lines. To understand the seriousness of the current crisis, it is instructive to listen to Vincent Lemieux and Léon Dion, two of the most respected voices of caution and moderation in the Quebec intelligentsia. In his brief to the Commission, Lemieux provided this succinct interpretation of our political drama of the last ten years: "Whereas in 1980 a majority of Quebecers said no to the party which was proposing a rupture with Canada, in 1990, this Canada said no to the party which suggested that Quebec should not break away from Canada."[3] Writing in *L'Analyste* in the fall of 1990, Lemieux argued that Canada and Quebec should become associate states,

---

2 Charles Taylor, "Le caractère distinct du Québec," paper prepared for a conference held at the University of Ottawa, 26-28 April 1990, p. 2, unpublished manuscript. In the words of Christian Dufour, "the failure of Meech Lake means that Canada is unable to accept that Quebec's distinctiveness should carry substantial political consequences." See Christian Dufour, *Le défi québécois* (Montréal: L'Héxagone, 1989), p. 140.

3 Vincent Lemieux, "Faire entendre les voix de la population," mémoire présenté à la Commission sur l'avenir constitutionnel et politique du Québec, December 1990, p. 2.

beyond federalism.[4] As a Quebec patriot, Léon Dion has been loyal to the Canadian federal dream for more than 40 years. His presentation to the Bélanger-Campeau Commission has been highly publicized in the English-speaking media. It was said that he wanted Quebec to give one more chance to Canada. However, the fine print of his brief is simply devastating for the federalist cause. Léon Dion writes that he rejects the constitutional reform of 1982 in its entirety, including the Charter of Rights and Freedoms.[5] This affirmation must be put in the context of the development of a new, Charter-based, Canadian nationalism in the 1980s. Alan Cairns and Peter Russell, among others, have studied this powerful legacy of the Trudeau era. Dion rejects the institutions and the symbols that have become dominant in the political culture of English-speaking Canada. In the concluding remarks of his discussion with the Commissioners, he repeated that the constitution of 1867 should be discarded as a starting-point for the impending negotiations between Quebec and Canada. Léon Dion himself, the federalist intellectual who contributed magnificently to the Royal Commission on Bilingualism and Biculturalism in the 1960s, and to the Task Force on Canadian Unity in the late 1970s, has moved beyond 1867 and 1982. In these circumstances a federal solution coming from Quebec is not impossible, but it appears extremely unlikely. The report of the Bélanger-Campeau Commission will provide a range for the more plausible options, from confederal models to those inspired by sovereignty-association and full-blown independence.

A PARLIAMENTARY COMMISSION TO PONDER THE FUTURE OF QUEBEC

John Locke, probably the most prominent liberal philosopher of all times, sees in the legislative power the soul of a political community. It is something sacred, of the utmost importance. In 1991, Quebec will be celebrating the bicentennial of its own parliament. As an outgrowth of this legislative power, the Parliamentary Commission on the Constitutional and Political Future of Quebec is provided with a unique opportunity to shape the contours of a majority French-speaking distinct society in America.

Events have evolved at a swift pace since the failure of the Meech Lake Accord. The agreement on the idea of an extraordinary Parliamentary

---

4   See *L'Analyste XXXI*, Fall 1990, p. 21. This view was expressed during a discussion on "Meech. L'avenir d'un échec," with V. Lemieux and a group of contributors to *L'Analyste.*

5   Léon Dion, "Pour sortir de l'impasse constitutionnelle," mémoire présenté à la Commission sur l'avenir politique et constitutionnel du Québec, December 1990, p. 6.

Commission was struck between Robert Bourassa and Jacques Parizeau in early July, a law was passed in early September, and the Commission inaugurated its public activities in the first days of November. The Commission will deliver its report at the end of March 1991. The underlying assumption that governs the life of the Commission is quite simple: Quebec now enjoys *de facto* sovereignty. All the options are on the table. In the immediate aftermath of the death of Meech Lake, Robert Bourassa said that Quebec was a free and distinct society, capable of assuming its own development. Later on, he specified that his government and his party would be guided in their actions by the superior interests of Quebec. This self-determination, within Canada or beyond federalism, is reaffirmed in the law creating the Bélanger-Campeau Commission. The co-chairmen have explicitly stated that they interpreted their mandate in such terms. In the conclusion of his book on the Meech Lake saga, Pierre Fournier has aptly captured the atmosphere of the times: "everything is now possible for Quebec."[6]

As an *ad-hoc* institution, the Bélanger-Campeau Commission is very much the product of partisan politics in a parliamentary democracy. Government and opposition bargained long and hard on every minute detail, from the nomination of the two co-chairmen to the establishment of a reasonably efficient process. The result was greeted at first with mixed opinions. Bélanger and Campeau were caricatured as the pawns of Bourassa and Parizeau. The composition of the Commission, with its 36 members, was strongly criticized. Such a forum, it was argued, was incompatible with the objective of serious and serene reflection. Many considered the process vitiated by the absence of adequate representation from minorities, from the aboriginal peoples and ethnic groups. Pierre Fournier has written that the Commission is an instrument used by Robert Bourassa to stifle an emerging sovereigntist consensus in Quebec.[7] Still others have deplored the exclusion of intellectuals.

After two months of intensive work, one has to recognize that the Commission has functioned like a well-greased locomotive. It received over 500 briefs from individuals and various organizations, with about 60 additional ones from experts. The Commission is based in Quebec City, where it has spent a considerable part of its time. It moved briskly through Montreal and took three weeks to tour the various regions of Quebec. The Commission operates with a secretariat managed by Henri-Paul Rousseau, an economist. Robert Bourassa's Liberal Party enjoys a slim majority on its steering committee.

---

6 Pierre Fournier, *Autopsie du Lac Meech. La souveraineté est-elle inévitable?* (Montréal: V 1b éditeur, 1990), p. 214.

7 Pierre Fournier, "Un guet-apens pour la souveraineté," *Le Devoir*, 5 November 1990, p. B3.

In the analysis of the life of the Commission, three dimensions have to be emphasized.

Dominance of the Economic Perspective

Considering that the founding fathers of the Commission, Robert Bourassa and Jacques Parizeau, are economists, that Michel Bélanger and Jean Campeau have respectively headed the National Bank of Canada and the Caisse de dépôts et placements du Quebec and that the secretariat is run by yet another economist and that many business leaders sit as commissioners, it is not surprising to note that the economic vision of politics enjoyed at first the status of dominant discourse.[8] This dominance has now been shattered by the economists themselves. I see this development as a turning point. In its presentation to the Commission, the Quebec Association of Economists has argued that economic considerations, although central in the transitional period between the current and future constitutional status of Quebec, whatever form it takes, should not be the main preoccupation.[9] Quebec could flourish economically either within renewed federalism, sovereignty-association or outright independence. In the long run, the science of economics is unable to predict which of these structural options would be most advantageous to Quebec. The economists have invited the Commission to give priority to cultural, political and strategic considerations. They have been heard. I would argue that the Commission is trying to answer two questions: What are the powers required by Quebec to preserve and promote its distinctiveness? and, How can these powers be attained?

The Powers of a Distinct Society

It took the Bélanger-Campeau Commission less than two weeks to demonstrate that Quebec had moved light years ahead of the set of demands included in the Meech Lake package. All observers expected the Commission to receive a significant proportion of prosovereignty presentations. However, the federalist and noncommitted members on the panel have been astonished by the number of briefs from individuals and groups representing all walks of life, refusing to take a firm position on the question of Quebec's status, but nevertheless demanding the immediate devolution of powers in areas of specific concern to

---

8   Gérard Bergeron, "Si la Commission B-C finit par démarrer, Ça va être tout un happening," *Le Devoir*, 28 September 1990, p. B8.

9   "Le rôle des considérations non économiques doit donc être — et sera — déterminant." See excerpts of the presentation of L'Association des économistes du Québec, in *Le Devoir*, 22 November 1990, p. B8.

them.[10] Many of these powers will find their way into the final report of the Commission. I would go as far as to make the following hypothesis: even if the Commission refuses to recommend a clear political and constitutional option to the government, the patriation of power, which it is bound to claim for Quebec will correspond to the dismantling of the federal system as we have come to know it.

To begin with, the Commission will probably recommend the abolition of all the special powers currently invested in the central government, powers that have given a quasi-federal flavour to the Canadian political system: emergency and residual powers, reservation and disallowance of provincial legislation, declaratory power and the power to spend at will in fields of exclusive provincial jurisdiction. The centrifugal thrust of the report is likely to affect the following matters: health and education, including higher education and the control of research and development; manpower, job training and unemployment; complete responsibility over immigration; transport and the environment; culture, including the arts and the broader aspects of communications; regional development; language policy; and justice, including ultimate control over the definition and interpretation of Charter-based rights. The Commission will obviously seek to patriate the economic powers that will enable Quebec to assume these new responsibilities. However, it will navigate prudently in these matters, in order not to imperil the objective of an economic and monetary union with Canada. The list of powers I have suggested is not exhaustive. It provides nonetheless a good idea of what is looming on the horizon: a massive restructuring of state machinery in Canada and Quebec.

Struggles Within a Commission

Ad hoc institutions such as the Bélanger-Campeau Commission are fascinating objects for political analysis. Their lives are short, intense, and full of uncertainties. Politicians create them with extreme care, for once on the road they develop their own rules and patterns, with an important dose of autonomy. This particular Commission is no exception. It must be noted after two months that Michel Bélanger and Jean Campeau, speaking and acting together, wield immense credibility and legitimacy. One can contemplate a situation in which

---

10 One of the most enlightening examples is the list of powers put forward by the Chambre de commerce du Québec. See excerpts of its brief in *Le Devoir*, 8 November 1990, p. B8. The recommendations of these briefs have already found their way into the Allaire report, with its list of 22 exclusive powers for Quebec. See Constitutional Committee of the Québec Liberal Party, *A Québec Free to Choose: Report of the Constitutional Committee* (Montreal: Québec Liberal Party, 1991).

a minority report, signed by the co-chairmen, would be the real report of the Commission.

The stature of Bélanger and Campeau, as well as the political weight of their final report, are enhanced by the untimely sickness of Robert Bourassa. The absence of the premier in late 1990 heightened the uneasy sense of confusion within the ruling Liberal Party. This party is simultaneously searching for a new constitutional position and anxiously reflecting upon the state of its current and future leadership. The consequences of this reality are two-fold: it paves the way towards a more radical report and it diminishes the capacity of the government to dissociate itself from the main thrust of such a report. It has been argued that a resignation of Premier Bourassa in March could give the government some room for procrastination. However, if the report is well received, as one can expect it will be, such a move could prove remarkably counter-productive for the Liberal Party.

Nobody in Quebec expects a unanimous report. The final report, or reports, will be produced by complex alliances between several groups. I wish to present a tentative list of these groups:

- The co-chairmen (M. Bélanger-J. Campeau) — 2
- The Liberal Party — 10
- The Parti Québécois — 7
- The Referendum Coalition (This group is structured around Lucien Bouchard, Claude Béland of the Mouvement Desjardins and the leaders of the unions; they appear to have a general consensus on sovereignty, and a firmer consensus on the idea of an early referendum) — 10
- The Business Coalition (This group seems to operate under the leadership of Ghislain Dufour of the Conseil du Patronat du Québec; it is trying to define a platform in support of a profound decentralization of the federal system) — 4
- The representatives of federal parties — (Liberal André Ouellet and Progressive Conservative Jean-Pierre Hogue) — 2
- The representative of the Equality Party (Richard Holden) — 1

It is expected that federalists will form the minority. There could be as many as three minority reports. It is hard to imagine the Conservative representative signing the same report as André Ouellet; the Conservative Party would commit suicide in Quebec if it allied itself with the party of Jean Chrétien. The pro-federalist business coalition will come up with decentralizing recommendations that Mr. Ouellet will have great difficulties to accept.

If a consensus emerges in the next couple of months, it could include about 24 members, with the co-chairmen providing the glue. Game-theorists could develop a plethora of complex scenarios to delineate all plausible alliances within the Commission and the most rational strategies for Quebec and Canada. My interpretation does not rely on such methodological tools. As I understand it, the members from the first four groups, and perhaps those from the fifth one as well, are becoming more and more aware of the unique opportunity that their Commission represents for the history of Quebec.[11] They have been invested with the responsibility of devising a blueprint for the flowering of a modern, liberal and pluralist, majority French-speaking society in North America. The pressure on them is enormous. I believe they will succeed in formulating a strong majority report, in part because the political price of a failure would be astronomical for the individuals or parties held accountable for it. At this crucial juncture, failure would be the equivalent of a breach of trust.[12]

In order to get out of the status quo, a common front between Quebec's two major parties is absolutely necessary. What could be the substance of such a consensus between the Liberals of Robert Bourassa and the Péquistes of Jacques Parizeau? Before entering into the discussion of structures and pro-cesses, some historical and strategic considerations must be factored into the equation.

HISTORICAL AND STRATEGIC CONSIDERATIONS

The full political sovereignty of Quebec is not an inevitable affair. It does not belong to the unchanging laws of history or social evolution. There are no such things. Nor is it a moral good in itself. However, there are reasons to believe that the aspiration towards sovereignty will be very difficult to contain. I sincerely believe that it is not in the interest of Canada to use its energy to stop this movement. Support for sovereignty has increased tremendously in Quebec since the failure of Meech Lake. Moreover, four major factors dampening the sovereigntist aspirations of Quebec have been set aside in the past couple of years. The more or less simultaneous disappearance of these hurdles creates a radically new historical context. I take the interpretation of this context to be

---

11 "Il est, dans l'histoire des nations comme dans celle des organismes, des occasions qu'il faut saisir au vol, des moments critiques où la vitesse d'exécution devient aussi importante que la décision elle-même." Such a Machiavellian understanding of the nature of fortune should encourage Quebec to act swiftly. See Jacques Dufresne, *Le courage et la lucidité. Essai sur la constitution du Québec souverain* (Sillery: Les éditions du Septentrion, 1990), p. 51.

12 This option has been expressed a number of times in the past year by political scientist Edouard Cloutier, of the Université de Montréal. See his brief, "La souveraineté du peuple comme stratégie de redéfinition du statut politique et constitutionnel du Québec," mémoire présenté à la Commission sur l'avenir politique et constitutionnel du Québec, November 1990, p. 7.

as important as the presentation of the specific options being considered by the Bélanger-Campeau Commission.

The apparent end of the Cold War removes the first of these major obstacles. Quebec and Canada are the neighbours of the United States, one of the most formidable imperial powers in the history of humankind. As long as the U.S. was locked into a confrontation with another imperial power, the Soviet Union, the sovereignty of Quebec and the destabilization of Canada could be regarded as strongly detrimental to their interests. Empires can be moved by the rhetoric of justice, but their actions reflect an understanding of their interests. The Greek historian Thucydides has taught us the importance of these words in international affairs.[13] Whatever the ethical and political justifications for the sovereignty of Quebec, the U.S. would not have allowed during the Cold War even the remotest possibility of a second Cuba to the North. Throughout the 1980s, the passion of Quebec for what Thomas Courchene calls "market nationalism" has proven that there would be no such second Cuba to the North. Moreover, and more importantly, the Cold War has been transcended. The Berlin Wall has disappeared, the reunification of Germany has changed the face of Europe, and the Soviet empire is facing more and more disintegration every day. The geopolitical nature of our world is undergoing substantial transformations. In this context, I would contend that a politically sovereign Quebec would not pose a threat to the U.S. In this context, the American giant will not encourage anything; neither will it intervene in the affairs of Canada and Quebec.

A second major obstacle had to do with economic considerations. Barely ten years ago, it could still be reasonably argued that federalism had been economically profitable to Quebec, or at least that the costs of independence were just too great to absorb. Since then, a number of studies have demonstrated the economic viability of a sovereign Quebec, with a Gross Domestic Product (GDP) comparable to those of Austria, Belgium and Denmark. In the words of Thomas Courchene, Quebecers now have not only the will but also the ability "to go it alone."[14] The argument is made more and more often that sovereignty would be economically profitable to Quebec. Although he does not personally support this political solution, Robert Young has explained its rationale with great cogency:

> This is the view that Quebec would have a higher G.D.P. and better prospects for growth were it to attain sovereignty, or at least to recoup from Ottawa extensive

---

13 Thucydide, *Histoire de la guerre du Péloponnèse*, vol. I (Paris: Garnier-Flammarion, 1966), Book One, Paragraph LXXV, p. 71. According to Thucydides, the behaviour of Athens, and of all empires, was guided by fear, honour and interest.

14 Thomas J. Courchene, "The Community of the Canadas," an invited submission to Quebec's la Commission sur l'avenir politique et constitutionnel du Québec, November 1990, p. 24.

powers over the economy. This argument is composed of the following strands:
(1) Quebec's balance of transfers with Ottawa is either zero or insignificantly
positive; (2) duplication and waste abound in areas of intergovernmental competition, and (3) in the current global economy, a small, flexible, consensual society
with a loyal business class, and with state policies tailor-made for it, is more
capable of success than is the same society when inserted within a larger unit where
adjustment is slow, government is inefficient, and policies — because they reflect
an inter-regional compromise, — are not suited to its requirements.[15]

There would inevitably be some transitional costs in the march of Quebec
towards sovereignty. The Quebec Association of Economists has argued that
these costs would be higher if the process happened to be governed by resentment on all sides. One cannot ignore the fact that the costs of a messy transition
would affect all economic and political actors in Quebec and Canada. It must
also be added that it could be economically rational for Quebec to absorb some
transitional costs and pursue its course on the avenue of sovereignty. Montreal
as an international city in the era of market globalization could be better served
by such a political shift, to repeat the famous argument of Jane Jacobs, and the
Quebec state could possibly manage public finances more efficiently than the
current Canadian federal state.[16]

Another impediment to the political independence of Quebec came from
ideological and philosophical sources. It was famously synthesized by Pierre
Elliott Trudeau. The aspirations of Quebec could be associated with retrograde
expressions of parochial nationalism.[17] This was incompatible with liberalism
and progress, and with universalism. Nationalism had led to massacres. A new
political humanism required its transcendence. The events of 1989-90 have
shown to all of us a different face of nationalism. They have demonstrated that
human beings do not easily renounce their national identities. They will resist
with great courage and ingenuity powerful attempts to homogenize and normal-
ize their communities in larger collective bodies. In a recent essay on the
question of nationalities in the Soviet Union, Kenneth Minogue and Beryl
Williams wrote that "From a Marxist point of view, the contemporary world is
a tangle of alienating particularisms waiting to be superseded by an essentially

---

15 Robert Young, "Solving the Constitutional Crisis by Transferring Powers over
   Language and Culture to the Provinces," unpublished manuscript, p. 1.
16 Pierre Fortin, "Québec peut gérer mieux qu'Ottawa," *Le Soleil*, 14 December 1990,
   p. 20. See also Jane Jacobs, *Canadian Cities and Sovereignty Association*, The
   XVIIIth Massey Lecture Series, Toronto Canadian Broadcasting Corporation, 1980,
   p. 12.
17 See, for instance, Stephen Clarkson and Christina McCall, *Trudeau and our Times*,
   vol. I, *The Magnificent Obsession* (Toronto: McClelland and Stewart, 1990), p. 181.

human identity."[18] Such a point of view can also be defended by modern forms of liberalism. In Poland, in the Baltic Republics and in the Ukraine, it would be hard to suggest that the promotion of national identities corresponds to the preservation of alienating particularisms. The question of Quebec can be interpreted from the prism of these developments. For Trudeau, Quebec nationalism remains a concrete manifestation of an alienating particularism. However, Europe, which is slowly being created, illustrates that attempts to promote national distinctiveness can be reconciled with universalism. Such efforts are not antithetical with the contemporary movements towards economic and political integration.

The fourth major obstacle to the autonomist aspirations of Quebec was the spirit of Canadian federalism. At its best, the federal regime in this country was based on productive tensions between a number of visions. In the practice of complex federalism from 1867 to 1982, there was enough room for ambiguity in the constitution and its interpretation for the visions to coexist. According to one of these visions, dominant in Quebec, the Confederation of 1867 was a pact based on the recognition of cultural duality. The founders of Canada, as Ramsay Cook saw it 25 years ago, had wanted to avoid the kind of uniformity and centralization that negates national differences.[19] The spirit of complex federalism has been demolished in Canada by the constitutional reform of 1982. The dualistic vision, which had always been important without exercising a symbolic monopoly, was sacrificed to facilitate the emergence of a new and homogeneous Canadian national identity. Such was the dream of Pierre Trudeau. The former prime minister struggled mightily against the Meech Lake Accord because he saw in the "distinct society" clause a menace to the absolute supremacy of his vision. The latter required all Canadians, from all parts of the country, to share an identical set of fundamental values.[20] There was, and there still is, no significant place whatsoever in this vision for the recognition of Quebec either as a distinct society or as a nation. The failure of the Meech Lake

---

18 Kenneth Minogue and Beryl Williams, "Ethnic Conflict in the Soviet Union: the Revenge of Particularism," in Alexander Motyl, *Building Bridges: Soviet Nationalities in Comparative Perspective*, (forthcoming). See also Jacques Rupnik, *L'autre Europe: Crise et fin du communisme* (Paris: Editions Odile Jacob, 1990), p. 355.

19 Ramsay Cook, *Canada and the French-Canadian Question* (Toronto: Macmillan of Canada, 1966), p. 165.

20 Pierre Elliott Trudeau, "Il doit y avoir un sens d'appartenance," in Donald Johnston and Pierre Elliott Trudeau, *Lac Meech Trudeau parle* (Montréal: Hurtubise HMH, 1989), p. 41. In a preliminary document, the Bélanger-Campeau Commission has identified this nation-building dream as a major hurdle in the restructuring of the relationship between Canada and Quebec. See "La Commission Bélanger-Campeau fait le point," in *La Presse*, 28 January 1991, p. B3.

Accord convinced a lot of Quebecers that Canada had become unable to accept their national identity. In the hearts and minds of these people, the Canadian federal regime of 1867 and 1982 died on 23 June 1990.

The movement towards greater political autonomy for Quebec has been considerably strengthened by the end of the Cold War, by the agony of complex and generous federalism, by the new world-wide legitimacy of nationalism and by the realization that Quebec would be economically viable as a sovereign entity. On the current mood of Quebec the words of Edmund Cape, a Toronto businessman, seem quite adequate:

> Quebec also has a remarkable soul. Its survival after the defeat of 1763 is evidence of an immensely tough and resourceful people. Quebeckers have nourished a society that is truly distinct, not just in Canada but in the world... Quebec is ready for independence. It has always thought of itself as distinct and is psychologically prepared to leave.[21]

As a historian, one can see the logic of a sovereigntist solution for Quebec some years down the road. As a political scientist, I must recognize that the more immediate conditions do not allow me to predict that the Bélanger-Campeau Commission will follow this route. Since the failure of the Meech Lake Accord, a number of events have made the situation more difficult than expected for Quebec: Canada has been hit by a recession, which may be deepened by the war in the Gulf. In Quebec, the Mohawk affair has rendered the equation even more complex. It has established clearly that Quebec will not be able to restructure its relationship with Canada unless it is prepared to put its own house in order more or less at the same time. In addition to these factors, two important question marks stand out: the Liberal Party and Robert Bourassa.

The Liberal Party has just stunned the whole country by publishing the most radically decentralizing constitutional document in its history. The Allaire report, unanimously signed by the members of the constitutional committee of the party, will be submitted to the Liberal convention, to be held in early March. In addition to a list of 22 exclusive powers for Quebec, the Allaire report recommends the abolition of the Senate, the elimination of the spending and residuary powers of the federal government, and a veto on constitutional amendments for Quebec along with a right to secede for all provinces. If the Allaire report was accepted by Canada, the Supreme Court would lose much of its jurisdiction in Quebec, and the Quebec Charter of Rights would exercise primacy over the federal one. The Allaire report also recommends the holding of a referendum in Quebec in December 1992 at the latest. Depending on the results of the negotiations between the governments of Quebec and Canada, the

---

21 Edmund Cape, "Planting new roots for Confederation," *The Globe and Mail*, 15 August 1990, p. A19.

population would be asked either to approve a new radically decentralized federal regime, or to support the march of Quebec towards political sovereignty.

The tone of the Allaire report is as revealing as its content. The report shows that the Liberal Party is about to accept the interpretation of recent constitutional history put forward by the nationalist and sovereigntist intelligentsia in Quebec:

> In Quebec, Confederation has always been perceived as a solemn pact between two nations, a pact that could not be changed without the consent of the two parties. Circumstances have made Quebec the "national state of French-Canadians", so it is easy to imagine the frustration felt by Quebeckers one morning in 1981 when they learned that their Constitution, the fundamental law of their country, would be amended without their agreement. Even more serious, an amending process was being institutionalized that would enable future amendments, again without the agreement of Quebec. Furthermore, this result contradicted a solemn promise of the Prime Minister of Canada. In a way, the Meech Lake Accord recognized the illegitimacy of a Constitution that failed to include Quebec.[22]

The meeting in March will be the most important in the history of the Liberal Party since 1967. The party could come out of it in shambles. Many hope that a healthy Robert Bourassa will be able to keep the Liberal coalition intact one more time. Whatever happens within the Liberal party is bound to have a major impact on the Bélanger-Campeau Commission. I suspect that if the Liberal Party holds together in early March, its members on the Commission would try to avoid the more hasty and radical scenarios. My own preference would be to see Robert Bourassa choosing the path of boldness. The hardening in attitudes in both Quebec and Canada, coupled to the spirit of the 1982 constitutional reform, have made a federal solution to our predicament practically impossible. Robert Bourassa, the man of caution par excellence, should listen to the voice of Machiavelli: "I believe, further, that he is prosperous who adapts his mode of proceeding to the qualities of the times; and similarly, he is unprosperous whose procedure is in disaccord with the times."[23]

FUTURE INSTITUTIONAL STRUCTURES FOR QUEBEC AND CANADA

The members of the Bélanger-Campeau Commission will have an easier time agreeing on such issues as processes and the powers required by Quebec than on specific institutional structures and the names given to them. The

---

22 The Constitutional Committee of the Québec Liberal Party, *A Québec Free to Choose.*

23 Nicolo Machiavelli, *The Prince* (Chicago and London: University of Chicago Press, 1985), chap. 25, p. 99.

deliberations of the Commission on these latter questions will be fraught with the perils of partisan politics. Neither the members linked to the Liberal Party nor those tied to the Parti Québécois will want to choose a name for the new structure too closely associated to the preferences of their political rivals. If the Commission fails to deliver a strong majority report, it will falter on this issue.

According to my interpretation, the Commission will move beyond the federal regime of 1867 and 1982. I doubt that the Commission will wish to give one more chance to federal structures. Thus, I think that the first five structural options listed by Ronald Watts in chapter 2 can be set aside rather rapidly. Status quo federalism is unanimously condemned. Bipolar federations suffer from chronic instability. A symmetrically decentralized federation, responding positively to the demands of Quebec, would diminish the powers of Ottawa to such an extent that its acceptance outside Quebec appears quite unlikely. Many in the political and intellectual circles of English-speaking Canada see the solution in a more radically asymmetrical federation. My response to this would be that such asymmetry is incompatible with the logic and the structures of the 1982 constitutional reform. Moreover, the elite opinion cannot sell such an asymmetrical solution in most parts of the country where the political culture fostered by the Charter has become dominant. I agree with Charles Taylor that the only chance of federalism in Quebec — a slim one, at best — resides in the complete and immediate abandonment of the constitutional frameworks of 1867 and 1982, in some form of return to the conditions of the 1864 Charlottetown Conference.

In its thinking about future structures, the Commission will most probably move from the ground up. It will start from its consensus on the powers required by Quebec and on the matters to be put in common with Canada. There seems to be a consensus on the need for a monetary and economic union, for the sharing of responsibilities over foreign policy and the armed forces. If it wishes to make such a decision, the Commission will eventually have to choose between confederal arrangements and forms of economic association between sovereign states. Both avenues require the establishment of its political sovereignty by Quebec. Thomas Courchene has presented the most systematic proposal for an asymmetrical and confederal restructuring of political life.[24] In his model, the members of confederation would be Canada East, Quebec, Ontario, Canada West and the First Nations. According to the proposal, Quebec would have full sovereignty on questions of language and culture. It is possible that such a scenario could emerge as a compromise in the future negotiations between Canada and Quebec.

Since the Liberal Party led by Robert Bourassa forms the government of Quebec, the proposals coming out of its ranks must be considered with the

---

24 Thomas J. Courchene, "The Community of the Canadas."

greatest attention. During the past years, the Liberals have given some indication that they would favour a European model, that is, an economic union between sovereign states. The youth wing of the Liberal Party adopted a platform along those lines at its meeting in the summer of 1990.[25] When he mentions the European model, Robert Bourassa talks mostly about the economic association and the political institutions going with it, much less about the prerequisites of sovereignty. However, it is my understanding that he is fully aware of the latter dimension.[26] I suspect that the Commission will prefer the idea of an economic association between states to the various confederal arrangements. The Liberal members are likely to insist on a greater degree of political integration than the one that currently exists in Europe.[27] At this moment, if it ever happens, real bargaining would start between the Liberals and the Péquistes. If they really want a strong majority report, the Péquistes will have to accept that the Liberal blueprint would constitute the first element of a referendum package. The other side of the compromise would be the following: if the negotiations with Canada, based on the structural preference of the Liberals, fail within the limits of an appropriate deadline, then political independence for Quebec would follow immediately. This would be the Liberal concession. I personally hope that the Liberal and Péquistes members will be wise enough to make such concessions. I now turn to the issue of processes.

PROCESSES FOR CONSTITUTIONAL AND POLITICAL CHANGE

The members of the Bélanger-Campeau Commission have spent a substantial portion of their time discussing questions of strategy and processes. They seek solutions that will show the firm resolve of Quebec, without closing the avenues of discussion with Canada. They have developed a consensus on the idea that it would be preferable for Quebec to have a strong economic association with Canada. The issue of political integration remains unresolved as I write these lines.

It is likely that the Commission will recommend the holding of a referendum in Quebec either in 1991 or in 1992. The Parti Québécois, along with the group that includes Lucien Bouchard and Claude Béland, clearly favour this process.

---

25 "Le nouveau défi national des Québécois," *Le Devoir*, 16 August 1990, p. B10. These are excerpts from the program of the youth wing of the Québec Liberal Party.

26 Gérard Bergeron, "Des stratégies et des hommes: sur le néo-supra-fédéralisme de Robert Bourassa," *Le Devoir*, 29 September 1990, p. B10.

27 Jean-Yves Grenon, "Pour une Communauté économique canadienne," *Le Devoir*, 3 November 1990, p. B8. See also Rodrigue Tremblay, "Au Québec de décider s'il veut la souveraineté," *Le Soleil*, 24 October 1990, p. A15.

They would prefer a referendum in 1991, whereas Robert Bourassa and the Liberals appear ready to wait until 1992. According to recent polls, over 70 percent of all Quebecers support the idea of a referendum. Some experts, such as Léon Dion, have suggested that the procedure of a referendum on independence should be used as a threat to force the rest of Canada into a new round of negotiations. I believe that after the failure of the Meech Lake Accord, the rest-of-Canada will need more than a threat to be moved into action. I also suspect that Robert Bourassa, if he was pressed sufficiently hard by public opinion, could surmount his hesitations and will ultimately side with the partisans of a referendum in 1991.

I see a number of advantages in an early referendum. It would help to convince the rest of the country that this time around, Quebec really means business. It would also alleviate some of the uncertainty that produces a climate of economic instability. I would suggest that the alternative, negotiations over a period of two years as recommended by the Allaire report, with uncertain results, could foster as much instability as an early referendum. Finally, it would enable Quebec to give Canada more time to organize an appropriate response. Many groups have urged the Commission to formulate scenarios that will settle the constitutional issues as soon as possible.[28] Some, such as the Confederation of National Trade Unions (CNTU) have mentioned June 1992 as a deadline. I expect the Commission to include some kind of deadline in the final report. I would endorse such a time-table. By December 1992 at the latest, Quebec will have to know whether or not a brand new arrangement is possible with Canada.

A hypothetical referendum package would undoubtedly include the proposition of a new arrangement with Canada. This structure, as we have previously seen, could take the shape of sovereignty-association, of an economic community, or of a confederal model. Will it also include a unilateral declaration of independence (UDI)? The members of the Commission have also been made aware of the dangers of a UDI[29] It could be too strong a medicine for the rest of Canada to swallow, thus preventing fruitful negotiations from taking place. However, the Commission has also heard groups and experts lamenting the near impossibility of reforming the Canadian constitution in a way that would be satisfactory to Quebec. This is not just a matter of the amending formula. It has also to do with the fact that the spirit of the 1982 constitutional reform is opposed to the dualistic and asymmetrical arrangements preferred by Quebec. Thus, the Commission faces the following dilemma: Quebec must declare its

---

28 Alain Dubuc, "Le souverainisme: vague de fond ou feu de paille," *La Presse*, 5 December 1990, p. B2. Dubuc believes, and I agree with him, that Quebec and the Commission should take their inspiration from the German model and proceed as swiftly as possible.
29 Courchene, "The Community of the Canadas," p. 26.

independence, and must acquire the sovereignty needed to decide in which fields it seeks exclusive jurisdiction, in order to liberate itself from the claws of the *Constitution Act, 1982*, and it must do so in a way that would not alienate the spirit of accommodation in the rest of the country.

The Commission is unlikely to recommend an early UDI, taking effect immediately after its proclamation by the National Assembly. It could opt for one of the following scenarios, always seeking their implementation through a referendum:

- A proposed new arrangement with Canada: if the negotiations fail within the appropriate deadline, then there would be a second referendum on independence. This is the solution of Léon Dion. Robert Bourassa and the Liberal Party will be extremely tempted by it. (The Allaire report gets rid of the first referendum.)

- A proposed new arrangement with Canada: if the negotiations fail, then the government of Quebec would have the mandate to proclaim independence, at a time it would judge appropriate. A constituent assembly would be set up, and the constitution of a sovereign Quebec would be adopted through a referendum.

- Independence is declared following a referendum by passing of legislation in the National Assembly, but does not come into effect until a later date. This date can either be explicitly specified in advance, or left to the discretion of the government. A constituent assembly is set up. An arrangement is proposed to the rest-of-Canada, but independence would be proclaimed no matter what at the agreed upon later date.

All these scenarios could be reinforced by the inclusion in a referendum package of the draft of a bill establishing the primacy of the laws of Quebec, following a suggestion of a group of professors from the University of Ottawa.[30] This would mean, for instance, that a substantially modified Quebec Charter of Rights, including many elements of a new social contract with minorities and aboriginal peoples, would be preponderant over the Canadian Charter of Rights and Freedoms. This seems to be the equivalent of an indirect softer UDI approach along the lines of the second scenario or the third one above. Such approaches are preferable because they would impose on the rest-of-Canada the necessity of a constitutional convention or of a constituent assembly to establish its own constitutional future. Canada is suffering from a case of institutional paralysis. For Canada, Quebec is simultaneously an important cause of sickness and a key to the cure. If the Bélanger-Campeau

---

30 Jean-Denis Archambault and four other professors from University of Ottawa's Law Faculty, "Décréter la primauté des lois du Québec," *Le Devoir*, 9 November 1990, p. B8.

Commission really wishes to move beyond the federal regime of 1867 and 1982, if it wants to help Canada find a way out of the present mess, it will have to choose one of the radical options.

A CHALLENGE AND A UNIQUE OPPORTUNITY

The sovereigntist locomotive which is gathering speed in Quebec can be slowed down, but I doubt that it could be stopped by the means available in a democratic and liberal polity. It could be crushed only by ways that would tarnish forever the international image of Canada. In many respects, the current showdown is not occurring at a good time for Canada. The leadership of traditional parties is discredited and the system of political parties is undergoing a process of fragmentation. The country is in a constitutional impasse. Its economy appears crippled by the combination of debt, deficit and recession. The economic and political troubles are matched by a profound malaise over symbols of identity. Anxieties and doubts concerning national identity have reached an unparalleled level. In this context, one can understand the attractiveness of the suggestion to push aside and forget for five years or a decade the constitutional issue and the fundamental questions raised by Quebec. If Canada took this course, I think it would make matters even worse for all of us. Gentle caring just will not be enough for Canada and Quebec in the years to come.

I believe it would be politically easier and economically less costly to negotiate immediately a new agreement between our two societies rather than five or ten years down the road. Procrastinating would not solve any of the problems that are asphyxiating Canada. In recommending swift action, I do not wish to ignore the immensity of the task. What Canada and Quebec are about to start undertaking, the systematic restructuring of two intricate welfare states, has never been done in such a way throughout modern history. Thus, there is no perfect model. The European example has been frequently mentioned by Robert Bourassa and by experts at the Bélanger-Campeau Commission. In chapter 2 of this volume, Ronald Watts writes that "It would be ironic, just at a time when Europe is evolving from confederalism, because of its inadequacies, towards its own unique form of federalism, for Canada to go in the opposite direction." I would like to express some reservations concerning the postulates of this argument. Are the two movements really going in opposite directions? Canada and Quebec have reached a degree of integration characterized by Georges Matthews as maximal federalism.[31] Such an arrangement has become suffocating for Quebec. However, it could well be that Quebec would be prepared to accept a degree of integration that Western Europe appears unlikely

---

31 Georges Matthews, "New Deal from Québec: A Canadian Community," *The Globe and Mail*, 22 May 1990, p. A7.

to reach before quite some time. The focus of the discussion should be on the mutually acceptable levels of integration. One must also note that the Western European countries have expressed no desire to abandon their status as politically sovereign nation-states. More importantly, I would argue that Canada and Quebec should stretch their imagination and move beyond the view that Western Europe is an appropriate model for them.

One often hears in English-speaking Canada that there is a presently palpable sense of exhilaration in Quebec, while anxiety and negative feelings reign in the rest of the country. This would change if only we could drop our reactive attitude towards Europe. The real challenge of the present times for both Canada and Quebec can be identified when we start thinking not only about Western Europe, but also about Eastern Europe and the Soviet Union. The whole of Europe, rather than being a model for us, appears to be seeking one. Europe is looking for ways to achieve high levels of economic integration, to provide meaningful and efficient political structures for its inhabitants, while preserving and promoting the flowering of national identities.[32] These goals will impose massive restructuring efforts upon many countries. I think that Canada and Quebec could be seen as models for the new Europe.

Quebec is not proposing to destroy the Canadian federal regime. The latter, as it now stands, has already entered into a state of obsolescence. Rather, Quebec poses a challenge that could give a new start if not to the federal regime of 1867-1982, then certainly to Canada. The report of the Bélanger-Campeau Commission is likely to propose the construction of a Canada-Quebec economic community, which fully respects national identities and sovereignties. If Canada and Quebec could calmly and lucidly restructure their relationship along such lines, they would have provided an edifying example for the Europe of tomorrow. It is perfectly plausible to imagine that some of the avenues of the future would be sketched for Europe by her own sons and daughters, by the French and English-speaking peoples who are valiantly trying to maintain their distinct political communities in North America.

CONCLUSION

Some months ago in Saskatoon, Gordon Robertson spoke eloquently of the need "to avoid the defeat of the transcendent purpose we have inherited of two peoples of different language and culture sharing and building a great country together."[33] This dualistic transcendent purpose has been expelled from the

---

32 André Fontaine, "Une Europe du possible," *Le Devoir*, 11 July 1990, p. 13.
33 Gordon Robertson, "What Future for Canada?" notes for remarks to the Conference "After Meech Lake," 3 November 1990 at the University of Saskatchewan, Saskatoon, Saskatchewan, p. 14.

federal regime of 1867 and 1982. Our challenge is to reestablish it in the structures of a new Canada-Quebec community. It is quite realistic to think at this time that the Bélanger-Campeau Commission will formulate such a project. This would be an extremely demanding and stimulating enterprise, with huge tasks at the level of the community, and comparable ones in each of the two societies. Canada and Quebec can survive and prosper without one another. The individuals and associations that want them to do things in common should recognize as soon as possible that the current arrangement is obsolete, that it must be not merely repaired, but transcended altogether.

7

Options for the Future of Canada: the Good, the Bad, and the Fantastic

Peter M. Leslie

Witnesses to the Bélanger-Campeau Commission generally portray Quebec's political options as ranging from *the status quo* (unacceptable to most) to *full independence*, or *independence without "economic association"* (unattractive to all but a few). Between these poles are said to lie a set of intermediate options. These are the ones that are drawing the most serious attention. Some of the intermediate options call for a new constitution designed to give Quebecers full control over their own social, cultural, and economic development while avoiding disruption or fragmentation of the Canadian economy. Others envision partial independence for Quebec, or sovereignty constrained by treaty-based forms of association with "Canada" or its several successor-states — arrangements that would preserve the economic union but dissolve the political one.

This portrayal of Quebec's political options is quite literally fantastic, in various old-fashioned senses recorded by my dictionary: "existing only in imagination, unreal; ... arbitrarily devised; ... eccentric, quaint, or grotesque in design or conception." I shall argue later why some of the supposed options meet that description.

First, a clarification. My message is emphatically *not* that Quebecers are deluding themselves about their capacity to overturn the status quo. If they choose full independence, and are willing to accept its risks and costs, only civil war or military repression could prevent that outcome.

"Solutions through force" I hope can be discounted. At issue, however, is the willingness and capacity of the rest-of-Canada (ROC) to play a new political game according to rules devised in Quebec. Quebecers are debating their preferences; but the ROC will not necessarily make a selection from the Quebec menu.

I do not mean that Quebec's options will (or can) be defined by the ROC. In this limited, essentially negative sense, Mr. Gil Rémillard and others are clearly correct in stating that Quebecers alone will determine the political arrangements under which, in future, they will live.

My basic point is that the whole idea of choosing from "menus of options" is based on a mistake. Quebec is well advanced in the exercise of developing a new set of minimum demands and perhaps a set of ultimate objectives. In the ROC voices are being heard saying: be ready to negotiate when Quebec is! Hardliners both in Quebec and in the ROC want to maneuver the "other side" into a position where it will have to select from their menu. Conciliators say instead: let both Quebec and the ROC draw up lists of options, define their respective goals and preferences, and then look for whatever common ground may exist. However, both hardliners and conciliators are leaving out the dynamics of a process that, like it or not, will ensure that there is never a full menu of options to choose from. There is real danger that irrevocable steps will be taken which will narrow the list of available choices to a selection that no one, literally no one, regards as an improvement over what has been destroyed.

Those who would avoid tragedy must recognize that defining the options and devising appropriate processes to achieve them are not separate activities. It is necessary, I believe, to give full forethought to sets of critical events that will, in all likelihood, simultaneously open up certain options and foreclose others — both for Quebec and for Canada as a whole. The negotiation and the subsequent hacking-down of the Meech Lake Accord are examples of such critical (i.e., path-selecting, options-narrowing) events in our recent past. There will be others in the future.

Options are not mere preferences, nor abstract models; they are realistically available choices that are credibly achievable. And credibility depends on having mapped out a route from the present to an imagined future. To do this one must take account of possible roadblocks along the way. One must shrewdly assess the ability of particular individuals, organizations, and groups to erect barricades at strategic locations. For this reason, every thought about constitutional options for Canada (or for Quebec) is inescapably time-bound; as events unfold, the options change.

Among future critical events the most significant would be a unilateral declaration of independence (UDI) by Quebec, accompanied by the enactment of Quebec laws purporting to nullify or override federal law. Other actions having similar effects or consequences might be almost as critical as a UDI; an example might be refusal by the Government of Quebec to acknowledge the binding nature of rulings of the Supreme Court of Canada — in other words, rejection of its jurisdiction within Quebec. From any such events there could be no easy turning back.

THE STATUS QUO AS THE DEFAULT CONDITION

As long as Quebec holds back from UDI or its equivalent, the Canadian constitution cannot and will not be amended, except according to rules set out in the *Constitution Act, 1982.* Changes to the division of powers can be made by resolution of Parliament and the legislatures of seven provinces containing half or more of the Canadian population; any of the three remaining provinces can opt out of amendments that would reduce its powers. Certain other changes, notably to the amending formula itself, require the approval of all ten provincial legislatures, as well as of Parliament.

These are substantial hurdles. Consequently, *the status quo is the default condition* or, barring legal discontinuity, *the base option.* The question facing Canada, at least for the present, is whether or not other options, representing modifications of the base (or built up from the base) are now available. What can be achieved within the confines of the *Constitution Acts* of 1867 and 1982?

Quebecers now in overwhelming numbers say the status quo is no longer acceptable. However, Quebec's capacity to set the agenda for constitutional change, even by threatening secession, seems to be slight. Opinion polls have shown that within the ROC, about a quarter of the population think Canada would be better off without Quebec (these data are several months old, but I am not aware of sharp swings that would materially alter the picture). Minorities, the history of Meech has shown, can torpedo proposed changes. It is therefore significant that various groups have their own constitutional agendas, and are beginning to define bottom-line positions of their own. Not only will their conceptions of a made-over Canada be set against those emanating from Quebec, they will be debated among the nine other provinces, and more generally among groups other than francophone Quebecers. The Government of Canada, provincial and territorial governments, partisans of Senate reform, and various aboriginal groups/nations — all will have their own constitutional claims to advance, and will refuse to defer them until after a new Quebec round. This, if nothing else, must surely be evident from the Meech debacle.

So we return to our basic question: what new arrangements can be built up, or built outwards, from the existing constitutional base, the status quo?

The first point to be made is that the federal system has greater capacity for change than is generally recognized, even without formally amending the constitution. Within a basically unchanged structure, Quebec transformed itself socially, culturally, and economically during and since the Quiet Revolution of the 1960s; the provincial government was the major instrument (as well as a main object) of change. Over the same period of time, Quebec assumed a far greater role, and came to exercise a far stronger influence, within the federation, partly because francophones acquired a prominence in federal politics that was far beyond their grasp until the 1960s. Similarly, Alberta — to take the second most striking example — acquired an entirely new position within the federation. In fact, the relative position of each of the regions changed; this had nothing to do with the written constitution, but the new constellation of regional forces transformed Canada. Other forces which similarly have nothing to do with the written constitution include the increased female participation in the workforce, and changed patterns of immigration.

A vital issue, then, is whether the constitutional framework significantly constrains the further or future development of Quebec and other provincial communities. On this point, it should be acknowledged that the division of powers has proved remarkably accommodating to the assumption of new policy roles by provincial governments. Matters like the regulation of financial institutions, or financial markets — an economic union issue, if ever there was one — show this dramatically.

A second issue is whether federal policy facilitates or hinders the achievement of provincial policy goals — something obviously subject to change without rewriting the constitution. Federal policy in areas such as energy, trade, and language has been vitally important for provincial governments and provincial communities. In each of these areas, federal policy has undergone wholesale redirection in recent years. If present policies are considered to be unduly constraining or apparently discriminatory, they can be changed without even touching the *Constitution Acts*.

In some areas (immigration and regional development being two of the clearest examples) federal-provincial agreements can adjust and indeed have adjusted the respective roles and responsibilities of the federal and provincial governments.

To take another challenge altogether, the policies of both federal and provincial governments shape the livelihood of the aboriginal peoples; it is a matter of judgement as to which route to change is the more effective or desirable, the legislative and administrative route, or the constitutional route.

Finally, fiscal arrangements underpin just about everything: the structure of the tax system, the role of the provinces in income support and major services such as health care (or generally, the future extension, redesign, contraction of the welfare state), interregional redistribution, and the viability of provincial finances.

In short, the constitutional status quo is a condition that is consistent with fundamental political change affecting all the groups or entities that are now demanding a constitutional solution to their discontents. The status quo is, as noted above, the default condition as long as the binding character of the *Constitution Act, 1982* is acknowledged; but adhering to the status quo does not have to mean stand-pattism. It has jokingly but truthfully been said, that in Canada we have a dynamic status quo.

TWO SORTS OF CHANGE

From one angle, it is essentially a technical matter whether or not formal amendment to the constitution is required to transform the federal system in some of the ways that are now being demanded from various quarters, notably (but not exclusively) from Quebec.

Whether constitutional innovation is formal or informal, it will be useful to distinguish two quite different sorts of change. First, there are potential or desired changes to the respective roles of federal and provincial governments; and second, there are potential or desired changes to the structure and operation of central institutions. Changes of the latter type could be expected to alter the relative political weight exercised by various groups (such as the residents of a particular province) in the workings of the federal government.

Policy Roles

Reassignment of federal and provincial policy roles could occur in any one, or any combination, of the following ways:

Quebec could gain a larger role than other provinces, resulting in a form of *asymmetrical federalism*. That is today's buzzword for what used to be called "special status" — but it is a less loaded and more precise term. Asymmetry can arise in several ways not requiring constitutional amendment: (a) through provincial opting-out from federal programs (as in aspects of social security); (b) through bilaterally-negotiated administrative arrangements (as in immigration); or (c) through relatively vigorous exercise of provincial legislative and administrative powers — especially in areas where, in practice, federal and provincial powers overlap. Examples of (c) are: industrial assistance and other programs for economic development, the regulation of consumer credit, and family allowances.

Other forms of asymmetry may require constitutional amendment. For example, an amendment could prescribe that in certain policy areas, when federal and provincial laws conflict, the provincial ones will prevail. This is known as "provincial paramountcy"; in 1964 provincial paramountcy was established with respect to old age pensions and supplementary benefits under section 94A of the (then) *British North America Act* (modifying a similar provision introduced in 1951). Asymmetry could also, conceivably, be achieved through a constitutional amendment permitting interdelegation of legislative powers, or one permitting Parliament to pass laws having application only to certain provinces, or to the residents of certain provinces. The last of these (hypothetical) types of constitutional amendment would clearly violate the principle of equality of the provinces, and would predictably generate opposition; but the introduction of asymmetry through other means might be less contentious. The main point is that some provinces (not necessarily Quebec alone) could seek and obtain a broader policy role than the remaining provinces, within a formal constitutional status that is similar for all provinces.

Across-the-board decentralization, expanding the policy role of all provinces and preserving the principle of equality of the provinces, is another possible direction for reassigning policy roles within the federation. Arguably, decentralization has been under way for about 30 years, achieved through the expansion of the role of government (but of the provinces more than of the federal government). Complementing this shift in policy roles, and essential to its coming about, has been the transfer of fiscal resources to the provinces. This has occurred through federal-provincial agreements and implementing federal legislation.

A more radical and quasi-permanent form of decentralization could be implemented through formal changes to the division of powers (transfer of jurisdiction to provincial legislatures). The arguments for decentralization are (a) that when government is "closer to the people" it is more responsive and more democratic, (b) that decentralization permits, within a regionally diverse country, adaptation of policy to local or regional needs, thus permitting the satisfaction of a higher percentage of the people's needs or wants; (c) that decentralized government is more efficient, partly because it permits more policy experimentation, and (d) a reduction in federal responsibilities and activities would reduce tensions and conflicts within the federation. However, certain governmental functions can be effectively performed only at a relatively centralized level. Examples are monetary management and interregional redistribution. Thus, across-the-board decentralization could weaken the federal government to the point where its policy capacity was dangerously low in areas for which the public holds it responsible. An ineffectual government loses respect, and therefore legitimacy.

A rebalancing of policy roles, with no further fiscal decentralization, is a possible alternative to across-the-board decentralization, and could be argued to be an essential element in "modernizing" the federation. A rebalancing process would transfer powers and/or policy responsibilities to the provinces in some areas, while transferring powers and/or policy responsibilities to the federal government in certain other areas.

Within the European Community (EC), the current principle to guide the assignment of functions to various levels of government is "subsidiarity." This means that governmental functions should be allocated wherever possible to the lowest (most local) level; only where local jurisdictions are incapable of acting effectively will policy responsibilities be assumed by the higher levels. Application of the principle of subsidiarity means that the national states belonging to the EC will (supposedly) devolve some of their powers to regional governments and municipalities, and other powers to the EC itself. Application or adaptation of the EC model to Canada would result in a rebalancing process, transferring certain economic powers from provinces to the federal government, while the provinces (and municipalities) acquire broader responsibilities in social and cultural fields.

In the allocation and possible reassignment of policy roles within the federation, traditional Canadian conceptions of what federalism means, or what a federal state looks like, should perhaps be reexamined. The particular form of federalism that exists in Canada is anchored in a division of legislative powers on a supposedly exclusive basis (except for three subjects specified to be concurrent: immigration, agriculture and pensions). In practice, the overlapping of federal and provincial powers, and certainly of their respective policy responsibilities, is far greater than a reading of the constitution would suggest. Perhaps the whole idea of two exclusive lists should be reexamined. Other forms of federalism exist. For example, in Germany the division of powers is relatively unimportant; it has been said that legislatively, Germany is virtually a unitary state. However, the central government (Bund) is broadly speaking dependent on the provinces (Länder) for the administration of federal laws — which the Länder have a significant role in enacting. Political and administrative relations between orders of government are the essence of the system. If we are thinking of restructuring federalism in Canada in a fundamental way, or of replacing federalism with a looser form of association among states or provinces (confederalism), attention to other concepts of federalism might be rewarding.

Central Institutions and "Les institutions fédératives"

In some respects, or to some groups of Canadians, it is more important to alter the structure and/or the operation of central institutions such as Parliament than to recast the formal division of powers. Of particular interest are what are known in French as "les institutions fédératives" and (less commonly) in English as federative superstructures.[1] These are institutions that have a balancing or linking role in the federation, affecting relations between the federal government and the provinces and/or relations among provinces and regions. The following central institutions might be considered for reform:

- In the past two or three years, attention has focused on the Senate as an instrument for sensitizing the federal government to regional needs and demands, and for rebalancing regional forces within the federation. This is the thrust that lies behind the Triple E movement (for an Elected, Effective, and Equal Senate), under which (as Premier Wells, an ardent advocate, has put it) two majorities would be required for every item of legislation except housekeeping matters: a majority of the people as

---

1   See Ronald L. Watts chapter 16, "The Federative Superstructure" in this volume.

expressed through the House of Commons, and a majority of the provinces as expressed through the Senate. Any redesign of the Senate would require formal constitutional amendment under the 7/50 rule (7 provinces containing 50 percent of the population).

- Another route to rebalancing regional forces within the federation would be to rewrite the electoral law and/or to give the smaller provinces (or less populated regions) relatively stronger representation in the House of Commons. Any significant departure from the principle of proportionate representation of the provinces in the House of Commons would require formal constitutional amendment under the 7/50 rule.

- Supreme Court of Canada: The composition, appointments process, working procedures, and jurisdiction of the Court are candidates for attention in a new phase of constitutional change.

- New structures to accommodate the needs and demands of aboriginal peoples could be put in place by legislation. A quasi-permanent commitment — entailing also rigidity — could be guaranteed through constitutional amendment.

- New institutions and processes could be created, generally without constitutional change and even without legislation, that would alter the relationship between the federal and provincial governments, or how they interact in forming policy. One type of change would be to involve provincial governments in the exercise of federal powers — as they have demanded, for instance in respect of trade policy. Consultation with the provinces during the negotiation of the Canada-United States Free Trade Agreement is a precedent and example. Its emulation in the future would no doubt be welcomed by some and cause dismay among others.

Another type of change would be to devise institutions or processes (habits or conventions) to achieve better coordination of federal and provincial activities in fields where policy is, in effect, a joint product of both orders of government. Fiscal policy, or economic stabilization, is a clear candidate for attention under this heading. It is of interest that, in Europe, Community-wide coordination of fiscal policy is widely regarded as a prerequisite for achieving monetary union.

Other procedural or institutional changes could have the effect of limiting the exercise of existing provincial powers, or the existing scope or range of provincial policies. An example (perhaps as a *quid pro quo* for provincial involvement in setting trade policy) would be agreements to constrain provincial policy-making in areas affecting interprovincial or international trade. More formal changes along the same lines could see the Supreme Court acquiring a new role, similar to that of the European Court in the EC, as guardian of the economic union; or they could involve the creation of a special tribunal or commission for this purpose.

Any of these types of change could give Quebec a unique role in the operation or functioning of the federation, reflecting its position as the only province of which a majority of the residents are francophone. Alternatively, ways might be found to address simultaneously the concerns of Quebec, and of the other provinces. For example, certain types of law (such as those in relation to language, immigration, regional development, or fiscal transfers to provinces) might require multiple majorities in the House of Commons, or other changes might be made to the simple-majority rule. Whatever the approach taken, changes in these areas would raise the symmetry/asymmetry issue in a different form.

LEGAL CONTINUITY AND THE RESTRUCTURING OF THE CANADIAN FEDERATION

Attempts to achieve change by working within the constitution will, if successful, lead to a restructured federalism comprising several elements that have been discussed here. The restructuring process will involve adaptations of existing arrangements in part through means other than constitutional amendment, and presumably in part through a set of formal changes that may establish or allow for some or all of the following:

- a degree of *asymmetry*, whether in the allocation of policy roles, or in the operation of federal institutions, or both;
- *decentralization* of policy responsibilities and fiscal resources on an across-the-board basis, or (in the alternative) a rebalancing of powers under which neither policy responsibilities nor fiscal resources flow, as along a one-way street, to the provinces;
- a new and more *flexible scheme for the division of powers*, with less emphasis on exclusivity and more on concurrency (overlapping);
- the redesign or *adaptation of central institutions* (institutions of governance, and "les institutions fédératives") to: alter working relations between the federal government and the provinces, and rebalance regional forces within the federation;
- changes in the content and/or application of the *Charter of Rights and Freedoms*; and finally,
- provisions specifically concerning *aboriginal peoples*, and perhaps other groups.

It does not any longer seem useful to me (although earlier I tried my hand at it) to set up specific categories such as "asymmetrical federalism," "decentralized federalism," etc. — as if any one such option could be selected in preference to others. Rather, each of the "options" identifies a possible direction of change that may be pursued to a greater or lesser degree, in combination with other changes. The goal is to restructure the federal system to take account of multiple objectives, and to respond to the needs and demands of multiple groups. Among these, francophone Quebecers are the largest and most impatient (and, in my personal opinion, have the best-founded constitutional grievance); but they are not the only demandeurs. On the other hand, they do most clearly have (as Pierre Trudeau noted in 1965) "the power to break the country"; and they are the ones that very largely will control the timing of a future crisis through their ability to go for a UDI.

Inevitably, the prospect of new attempts to restructure the federal system induces fatigue, discouragement, and impatience. The Quebec government, supported by numerous witnesses before the Bélanger-Campeau Commission, have insisted that Quebec will never again enter into constitutional negotiations with 11 parties at the table. There may be ways of finessing this problem, but ultimately (if the constitution is to be respected) it will be necessary to have the required number of legislative resolutions to achieve formal change.

Thus it must be acknowledged that the constitutional reform enterprise may never be seriously launched; and if it is, it may fail. Such changes as are achieved may be judged inadequate. The balancing of regional forces, and the devising of new arrangements acceptable to major ethnic, cultural, or linguistic groups, may prove impossible. Demands for constitutional recognition by one group (as in the "distinct society" clause of the Meech Lake Accord) may merely provoke resistance and generate counter-demands from other groups, producing what Alan Cairns has called "constitutional minoritarianism."

And the most fundamental fact of all: federalism may be, as most of the Bélanger-Campeau witnesses have been saying, over and done with as far as Quebec is concerned. Many former federalists now recommend secession by UDI. They have cast in their lot with those who have said for years: declare independence, and then see what form of economic association can be negotiated.

This step would represent repudiation of the *Constitution Acts*. It would bring about legal discontinuity — of which the consequences are unknowable, but presumably vast, tumultuous, and economically devastating.

LEGAL DISCONTINUITY AND THE HUMPTY-DUMPTY OPTIONS

With the secession of Quebec, assuming it to be decisively accomplished (not to be taken for granted: but that is another subject), the default condition becomes that of "independent successor-states." Let us trace that through.

If Quebec secedes, the *Constitution Acts* are likely to become "a dead letter," even outside Quebec. This is so primarily because Quebec is simply too integral to the structure and operation of the existing central institutions to imagine they could continue to function without challenge. Parliament would lose a quarter of its members, and the Supreme Court a third. It is hard to see how they could continue on as before without being reestablished on a new basis. In the interval, the federal government could easily have lost its capacity to govern, whether for strictly legal or constitutional reasons, or through lack of legitimacy.

In all likelihood, it would be necessary to construct new institutions, or to redesign the old ones, if links among some or all of the nine provinces (and the territories) were to be preserved. This would imply building a new state, or some form of association of states, from the ground up.

It is possible and even probable that the process of reconstructing new political arrangements, with Quebec out of the picture, would fail. The main reason for this is that a hypothetical new CWQ (Canada-without-Quebec) would be torn by debilitating regional conflict. Such conflict would take the following forms:

- Ontario, which would constitute about half the population of CWQ, would dominate economically and politically. I cannot imagine this being tolerated in the western provinces, particularly not in Alberta. On several key economic issues, Quebec and the resource-rich provinces of the west have tended to support each other; and Quebec votes were essential to creating an electoral majority for Canada-U.S. free trade. In other words, Quebec has been an essential counterbalance to Ontario; in its absence, western demands for a rebalancing of regional interests within Parliament — whether through a Triple E Senate or some other device — would become irresistible. But what could possibly induce Ontario to see its interests subordinated within national institutions to other regional interests in the rest of this now-truncated country?

- Without Quebec, the political coalition supporting interregional redistribution would probably disappear. Ontario, as Thomas Courchene has repeatedly argued, is increasingly disinclined to continue supporting the present degree of wealth-transfer to other regions, as north-south economic links strengthen relative to east-west ones. This attitude would be strongly reinforced by Quebec's departure, and the western provinces are unlikely to take a different attitude. With waning support in CWQ for equalization and other transfers, the Atlantic region would suffer great hardship, and would surely want to reassess its options — as reportedly it has already been doing to some extent.

- Conclusion: In different ways, Quebec's membership in the federation is essential to the interests both of the west and of the Atlantic provinces.

Remove Quebec, and the ROC would break apart under its own regional strains.

I acknowledge that at present, sentiment in the ROC favours sticking together as a federation, if Quebec were to secede. But the obstacles to creating a new form of union would be formidable and, in the end, the incentive slight. Wherein would lie the benefit, and for whom? The "Canada-would-be-stronger-without-Quebec" line of thought is dubious indeed. Rather, with Quebec's secession, the break-up of Canada into several successor-states (more than two) might appear preferable to many, if compared with a too-constraining form of union on the one hand, or an ineffectual one on the other.

Canada after UDI would, in all probability, break up altogether. Under this scenario, the obvious question arises: could the pieces of this shattered vessel be put back together again, albeit in some new form? Some say yes: they think that in order to build a new and stronger (but different) Canada, it will be necessary first to break apart the old one. They put their faith in what I call "the Humpty-Dumpty options."

There are three Humpty-Dumpty options. They are: (a) sovereignty-association, (b) an association of several regional states, and (c) "reconfedera-tion." All three are fantastic — abstract models that either are inherently unworkable (nonfunctioning, unstable, incapable of producing effective gov-ernment) or are, given political forces in Canada, absolute nonstarters: unat-tainable, because you can't get there from here. (In practice, there may not be much of a distinction between the unworkable and the unattainable: models that are perceived to be incapable of producing effective government will be nonstarters, and models that ignore political realities in Canada are unlikely to be workable.)

SOVEREIGNTY-ASSOCIATION

Sovereignty-association refers to a two-member confederacy or quasi-federation comprising Quebec as one unit, and "Canada" (obviously, without Quebec) as the other. The concept was spelled out in some detail by the Parti Québécois government in 1979. Its proposals called for a customs and monetary union without a central legislature; no "Canadian" laws would apply in Quebec; Quebecers would pay no taxes to "Canada"; joint institutions, such as a central bank, would be set up on the basis of *parity*, or equal representation from Quebec and "Canada" (a principle that the PQ later indicated need not be strictly applied). However, as Daniel Soberman argues in another chapter in this volume, the ROC could not possibly accept Quebec's claim to parity — but unless it did, sovereignty-association would be of no attraction to Quebec. In short, this abstract model is utterly unworkable: a contraption that won't fly.

A great many Quebecers are deluding themselves on this point. It will be recalled that at the Bélanger-Campeau Commission, it is the intermediate options that are receiving most of the attention, since the status quo is unacceptable and full independence is unattractive. But in putting forward the intermediate options, witnesses are making unwarranted and unrealistic assumptions about the willingness and ability of CWQ to make a deal. For example, even the former Deputy Minister Louis Bernard, probably the most experienced person in Quebec in intergovernmental relations and constitutional affairs, has emphasized that Quebec must do everything it can to ensure that the ROC sticks together as a single country, because a Quebec that was independent and failed to enter into an economic association with "Canada" would be vulnerable to American domination. However, he and many others have been putting forward proposals for ensuring a single ROC based on quite unwarranted and indeed unrealistic assumptions.

It is difficult to imagine how, under a legal discontinuity scenario in which Quebec secedes, any new bilateral structure, whether constitution-based or treaty-based, could be created. If my analysis of regional strains within a hypothetical CWQ is valid, there would be no entity with which Quebec could enter into negotiations. Sovereignty-association would be unattainable, because it presumes two viable political entities that have a mutual interest in economic integration. You can't get there from here.

All right then: how about finding a different path? Suppose negotiations precede, rather than follow, Quebec's secession? Under this scenario, Quebec indicates its intention to declare itself independent by a certain date, but also says it wants to negotiate sovereignty-association first.

I cannot see how that would make much difference. Admittedly, the level of antagonism and the desire for revenge — potent emotions when a country is broken up — might be somewhat lower. However, the basic problem of the viability of CWQ would remain. It would be, in my view, an insuperable obstacle. But an even more immediate problem is, with whom would Quebec negotiate?

We are imagining here new political arrangements under which there is no directly-elected central legislature with both lawmaking and taxing powers. It follows that negotiations towards a confederal or quasi-federal arrangement — whether constitution-based or treaty-based — would have to be conducted between Quebec and some entity other than the Government of Canada, which derives its authority from Parliament. The present government would lack a majority in a parliament from which the Quebec members were absent; several ministers, including the prime minister, would have to absent themselves from the process. The current Government of Canada could not negotiate sovereignty-association — or the terms of Quebec's secession, under any new arrangements whatever — unless first reconstituted on a basis that excluded all

Quebecers. The current Government of Canada has no mandate to negotiate Quebec's secession, and (if my analysis above is correct) no means of obtaining such a mandate. I do not even see what incentive it would have in trying to get one.

The essence of legal discontinuity is that established rules and procedures no longer apply; all is in flux. That is why UDI, or indeed any initiative aiming at negotiated dismemberment (with UDI as the threatened default outcome), would have tumultuous and economically disastrous results.

AN ASSOCIATION OF REGIONAL STATES

Our second Humpty-Dumpty option is a confederacy or quasi-federation comprising several regional states. The number of member states is uncertain, as some of the existing provinces might amalgamate — while on the other hand, some might not join in.

It must be recalled that each of the provinces is situated within North America, on the periphery of an economic giant. The provinces are not like the member states of the European Community, which are each others' most important trading partners, and have formed the core of one of three major economic blocs of a globalized economy. Canada today, as an economic and political union, is a junior partner of the United States; its capacity to bargain with or influence the United States depends on a federal structure that, in most aspects of trade policy, gives it the capacity to act as a single unit in relation to foreign countries. However, without political union, each of Canada's successor-states would give top priority to retaining and perhaps improving its access to the American market; north-south bilateral relationships would be crucial to them. To the extent that the sucessor-states were to remain economically integrated, that would probably be a by-product of the ties they individually built up or retained with the United States. To use a European analogy, Canada's successor-states would be like the EFTA (European Free Trade Association) countries — Switzerland, Austria, Sweden, Norway, Finland, and Iceland — each of which is linked functionally and by treaty to the EC, and in consequence, able to maintain free trade with the others. But the EFTA is not a cohesive unit, and several of its member states have opted for membership in the EC, if they can get in. Because the EC is an economic magnet, the EFTA countries have no incentive to integrate further with each other (although cooperation among the Nordic countries is an interesting phenomenon). The cohesiveness of any grouping of Canada's successor-states would be subjected to strain resulting from bilateral relationships with the U.S.

The question of incentive to create an economic association among Canada's successor-states (whether on a bilateral or a multilateral basis: sovereignty-association, or a multimember confederacy) is closely linked to the question of workability, or capacity to function as intended, given the purposes of maintaining an integrated economy, which are:

- To avoid the fragmentation of markets, not only for goods, but for services and for factors of production (labour and capital);
- To achieve or preserve economic diversification, in order to diminish the effect of price shocks, trade wars, or other accidents at the level of the global economy — in effect, to set up and maintain a mutual insurance scheme for economically specialized regions; and
- To exercise some weight within the continental and global economies, now symbolically recognized in Canada's membership in the Group of Seven (G-7).

All three purposes are supported by monetary union; by the implementation of common policies in areas such as competition law, market regulation, and economic stabilization; by the creation or retention of some capacity for interregional redistribution; by policies for economic development (e.g., transportation and other infrastructure, and technological innovation); and by having a single policy for all foreign economic relations (not just a common external tariff). EC countries have discovered that completion of the internal market (Europe 1992) and progress towards monetary union will require further political integration as well. Indeed, one of the great lessons of recent European experience is that economic union cannot be achieved without a significant degree of political union, probably crossing the threshold from confederalism to federalism. It is utterly unrealistic to imagine that the even wider economic purposes envisioned for "economic association" between Quebec and CWQ could be achieved while breaking apart the existing political union.

"RE-CONFEDERATION"

There has been some discussion of possible bilateral negotiations between Quebec and Ontario, either preceding or subsequent to UDI by Quebec. The two central provinces would, under this scenario, strike a new federal bargain through a process of re-Confederation. Once struck or even partially sketched out, the Ontario-Quebec agreement might then be extended to other comers, east and west.

Of the three Humpty-Dumpty options, re-Confederation is the one to be taken most seriously. It would be the easiest to negotiate, since most of the bargaining would involve only two partners. (However, agreement certainly would not be easy, particularly as emotions would no doubt be running high.)

The viability of the new arrangement would depend on what was negotiated, and on which other provinces joined in. If the new entity were a two-member federation, it would almost certainly be unstable because one member state would tend to dominate, or would feel it had the right to be "senior partner."

Thus a strictly bilateral deal would probably be unworkable; on the other hand, it seems doubtful that if Quebec and Ontario were near to an agreement, any of the other provinces (or groups of them, if there were amalgamations) would want to sign on. What joint purposes could be achieved, if the new arrangements were merely confederal or quasi-federal? And if a new federal union were envisioned, would not the west want to stay clear of it? Westerners already complain about the domination of the "east"; buying into a ready-made Quebec-Ontario deal would be an acknowledgement of impotence.

THE HUMPTY-DUMPTY OPTIONS: CONCLUSION

Under any scenario involving the destruction of Canada as a federal state, the obstacles to a subsequent rebuilding process would be formidable. Federal outcomes would more easily be achieved by modifying, not breaking asunder, the existing federal structure. With Quebec's secession, there would be a legacy of bitterness to contend with; transition costs to any new arrangements would probably be high, and several stumbling-blocks would be strewn along the route (agreement on dividing up the national debt and making provision to service it in the future, etc.)

It seems clear, then, that nonfederal (confederal or quasi-federal) options for Canada — thinking of "Canada" as an economic union but not a political one — are merely fantastic. There is no way in which any of these options could credibly be achieved; there is little incentive to want to achieve them; and were they achieved, they would not work.

CONCLUSIONS

There will be many people who will ask, now that federalism is so widely reviled in Quebec, why I have considered it at all. My answers are:

- Federalism has lasted a long time, and has provided a framework within which Quebec has transformed itself over, especially, the past 30 years — not only economically, but socially and culturally as well. A system that was all bad could not have kept going this long.
- As long as Quebec does not go the UDI route, the status quo is the default condition. That may not last long, but while it does, it is the base from which formal constitutional change may yet be brought about.
- All imaginable options not involving legal discontinuity are federalist.

To restructure the federation in ways that will make it acceptable to Quebecers will be difficult, and may easily prove impossible. The process may not even be seriously engaged. Canadians outside Quebec bear responsibility for facilitating and contributing to the restructuring process, giving Quebec less incentive to storm out of the house. To believe that Canada would be stronger without Quebec is unbelievably foolish; CWQ probably would not even be viable. In any case, it is an experiment not worth making.

A restructured federalism can be brought about partly through means other than constitutional amendment. There is no point waiting until agreement on a set of amendments can be reached, before beginning the restructuring process.

It is not necessary to choose between distinct models of a restructured federal state, such as asymmetrical federalism, decentralized federalism, etc. A restructured federalism could include changes in several areas, which could be combined in various ways. Possible directions for change include:

- a degree of *asymmetry*, whether in the allocation of policy roles, or in the operation of federal institutions, or both;
- *decentralization* of policy responsibilities and fiscal resources on an across-the-board basis, or (in the alternative) a rebalancing of powers under which neither policy responsibilities nor fiscal resources flow, as along a one-way street, to the provinces;
- a new and more *flexible scheme for the division of powers*, with less emphasis on exclusivity and more on concurrency (overlapping);
- the redesign or *adaptation of federal institutions* (institutions of governance, and "les institutions fédératives") to: alter working relations between the federal government and the provinces, and rebalance regional forces within the federation;
- changes in the content and/or application of the *Charter of Rights and Freedoms*; and finally,
- provisions specifically concerning *aboriginal peoples*, and perhaps other groups.

Several assumptions commonly if not universally made in Quebec today appear shaky and should, at a minimum, be reexamined:

- That independence could be achieved without significant economic disruption.
- That a way exists, or could be created, through which federalism could be replaced by a nonfederal arrangement, which would come into effect simultaneously with Quebec's secession.
- That an independent Quebec could rejoin "Canada" economically, or preserve the economic union while dissolving the political one, whether through sovereignty-association, or through the creation of an association of regional states.

Those who start a process of dismembering a state are unlikely thereafter to be able to control events. They cannot simply stop the process at a point they find convenient.

Under a legal discontinuity scenario, the default condition is independent successor-states. This, realistically, is the most likely outcome if Quebec secedes. It would be better to accept this outcome than to create an unworkable structure — notwithstanding the fact that, as has widely been recognized in Quebec, the breakup of Canada would entail the dissolution of the economic union, and would be an unambiguously *bad option* for everyone. Confederal or quasi-federal forms of political union are unattainable (cannot credibly be brought about) and inherently unworkable. On both counts these intermediate options (abstract models lying between federalism and full independence) are best regarded as merely *fantastic options* ("existing only in imagination, unreal, ..."). Without exception, the *good options* for Canada are federalist — with Quebec being one of the provinces. I believe this is as true for Quebec as for the ROC. Only federalism is capable of meeting the economic purposes of remaining together at all — not to mention noneconomic ones, of which it has become unfashionable to make mention in Quebec.

Postscript

In the discussion following the presentation of this paper, one person remarked that the right balance must be struck, over the next few months or years, between realism and fantasy. It was said that if in 1864-67 the Fathers of Confederation had paid too much attention to the obstacles that lay before them, Canada would never have been created.

To the plea for imaginative solutions to our present difficulties, I respond: Yes! It is essential that we should be maximally inventive. Anything less, and Quebec will secede: Quebec needs evidence that Canadians everywhere are committed to a restructuring of their country, so it will respond better to the needs both of francophone Quebecers and of other groups. Let us, then, be as daring as Wilbur and Orville Wright; let us defy gravity. But let us also be realistic — there is no contradiction between realism and daring. Realism demands that we recognize the distinction between an airplane and silly contraptions that won't fly. It also demands that we take care not to destroy what Canadians of past generations have created, but to adapt and rebuild.

8

Towards a New Constitutional Process

Peter H. Russell

THE IMPERATIVES OF CONSTITUTIONAL POLITICS

> The demand for constitutional change itself represents lack of consensus about
> some important aspects of the system; but since the rules governing constitutional
> change normally require a high degree of consensus, it is often impossible to
> mobilize sufficient consent to bring the issues to a close. Lack of consensus makes
> constitutional change necessary. The same lack makes resolution supremely
> difficult.[1]

Canada's experience with constitutional politics over the past 25 years
demonstrates the accuracy of these words of Banting and Simeon at the
beginning of their book on constitutional politics in industrial countries. We
Canadians should know by now how tough and how frustrating constitutional
politics can be. Constitutional politics are usually waged in symbolic terms
which touch the deepest wells of civic passion — the individual's sense of
identity and self-worth. Canadians are now deeply divided on these symbolic
issues. Meech Lake revealed and exasperated deep divisions between the
majority of Quebecers and the majority of Canadians on questions of constitutional justice and on the nature of the political community to which they wish
to give allegiance. Oka did much the same with respect to Canada's aboriginal
and nonaboriginal populations.

Meech Lake also demonstrated that we had allowed our political leaders in
1982 to lock us into a most unsatisfactory set of procedures for amending the
Canadian constitution. We found truly what is meant by "the tyranny of
unanimity." Further, during the constitutional politics of the 1980s, we
Canadians made our predicament more intractable by undergoing a democratic

---

1 Keith G. Banting and Richard Simeon (eds.), *Redesigning the State: The Politics of
   Constitutional Change in Industrial Nations* (Toronto: University of Toronto Press,
   1985), p. 25.

mutation in our constitutional culture. This has caused us to repudiate the elitist nature of the traditional negotiating process used by the first ministers to work the rigid rules built into the *Constitution Act, 1982*. Eager as we Canadians now are to do our constitutional politics democratically we must recognize that, given our deep divisions, negotiating a popular accord will be ever so much more difficult than rejecting an elitist accord.

So, in light of all this, why go on to yet another round of constitutional politics? After all, if polling evidence is to be believed, a majority of Canadians both within and outside Quebec would prefer to set constitutional issues aside at this time. Why not, then, accede to this view and abandon constitutional politics for a few years at least?

The answer is that we Canadians simply have no choice and that *in one way or another* we will soon be forced by the pressure of events, much sooner than most of us may like, to engage in another very heavy round of constitutional politics. My reason for saying this is that I believe a majority of politically active Quebecers and politically active aboriginals are so dissatisfied with their constitutional status that they will generate demands for fundamental change, demands that will be too powerful to ignore or finesse. The choice will be to respond through procedures that are peaceful, legal and mutually acceptable or through extra-legal processes fraught with uncertainty and the risk of short-term chaos.

This paper is built on the assumption that the constitutional status quo is not now a politically viable option for Canada. Those who reject this assumption and believe that Quebecers and aboriginal groups will, if not responded to, just quietly abandon their constitutional projects, need not read on. But supporters of such a strategy of benign neglect should think about the price we will pay if they are wrong and we are forced into a constitutional struggle with no mutually acceptable procedures in place for endeavouring to resolve the conflict.

AN ALTERNATIVE PROCESS FOR ABORIGINAL PEOPLES

Constitutional negotiations with aboriginal peoples are already taking place. I refer to the land claims negotiations now in process in many parts of Canada and the discussion of a modern treaty recognizing the right of Ontario native peoples to self-government.[2] In 1984, the first amendment made to the Canadian constitution since patriation gave rights established through land claims agreements the same constitutional status as treaty rights. Modern treaties and land claims agreements fashioned through bilateral or trilateral negotiations and

---

2   *The Globe and Mail*, 4 October 1990.

tailored to the special circumstances of different aboriginal peoples is a constitutional process that is now under way in many parts of Canada.

This modern treaty approach has the great advantage of being readily at hand and not dependent on the resolution of the major constitutional issues dividing nonaboriginal Canadians. Unfortunately, however, the federal government's approach to what it calls the "comprehensive land-claims process" is thoroughly flawed. These flaws have been fully documented by a federal task force headed by Murray Coolican. The Coolican Report[3] was well received by aboriginal peoples but its principal recommendations have not been acted on by the government. In particular, federal negotiators have continued to insist on the total extinguishment of aboriginal rights as a condition of any agreement. They have also refused to make the process accessible to aboriginal peoples who are still living on their ancestral lands and have never entered into any agreement with British or Canadian authorities but whose claim in the government's view has simply been "superseded" by the imposition of nonaboriginal law and settlement. For a country that purports to believe that government should be based on consent this policy should be intolerable. It is also intolerable to make reform of the land-claims process a hostage to the resolution of what one native leader has aptly referred to as the "dispute between thieves" — i.e., the major constitutional disputes among nonaboriginal Canadians. Reform of the land-claims process should proceed forthwith.

Over and beyond what might be achieved through modern treaties with particular aboriginal nations, there is much to be done overall to strengthen and clarify the position of aboriginal peoples in the Canadian state. Some of these possibilities are examined by Brad Morse and David Hawkes in their contribution to this volume. Constitutional amendments of this general kind could be negotiated through a resumption of the special conferences that were held under section 37 of the *Constitution Act, 1982* or through aboriginal participation in the constituent assembly process proposed later in this paper. The choice of negotiating fora should be made by the aboriginal peoples.

PUBLIC DISCUSSION: STAGE ONE OF A THREE STAGE PROCESS

A new constitutional process must overcome the two basic faults of the Meech Lake process: its undemocratic quality and its inefficiency. There was very little public discussion of constitutional alternatives before political leaders committed themselves to the Meech Lake Accord. Participation in the negotiating

---

3 *Living Treaties: Lasting Agreements* (Ottawa: Department of Indian Affairs and Northern Development, 1985).

process was unduly limited and closed. The unanimity rule was unnecessarily extended to all parts of the Accord. No sensible timetable for ratification was established.

An improved constitutional process should aim to overcome these deficiencies through the three basic stages of the constitutional process. These stages are:

- public discussion,
- negotiations, and
- ratification.

We are now in the public discussion phase. Already, the Bélanger-Campeau Commission and the constitutional review being conducted by the Quebec Liberal Party have stimulated much more discussion and debate in Quebec about constitutional options than preceded Meech Lake. Alberta, British Columbia, Manitoba, New Brunswick and Ontario have established committees or commissions to conduct public consultations on the constitution.[4] Still more provinces and territories are likely to do the same. At the federal level the Citizen's Forum on Canada's Future, led by Keith Spicer, has a mandate to consult Canadians on the future of the country and a special parliamentary committee to be chaired by Mr. Jim Edwards and Senator Gerald Beaudoin has been established to study ways of improving the process of constitutional amendment. Besides these governmental initiatives private sector organizations and universities in all parts of the country have been sponsoring conferences on Canada's constitutional future. The BCNI symposium for which this paper was prepared is part of this activity.

Not since the pre-Confederation period has there been, *prior to constitutional negotiations*, as much public discussion of constitutional options by non-politicians. Still, no one could pretend that the general public have been much involved in these discussions — even in Quebec. The participants are mainly what the political sociologists refer to as "elites" — politicians, interest group leaders, journalists, lawyers, corporate executives and academics. Even this degree of prenegotiation discussion has gone some way to opening up the constitutional process. However, as we enter 1991, it is all too apparent that public discussion of Canada's constitutional future in the post-Meech period continues to be gravely asymmetrical. The level of constitutional interest and concern in Quebec is not even closely matched in the rest-of-Canada.

This asymmetry is perfectly satisfactory for those who look forward to Canada breaking up into two or more independent states. If the asymmetry is

---

4   For a recent listing, see *Toronto Star*, 20 December 1990, p.2. Manitoba's commission has been announced since then.

not overcome soon, the opportunity of giving serious consideration to any option short of the complete separation of Quebec from Canada will be foreclosed. There is relatively little awareness in Canada outside Quebec of just how radical a restructuring of Confederation might be necessary to win majority support in Quebec for remaining under a Canadian constitution. When English-speaking Canada wakes up to the radical nature of Quebec's constitutional aspirations, it is likely to be in an angry mood and unprepared to support the negotiation of Quebec proposals which are much more autonomist than anything contained in the Meech Lake Accord.

If the public discussion stage is to lay any of the groundwork for constitutional negotiations capable of saving the Canadian union, some progress must be made in making different parts of the country more aware of one another's constitutional concerns and aspirations. Spicer's Citizens' Forum is the public instrument with the most potential for doing this. Unfortunately, the Forum was established by the Mulroney government without consulting the opposition parties. This has given it a sour launch. But if I am right about the crisis which this country is rapidly approaching, we cannot afford to play ordinary partisan politics with the constitution or to indulge in cynicism. Spicer's fellow commissioners are not partisan. They strike me as decent and thoughtful Canadians. The Forum is the best vehicle at hand for transcending the dangers of introspective balkanization and helping ordinary Canadians explore the common grounds on which they might share a constitution.

There is not much time for Spicer or any alternative to do this work. The Quebec Liberal Party's constitutional committee has now reported.[5] Bélanger-Campeau reports at the end of March. Spicer reports in June. By that time or not long thereafter Quebec will likely make a dramatic constitutional move. Quebec might move right away to an election or referendum to test public support for the Quebec government's constitutional proposal. What now seems more likely is that a date will be set for a referendum to endorse an agreement Quebec has made with the rest-of-Canada or, in the event that no such agreement is reached, to endorse Quebec's independence.[6] The choice then for the rest-of-Canada will be to begin to work on a new Canadian constitution that includes Quebec or one that does not. This author prefers, for now, to work on the former.

---

5 Constitutional Committee of the Québec Liberal Party, *A Québec Free to Choose: Report of the Constitutional Committee* (Montreal: Québec Liberal Party, 1991).

6 This is indeed the procedure recommended in the report of the Constitution Committee of the Quebec Liberal Party. The report recommends that the referendum be held in late 1992.

THE UNLIKELIHOOD OF CONTAINING THE NEGOTIATING AGENDA

Constitutional negotiations would be much easier to conduct if they were confined to a very limited agenda. Under section 43 of the amending formula, (*Constitution Act, 1982*) changes in the powers of one or more but not all of the provinces require approval of the federal House of Commons and the legislatures only of the provinces affected.[7] Amendments under this section applying only to Quebec could be agreed to through bilateral negotiations between Ottawa and Quebec. But it is very dubious that section 43 could be used as a basis for transfers of jurisdiction to Quebec alone (or to Quebec and several other but not all provinces). Because such amendments would modify the list of federal legislative powers they would seem to be well beyond the scope of section 43.[8]

Alternatively, Quebec autonomy could be significantly enhanced without any formal constitutional changes through administrative adjustments in federal programs. The dismantling of federal cultural and language programs, opening up more tax room and withdrawing from social and regional development programs in Quebec could go a long way towards giving Quebec, *de facto*, distinct society status within the federation.

Attractive as such measures may be in terms of negotiating ease, it is most unlikely that they will satisfy Quebec's aspiration for constitutional change or be politically acceptable to the other provinces. The most modest proposal that can be expected to come out of Bélanger-Campeau and the Quebec referendum which likely follows will be for a restructuring of federalism so extensive as to require changes in federal institutions and federal legislative powers. Constitutional changes in the structure of federal institutions and the division of powers are well beyond the ambit of section 43 and require the agreement of at least six other provinces besides Quebec. Further, the Meech round demonstrated the populist appeal of the principle of "provincial equality" outside Quebec. A policy of providing special arrangements for Quebec entails political risks which federal leaders will be loathe to assume. We also learned through Meech how unacceptable a purely Quebec round of constitutional change is to the rest-of-Canada. Once Quebec proposals requiring the approval of other provinces are on the table there is virtually no possibility of confining the agenda

---

7   For a discussion of the advantages of using section 43 and nonconstitutional adjustments, see Patrick Monahan, "After Meech Lake," The Inaugural Thomas G. Feeney Memorial Lecture, University of Ottawa, 13 October 1990, published in a revised form as *After Meech Lake: An Insider's View*, Reflections, no. 5, (Kingston: Institute of Intergovernmental Relations, Queen's University, 1990).

8   For a discussion of section 43 and its possible use, see Peter W. Hogg, *Constitutional Law of Canada*, 2d ed., (Toronto: Carswell, 1985), pp. 66-69.

to these. At the very least western provinces and Newfoundland will insist on including reform of the Senate.

In the process of establishing the new parliamentary committee on the constitutional process, the suggestion has been made that the constitution amending rules might be changed before proceeding with any other constitutional changes. This suggestion is most unrealistic. Any change in the amending formula, even simply reducing the three year deadline, requires the approval of all ten provincial legislatures plus the federal House of Commons. The prospects of Quebec being willing to participate in a mini-round of constitutional amendment devoted exclusively to the amending formula are virtually nil.

Thus we should give up the illusion that the post-Meech round of constitutional politics now underway can be concluded by some simple federal deal with Quebec or through new amending rules that are somehow magically transformed without touching anything else in the constitution. If constitutional change is to be negotiated within the existing constitution of Canada, we will have to find a way of working within the constitution, a way that is both more democratic and more efficient than the Meech negotiating process. The alternative will be a negotiation that takes place outside the framework of any rules authorized by Canadian law.

THE THREAT OF NEGOTIATING OUTSIDE THE CONSTITUTIONAL RULES

A unilateral declaration of independence (UDI) by the Quebec government is a real possibility before the end of 1992. Submissions to the Bélanger-Campeau Commission indicate that there is a good deal of support for UDI within the independentist movement. The Quebec Liberal Party's recent report makes it clear that independence is the option many members of Quebec's governing party will turn to if Quebec cannot secure much more autonomy within Confederation. If UDI were to occur, Quebec would claim to be an independent nation-state and then insist on negotiating within the rules of international law, not the rules of the Canadian constitution. One could not be optimistic about either the ease of such negotiations or their outcome — particularly if a desired outcome is some continuing association between Quebec and Canada.

In world history the experience of unilateral secessionist movements is not a happy one. Apart from such cases as Switzerland (1847), the United States of America (1860), Nigeria-Biafra (1966-70) and the Southern Sudan (1960s and 1970s) which resulted in civil wars with unity reimposed by force, the West Indies Federation and the Federation of Rhodesia and Nyasaland simply proceeded to disintegrate further and East and West Pakistan have remained quite separate. The common currency shared by the Irish Free State and Britain from independence to 1973 might be considered an exception to the general pattern, but the price Ireland had to pay was having its budget approved by Britain before being presented to the Irish Parliament.

A unilateral declaration of independence by Quebec before even attempting to negotiate new constitutional arrangements is bound to have very adverse economic and social consequences. The climate of uncertainty and tension generated by such a move will reduce international confidence and put severe strain on the Canadian economy. Even if UDI were supported by a substantial majority of Quebecers, some of those who opposed it, particularly within the anglophone and aboriginal communities, might insist on federal protection of their rights against a Quebec government operating outside Canadian law. Civil disobedience and violence cannot be ruled out. Besides these negative short-term consequences, the heat and emotion that erupt on both sides in the wake of UDI will create a very hostile atmosphere for subsequently negotiating a new association.

A declaration of Quebec independence without any constitutional negotiations would throw into question the position of the Prime Minister of Canada and his Quebec parliamentary colleagues. If the prime minister were to accept Quebec's independence as a *de facto* reality, then what is his status? Who do he and his Quebec colleagues represent if Quebec is no longer part of Canada? A softer unilateral option which reduces this problem is the proposal that Quebec simply declare the primacy of Quebec laws, but leave institutional arrangements intact.[9] While this kind of unilateralism would create less havoc, it would still cause a great deal of uncertainty and would soon be subjected to legal challenge.

So for those who wish to see some continuing relationship between Quebec and the rest-of-Canada, the first choice of negotiating procedures should not be an attempt to enter into negotiations after a unilateral declaration of Quebec's independence or a unilateral break from the supremacy of the constitution of Canada. However, it is precisely through the trigger of one or other of these unilateral Quebec moves that negotiations are likely to be initiated, if an acceptable method of negotiating within the rules of the Canadian constitution is not available. If it appears that the only process available is the discredited Meech Lake process, it would not be unreasonable for Quebecers to shun negotiations within the Canadian constitution and act unilaterally. That is why it is so essential now to try to design a mutually agreeable way of negotiating within the provisions of the *Constitution Act, 1982.*

---

9   See the submission of Jean-Denis Archambault, André Braën, Jean-Paul Lacasse, Michel Morin and Daniel Proulx to the Bélanger-Campeau Commission, *Le Devoir*, 9 November 1990.

BYPASSING THE CONSTITUTION BY REFERENDUM

Another proposal has recently been put forward for settling the constitutional impasse by extra-legal means. This is the idea of conducting a country-wide referendum to settle constitutional issues without any authorization for such a referendum in the constitution. Apparently this is one of the options which Prime Minister Mulroney has asked the recently appointed special parliamentary committee on the constitution amending process to consider.[10]

To put the matter kindly, this is a rather mad-cap proposal. Obviously a referendum not authorized by the constitution could have no formal legal effect. It could provide political legitimacy for constitutional change only if all parts of the country participated in it and accepted the referendum as a legitimate exercise. Already, both the government and opposition parties in Quebec have expressed their opposition to the proposed federal referendum. It would, indeed, be a daring roll of the dice for federal leaders to attempt to go over the heads of Quebec's provincial leaders and involve the Quebec people directly in constitutional change.

The key question for any referendum dealing with the constitution is what constitutes a binding majority. Obviously, Quebecers would be reluctant to put their constitutional destiny in the hands of a simple numerical majority of Canadians. Aboriginal peoples who have not yet decided whether they wish to be part of the Canadian people would also object to simple majority rule. Just as obviously, many Canadians outside Quebec would object to giving Quebec voters a constitutional veto. And perhaps even more Canadians would object to a referendum rule requiring majorities in every province, the northern territories and within aboriginal nations.

Settling the question of which majorities should be constitutionally sovereign takes us to the very heart of the Canadian constitutional dilemma. For it raises the question of what kind of "a people" are we? Are we a people sufficiently homogeneous and trustful of one another to place our constitution, our highest law, in the hands of a simple majority? Or are we a people divided in some fundamental ways that must be reflected in the process that shapes the law governing our collective existence. And if we are the latter, then what divisions are to count? If we Canadians in all parts of the land could agree on the answers to these questions, we would surely have solved our basic constitutional issue. We would, at last, have constituted ourselves a people capable of sharing a constitution based on popular consent.

There is much to be said for writing referenda into our constitutional amending rules. But, as I have argued earlier, it is most unlikely that the negotiations needed to effect this constitutional change could be confined to

---

10 *The Globe and Mail*, 14 December 1990.

the amending process. To go ahead with a referendum before negotiating either the rules governing such a referendum or any matters of substance is indeed to put the cart before the horse. One circumstance, however, in which an extra-constitutional referendum becomes a more reasonable option is if it appears to be the only way to overcome deadlock in negotiations conducted within the constitution.

A BETTER WAY OF NEGOTIATING WITHIN THE CONSTITUTION

A Constituent Assembly

It is essential to recognize that the formal amending rules in the *Constitution Act, 1982* do not lay down a negotiating procedure. The Meech Lake procedure — that is first ministers meeting behind close doors with almost no prior public discussion — was not mandated by the constitution. The challenge is to design a procedure that is both more democratic than Meech Lake and has a better chance of producing positive results.

A procedure that might best satisfy these criteria is a constituent assembly made up of delegations from the ten provincial legislatures and the federal parliament.[11] Historically, there is nothing new about such a procedure. When fundamental constitutional change was undertaken in the United States in the 1780s, in British North America in the 1860s and in Australia in the 1890s, the negotiating instrument in each case was a meeting of delegates representing the elected legislatures of the constituent political communities. The political legitimacy of such meetings is greatly enhanced if they take place after extensive public discussion and the delegations include opposition as well as government leaders. The key to the success of such assemblies is that, if all the major political groups are adequately represented, then any agreements reached are likely to be ratified by the legislative bodies to which the delegates are accountable.

---

11 The Committee for A New Constitution of which I was a member called for a constituent assembly in 1977. See "Canada and Quebec: A Proposal for a New Constitution," *Canadian Forum*, June-July 1977, pp. 4-5. The proposal presented here has much in common with a proposal made in 1987 by Mr. John Holtby to the Special Joint Parliamentary Committee on the Meech Lake Accord. Mr Holtby proposed a continuing National Joint Committee on Constitutional Amendments composed, so far as it is practical, of members of each party of each House. Mr. Holtby renewed this proposal in his submission to the (Charest) Committee on the Proposed Companion Resolution to the Meech Lake Accord.

In addition to delegations from the federal and provincial legislatures which under the existing constitution must ratify constitutional changes, the northern territories and aboriginal nations should be asked to send delegations if they wish such a constituent assembly to deal with their constitutional interests. If they do not, then the constituent assembly should not consider proposals that impinge directly on their interests. To go ahead with constitutional changes concerning northerners or aboriginals in the absence of their legitimate representatives would mean abandoning any pretense of a constitution based on consent with respect to these people.

The kind of constituent assembly proposed here is different from the model described in the recently published federal discussion paper on amending the constitution.[12] That model is put forward as an alternative amending procedure to the procedure provided for in the *Constitution Act, 1982*. The constituent assembly procedure I am proposing is a negotiating instrument to be used within the rules of the *Constitution Act, 1982*. A constituent assembly of this kind is hinted at in the federal paper when it suggests, in the context of negotiating within the existing amending rules, that "there might be merit in establishing a special body of government and opposition members of all legislative bodies" to sensitize federal and provincial legislators to the concerns of Canadians in all regions of the country.[13] Also, the fact should not be overlooked that earlier this year all of the first ministers in their abortive attempt to settle Meech agreed to establish a commission representing all constituent legislatures as a method of working out constitutional proposals on Senate [14]

The detailed features of the constituent assembly will have to be carefully planned. It is to be hoped that some of the constitutional commissions and committees now in process, especially the Edwards-Beaudoin parliamentary committee on the amending process, will give careful consideration to how such an assembly might best function and will obtain public input on such a proposal. I will suggest only a few general guidelines here.

As for the size and shape of the delegations, there is much to be said for flexibility rather than a standardized formula. That was certainly the case in the historical precedents. Indeed, I would favour letting each legislature decide how it wishes to be represented. Some might favour including nonpoliticians in their delegations. Some might wish to have delegates directly elected by the people. The crucial requirement is that each delegation have a high degree of political legitimacy with the jurisdiction it represents.

---

12 Government of Canada, *Amending the Constitution of Canada*, (Ottawa: Federal-Provincial Relations Office, 1990), pp. 18-20.
13 Ibid., p. 11.
14 *The Globe and Mail*, 11 June 1990.

Some time parameters for the constituent assembly must be agreed to in advance. Obviously more time would be required than the two or three days usually scheduled for a First Ministers' Conference. At least several weeks would be needed. If government leaders with heavy executive responsibilities are to participate (and I think it is essential that they do), one or two recess periods should be scheduled. These recesses would also provide an opportunity for public feed-back to the delegates on proposals discussed in the assembly. But the assembly should not drag on for too long. There is a limit (one hopes) to the length of time the country and its leaders can be tied up in constitutional debate. One or two months should be the outer limit. Setting such a time limit should provide some discipline to the assembly's deliberations.

Many of the assembly's proceedings must be open and subject to full media coverage. The almost totally closed nature of first ministers' meetings is unacceptable to the Canadian people. Nonetheless, it is essential that there be opportunities for bargaining out of the eye of the media. Although the meeting at Philadelphia in 1787 was somewhat more open than the meetings of our own founding fathers at Charlottetown and Quebec City, nonetheless the delegates at Philadelphia found it necessary to nail planks across the windows so that they could negotiate in private. It is against all we know about human nature to expect negotiations to proceed in full public view. This is especially so among politicians who are being watched like hawks by the media for the slightest sign of weakness. The conditions for what Michael Stein calls "integrative bargaining" will require a deft combination of open and closed meetings.[15]

The toughest constraint on bargaining within the rules established by the *Constitution Act, 1982* is the requirement of unanimity for certain constitutional changes. But the scope of the unanimity rule should not be exaggerated. That rule applies only to a few parts of the constitution, the most important of which are the amending formula, changes in the composition of the Supreme Court and the monarchy. The more flexible 7 province/50 percent of the population rule applies to most other amendments — including the federal division of powers, the Charter of Rights and Freedoms, and Senate reform. By keeping this point in mind as it proceeds, the assembly can avoid the mistake of Meech and not lump together proposals subject to different sections of the amending formula. This could give it considerable relief from the tyranny of unanimity.

The voting rules for the constituent assembly should reflect the reality of its participants' mandate. The assembly proposed in this paper is not a final decision-making body. Proposals agreed to in the assembly would have no binding legal force until ratified by legislatures. Accordingly, what should be

---

15 Michael B. Stein, *Canadian Constitutional Renewal, 1968-1981: A Case Study in Integrative Bargaining*, Research Paper no. 27, (Kingston: Institute of Intergovernmental Relations, Queen's University, 1989).

counted in such an assembly is not the votes of individual delegates, but the votes of whole delegations. A few dissenting votes within delegations would be tolerable, but there would be no point in proceeding to the ratification stage unless a broad consensus had been reached within and among the delegations of the legislatures required for ratification.

A One Stage or Two Stage Assembly

It would be preferable if all the provinces and the federal parliament participated in the constituent assembly from the beginning. This way there would be full and continuing awareness of the various positions that must ultimately be accommodated. However, some provinces, particularly Quebec, might not be willing to participate at the outset. In this case, the constituent assembly would have to be organized in two stages. In the first stage, delegations from at least seven provinces representing 50 percent of the population and the federal parliament would attend. If they could reach an accord on a significant group of proposals, then other provinces, including Quebec would be invited to attend the second stage of the constituent assembly.

The Premier of Quebec and Quebec's Minister of Intergovernmental Affairs are on record as being willing to negotiate only with the Prime Minister of Canada. They will have to realize that the prime minister has neither the legal power nor the political authority to commit the rest-of-Canada to fundamental constitutional change. Premier Rae has stated that "Ontario does not for one moment accept the proposition that the federal government speaks for 'English Canada' while the government of Quebec speaks for itself. Each government speaks for itself and for the people in its jurisdiction."[16] This view, I expect, would be shared by all Mr. Rae's fellow premiers.

The only response Prime Minister Mulroney could make to a request from Premier Bourassa to negotiate Quebec's constitutional proposals would be to confer with his own federal parliamentary colleagues and the other provinces. The best vehicle for such a conference would be the first stage of the constituent assembly as proposed in this paper. Even though delegates of the Quebec National Assembly did not participate in this first stage, their constitutional aspirations, to the extent that they were declared and perhaps confirmed by referendum, would be known to the delegates who did attend. Thus Quebec's objectives might be taken into account but not to the exclusion of constitutional proposals emanating from other parts of Canada.

Quebec must understand that it cannot force a centralized and undemocratic form of constitutional politics on the rest-of-Canada. Some Quebecers may want what they call "English Canada" to behave as if it were a monolithic and

---

16 *The Globe and Mail*, 20 December 1990, p. 1.

unitary state. But "English Canada" is not like that now. Nor is "English Canada" likely to be like that if it "gets its act together" through something like the first stage of a constituent assembly. Quebecers are clearly committed to a democratic process of constitutional politics for themselves. So are Canadians outside Quebec — for themselves. The best way of meeting the aspirations of all Canadians for negotiating their constitutional future in a democratic manner is not through bilateral Ottawa-Quebec meetings nor through meetings of first ministers, but through the constituent assembly process.

As we enter 1991, there is no will among the people of Canada for their elected leaders to participate in a constituent assembly. Quebecers are preoccupied with defining Quebec's constitutional future. Most other Canadians do not have any sense that the constitutional status quo cannot hold. However, the process of constitutional discussion now going on throughout Canada may change the condition of public opinion. It is possible that over the next few months the need for constitutional negotiations on the fundamental shape of the federation will become widely recognized, thus giving elected leaders in all parts of Canada a mandate to participate in a constituent assembly. This would be the ideal way — a truly wonderful way — to initiate the process.

But of course this may not happen. The formation of constitutional opinion may continue to proceed in Quebec at a pace that is not even remotely matched elsewhere in Canada. It may be that the only way Canadians outside Quebec can be woken up is by a dramatic constitutional event in Quebec. This event is likely to be a majority report of the Bélanger-Campeau Commission backed by the Quebec Liberal Party calling for a radical change in Quebec's constitutional status and the scheduling of a Quebec referendum. For those who wish to preserve legal continuity through the negotiating process, it is to be hoped that at this stage the government of Quebec would still be willing to undertake constitutional negotiations within the existing constitution at least for a period of time rather than attempting immediately to act unilaterally outside the constitution.

One cannot be optimistic about the public's attitude outside Quebec to constitutional negotiations in the circumstances I have just described. People are usually in a very foul mood when they are woken up with a pail of cold water. No one likes to negotiate with a gun pointed to their head. The first reaction of a great many Canadians confronted by a Quebec proposal for a much more autonomous status within Canada will be "if that's what they want, let them go." It will take exceptional political leadership, on a nonpartisan basis, not to concede the future to separatists both within and outside Quebec. It would be much better to prepare Canadians now for a process of democratic constitutional discussion of optional ways of living together short of division into totally independent states.

Ratification

The existing amending rules permit up to three years for ratification of constitutional proposals. The Meech Lake experience demonstrated that this is too long a time period for ratification. It is most unlikely that the three year rule could be changed quickly and independently of any other constitutional changes. The only way to mitigate its effect would be for the delegations which reach an accord in the constituent assembly to agree on a timetable for placing their agreement before their respective legislatures. This timetable must respect the procedures established by legislatures for consideration of constitutional proposals. Even so, it need not and should not allow more than a month or two for a legislative vote on ratification to take place. The constitutional rules stipulate that, unless each provincial assembly votes earlier, a constitutional amendment cannot take effect until a year after the first legislature has given its approval. The timetable for ratification votes should fall well within the year.

Ratification should follow a successful constituent assembly relatively smoothly. In contrast to the first ministers' meeting that produced the Meech Lake Accord, the constituent assembly would take place after an extensive period of public discussion. Any accord it produces will have been reached much more openly and by delegations representing major opposition groups as well as governments. The legislative bodies to which it is submitted for ratification should be well prepared for proposals agreed to in the assembly.

Technically, a package of constitutional proposals concerning such important matters as the division of powers, the Charter of Rights and the Senate could be ratified by the House of Commons and the legislatures of seven provinces constituting 50 percent of the population. If the accord reached in a constituent assembly is not unanimous but enjoys the support of delegations representing the vast majority of English- and French-speaking Canadians, there would certainly be merit in taking advantage of this more flexible rule.[17] On the other hand, it would make sense to ratify amendments lacking Quebec's support only if these amendments were designed for a Canada without Quebec. Similarly it would be wrong to ratify amendments concerning aboriginal peoples or northerners that were not supported by their representative institutions.

A NEW SOCIAL CONTRACT OR SEPARATION

Most Canadians believe in the self-determination of peoples. Canadians are now engaged in the process of discovering whether they are a people capable

---

17 Under section 40 of the *Constitution Act, 1982*, dissenting provinces could opt out of any amendments transferring jurisdiction over education or other cultural matters to the federal parliament.

of sharing a constitution based on their mutual consent. The constitutional process outlined in this paper is designed to facilitate this inquiry. If, at the end of this process, the answer was in the affirmative and there was broad agreement among elected representatives on the terms of a new constitutional structure, then the process could be taken to its logical conclusion and ratified by popular referendum. If there had been agreement on writing a referendum process into the amending rules, a referendum conducted according to this new procedure would be an apt finale to the constitutional process. We would then truly have constituted ourselves as a people.

But there is the possibility of a very different outcome. An accord might not be reached through the constituent assembly process. At the end of the allotted time, we may only have agreed to disagree about our constitutional future. In this case, the consequences must be faced and Canadians should be prepared to enter into a new set of discussions to reorganize what is now Canada into two or more separate states. For many of us this will be a very sad ending. But it would be, perhaps, a little more acceptable if it were a conclusion we came to only after having tried through a decent and democratic process to resolve our differences within the existing constitutional framework.

9

Riding the Constitutional Rollercoaster:
A Commentary

Patrick Monahan

When Premier Frank McKenna emerged from the Conference Centre in Ottawa on 7 June 1990, after four-and-a-half days of being locked in a windowless room with the other first ministers and with two-and-a-half days to go, he described Meech Lake as a kind of constitutional rollercoaster. You keep going from low points to high points, and back to low points McKenna told a throng of reporters crammed behind steel barricades on the sidewalk outside the Conference Centre. The ashen-faced McKenna said the dips and the curves on the rollercoaster were taking a severe toll and that he had almost lost his stomach on that day's ride.

Reviewing the preceding chapters I had flashes of a similar experience. A common theme running through all the papers in this volume is the extreme seriousness and life-threatening character of the current political and constitutional situation. Thankfully, all of the authors attempt to propose very thoughtful and considered solutions to the impasse they identify. These are the high points on the rollercoaster, the moments when it seems that everything will turn out all right in the end. But these bursts of optimism tend to be short-lived and sporadic. Typically, the very next chapter explains why the solution that has just been proposed is either unrealistic or undesirable. This triggers a very steep and hair-raising ride back down the rails of the rollercoaster, and it is at this point that we recall Frank McKenna's description of the consequences for the stomach of such a high-speed descent.

Consider, as an example of the process I am describing, the two superb papers by Professors Guy Laforest and Peter Leslie on our future constitutional options. Professor Laforest begins his analysis by informing us that the federal cause in Quebec has been damaged beyond repair and is now "bankrupt." Professor Laforest's solution to this profound impasse is not to abandon all links between Quebec and Canada, but rather to "reinvent a Canadian dream that would include Quebec in a significant fashion...." This new "Canadian dream" would involve political sovereignty for Quebec, accompanied by some kind of economic association or confederal arrangement with the rest-of-Canada. These links might include a monetary and economic union, as well as the sharing of responsibilities over foreign policy and the armed forces. Describing this confederal arrangement as a "compromise in the future negotiations between Canada and Quebec," Professor Laforest talks in glowing terms of such an arrangement providing an inspiration for the future political developments in the European Community.

Suitably uplifted, I turn to the succeeding chapter by Professor Peter Leslie. Here, I am almost immediately doused with cold water. Professor Leslie's very compelling analysis demonstrates that the proposed new "Canadian dream," which Professor Laforest has defined as the only possible salvation from our current difficulties, is simply unattainable. Professor Leslie's argument is that the only realistic options for Canada are some form of restructured federalism or complete independence for Quebec. Any of the "intermediate options," which would include the confederal arrangements proposed by Professor Laforest, are described by Professor Leslie as "merely fantastic," which he defines as "eccentric, quaint, or grotesque in design or conception." Professor Leslie's argument is that any confederal arrangement requires two parties at the table, and it is unlikely that Canada without Quebec will be capable of getting its act together in time to even begin any such negotiations.

I should indicate that I agree very much with Professor Leslie's conclusion on this point, although not necessarily for the reasons that he identifies. Of all the possible options for Canada's future, it seems to me that the "confederal arrangements" which Professor Laforest describes are perhaps the least likely to occur. But before I elaborate further on my reasons for coming to this conclusion, let me highlight a few of the other important insights which Professor Leslie has identified in his chapter.

First, Professor Leslie reminds us that our discussions must be grounded firmly in political reality. Politics, including constitutional politics, is the art of the possible. There is little practical value, and substantial risk, in focusing attention on options that are theoretically possible but practically unattainable or unworkable.

Second, Professor Leslie makes the very important distinction between formal changes to the constitution and informal political and administrative arrangements that are quasi-constitutional in nature. He provides us with the important insight that the status quo, in terms of the formal constitituion, is compatible with very substantial modifications in these quasi-constitutional arrangements. In this sense, the supposed dichotomy between the status quo on the one hand, and substantial constitutional change on the other, may be an entirely false one.

My regret is that Professor Leslie's discussion of the possible "federalist options" does not include an assessment of which, if any, are politically possible or desirable. Such a practical weighing of these options is essential, for the reasons that Professor Leslie himself identifies. Perhaps, as a supplement to his discussion, I might offer a few thoughts on this score.

As the discussion thus far has demonstrated, the possible theoretical options for Canada's future are so numerous as to be almost mind-boggling. But we should not be overly concerned with the length or complexity of the list of theoretical options. The reality is that the practical options are very limited and the choices that all of us have to consider can be stated in fairly precise terms.

If the Meech Lake debate made anything clear, it was that Canadians outside Quebec were committed to the formal equality of the provinces. With suitable apologies to Professor Charles Taylor, who earlier pointed out the different possible variations in the meaning of "equality," the term is defined for the purposes of the present discussion as having the same "status and rights as a province of the federation."[1] Sentiment on this point outside Quebec has, if anything, hardened in the aftermath of the failure of Meech. The recent *MacLean's*-Decima poll is representative of the very uniform findings on this point.[2] Decima asked Canadians whether they would support the negotiation of a new constitutional deal with Quebec that would give the province "special powers that would allow it to make more decisions on its own." Fully 74 percent of those polled outside Quebec indicated that they would be opposed to any such "new deal." When asked to choose among six possible constitutional options, a federal system giving Quebec special powers was the *least popular option* among Canadians outside Quebec, receiving the support of only 3 percent of respondents. In short, I do not think it is very productive to spend a lot of time contemplating formal constitutional amendments involving what has been described as "asymmetrical federalism."

The same opinion research tells us that public opinion within the province of Quebec is running overwhelmingly in favour of substantial enhancements to Quebec's constitutional authority. This is one of the main messages of Professor Laforest's very lucid account of the current situation in Quebec. This suggests that the only possible *federalist* resolution of Quebec's claims lies in some form of decentralization in favour of all provinces. As we can all (painfully) recall, this was the strategy employed at Meech Lake. It seeks to accommodate Quebec while respecting the principle of the formal equality of the provinces by

---

1   See Letter from the Honourable Clyde Wells, Premier of Newfoundland and Labrador, to the Right Honourable Brian Mulroney, Prime Minister of Canada, 18 October 1989, p. 2.
2   See "A Shaken Nation Bares Its Anger," *MacLean's*, 7 January 1991, p. 10.

ensuring that whatever is offered to Quebec is also available on equal terms to all the others.

Professor Laforest cautions that this approach is a nonstarter, since Quebec's demands for additional powers are likely to be so substantial as to preclude any attempt to generalize those concessions to the remaining provinces. Certainly it is clear, for example, that the Allaire report goes far beyond what would be acceptable to the country as a whole.[3] It is evident that any decentralization will have to be relatively modest, at least in terms of formal constitutional change, and leave the federal government with the tools necessary to manage the national economy effectively. Whether this type of "rebalanced federalism" could eventually form the basis of a national consensus is difficult to predict in advance.[4] For my own part, however, I am not at all certain that such a strategy should be ruled out in advance. I would note in passing that the same *MacLean's*-Decima poll indicated that by far the most popular constitutional option among Canadians outside Quebec was a federal system giving all provinces much more power.[5] Fully 41 percent of respondents selected this as their preferred option. No other proposed change in the system received the support of more than 14 percent of respondents outside Quebec.[6]

Turning very briefly to what Professor Leslie describes as the "legal discontinuity" options, I have some difficulty with his conclusion that a Canada without Quebec is probably not viable. I agree that the difficulties in creating such a new entity are very formidable, for precisely the reasons he describes.[7] What I think he has failed to weigh adequately in the mix is the very substantial public sentiment in favour of some new form of political entity involving the remaining nine provinces in the event that Quebec chooses to leave. This sentiment will be reinforced by the realization that some form of reconstructed Canada is the only viable alternative to eventual absorption by the United

---

3   See Constitutional Committee of the Québec Liberal Party, *A Québec Free to Choose: Report of the Constitutional Committee* (Montreal: Québec Liberal Party, 1991).

4   I use the term "rebalanced federalism" because it is evident that any constitutional accommodation that might prove generally acceptable will have to deal with the demands and concerns of all parts of the country, not those of Quebec alone. It will have to be a comprehensive package that is seen to be "balanced," not simply a federal "giveaway" of powers to the provinces. For a more developed analysis of what this might involve, see Patrick Monahan, *Meech Lake: The Inside Story* (Toronto: University of Toronto Press, forthcoming) chap. 10, "The Way Ahead."

5   See *MacLean's*, 7 January 1991, Chart: "Weighing the Options," p. 19.

6   Of some interest is the fact that the second most popular option is the status quo — favoured by one-quarter of respondents.

7   For a discussion of the difficulties involved see Patrick Monahan, *After Meech Lake: An Insider's View*, Reflections Paper no. 5 (Kingston: Institute of Intergovernmental Relations, Queen's University, 1990), pp. 33-34.

States. The possibility that the remaining nine provinces might succeed in fashioning a new political order out of the ashes of the old Canada should not be dismissed out of hand.

I entirely accept Professor Leslie's conclusion that any type of confederal arrangement involving a sovereign Quebec and a reconstituted Canada is highly improbable. If Quebec decides to leave, the only realistic outcome is a fully independent Quebec without any "political superstructure" linking it to the rest-of-Canada. The main reason has to do with the difficulties of constructing confederal arrangements involving only two parties.[8] What I find rather remarkable and somewhat troubling is that Professor Laforest does not even discuss a scenario in which Quebec opts for total independence. His analysis simply assumes that a new type of confederal arrangement can be establised between Quebec and the rest-of-Canada following the demise of federalism. But this option is in all likelihood simply unattainable. How, if at all, does this fact affect the calculation of the relative merits of the various options that is now taking place in Quebec? It is striking that the question does not seem even to feature in the current Quebec debate, as Professor Laforest's paper illustrates. This is, in fact, one of the most disturbing features of the current Canadian situation.

Professor Russell's proposal for a constituent assembly is attractive in the sense that it promises a more democratic and accessible process for defining our new constitutional arrangements. But Russell's use of the term "constituent assembly" is somewhat misleading, since he makes it clear that each provincial delegation would vote as a single unit, rather than as a collection of individuals. Russell also argues, correctly in my view, that there must be an opportunity for private negotiations, although a good part of the proceedings could be open to the public.

There is already some precedent for the approach that Russell is suggesting. At the meeting of first ministers in June of 1990, the Manitoba delegation included the two opposition leaders from that province. Russell's proposal would build on this experience by generalizing it to all provinces as well as the federal government. Each provincial delegation would include representation from all the parties in the provincial legislature. One advantage to this approach is that it provides for greater representation of interests and constituencies without compromising the effectiveness of the process. A second advantage is

---

8   Any attempt to construct new arrangements will founder on the issue of whether Quebec is to be treated as an "equal" or as a junior partner in the new political structure. Quebec will no doubt insist on some right of veto over important decisions, a demand that will prove unacceptable to the rest-of-Canada. At the same time, Quebec will be unwilling to associate itself in a wider political arrangement in which its basic interests could be overridden by a Canadian (i.e., non-Quebec) majority. This would represent a net loss from Quebec's current position in the existing federation.

that it seems to offer a solution to the problems posed by the three-year time period for ratification of constitutional amendments. As the Meech process demonstrated, the problem with a three-year limit is that governments are likely to change during this period. The new government will inevitably want to start the negotiations all over again, rather than continuing the ratification process. But this difficultly can be minimized if the opposition leaders are included in the original negotiations. This will ensure that any negotiated agreement will be written in a way that is acceptable to both the government and the opposition in each legislature. In short, Professor Russell's suggestions seem to offer very significant improvements to the process of amending the constitution.

10

Alternative Methods for Aboriginal Participation in Processes of Constitutional Reform

David C. Hawkes and Bradford W. Morse

INTRODUCTION

We have yet to find a successful process for involving the aboriginal peoples of Canada — in a sense, the first citizens of this country — in constitutional discourse. The matter is an issue of moral, ethical, and political import in its own right, and a major challenge to nation-building — to "completing the circle of confederation" as the Inuit have phrased it. It is doubly important, in our view, because we believe that the resolution of the "aboriginal question," in constitutional terms, is directly tied to that of the "Quebec question." For these reasons and others, this task has become a national priority, an integral element in the rebuilding and renewal of the Canadian federation.

In this chapter we present alternative methods for aboriginal peoples to participate in processes of constitutional reform. The substance of the constitutional amendments is not addressed, only the alternative processes by which such amendments might be arrived at. To set the topic in context, we begin by providing brief background information on relations between aboriginal peoples and Canadian governments, principally the federal government, focusing on recent efforts at constitutional reform involving aboriginal peoples. Second, we briefly examine the impact of the Meech Lake Accord, the reasons for aboriginal opposition to it, and the parallels between Quebec and aboriginal self-determination. Our third task is to construct a "test" for workable constitutional reform processes involving aboriginal peoples. In constructing such a test, we explore the lessons of the Meech Lake process, and those of the process

We wish to thank Daniel Lavery and Abhimanga Jalan for their research assistance, and the many people from the academic, government and aboriginal communities who provided us with their comments on an earlier version of this paper.

of First Ministers' Conferences on Aboriginal Constitutional Matters — better known as the "section 37" process, after its constitutional mandate — which took place between 1983 and 1987. Fourth, we present alternative methods for involving aboriginal peoples in processes of constitutional reform, in each case analyzing the alternatives against the test criteria. Finally, we draw some conclusions as to which alternatives may be the most effective, considering both short- and long-term implications, desirability, feasibility and practicality.

BACKGROUND

In order to place into perspective relations between aboriginal peoples and the federal government, one does not have to reach far back into history. Just over 20 years ago, in a federal government White Paper released in 1969, then Minister of Indian Affairs Jean Chrétien proposed to bring status Indians into the "mainstream" of Canadian society. The paper, an outcome of Pierre Trudeau's call for a "just society," sought to end the collective rights of aboriginal peoples in favour of individual rights. Among other measures, it proposed terminating the special legal status of Indian peoples, discontinuing the federal government's "special relationship" with Indian peoples,[1] eliminating protection for reserve lands, and having services delivered to Indians by provincial governments. The strength of Indian opposition from across the country forced the federal government to abandon the policy officially, although doubts linger among aboriginal communities as to the government's true intentions.

The 1969 White Paper and federal government initiatives in the field of constitutional reform beginning in the late 1970s served to mobilize aboriginal peoples from coast to coast. Without the unifying opposition to government policy regarding aboriginal and treaty rights, land claims and Meech Lake, it is arguable that aboriginal peoples in Canada could not have achieved such solidarity and cohesion at the national level.

Aboriginal Peoples and Constitutional Reform: Recent History

In 1978, in the aftermath of the election of the first Parti Québécois government in Quebec, the federal government introduced its proposals for constitutional reform, entitled "A Time for Action," and its companion legislation Bill C-60. The proposals contained, for the first time, a Charter of Rights and Freedoms, and a provision that would shield certain aboriginal collective rights from the general application of the individual rights contained therein.[2]

---

1   The "special relationship" has been characterized as a fiduciary obligation, similar to that imposed on a trustee.

Following the defeat of the short-lived Conservative government of Joe Clark (which placed aboriginal issues on the constitutional agenda for the first time), the victory of the federalist forces in the Quebec referendum on sovereignty-association, and the failure of a First Ministers' Conference (FMC) on the Constitution in September of 1980, the reinvigorated Trudeau government decided to act unilaterally to patriate and amend the constitution. Three sections of the new proposal affected aboriginal peoples. A proposed section 25 provided for the nonderogation of aboriginal, treaty and other rights and freedoms with respect to the Charter of Rights and Freedoms, ensuring that the Charter would not detract from these rights. Section 34 proposed to entrench aboriginal and treaty rights in the constitution, and section 37 proposed one further meeting of first ministers and aboriginal leaders to define aboriginal and treaty rights in the constitution.

The action to patriate was opposed by eight provincial governments and many aboriginal peoples, most notably the National Indian Brotherhood. The latter was concerned that the federal proposals would endanger the special trust relationship between aboriginal peoples and the Crown. The Supreme Court decision in September of 1981 on the Constitutional Reference brought before it by provincial government legal challenges had the effect of forcing the first ministers back to the bargaining table.

At a conference held in November of 1981, the federal government and nine provinces reached a political accord on the constitution. Quebec would withhold its consent, and the accommodation would remain incomplete until the ill-fated Meech Lake Accord of 1987. During the negotiations in 1981, the amendments relating to the rights of aboriginal peoples had been deliberately deleted at the last minute. Canadian women were also upset at the result, since they feared that their hard-won gender equality rights might be made ineffectual by the "notwithstanding" clause, section 33. Through the determination and lobbying of both groups, their concerns were partially addressed, although in the case of aboriginal peoples, the word "existing" was placed before the clause "aboriginal and treaty rights" — a signal, among other things, of provincial concern regarding the uncertain legal ground being ventured onto and the desire to maintain the status quo.

The *Constitution Act, 1982* was proclaimed on 17 April 1982, and three sections of it related directly to aboriginal peoples. Section 25 guaranteed that the Canadian Charter of Rights and Freedoms will not

... abrogate or derogate from any aboriginal, treaty or other rights or freedoms that pertain to the aboriginal peoples of Canada, including:

---

2 For further detail, see for example, Roy Romanow, John Whyte and Howard Leeson, *Canada...Notwithstanding: The Making of the Constitution 1976-1982* (Toronto: Carswell/Methuen, 1984), chap. 1.

(a) any rights or freedoms that have been recognized by the Royal Proclamation of October 7, 1763; and
(b) any rights or freedoms that may be acquired by the aboriginal peoples of Canada by way of land claims settlement.

Section 35 stated that:

(1) The existing aboriginal and treaty rights of the aboriginal peoples of Canada are hereby recognized and affirmed.
(2) In this Act, "aboriginal peoples of Canada" includes the Indian, Inuit and Metis peoples of Canada.

Section 37 provided for the convening of a single First Ministers' Conference on Aboriginal Constitutional Matters to identify and define aboriginal rights, and for the participation of aboriginal peoples' representatives and delegates from the territorial governments in those discussions.

That First Ministers' Conference was held in March of 1983, and resulted in the first — and to date only — set of amendments to the newly-patriated constitution. Section 25 (b) was amended to protect future and existing land claim settlements. Two new subsections were added to section 35: one guaranteed aboriginal and treaty rights equally to male and female persons; another clarified the definition of "treaty rights" to include existing and future land claims agreements. Section 35.1 was also added to provide for a First Ministers' Conference to be convened, including the participation of aboriginal peoples, before any amendment is made to the constitution that directly affects them. Section 37 was amended as well, including a provision (supplemented by a Constitutional Accord commitment) for at least three more First Ministers' Conferences on Aboriginal Constitutional Matters, in 1984, 1985 and 1987.[3]

These three First Ministers' Conferences — all of them focused upon the aboriginal right to self-government — ended without agreement in March of 1987. The next month, on 30 April 1987, the Meech Lake Accord was signed by the prime minister and all provincial premiers.

THE IMPACT OF THE MEECH LAKE ACCORD

The Meech Lake Accord had a direct impact on aboriginal peoples, and at several different levels. The first level was symbolic. The irony of the developments was overwhelming — first ministers could accept the vague notion of a distinct society for Quebec after a rather short negotiation, but not the similar concept of "self-government" for aboriginal peoples after five years of

---

3   For a fuller description and analysis of the section 37 process, see David C. Hawkes, *Aboriginal Peoples and Constitutional Reform: What Have We Learned?* (Kingston: Institute of Intergovernmental Relations, Queen's University, 1989).

intensive discussions. If aboriginal peoples were not distinct, who were? The Accord failed to recognize the contribution of aboriginal peoples to Canadian society.

A second level was substantive, in that some parts of the Accord did little to assist, and in some cases directly diminished, the constitutional aspirations of aboriginal peoples. For example, under the terms of the Accord, it would be more difficult for northern territories, which are heavily populated by aboriginal peoples,[4] to attain provincial status, since the unanimous consent of the federal government and all provincial governments would be required. As well, the Accord proposed that appointments to the Supreme Court and the Senate would come from nominees supplied solely by provincial governments, effectively ignoring any input from Northerners.[5] Concerns were also voiced over possible negative repercussions from other clauses, such as opting-out of national programs, and entrenching an annual First Ministers' Conference on the Constitution without aboriginal participation.

A third level was in terms of process — comparisons were made between the apparently "successful" Meech Lake negotiation process and the "failed" section 37 negotiation process. This aspect will be addressed in the next section, where we examine the lessons to be learned from the two processes.

The Meech Lake Accord sowed both seeds of unity and disunity. It deepened some cleavages already well-established in Canadian society, such as those between Quebec and non-Quebec (territorial), between anglophone and francophone (linguistic), and between aboriginal peoples and the Quebec government (cultural). On the other hand, it provided new solidarity to aboriginal peoples, francophone Quebecers, Northerners, and Atlantic Canadians.[6]

Canadians saw, for the first time, the striking similarity between the demands for self-determination of the Québécois and aboriginal peoples. While the nationalism of Quebec was viewed as legitimate by first ministers, the self-determination of aboriginal peoples was not. "The story played very

---

4   The aboriginal peoples account for about one quarter of the population of the Yukon Territory, and over one half of the population of the Northwest Territories. See Allan Maslove and David Hawkes, *Canada's North: A Profile* (Ottawa: Statistics Canada, 1990).

5   See Lorne Ingle, *Meech Lake Reconsidered* (Hull: Voyaguer Publishing, 1989), Chaps. 10 (Donald Purich) and 13 (Tony Penikett).

6   For a fuller treatment of how this affected the solidarity of aboriginal peoples, see David C. Hawkes and Marina Devine, "Aboriginal-State Relations: After Meech Lake and After Oka" in Frances Abele (ed.), *How Ottawa Spends, 1991-92* (Ottawa: Carleton University Press, forthcoming). Since the failure of the Meech Lake Accord, Newfoundland Premier Wells has indicated a willingness to discuss closer association among the Atlantic provinces, while Premier McKenna of Neᵛ Brunswick has proposed an economic union among the Maritime provinces.

differently," as the media and pollsters phrase it, among the general public. The aboriginal and Quebec constitutional issues are joined in the public perception. Both demand a constitutional status as distinct societies, both define themselves in national terms (e.g., the Assembly of First Nations and the Quebec National Assembly), both seek protection for their languages and cultures, both are minorities with constitutional legal standing, and both, in different definitions of the phrase, are "founding peoples."

Pollster Angus Reid, in recent opinion surveys on native issues, found that among English-speaking Canadians there was strong support for greater sovereignty, including aboriginal self-government. Based on his data, he suggested that aboriginal and Quebec constitutional issues have become linked in the public's view, and that, in seeking to address these matters, governments must consult not only Quebecers and aboriginals, but also the Canadian public at large.[7] To renew Canadian federalism, he suggested, both must be resolved at the same time.

CRITERIA FOR A WORKABLE CONSTITUTIONAL REFORM PROCESS

It is a creative, albeit relatively straightforward task to describe alternative methods for involving aboriginal peoples in processes of constitutional reform. We do this in the next section. What is more difficult, however, is to find a way of judging which of these alternatives is likely to be the most effective. In this matter, there is little guidance.

It is appropriate, therefore, if not imperative to our task, that a "test" be designed, so that these alternatives may be measured against some objective criteria. In choosing the criteria for a workable constitutional reform process involving aboriginal peoples, we return to the two recent failed initiatives — the section 37 conferences on aboriginal self-government and the Meech Lake process — to see what lessons can be learned from past mistakes. These experiences may have application, as well, to the matter of constitutional reform more generally.[8]

---

7 From an address by Angus Reid to the "National Caucus on Aboriginal-Federal Relations," Ottawa, 25 September 1990.

8 For two quite divergent views on the efficacy of the Meech Lake process, see Louis Bruyere, "Aboriginal Peoples and the Meech Lake Accord" in the *Canadian Human Rights Yearbook*, 1988 and Senator Lowell Murray, "The Process of Constitutional Change in Canada: The Lessons of Meech Lake" in *Choices*, Institute for Research on Public Policy, February 1988.

Lessons from the Section 37 and Meech Lake Processes

It will become evident over the next few pages how different these approaches were. The section 37 process was relatively formal, with a fixed number of constitutionally-mandated First Ministers' Conferences. The Meech Lake process was informal, with no previously established timetable of meetings. The section 37 process featured large, multilateral (federal/provincial/territorial/aboriginal) conferences of first ministers and aboriginal leaders, with unclear and at times long agendas. The Meech Lake process was marked by small, bilateral (interprovincial and federal-provincial) and multilateral meetings, with a limited and clear agenda. The section 37 process was open and public, most of it broadcast live on national television. The Meech Lake process was closed and private, almost none of it seen in the media.[9]

The evolution of the two processes was different as well. In the Meech Lake process, Gil Rémillard, the Quebec Minister of Intergovernmental Affairs, visited each provincial capital to meet privately with the premier or designated minister, in order to assess the likelihood of fruitful negotiations. He was followed by Senator Lowell Murray, the federal Minister of Federal-Provincial Relations, who also held a series of private, bilateral meetings. It was only after many closed bilateral and multilateral meetings of federal and provincial ministers and officials that the federal government was willing to bring first ministers together at the secluded Meech Lake retreat near Ottawa. The meeting was private, and closed to the public and the media. The first ministers' meetings which followed, at the Langevin Block in Ottawa during June of 1987, and the week-long meeting at the Government Conference Centre during June of 1990, were also closed.

The section 37 process was marked by early success. First ministers and aboriginal leaders agreed upon on aboriginal rights package at the conference in 1983, and the constitution was subsequently amended to reflect this agreement. The conference in 1984 failed to reach any agreement, with the 1985 conference coming close to an accommodation. During this time, informal conventions developed as to the rules of the process. Bilateral meetings and federal-provincial meetings (excluding aboriginal peoples) were viewed as inappropriate. Although private meetings of government ministers and aboriginal leaders were held, they were viewed with suspicion. This led to stylized First Ministers' Conferences carried on national television, with set opening addresses by first ministers and aboriginal leaders, and with little opportunity for dialogue and negotiation. Momentum slipped away during the remaining

---

9 For further analysis, see Hawkes, *Aboriginal Peoples and Constitutional Reform: What Have We Learned?* Chaps. 5, 6 and 7.

two years of the process, with little effort made by the governments during the 1985-87 period.

It is interesting that government officials characterized the section 37 process as a "failure," while aboriginal peoples were reluctant to do so. They favoured an open and public process, since it put pressure on governments and provided an opportunity to educate the public as to the issues at stake. It was assumed that if Canadians knew more about the issues, they would be more likely to support the positions of aboriginal peoples.[10]

Both processes failed, but for very different reasons. In a sense, the section 37 process was too open (and politically naive), while the Meech Lake process was too closed and elitist (and therefore lacking legitimacy). In the case of the Meech Lake process, some of the characteristics that supposedly led to its success — its closed and private nature, the lack of public input — appear to have contributed to its ultimate undoing. First ministers failed to understand that constitutional reform is no longer the exclusive concern of governments, and that executive federalism is no longer seen as an appropriate decision-making process for constitutional change. The changes brought about in 1982, including the Charter of Rights and Freedoms and a "made-in-Canada" amending formula and procedure, made constitutional change a concern of all Canadians, who expect to participate in the process.[11]

Although the section 37 process was more open, it too lacked public input. Its major failing, however, is that it was ineffective in reaching an agreement. The high profile and public nature inhibited negotiation. It is politically naive to expect first ministers and aboriginal political leaders to alter their positions on national television. In *realpolitik*, leaders are more apt to speak to their constituencies through the media, instead of to one another; and to be seen to be defending the interests of their people, rather than the interests of the country.

The exclusive reliance on large, formal, multilateral conferences provided no scope for the building of trust among the parties to the negotiations, a key element that can be engendered through smaller, private, informal meetings. It should also be noted that the section 37 approach was a "one shot, all or nothing" attempt to deal with the constitutional aspirations of aboriginal peoples, whereas in dealing with the problems that confronted it, Quebec had a permanent place at the first ministers' table. The former process pressured aboriginal leaders to put everything on the table, which led to an agenda

---

10 See Hawkes, *Aboriginal Peoples and Constitutional Reform: What Have We Learned?* p. 39. There is reason to support this assumption, based on polling data gathered by Decima Research for the Inuit Committee on National Issues.

11 See Alan C. Cairns, "Citizens (Outsiders) and Governments (Insiders) in Constitution-Making: The Case of Meech Lake" in *Canadian Public Policy*, XIV Supplement, September 1988, pp. S121-S145.

overload and made the stakes too high for aboriginal leaders to agree to any significant compromises.

Criteria for Workable Processes

Based on this analysis, we have identified the following criteria to be built into our test for workable processes of constitutional reform involving aboriginal participation. We hasten to add that the test is only partial — these conditions are necessary but not sufficient. These criteria are:

- public consultation with the wider Canadian community prior to entering negotiations, or in the very early stages (participatory, educational, informing of public support);
- public and private meetings (public for education, private for negotiation);
- clear and agreed agenda (short, priorized, guiding set of principles);
- bilateral and multilateral meetings (encourages creativity, building momentum, problem-solving);
- more private, informal, and smaller meetings (build trust ties among parties to negotiations, mutual understanding and candor);
- legislative review, involving public input, of any proposed constitutional resolution; and
- security of a place at the negotiation table (encourages the adoption of a limited and workable agenda).

To these conditions must be added the following considerations: whether the benefits of the alternative process are likely to be short or long term; the practicality and feasibility of the approach; and the innate desirability of the method (e.g., based on principles such as responsible and democratic government, fair representation, and accountability to the public).

The federal government has recognized the need to address the role of the Canadian public in constitutional reform. In December 1990 a Special Joint Committee of the Senate and the House of Commons was established "to consult broadly with Canadians ... upon the process for amending the Constitution of Canada."[12] In addition to examining the role of Canadian citizens, the Joint Committee is charged with assessing the effectiveness of the existing process and formulae, as well as exploring alternatives.

---

12 *Hansard*, House of Commons, 11 December 1990.

ALTERNATIVES

The alternatives proposed below are in two categories: (a) those that would entail the use of existing processes to affect a constitutional amendment concerning aboriginal peoples; and (b) those that would require institutional change or would restructure the relationship between aboriginal peoples and governments in Canada. The timing and other aspects concerning the feasibility and desirability of any of these alternatives is assessed in the concluding section of the paper.

Existing Processes

SECTION 37 PROCESS REVISITED

One alternative would be to return to a renewed section 37 approach, having learned from past mistakes, and incorporating the criteria noted above. The obvious benefit would be that the approach would be more easily understood, and that parties to the negotiations could pick up where they left off, so to speak. It would be relatively easy, in the short term, to restart negotiations. In fact, this was the proposed agreement of first ministers in June of 1990, when they proposed a permanent process of constitutional meetings on aboriginal issues every three years. More private meetings could be added, the agenda could be clarified and agreed upon, and a set of principles could guide negotiations.

Before relaunching this process, however, it would be necessary to engage Canadians in constitutional discourse regarding the rights of aboriginal peoples and what might be placed in the constitution in this regard. Thus, a first step would be a public consultation process, perhaps through a royal commission on aboriginal affairs, as the prime minister offered in June of 1990,[13] or through a joint parliamentary committee or task force, or through some vehicle jointly designed by aboriginal peoples and federal and provincial governments.

Not all of the past problems with the section 37 approach are easily addressed. For example, some aboriginal peoples felt unrepresented in the process — in fact, many either never joined in, or withdrew from it and boycotted the meetings. This limits the legitimacy of the process in the eyes of some aboriginal peoples. Nor can other barriers, such as the lack of understanding among parties to the negotiations, or the absence of political will, be overcome solely by redesigning the process.

---

13 In a letter to Chief Phil Fontaine, Provincial Leader of the Assembly of Manitoba Chiefs, dated 18 June 1990, the prime minister sought to facilitate the procedural blockage of federal initiatives "with a view to securing that justice for aboriginal peoples while enhancing the cause of national unity."

LITIGATION

A further method by which aboriginal people can obtain a role in the process of constitutional reform is through the courts. Aboriginal groups gave considerable thought to initiating a lawsuit during the Meech Lake process to challenge the validity of the Accord on the basis that it would affect their section 35 rights (*Constitution Act, 1982*) such that the constitution was being violated by the prime minister's failure to convene a First Ministers' Conference under section 35.1. This argument would primarily have hinged on the inadequate scope of the nonderogation clause (section 16) within the proposed *Constitutional Amendment, 1987*. An additional ground of attack would require a very expansive interpretation to be given to section 35 whereby any fundamental realignment of Canadian federalism could be said to infringe the "existing aboriginal and treaty rights of the aboriginal peoples" such that their consent to the changes are necessary. This latter assertion would naturally remain open as applicable to any future amendments of significance.

A further argument emanates from the fiduciary obligation residing in the Crown. The Supreme Court of Canada declared in May 1990 in the *Sparrow* decision, that both federal and provincial governments are subject to this fiduciary duty and that it benefits all aboriginal peoples.[14] While the precise scope of this legal concept is unclear, the Court has indicated that it expects the honour of the Crown and the special, historic relationship with aboriginal peoples to be placed above the interests of other Canadians. It is at the very least arguable that any constitutional amendments that diminish the rights or unique legal position of the indigenous population would be contrary to this common law doctrine that has now, according to the Supreme Court, been incorporated into the interpretation of section 35.

Litigation may also provide a further avenue for aboriginal participation in constitutional reform. As opposed to lawsuits designed to strike down amendment proposals or to compel consultation, litigation that results in a broader elaboration of aboriginal and treaty rights would indirectly and unofficially introduce constitutional change. For example, if the courts declare that the Gitskan and Wet'suwet'en peoples of British Columbia have the authority to govern their own affairs and regulate the usage of their territory under their traditional law, then the predominant interpretation of the constitution held by federal and provincial governments would have to be jettisoned. This would obviously affect the current practice of federalism in Canada and it might minimize, if not eliminate, the desire for an amendment recognizing a right of self-government.

---

14 *R.* v. *Sparrow* (1990), 46 B.C.L.R. (2d) 1 (S.C.C.).

Litigation is, of course, a costly and unpredictable exercise for all sides. Although it is patently not the first choice of aboriginal peoples, it does remain a viable option — and one of the few that they can pursue in the face of intransigence on the part of the federal and provincial governments.

DECLARATIONS OF SOVEREIGNTY

Another alternative is a declaration of sovereignty by an indigenous group that is able to meet the standard for nationhood. The normal test at international law is to occupy a distinct territory, to have a population, to possess common linguistic or cultural attributes, and to operate a government. While many aboriginal groups can meet this basic test, the real hurdles are to obtain political recognition from other states and then to translate this official status into political reality. Lithuania, Estonia and Latvia are all currently wrestling with the first hurdle. The Palestine Liberation Organization is struggling with the latter as the territorial claims of the Palestinians are effectively blocked by the challenges of Jordan and Israel.

The International Court of Justice is of no help in this regard as it can only hear cases brought by states that are already recognized as nations by the international community. Although the United Nations Human Rights Committee can receive complaints against Canada for violating the International Covenant on Civil and Political Rights under the Optional Protocol, including the right of self-determination of all peoples,[15] the Micmac have already discovered the frustrations and limitations of that option.

Asserting sovereignty in the sense of independence is an exceedingly difficult task. Securing internal sovereignty, as Indian tribes in the U.S. have under the label of "domestic dependent nations,"[16] is more readily obtainable, but it requires invoking the jurisdiction of the domestic courts or receiving the concurrence of the federal and/or regional governments. Either method leads one back to the previously discussed alternatives. Thus, a declaration of sovereignty is truly a different option only when it can be implemented unilaterally through the force of arms or with the acceptance of the international community in a meaningful way. Developments within the United Nations towards a Declaration of the Rights of Indigenous Peoples through the efforts of the UN Working Group on Indigenous Populations may improve the viability of this

---

15 For a detailed discussion of this topic as it relates specifically to indigenous peoples, see Barbara Hocking (ed.), *International Law and Aboriginal Rights* (Sydney: Law Book Company Ltd., 1988).

16 This doctrine emanated from the decisions of Chief Justice Marshall in the landmark Cherokee cases. See, for example, *Worcester* v. *Georgia* (1832) 6 Peters 515 (U.S.S.C.).

strategy, although it appears that it is likely only to increase the stature and content of indigenous rights at the international level.

REGIONAL AMENDMENTS

A variation on several of the alternatives previously discussed is to initiate reform on a provincial or regional basis. Section 43 of the *Constitution Act, 1982* authorizes amendments that apply only to "one or more, but not all, provinces" where approved by Parliament and the relevant provincial legislature(s). It has already been used in 1987 concerning denominational school rights in Newfoundland and has been the subject of extensive consideration regarding proposed amendments to the *Alberta Act* to entrench the Metis settlements.

Given Premier Rae's public pronouncements that the Government of Ontario now recognizes aboriginal people as possessing an inherent right of self-government, one could envision a proposed amendment that reflects this commitment and understanding emanating from his government that would apply only to this province.

TREATY PROCESS

Another method whereby aboriginal people could obtain their constitutional objectives for greater self-determination within the Canadian federation is through the treaty process. The Crown has been negotiating treaties with First Nations for over 300 years. This exercise continues under the name land-claims agreements. These settlements are regarded as treaties in constitutional terms by virtue of section 35(3) of the *Constitution Act, 1982*. It is clearly possible for the federal government and appropriate Indian, Inuit or Métis groups to negotiate and conclude treaties that resolve jurisdictional issues, including an articulation of powers and authorities for aboriginal governments. These treaties could be phrased so as to reflect the inherent sovereign rights of aboriginal peoples or could be couched in neutral language such that the treaties themselves might be viewed as the source of self-government powers. Either way, the treaties would receive constitutional protection under section 35 so as to become part of the "supreme law of the land" with the result that federal or provincial laws that conflict with the terms of the treaties would be "of no force and effect" pursuant to section 52 of the *Constitution Act, 1982*. It may, however, be possible for otherwise valid federal or provincial statutes to restrict these treaties in limited circumstances in light of the Supreme Court of Canada's decision in the *Sparrow* case.[17]

---

17 *R.* v. *Sparrow* (1990).

It is also possible, at least in theory, for such treaties to be negotiated without provincial involvement, as has been the case in the vast majority of Indian treaties both before and after Confederation. The likelihood of this occurring in the face of opposition from a provincial government is rather low at present.

Not only does the treaty process strike a responsive chord among aboriginal peoples as the appropriate mechanism for a nation-to-nation approach to constitution-making, but it also permits a high degree of flexibility and diversity to occur. That is, treaties could be negotiated separately with the three distinct aboriginal peoples (Indians, Inuit and Métis) or collectively but on a regional basis. This suggestion is not entirely unprecedented as the Commonwealth Government of Australia committed itself in 1988 through the Barunga Statement of Prime Minister Hawke to negotiate a national treaty with the aboriginal and Torres Strait Islander population.[18]

Institutional Change

REFERENDA

Another process for constitutional reform involves the use of a referendum. Referenda can be conducted either on initial issues or questions of principle (as was the case in Quebec in 1980) or as the final element in the ratification process of proposed amendments (as in Australia). In the aboriginal context, referenda are used to ratify land surrenders under the *Indian Act*, and to ratify land claims agreements. While it is conceivable that referenda might be used only in relation to constitutional amendments on aboriginal issues, or to gauge the reaction solely of aboriginal people, it is unlikely for such a departure from Canadian tradition to be made for limited purposes.

Furthermore, the primary rationale for considering a referendum process at present is to assuage the general public's demand to have a major role in all aspects of constitutional change. Therefore, the attractiveness extends to all amendments rather than just to aboriginal people or issues. We would anticipate that aboriginal organizations might be somewhat anxious over how referenda might be used, since referenda tend to favour majoritarian interests. It would be reasonable to anticipate that they would seek involvement in the drafting of the question or amendment, a veto on matters that would directly affect them, or both.

---

18 Garth Nettheim and Tony Simpson, "Aboriginal People and Treaties" *Current Affairs Bulletin* no.6, 1989, p. 18.

CONSTITUENT ASSEMBLY OR CONSTITUTIONAL CONVENTION

Constituent assemblies are bodies specially created to be broadly representative of the country as a whole. They are separate from the existing regional or national governments. The members are chosen either by popular election or by provincial legislatures, to meet in exceptional circumstances to develop or ratify a complete constitution or amendments to an existing one. The expression "constituent assembly" implies that the broad spectrum of society is represented through this body and that it exists primarily for this purpose.

Constitutional conventions are designed solely to address constitution-building or amendments, and are usually comprised of a select group of existing legislators nominated to serve in this added capacity by their colleagues. This latter concept does not necessarily involve the public at large in the election of the members of the convention.

The United States Constitution was devised by a constitutional convention meeting in Philadelphia from May to September of 1787 consisting of individuals chosen by their respective state legislatures as their delegates. The final draft of this convention was submitted for ratification by each state to constituent assemblies specifically elected for this purpose. The current amending formula in the U.S. Constitution creates optional processes whereby the existing state legislatures and Congress vote on changes (which has been the approach used in all but one case), or special conventions can be called at the national or state level.[19]

The constituent assembly model was used to develop the new constitutions of India and Pakistan after World War II. Initially one assembly was elected for the entire subcontinent, but the Muslim delegates boycotted it and were successful in persuading the British government to convene two constituent assemblies for the two newly independent countries. The Indian Constituent Assembly met from 1947 to 1949 consisting of delegates chosen on a proportional basis reflecting the population of the three main communities (Muslim, Sikh and General). Members of each community within the existing provincial legislative assemblies elected their own representatives.[20] The initial Pakistan Constituent Assembly was similarly selected by the already existing provincial legislative assemblies. In both countries the Constituent Assembly also served as the interim national parliament until the new constitution came into effect.

Various other countries have used the constituent assembly approach to devise a founding or new constitution. Not only does it provide a vehicle to focus attention exclusively on constitutional issues, but it also can

---

19 Canada, Federal-Provincial Relations Office, *Amending the Constitution of Canada — A Discussion Paper* (Ottawa: Minister of Supply and Services, 1990), pp. 18-19.

20 D.D. Basu, *Introduction to the Constitution of India* (Delhi, 1971), pp. 17-20.

accommodate diverse ethnic, racial, religious, cultural or linguistic groups within the country by providing for distinct representation. The most recent examples of utilizing a constituent assembly were in Namibia and Nicaragua, in which the indigenous populations elected their own delegates.

Establishing a constituent assembly for Canada could obtain broad popular appeal for many obvious reasons. For aboriginal people, however, it could generate some mixed emotions even if they obtained a guarantee of representation, for a scheme of representation based on population alone would likely leave them with at most 5 percent of the delegates. (It is, of course, possible to provide aboriginal people with a higher percentage to reflect their unique position, since precise proportional representation may not be mandatory.) Unless representation is based on the aboriginals' unique position, there will be a sense of concern that current achievements might be dissipated. On the other hand, the status quo provides no long-term security either, as aboriginal demands for a veto over future constitutional changes that would affect them have been repeatedly rejected with only a requirement to hold a First Ministers' Conference pursuant to section 35.1 (*Constitution Act, 1982*) providing any comfort. This model could, at the very least, involve aboriginal people as a unique component of Canada in all future constitutional decisions. It is interesting to note that the recent federal discussion paper by the Federal-Provincial Relations Office, *Amending the Constitution of Canada*, not only discusses this option at some length, but also raises the possibility of separate representation for aboriginal peoples.[21]

SENATE REFORM

It is almost certain that the issue of Senate reform and a Triple E Senate (i.e., Elected, Equal and Effective) will be debated during the next round of constitutional deliberations. In an effort to redesign the Senate's mandate and composition, and to make it more equal and more effective, it is quite likely that calls for a redistribution of Senate seats will be forthcoming, and that proportional representation will be considered. A possibility well worth considering would be for aboriginal peoples to be allotted a number of Senate seats, based upon their proportion of the Canadian population, or as a reflection of their special status as the original owners of Canada.

GUARANTEED REPRESENTATION

Aboriginal people have asserted for many years that the Canadian version of parliamentary democracy has effectively excluded them from possessing a

---

21 Federal-Provincial Relations Office, *Amending the Constitution*.

voice within the legislatures of the land. Registered Indians were denied voting rights in federal elections until 1960 — hence the expression "enfranchisement" being used to describe the process whereby Indian people voluntarily relinquished their status, or had it taken from them under the provisions of the *Indian Act*, in order to acquire the electoral franchise through ceasing legally to be "Indians." Guaranteeing voting rights to all adult aboriginal men and women does set Canada apart from South Africa, to which parallels have increasingly been drawn in recent years, but this is of little comfort outside the north, as aboriginal people possess limited electoral clout due to their small and widely scattered population. There are, of course, individuals who have gained particular prominence through mainstream elections, such as Elijah Harper and Ethel Blondin. Nevertheless, their numbers have been very small indeed and restricted geographically to locales with significant aboriginal voting strength.

In light of these demographic facts, coupled with a desire to obtain a practical form of official recognition as a "founding people" and to ensure that aboriginal concerns are heard consistently, some aboriginal organizations have repeatedly called for guaranteed political representation within Parliament and provincial legislatures.

The best known case of guaranteed representation for an indigenous minority is that of New Zealand. Almost immediately after the establishment of an elected colonial legislature, a system was introduced whereby four seats were dedicated to the Maori people. This scheme was initially devised so that the minority white settlers would dominate the government by restricting the political power of the majority Maori population to a handful of seats. Its effect has changed considerably over time, however, as it now serves to guarantee that Maoridom (who are approximately 13 percent of the population) will always have a voice in the national Parliament, thereby reflecting their unique standing as originally both the owners and exclusive sovereign rulers of New Zealand.

Under this system the country is divided into four ridings as far as the Maori seats are concerned. Each Maori voter then has the option to register on the Maori roll for their region or on the general electoral list for the constituency in which they live. The Maori seats are contested by the major mainstream political parties as well as a Maori party. While many Maori voters opt for the general electoral rolls, thereby increasing their overall political influence, the four guaranteed seats assure that Maori from all parts of the country have a voice in Parliament through Maori representatives.

Another example closer to home is in the state of Maine where the Penobscot and Passamaquoddy tribes each elect a representative to sit in the state legislature. This system, first created in the nineteenth century (but allowed to lapse and reborn only recently), also guarantees that the perspectives of both tribes are heard on all issues. These representatives do not vote on bills before the Legislature, which was a decision taken by the tribes, but they possess all other rights as members including sitting on committees, speaking on any issue, and receiving the normal benefits of an elected legislator (e.g., salary, office, expenses, support staff). The Republican and Democratic parties both support this creative initiative, but neither is involved in the tribal elections.

The appeal of this alternative stems from its practicality as it is easily understood, already known, and possible to accomplish in the short term. It could be implemented readily through amendments to the relevant legislation that governs the structure of Parliament or provincial legislatures. This approach would, of course, be vulnerable to erosion or elimination in the future through simple legislative change. It would also have to be implemented with great care and subject to the restrictions present in sections 41 and 42 of the amending formula in the *Constitution Act, 1982* regarding the method of selecting Senators (section 42(1)(b)), the number of MPs (section 41 (b)) and the principle of provincial proportionate representation in the House of Commons (section 42 (1)(a)). A more enduring mechanism or fundamental restructuring would entail a constitutional amendment. The Royal Commission on Electoral Reform and Party Financing has received several submissions on this issue and may address the subject in its final report.[22]

ABORIGINAL PARLIAMENT

Several alternatives would involve creating new institutions of governance or reforming existing ones. One that appears especially desirable is an aboriginal parliament, perhaps designed along similar lines to the Saami Parliaments in Scandinavia. The Saami (or Lapps) are the indigenous people of what was formerly called Lapland (now Saamiland), which is divided among Sweden, Norway, Finland and the Soviet Union. Although the Saami have no autonomous territory, some of their aboriginal rights were protected in a document known as the Saami Codicil of 1751, which was an addendum to a treaty between Sweden and Denmark-Norway. It allowed for the free movement of Saami reindeer herders, recognized the customary law of the Saami, and acknowledged a "Saami Nation," with exclusive jurisdiction of Saami courts over Saami disputes.[23]

---

22 The Native Council of Canada, the Assembly of First Nations, the Grand Council of the Crees (Quebec), the Assembly of Manitoba Chiefs, the New Brunswick Aboriginal Peoples Council, the Metis Society of Saskatchewan, the Shuswap Nation Tribal Council, the Dakota Objibway Tribal Council and Senator Len Marchand, among others, have suggested such an approach to the Royal Commission on Electoral Reform and Party Financing. Earlier calls for guaranteed representation were made by Louis Riel in 1870 and by the Malecite Nation in 1946.

23 Tom G. Svensson, "The Attainment of Limited Self-Determination Among the Sami in Recent Years," paper presented to the Commission on Folk Law and Legal

The Saami Parliament in Norway, the Samething, is in large part the result of the Norwegian Saami Rights Committee, which was formed in 1980. The committee had 18 members, representing different interests and settlements, and was given the mandate by the Norwegian government of assessing the political, economic and cultural needs of the Saami. Among other measures, it recommended the creation of an elected body for the Saami. In 1987 the Norwegian assembly passed the *Saami Act*, which for the first time recognized the Saami as a distinct people entitled to special rights (language, culture and social life), and allowed for a Saami parliament. Each of 13 constituencies returns three members, elected directly by those on the Saami electoral register (i.e., those who identify as Saami and use Saami as their home language or have a parent or grandparent who does). The first election was held in 1989. The Act enables the Saami Parliament to bring matters before public authorities and private institutions, and encourages public bodies to consult the Saami Parliament on appropriate matters.

The Finnish Saami Parliament, officially called The Delegation for Saami Affairs, was established in the early 1970s. It has 20 members, 12 elected from four Saami constituencies, and two each from four Saami local councils. Although elected, it has no legislative function.[24]

In this model, aboriginal peoples in Canada would elect, to an aboriginal parliament, individuals to represent them in national decision-making, including participating in constitutional reform processes. The parliament would have no territorial base, but it would provide a method for enabling aboriginal peoples across Canada to participate in national decisions affecting them. Each aboriginal person in Canada would have one vote, which could be cast individually or, should a collective decision be desired, could be cast as a group. Alternatively, seats in the parliament could be allocated proportionately among Indian, Métis and Inuit peoples, with these peoples deciding among themselves as to how they will select their members and hold them accountable.

Either the single vote or proportional approach would require a roll or list of voters, and the enumeration of aboriginal Canadians. This would help to ensure that the process and the parliamentarians are representative, as well as provide some long-term, institutionalized, and higher profile processes for involving

---

Pluralism, Ottawa, August 1990. See also Peter Jull, "Politics, Development and Conservation in the International North" (Ottawa: Canadian Arctic Resources Committee, Policy Paper 2, March 1986).

24 Pekka Aikio, "Experiences Drawn from the Finnish Sami Parliament" in *Self-Determination and Indigenous Peoples: Sami Rights and Northern Perspectives* (Copenhagen: International Working Group on Indigenous Affairs, 1987).

aboriginal peoples in constitutional reform. However, since its decisions would be only advisory, governments would not be bound by its recommendations.

CONCLUSIONS AND RECOMMENDATIONS

We have attempted in this paper to canvass the full range of alternative methods for enhancing aboriginal participation in constitutional reform processes in as detailed a fashion as possible given the space and time constraints. None of these alternatives is meant to undermine or replace the necessity for explicit constitutional amendments on aboriginal matters, such as those designed to develop a third order of government in Canada. While all of these alternatives are theoretically possible, it is apparent that several are far more probable than others. The difficulty in offering prescriptions in this area is that the presence of political will and the personalities of key individuals play such decisive roles.

Currently Available Avenues

While litigation is not a preferred strategy that we would advocate, we antici-pate that major court cases will continue at an ever-increasing rate, at least over the next few years. This reflects a perception held by many aboriginal organi-zations and First Nations that the current decision-makers in Ottawa, and in many provincial capitals, are simply unwilling to implement fundamental, structural changes in the Crown-aboriginal relationship. This belief is also coupled with a more optimistic assessment of the Canadian judiciary in light of decisions taken recently by the appellate courts of Nova Scotia, Quebec and British Columbia as well as by the Supreme Court of Canada (although similar positive views are not shared by all, nor do they apply to the appellate courts in Ontario and the three prairie provinces).[25] Finally, many aboriginal commu-nities feel that they are facing immediate threats to their survival from major resource developments such that strategies involving lobbying, civil disobedi-ence and defensive lawsuits are inevitable.

Our analysis of the current dynamics also leads us to believe that declarations of sovereignty will not, in and of themselves, lead to greater aboriginal partic-ipation in constitutional reform. These declarations have already been pro-claimed (e.g., by the Haida Nation) and more can be anticipated. Their significance, at present, is the effect they have on public opinion (which is

---

25 This assessment reflects a number of recent decisions, such as *Sparrow, Saanichton Marina, Mullin, Sioui* and *Denny* cases which support aboriginal and treaty rights strongly; versus the *Bear Island, Agawa, Dumont, Eninew, Horse* and *Horseman* judgements which were negative at the court of appeal level in these latter four provinces.

largely negative) and on Canadian governments (who choose to ignore them). Nevertheless, they do attract media attention and consolidate support within the aboriginal population. Furthermore, in light of the incredible developments in Eastern Europe over the last two years — and the pace of change in Canadian politics (particularly given the rise of nationalism in Quebec, discussion of union in the Atlantic provinces, and massive public dissatisfaction with parliamentary democracy as currently practised) — one cannot too quickly discount the possible importance of declarations of sovereignty.

It cannot be assumed that a unilateral declaration of independence by Quebec would encompass aboriginal peoples and their lands, given the federal head of power through section 91(24) of the *Constitution Act, 1867*, "Indians, and Lands reserved for Indians," and the special, historic relationship of aboriginal peoples with the Crown. Moreover, aboriginal peoples in Quebec could declare internal sovereignty, and do so within either Canada or Quebec. They could initiate discussions with both Quebec and Canada to discern which would be most open to aboriginal self-determination. It is possible that aboriginal peoples in Quebec would choose to remain linked to the aboriginal peoples in the rest-of-Canada, and with their aboriginal rights now embedded in the Canadian constitution. Recent experiences in aboriginal-Quebec relations, such as the conflict at Oka and the debate over the James Bay II hydroelectric project, reinforce this likelihood. The possibility exists, therefore, that a unilateral declaration of sovereignty by Quebec could put it on a collision course with aboriginal peoples and environmental interests in that province. In addition, we expect that Canadian courts would rule, if asked, that aboriginal communities are internally sovereign and that this sovereignty is protected by section 35 of the constitution, while also subject to constitutional constraints.

There are three remaining alternatives within the existing process to achieve constitutional reform, namely: (a) a revival of the section 37-style First Ministers' Conference (FMC); (b) the regional amending formula; and (c) treaty-making. The first of these is completely dependent upon the presence of a high degree of political will among first ministers to be successful, which is not readily apparent among the current group of 11 men. Moreover, Quebec Premier Robert Bourassa has stated that his province would not participate in any more one-of-eleven FMCs. It is difficult to imagine that the prime minister would convene a FMC on aboriginal constitutional matters, which can be done politically at any time even though sections 37 and 37.1 have expired, unless it is part of a package that accommodates Quebec's aspirations. It is perhaps easier to envision such a FMC being held to consider an amendment passed by a supportive province like Ontario or Manitoba. Section 35.1 would be triggered, thereby requiring the prime minister to call a FMC to debate the resolution.

The more promising scenario in the short term, for political reasons, is the option of section 43 (*Constitution Act, 1982*). Any province can initiate an appropriate amendment, presumably in conjunction with aboriginal peoples, that would change the Canadian constitution as it applies within that province. We already have a great deal of diversity stemming from the terms on which different parts of the country achieved provincehood, and therefore this suggestion should not be viewed with alarm. The federal government's consent is necessary for this approach to work, however, and such approval may be hard to obtain. Nevertheless, the events of the past summer render all standard political calculations unreliable. This avenue does permit speedy progress to occur with willing provinces. Such examples would provide a demonstration role and help to reduce concerns held in other quarters. In addition, federal reluctance over Quebec's possible reaction to such an approach may dissipate if section 43 were to be used in the near future to entrench some of Quebec's constitutional proposals.

The final option — the treaty process — is both highly workable and flexible so as to be the most attractive of the existing approaches. It is also the most desirable from an aboriginal perspective for several reasons. Not only is this approach the only one in which aboriginal agreement is mandatory, but it is also entirely in keeping with our history. One must remember that the first one hundred years of Indian treaties, as well as many later ones, had nothing to do with land surrenders but instead focused on political and economic relations. This approach meets the aboriginal objective of seeking to rebuild the nation-to-nation relationship while allowing the maximum opportunity to accommodate tribal or local variations. Although treaties have generally involved the federal or Imperial Crown in bilateral agreements with First Nations, the Inuit, Métis and Ontario governments have all had some treaty relations. The *Sparrow* decision of the Supreme Court increases the possibility for provincial-aboriginal treaties on suitable subjects.

New Institutions of National Decision-Making

The alternatives in this category address not only constitutional reform, but the prospect of rebuilding Canada's relationship with aboriginal peoples. They could provide a permanent and ongoing role for aboriginal peoples in institutions of national decision-making, and across all policy sectors. Alternatives requiring institutional change naturally demand both political will and concrete action before the new institutions would be created that could in turn consider further reforms. This tends to diminish their likelihood in the very short term, although this does not undermine their legitimacy, innate desirability, ease of implementation or long-term prospects. It should also be realized that practical gains can be achieved to effect many of these changes through political commitments or legislation without having to obtain constitutional amendments as preconditions.

This collection of options can be further subdivided in practical terms between those directed towards aboriginal peoples alone (i.e., guaranteed representation and an aboriginal parliament) and those affecting all Canadians in which aboriginal people would want distinct involvement (i.e., a constituent assembly or constitutional convention, referenda and Senate reform). The latter three are driven by nonaboriginal imperatives. Each can be implemented immediately, albeit at a limited level. The prime minister can seek federal legislation authorizing referenda that would not have a binding effect on Parliamentary consideration of constitutional initiatives, somewhat akin to a massive opinion poll. A constituent assembly could also be elected pursuant to federal statute to debate and draft constitutional resolutions for possible action by Parliament. Likewise the House of Commons could appoint a constitutional convention from among its midst, possibly supplemented by nonmembers of Parliament, similar to past practice with special committees (e.g., the Penner Committee on Indian Self-Government in 1982-83, or as in the case of the Bélanger-Campeau Commission in Quebec). The provinces could also develop parallel initiatives.

Another device would be for the prime minister to announce a personal commitment to exercise his power to appoint Senators in the future based upon clearly enunciated criteria of representiveness (e.g., encompassing linguistic, ethnic, racial and aboriginal factors) or popular will through special elections (as in Alberta). All of these approaches would be subject to termination in the future by a new government unless entrenched through a constitutional amendment.

There are, as well, potential linkages among these options. Guaranteed representation for aboriginal people in legislatures and Parliament could obviously interconnect with revisions to the method of selecting Senators. An aboriginal parliament might be the ideal body to choose the aboriginal members of the Parliament of Canada or any general constituent assembly or constitutional convention. A new national aboriginal institution like a parliament elected by all Indian, Inuit and Métis peoples, although with carefully crafted electoral boundaries to ensure that all regions and each of the three distinct groups are included, should naturally have some interface with the existing Parliament. It would, in our view, be preferable to reduce the possibility of strongly competing views between the aboriginal parliament and those occupying the guaranteed seats in the House of Commons and Senate, as this could drastically undermine the legitimacy of the new institution arising from fights over who truly represents the aboriginal perspective. Empowering the aboriginal parliament to elect the representatives to the Parliament of Canada would not eliminate all disagreements, as occasional differences of views are both human and healthy. It would serve, however, to minimize conflict while enhancing the influence and representativeness of the aboriginal parliament.

It is our opinion that the aboriginal parliament should have an important role in setting the national agenda on aboriginal issues. It would not be another lobby group, or even a replacement for existing aboriginal organizations, as they would continue to have valuable functions to exercise in representing the interests of their own constituents to the federal and provincial governments and the public at large. In addition, national aboriginal organizations would continue to represent the interests of their distinct constituencies at any future First Ministers' Conferences on the constitution.

We believe that the Scandinavian experience provides useful guidance as to both pitfalls to avoid and benefits to be gained from an aboriginal parliament. It needs three basic powers. First, it requires the capacity to develop initiatives and draft legislation on its own for referral to Parliament for mandatory debate and voting. While the Canadian Parliament would not be bound to adopt the proposals of its aboriginal counterpart, it should at least be compelled to consider these proposals seriously.

A second power would entail the authority to receive references from Parliament for investigation. A third power would be to review all federal legislation that expressly affects aboriginal people or their lands before passage. The former would enable the Parliament of Canada to benefit from the detailed assessment by aboriginal representatives of major policy or legislative matters in a formal way before the possible new initiatives are very advanced. This could be analogous to the occasional use made of law reform commissions. The power to review bills, perhaps with an appropriate time frame in which it would occur, would not tie Parliament's hands to any particular outcome. It would, however, ensure that a careful clause-by-clause analysis of legislation from an aboriginal perspective had been conducted before the House of Commons made its final decision on a new law.

Neither of these functions would eliminate the role of the current Senate and Commons Standing Committees on Aboriginal Affairs, as they provide opportunities for Parliamentarians to supervise the general operation of federal programs for aboriginal peoples and to consider new legislation in light of the evidence presented by witnesses. Instead, this proposal is designed to augment the importance and influence of aboriginal people in national decision-making in a manner that benefits all Canadians. It is intended to supplement the constitutional amendments on substantive rights rather than substitute for them.

Recommendations

In conclusion, our recommendation is that immediate constitutional reform concerning aboriginal issues be considered both warranted and critically necessary. It is vital in its own right but it could also play a crucial role in improving the likelihood that Quebec's legitimate aspirations can be realized.

The preferable manner of obtaining substantive changes is through the treaty process at the national and regional levels, resulting in agreements that obtain constitutional protection pursuant to section 35(1) of the *Constitution Act, 1982*. A second highly viable choice is to utilize the bilateral federal-provincial amending formula provided by section 43 in those areas of the country in which agreement is possible on such issues as aboriginal language rights, cultural protection and the inherent right to self-determination. These approaches lead us to substantive amendments and the protection of aboriginal rights. Alone, however, they fail to address the more fundamental requirement of restructuring relations between aboriginal peoples and Canadians.

For this reason, we believe that structural changes are also necessary to our existing decision-making institutions so that aboriginal people have a permanent voice in processes of national decision-making, including all laws and programs brought before Parliament. This can best be achieved, in our view, by guaranteeing a minimum number of seats in provincial legislatures, the Senate and the House of Commons for representatives of the aboriginal peoples of Canada. This should further be supplemented by the establishment of a national aboriginal parliament, which would elect from among its members the guaranteed MPs and Senators. Linking these two initiatives, guaranteed representation and an aboriginal parliament, would ensure that the aboriginal peoples of Canada fully participate in our national governing institutions.

The general agenda for constitutional revision including the accommodation of Quebec cannot be advanced without at the same time addressing the constitutional aspirations of aboriginal peoples. In this paper, we have identified methods for enabling substantive changes to the constitution regarding aboriginal issues that should be pursued immediately. However, it is our view that aboriginal peoples require a permanent and ongoing role in national decision-making, and that this can only be achieved through structural reform of our governing institutions. Utilizing both strategies would go a long way to renewing the relationship between aboriginal peoples and the Canadian state.

V

Models for Future Structures

11

European Integration:
Are There Lessons for Canada?

Dan Soberman

The origins and evolution of the European Community must be examined before we can make any useful comparisons with our current dilemmas about the future of Canada.

A BRIEF HISTORY OF THE COMMUNITY

The beginnings of the Community can be traced to the early 1950s, when western Europe was in the midst of reconstruction after World War II. With help from North America, Europeans made rapid progress, especially in West Germany. An important question, gnawing at the soul of Europe, was how to prevent a recurrence of the increasingly terrible wars of 1870, of 1914 and of 1939. That question translated into how to make war between France and Germany impossible.

The coal and steel industries were viewed as the heart of the war machine in the first half of the twentieth century; if production of these two commodities in France and West Germany could be integrated within a single market, controlled by a supranational body, another war between the arch rivals would become impossible. In 1951, this idea found its expression in the Treaty of Paris, by which France, Italy, West Germany and the three Benelux countries (Belgium, The Netherlands and Luxembourg) formed the European Coal and Steel Community (ECSC). The Treaty created a number of central institutions including a court, but it was the "High Authority" that wielded supranational powers to supervise the coal and steel market. The ECSC became the model that set the mould for future integration.

Professor Charles Pentland acted as consultant to the author and provided invaluable advice and suggestions.

In the postwar era, the United States of America was viewed by the mainstream of European political thought as the ideal political and economic state — a democracy with the most powerful economy in the world, able not only to win the War but also to finance the reconstruction of Western Europe. It had unquestionably become the leading nation in the West. If the early progress of the ECSC was any indication of the benefits to be gained by emulating the United States, then its member states should be able to make dramatic gains in economic strength and political stability by accelerating the movement towards federalism. The six members of the ECSC retained a continuing concern to make war within Western Europe impossible and also aspired to become the third superpower; they concluded that the natural next step was to integrate their defence forces. They moved remarkably quickly: in May 1952, they signed the Treaty of the European Defence Community (EDC), and within a few months negotiated the Treaty of the European Political Community with a democratically elected "federal or confederal structure."

Unhappily for the strong European federalists, it soon became evident that the new moves towards integration had come much more quickly than many Europeans were prepared to accept; in particular, most French political parties feared direct surrender of so much political sovereignty to a new, untried central parliament — and they worried about West German domination. In August 1954, the French National Assembly refused to ratify the EDC Treaty and with it the movement towards a political community also died.

However, the ECSC had begun the process of economic integration, and thus had created new incentives for further removal of barriers. In a modern industrial economy different forms of energy had become interchangeable — coal with petroleum, natural gas or nuclear power. So too, had different materials — steel with other metals and plastics. As a result, the effectiveness of the ECSC's regulation of its own part of the market was limited. Moreover, a growing belief in the importance of a larger European market pressed the six towards integration. Less than a year after the failure of the EDC, the member states met again to discuss a more comprehensive form of economic integration, without the elements of defence or of more openly federal central institutions.

Paradoxically, the proposal for a "merely" economic community accommodated the opposing views both of those leaders concerned to protect member-state sovereignty and of European federalists. The sovereignty supporters believed that the major benefits of economic integration could be gained with little, if any, surrender of political power to central institutions, especially if a veto were retained by national governments; at the same time the federalists believed in a form of "economic determinism" — political power would ultimately have to follow economic power in order to maintain democratic control over central bureaucracies, even if it took decades for this to happen — and they were prepared to wait. In March 1957, the six member states signed the Treaty of Rome, establishing the European Economic Community (EEC), and also the Treaty creating the European Atomic Energy Community (Euratom). All six ratified the treaties within a few months and it came into force on 1 January 1958.

The EEC Treaty was a pioneering effort, taking into account modern economic theories of integration.[1] First, like the ECSC, it created a number of permanent supranational institutions, to be described briefly in the next section.

Second, it contained a long-term plan for economic integration in three stages, charting the stages over a decade and a half.[2] Thus it was an action plan that set out objectives rather than simply establishing areas of jurisdiction for EEC institutions. An important consequence has been that, rather than remaining static, the legal powers and jurisdiction of the Community have expanded to meet its growing role, first at each of the three stages, and subsequently, as integration progressed.

Third, the Treaty went far beyond the modest, traditional arrangement of creating a free trade area, and well beyond even the next stage of integration, a customs union in which the member states share a common outer "wall" of mutually agreed standard tariffs and quotas: it required the progressive elimination not only of all internal tariffs and quotas but also of "all other measures of equivalent effect." It thus recognized, and set out to deal with, other more sophisticated tools used by governments and business enterprises to restrict competition from foreign goods and services.

Most important, the goal of the Treaty was not limited to ensuring the free movement of goods and services behind a common tariff wall. Its purpose was also to permit free movement of the major "factors of production," that is, of workers (including qualified tradespeople and professionals) and of capital, and to permit all businesses from one member state to establish themselves in any

---

1 Three major contributors to the literature on "trade diversion" and "trade expansion," that influenced ideas on free trade areas and customs unions, were J. Viner (1950), J.E. Meade (1953, 1955) and R.G. Lipsey (1957). For a full discussion of this development, see John Pinder, "Positive Integration and Negative Integration: Some Problems of Economic Union in the EEC," and Nils Lundgren, "Customs Unions of Industrialized Western European Countries," in M. Hodges (ed.), *European Integration* (Harmondsworth: Penguin Books, 1972), pp. 124-183.

2 The Treaty set out detailed requirements that the Community and its member states undertook to implement in three four-year stages, with flexibility to increase each stage by one year. The main matters that had to be dealt with in an overlapping scheme (some required to be completed ahead of others) were: free movement of goods (including creation of common external customs barriers), common agriculture policy, free movement of persons, services and capital, common policies on transport, competition rules, and tax provisions, "approximation" of laws affecting the common market and a common social policy.

or all of the others. This stage of integration has become known as a "common market."

COMMUNITY INSTITUTIONS

Before discussing the further stages of economic integration of the Community it will be helpful to outline the Community's main institutions.

The European Parliament. Originally called the "Assembly," from 1958 until 1979, it consisted of "delegates who shall be designated by the respective Parliaments from among their members..." Its role was largely advisory, although it had some small budgetary responsibilities. And, of course, sitting in the assembly was clearly a secondary job: members had first to be elected to their own legislatures which commanded their main allegiance and effort. Since 1979, its members are directly elected and its powers have expanded moderately, particularly with respect to the Community budget. As we shall see, further increases in its powers may depend on further economic integration in the Community.

The Council. Consists of 12 members — a cabinet minister from each member state — who attend according to the main subject to be discussed and decided. It might be, for example, ministers of transport, agriculture or finance. When the Council meets with the heads of state sitting it is called the "European Council." The Council is an unusual body in that it has legislative power, although normally it acts only in response to proposals made by the "Commission," described below. It also works to coordinate member- state economic policies, and to resolve disputes among the member states.

The Commission. Its has 17 members, at least one from each member state, but not more than two from any state. It duties are "to ensure the proper functioning and development of the common market." It is the watchdog that makes sure the Treaty and all subsequent legislation is complied with. It formulates proposals to achieve the objectives of the Treaty and it devises detailed rules to implement legislation approved by the Council. Its members are expected to be completely independent, and "they shall neither seek nor take instructions" from their home governments. Their independence is similar to that of judges. The Commission is a unique body, unlike that in any federal or unitary state.

The Court of Justice. The Court has 13 judges, "appointed by common accord" of the member states, but in fact one judge ordinarily comes from each state. The Court hears cases to review the conduct of Community institutions and to ensure that the Treaty is observed by member states. Although the Treaty does not give the Court direct powers over the laws of member states, the Court itself took the initiative, especially in the first two decades of the Community's life, to establish firmly a set of principles similar to those found in federations like the United States and Canada. These principles stipulated that: where the Treaty gives powers to Community institutions, their decisions prevail over conflicting laws of member states; where there is a dispute between courts of member states and the Court of Justice as to whether a particular matter falls within the powers of the Community, the member state courts must accept the decision of the Court of Justice; and, that member states must accept interpretation of Community laws by the Court of Justice so that those laws will be uniform within each member state. It is generally agreed that the Court of Justice has been the most centralist of the institutions and has been essential to the economic integration of the Community.

"NEGATIVE" AND "POSITIVE" INTEGRATION

Some European commentators have noted that the early stages of the process were mainly "negative" integration — the *removal* of tariffs, quotas and thinly disguised barriers, such as rigid health and safety regulations that deliberately conflict with the regulations of neighbours. As those measures progressed, the EC became increasingly concerned with integrating the factors of production, especially the free movement of workers, and gradually concentrated more on aspects of "positive" integration — the *creation* of more complex central schemes to create community-wide standards for eligibility for health care, schooling, pensions, common qualifications for trades and professions, etc. This process required larger central bureaucracies to arrange meetings among experts from EC member states, and to write ever more complex sets of regulations.

Inevitably, the result has been to affect directly the daily lives of EC citizens, although generally speaking, they are not aware of the consequences of Community actions; virtually all restraints and benefits are conferred directly by national governments. As a leading writer on the Community said in 1980, "the EC bites deeply into national policy processes. It sets constraints on national freedom of manoeuvre... the autonomy of national governments is circumscribed by their obligations to each other and by a shared commitment to preserve the common ground that has been established."[3]

---

3   Helen Wallace, "National Politics and Supranational Integration," in D. Cameron (ed.), *Regionalism and Supranationalism* (Montreal: Institute for Research on Public Policy, 1981), p. 113.

CREATING A SINGLE EUROPEAN MARKET

The Community has gone through cycles of pessimism and inactivity — almost to the point of stagnation — in the mid-1960s, in much of the 1970s, and again in the early 1980s.[4] Each of these low points was precipitated by quite different political and economic events, but in the period immediately after each low point major advances in integration occurred. It can be persuasively argued that the most significant advances occurred following the pessimism of the early 1980s, when the member states agreed on two major steps in integration:(a) the creation in February 1986, of a *Single European Act*[5] to amend and consolidate the separate treaties covering coal and steel, atomic energy and general economic arrangements; and (b) the move to a "Europe without frontiers" — a truly single integrated economic market by 31 December 1992 — as proposed in the White Paper of the Commission of the EC, "Completing the Internal Market," in June 1985.[6]

The Single European Act

A major crisis occurred in the Community in 1965, when the veto given to each member state during the transitional period of the first eight years was about to expire; the French government of Charles de Gaulle rejected the prospect of being bound by decisions of a qualified majority vote in the Council, as set out in the Treaty of Rome; it insisted that France retain a veto. The French representative refused to attend meetings of the Council — it was the time of the "empty chair." The crisis was resolved by an informal convention, reached in Luxembourg in January 1966, agreeing that any member state would have a veto over new measures if the dissenter declared the matter to be of vital interest to it.

The *Single European Act* of 1986 made it clear that a qualified majority system would prevail over the conventional veto in most of the further stages of integration.[7] That position has now been accepted by all member states.

---

4 In 1967, the three communities — the ECSC, the EEC and Euratom — merged their executive bodies, the Council and the Commission. The merged organization became known simply as the "European Communities" (EC), or as the "Community."

5 Official Journal 1987 L 169/1.

6 White Paper from the Commission to the European Council, Luxembourg, June 1985, COM (85) 310 final.

7 The qualified majority system assigns weighted voting to each member state roughly according to its population. The four largest states (France, Germany, Italy and the United Kingdom) each have ten votes. The remaining eight members range from eight votes (Spain) to two votes (Luxembourg), for a total of 76 votes. Matters are divided into three categories: the strictest requirement is for proposals relating to

The European Community Without Borders, 1992

The complex, detailed and numerous provisions (some 300) agreed on in the 1985 White Paper, set out a plan to remove:

- physical barriers at frontiers and thus eliminate entirely, or make negligible, virtually all remaining physical checks at border points for goods moving between member states;
- technical barriers to the movement of goods, services and capital — in particular, by making it easier for "labour and the professions" to move from one member state and establish themselves in another, and by freeing the movement of capital through "the decompartmentalization of financial markets";
- fiscal barriers, especially through the approximation of value-added and excise taxes, making the movement of capital much freer.

It was the intention of the White Paper that as result of these measures, member states would at most retain a very limited ability to regulate their own capital markets, using only temporary safeguard measures. An immediate consequence of these goals for 1992 was to make the largest remaining barrier to integration loom even larger — the existence of separate currencies and exchange regulations. Even limited control over money supply and exchange rates can have significant effects, distorting a member state's internal market by impeding the ability to pay for imported goods and services. Thus the natural next step was to propose the creation of a central European bank and a common currency among all 13 member states, that is, "monetary union."[8]

IMPLICATIONS OF A MONETARY UNION FOR THE AUTONOMY OF MEMBER STATES

A member state's control over money supply, exchange rates and interest rates — constrained as it may already be among interdependent economies — would virtually disappear in a monetary union.[9] Not surprisingly, a vigorous

---

certain specified matters to be adopted by 54 votes and at least eight members in favour; other matters require 54 votes without a stated minimum number of members; all other proposals require only a simple majority of members in favour, unweighted. Official Journal, 1987 L 169/1, Article 8 B.

8   "...it is hard to imagine a Community with full capital mobility being able to live with the very incomplete degree of monetary integration that we have today." T. Padoa-Schioppa, "Questions About Creating a European Capital Market," in Roland Bieber, Renaud Dehousse, John Pinder and Joseph H.H. Weiler (eds.), *1992: One European Market?* (Baden-Baden: Nomos Verlagsgesellschaft, 1988), p. 285. Mr. Padoa-Schioppa is Deputy Director-General of the Bank of Italy.

debate was soon underway about the effects of this loss of monetary control on the fiscal autonomy of member states. The anti-federalists argued that the implications for a state's policies regarding taxation and the funding of its social priorities would be substantial — there would be a severe diminution in a state's ability to make its own decisions, especially when they run counter to the dominant priorities of the Community.[10]

The fear is sometimes expressed in terms of a serious erosion of national values and identity. Those who oppose monetary union call the loss in member-state autonomy a "transfer of sovereignty" to EC institutions. Prime Minister Margaret Thatcher had no doubts about the loss of sovereignty for the U.K. Parliament; she expressed her opposition to monetary union in uncompromising terms, and her stand became one of the factors in her downfall. There were two elements to Thatcher's opposition. On the one hand, she opposed a transfer of power to the "Eurocrats" in Brussels, a democratically unaccountable bureaucracy that can impose its priorities on democratically elected national legislatures. On the other hand, she was perhaps even more adamantly against a transfer of power to a democratically reformed Community institution, whether it be the European Parliament or the Council, because the transfer would then have more legitimacy.

Even strong supporters of monetary union acknowledge that member states will be subjected to a severe "fiscal discipline" and will not be able to ignore economic realities.[11] However, they argue that the discipline resulting from member states losing control over monetary policy — and thus over some basic tools to protect local industries — will lead to healthy competition and better allocation of resources. It is also asserted that the EC has become accustomed to a collaborative approach towards resolving problems, and that the best way to ensure mutually acceptable solutions to monetary problems is to create a

---

9   "Even apart from political difficulties, it is hard to see how a transnational unified common marketplace could be created and remain viable without adequate monetary and fiscal powers. Thus,... the achievement of the single market will necessitate far greater attention to the formation of common economic policies and major changes in the decisional processes of the Community." Bieber, Dehousse, Pinder & Weiler, "Introduction, Back to the Future: Policy, Strategy and Tactics of the White Paper on the Creation of a Single European Market" in *1992: One European Market?* p. 14.

10 There has been some discussion among Europeans about the ability of individual states or provinces in federations to implement divergent fiscal priorities but, I would suggest, much more is needed. (See, *The Economist*, 15 December 1990, pp. 14-15 and 69).

11 However, complete uniformity is not required: "As for the harmonisation of [Value Added Tax or "VAT"] rates, the White Paper points out that all Member States' general rates of value-added tax are within the range of 14-19 percent, apart from Denmark, the Irish Republic and Luxembourg, which is less than the difference among Canadian provinces or US states," *1992: One European Market?*, p. 27, n. 8.

central bank structure that continues and encourages this approach. The Community may well have to adapt its institutions to reassure those members states that feel insecure about too great an initial transfer of their own powers. It may take time to build their confidence in central decision-making that will be sensitive to their needs.

However, assuming monetary policy issues can be resolved satisfactorily and a more highly integrated market with a common currency results in a substantial increase in Community productivity, to the benefit of its citizens as a whole, there will be a price to be paid. Fritz Franzmeyer has observed that:

> There may certainly be net losers at [the] regional level, and even at [the] national level primary net advantages might be very unevenly distributed. Empirical studies for the regional level show, for example, that the peripheral zones will be handicapped by economic integration in structural terms. ...in a free exchange of goods and services the more central regions develop into gravitation centres of economic activity... [This activity] improves the chances of employment and, in the wake of a higher wage level, leads to a net migration of workers. In this way the outlying regions often lose the very people who are the most mobile and dynamic.[12]

and:

> The market integration process will result in a reallocation of unemployment...where entire countries are affected by the reallocation the EC as a collective community is also challenged.[13]

The Community is left, then, with the problem of compensating some member states, for it cannot justify overall gains that leave those states as long-term net losers. Franzmeyer notes that:

> Since the most important decisions regarding integration policy are taken as a consensus of the governments of the Member States, it is important that there should not be a net gain only at [the] Community level, but that each individual Member State can regard its overall result as positive, at least after the "redistribution round."[14]

He further observes that current compensatory arrangements through the Regional Fund will be inadequate to provide compensation after more complete integration is achieved in 1992, and that new sources of income, revenue generated by the Community itself, will be required.[15]

---

12 Fritz Franzmeyer, "Economic, Social and Political Costs of Completing the Internal Market," *1992: One European Market?* p. 59.

13 Ibid., at p. 70.

14 Ibid.

15 We should note that the differences in per capita income between the richest and poorest regions in Canada are much smaller (about 1.6 to 1) than in the European

At this point, the early thesis of the federalist, economic determinists of 1957 seems to be borne out by the development of the 1980s. In summary:

- The Treaty of Rome's purpose, to create an integrated market for goods and services, necessarily advanced — as contemplated by the Treaty — to deal with the free movement of labour and ultimately of capital.

- The original mechanisms proved inadequate to accomplish the task; recognition of this state of affairs led to intensive reinterpretation of the problem and the additions of the White Paper and the *Single European Act* of the mid-1980s.

- The anticipated success of the new initiatives has confronted the Community with the need for monetary union.

- If the creation of a single market along with monetary union should take place, two further challenges arise —
  1) member states will have surrendered much of their autonomy in fiscal policies, that is, decisions about taxation and internal social priorities;
  2) at the same time, some members may well have become long-term net losers, when compared with the average gains, and will be unable to create their own policies and programs to counter the negative effects.

It is the last point, that leads to the greatest challenge for the EC. A final quotation from Franzmeyer puts the issues clearly:

As the internal market is completed [including monetary union]... more and more legal and decision-making powers will pass over to the Community level. By and large these functions will be exercised by the Council or Commission, which brings us to a basic "question of cost": the question of loss of democracy as a result of integration. Neither institution is directly elected or appointed by the directly-elected European Parliament. In the long run this is bound to lead to a legal crisis out of all proportion with the increase in efficiency and welfare. This would mean a real "loss" through integration for all concerned and can only be avoided if

---

Community (between 4.4 to 1, and 6.0 to 1). See "Income Distribution by Size in Canada," 1979 Catalogue 13-207. (Ottawa: Statistics Canada, May 1981), p. 94; D. MacDougall et al., "1 Report of the Study Group on the Role of Public Finance in European Integration" (Brussels/Luxembourg, EC Commission, Office for Official Publications, of the EC, 1977), p. 27, (the MacDougall Report). While this data is not up-to-date, there is no recent evidence to make one believe that there have been substantial changes in the comparisons.

It is generally accepted that two factors are mainly responsible for the narrower gap in Canada: labour mobility from poorer to wealthier regions, and the much larger redistribution of income through federal programs (over 15 percent of Canada's gross domestic product (GDP), compared to 1 percent of GDP in the Community).

Parliament, given the federal structure of the Community, is fully involved in legislation and financial control.[16]

Franzmeyer thus asserts that a democratically accountable legislature, sensitive to regional needs, must have it own resources — taxation power — to raise funds and redistribute them through taxation to loser regions. And he emphasizes that it is crucial for legitimacy to have such a democratic process.

GENERALIZING FROM THE EUROPEAN EXPERIENCE: IS THERE A NATURAL SEQUENCE IN ECONOMIC INTEGRATION?

It is my thesis, based on studying the European experience, that monetary union is at the apex of economic integration, the keystone needed to hold it together, and at the same time such complete integration will create the drive for central democratic institutions with substantial revenue raising capabilities. While the European federalists of the 1950s probably did not foresee the details of this evolutionary process, with hindsight we can see how it has come about. An interesting element in the process has been the "spill-over" effect: as economic interest groups — industries, farmers, trade unions and others — gradually recognized the growth of decision-making power in Community institutions they organized themselves to lobby for their favoured policies and regulations. This development has reinforced EC powers and increased member state interest in influencing Community decisions. Many other ongoing informal arrangements have supplemented and encouraged the growth of formal Community powers.

Does the EC present the only viable model for integration among a group of modern industrialized states? Need monetary union be the ultimate stage or could it occur at a much earlier stage in integration, or indeed, merely be a minimalist arrangement, with shared decision-making only about monetary policies? I know of no examples where this minimalist approach alone has been used. It is true that the colonies of the French and British empires often shared a common currency with the imperial power but it was not the colonies that made decisions about monetary policy. And there were preferential trade arrangements among members of the empire, so that common currency arrangements did not subsist alone. Thus, a common currency has existed along with relatively low levels of economic integration where one party was clearly dominant. Of course, when the dominance of the imperial power ceased as a result of decolonization, most of these arrangements also came to an end.

---

16 *1992: One European Market?* p. 72.

In any event, we may ask, what is the point of a monetary union without any other significant elements of economic integration?[17] Each member state would pursue its own priorities and macroeconomic policies, inevitably resulting in continual conflict about monetary policies. There would be no gain to any of the parties. But if in addition to monetary union, the parties agree to other significant elements of economic integration, I would submit that, based on the dynamics of the EC, strong pressures towards further integration would apply.

THE DANGERS IN A TWO-PARTY ASSOCIATION

There are two twentieth century examples of monetary unions between two parties, those of Ireland and Britain, and of Belgium and Luxembourg. In both cases one party was many times larger than the other both in population and in wealth, and that party made its own decisions about monetary issues, much as did an imperial power for its colonies. The smaller party had no expectation of substantial influence in those decisions and adhered to the arrangement because it was advantageous: the smaller state believed that it needed the stability of the much larger currency area.

Bipolar monetary unions with each party having an equal say, that is, each having a veto, are rare — if indeed there are any at all — because they are inherently unstable. The risks of impasse and frustration leading to paralysis mean they are unlikely to last. Moreover, the inducements to enter into such an arrangement in the first place must be negligible: the larger and wealthier member state would ordinarily have little incentive to give the smaller partner a veto, thus limiting its own autonomy for no net gain; conversely, for the smaller partner there would be little incentive to agree to be a supplicant that ultimately had no role other than to adhere to the decisions of the dominant member. The scenario is rather stark — either a veto and the unpalatable risks of impasse, or one party being a mere supplicant with the danger of regularly being the loser in any disagreement. The United Province of Canada (East and West) 1841-1867, is an example, where these difficulties became a major factor leading to federation among several British North American colonies.[18]

---

17 I am here disregarding the negative reason why members states that terminate an economic union may wish to retain monetary union: fear of the adverse economic consequences of a monetary separation. If my observations about the pointlessness of retaining only a common currency are correct, then informed investors will see through its artificial retention as creating only a false security.

18 The *British North America Act* granted the federal government broad powers of taxation, with the capacity to redistribute wealth so raised from the centres of economic gravity, to the regions that obtained the least benefit from economic integration. There is, of course, a continuing debate about the system, on the one hand in terms of the representativeness of our institutions and their decision-making

By contrast, in a multiparty union, alliances among member states shift according to the interests they perceive will be affected by decisions of the central institutions. A member state will sometimes be on the winning side and at others on the losing. But so long as it anticipates that it will more often win than lose (because in many decisions there will be a consensus, with no losers), it will feel better off to be part of the union than not to be.[19]

THE APPLICATION OF THESE OBSERVATIONS TO THE CANADIAN SITUATION

Two-Party Sovereignty-Association

The suggestion has been made that an independent Quebec might seek as a minimum to maintain only a common currency and central bank with the rest-of-Canada. My observations about the instability of bipolar arrangements would apply to such an association. It seems highly improbable that after the rest-of-Canada had bid an independent Quebec farewell, it would immediately grant a new smaller state a veto over its own economic decisions. Conversely, Quebec would be highly unlikely in one breath to declare its independence and in the next breath to agree to become a mere supplicant in major economic matters. With only two parties this stark scenario cannot be avoided.

Indeed, in any expanded two-party arrangement between Quebec and the rest-of-Canada — a common market that comprised a free trade area, customs union, integrated transportation policy and free movement of the factors of production — granting to an independent Quebec full equality in the form of a veto in all these areas would be even more unlikely; the higher the level of economic integration that the parties contemplate, the more unpalatable such a bipolar arrangement becomes.[20] In my view, such arrangements are viable *only* in a multiparty union.

---

ability, and on the other hand, in terms of the substance, the fairness and wisdom, of the redistribution.

19 While Germany is the dominant economic power in the EC, its dominance is not total; in population and wealth the combination of France, Italy and Britain is greater than that of Germany. The situation is not dissimilar to that of Ontario in Canada. For a further discussion of this subject, see D.A. Soberman, "The Parti Québécois and Sovereignty/Association," The Law Society of Upper Canada, *The Constitution and the Future of Canada.* (Toronto: Richard DeBoo, 1978), p. 65 at pp. 79-81.

20 A counter to this assertion is to cite the Canada-U.S. Free Trade Agreement. In my view, the jury is still out regarding both its merits and its stability. See D.A. Soberman, "Free Movement of Goods in Canada and the United States," *Cahiers de Droit,* vol. 29, 1988, p. 291, at pp. 319-22. The dynamics of the Free Trade Agreement might be altered dramatically if Mexico were to joint in a tripartite pact.

The Substance of a New Economic Association

A reconstituted union, whether it be the current ten members of the Canadian federation or fewer regional groupings, must confront the same political-economic issues as the European Community has been facing:

- which member state or states, if any, should have a veto over which matters falling within the central jurisdiction of the union?

- regarding other matters within the central jurisdiction, what proportional vote should each member state have, and what majority beyond a simple majority should be required for which matters?

- which matters generally, in modern industrial states should be left for member-state decisions? (Europeans have rediscovered the question of the distribution of powers between central institutions and member states under the label of "subsidiarity.")[21]

As in Europe, these issues need to be reexamined in the context of modern industrialized economies and — in Canada's case — with an already highly integrated economy in areas such as financial institutions and transportation among others.

We have noted that Canada has a central government with broad powers of taxation and a system to redistribute a substantial portion of its national revenue to governments and individual citizens in poorer regions of the country. In terms of the European model of integration, these attributes of Canada's federal government appear to be the EC's next stage for the enhanced role of central institutions of the Community in completing the single market. However, as a number of studies have pointed out, Canada's success in implementing the *earlier* stages of market integration is mixed.[22] In many instances, we have not

---

21 The term "subsidiarity" dates from late nineteenth century Catholic philosophy which asserted "that decisions should be taken as far down a hierarchical power structure as possible, as close to those affected as possible. It is therefore closely related to the concepts of participation and democracy." (See, Clifford Longley, "Popes against Eurocrats," *The London Times*, 17 November 1990.) In the Canadian context, the principle of subsidiarity could be used to examine whether matters currently under federal jurisdiction could not be better managed by the provinces with little or no loss of efficiency.

22 See, M.J. Trebilcock, G. Kaiser and J.R.S. Pritchard, "Restrictions of the Interprovincial Mobility of Resources: Goods, Capital and Labour," *Intergovernmental Relations* (Toronto: Ontario Economic Council, 1977), p. 101; Minister of Justice, *Securing the Canadian Economic Union in the Constitution* (Ottawa: Minister of Supply and Services Canada, 1980); F.R. Flatters and R.G. Lipsey, *Common Ground for the Canadian Common Market* (Montreal: Institute for Research on Public Policy, 1983); R.E. Haack, D.R. Hughes and R.G. Shapiro. *The Splintered Market* (Toronto: James Lorimer & Co., 1981).

progressed as far in 123 years, as the Community has in 33 years. Accordingly, there are likely to be a number of areas where a renewed Canadian union should further integrate its markets and factors of production.

On the other hand, there are also likely to be a number of areas where uniformity and/or central control and regulation are unnecessary or can be limited to protecting certain national interests. Indeed, by citing the European principle of subsidiarity, it may be argued that central control is harmful simply because it interferes in matters better left to decisions that can reflect local priorities. Thus, in the field of communications, technical standards and negotiating international arrangements about use of channels, etc., would best be left to federal authority. In addition, a certain number of country-wide channels for television and radio could be reserved for country-wide networks (say a half dozen) and would be federally regulated; provinces choosing to regulate and/or sponsor all remaining channels would have the power to do so.

Also, some areas now unnecessarily divided between federal and provincial jurisdiction could be allocated to the provinces. For example, the whole area of family law, including marriage and divorce as well as family support, custody of children and division of assets, should be provincial.

CONCLUSION

A monetary union between an independent Quebec as one member state and the rest-of-Canada as the other is not feasible for two reasons. First, there does not appear to be any point to such an arrangement when the two parties are pursuing their own fiscal priorities and macroeconomic policies. Second, in a bipolar arrangement either there must be equality and a veto in policy-making for each party, or one party must accept to be merely a supplicant and adherent — and both alternatives are unworkable.

The stark bipolar alternatives also make more substantial economic integration unworkable, leaving a multiparty arrangement as the only feasible approach. If negotiating parties were to start with a clean slate, but keeping in mind the lessons learned both from the European Community experience and from our own history, I believe they would draft a radically different constitution from our present model, both as regards division of powers (of which I have given but brief examples in the preceding section) and also the design of central institutions. While the European Community institutions are not likely to be models we would directly adopt, they do illustrate the ingenuity that can be used to create institutions suited to their tasks.

Our hope for the future lies in renegotiating the terms of Confederation, approached with a generosity of spirit and a willingness to understand the needs and aspirations of our disparate regions, and especially of Quebec. Radical changes may well be necessary, but an accommodation is much more likely to be reached within a federal framework than in a two-party negotiation.

12

Other Federal and Nonfederal Countries: Lessons for Canada

Alain-G. Gagnon

INTRODUCTION

There is a growing consensus that neither the status quo nor the complete separation of Quebec are optimal trajectories for contemporary Canadian federalism. While this much is agreed upon by the principal actors engaged in the current debate, there is little agreement concerning the future institutions or relationships that need to be developed if Canada is to remain a dynamic and competitive country in a changing global environment. The following discussion examines some of the current trends affecting Western Europe and the Third World in order to understand what models might have application in the Canadian context. This is accomplished by discussing some of the options that have informed efforts to transform Canadian federalism, followed by three comparisons: Third World multicommunal federal states (India and Malaysia), unitary states in Europe currently undergoing a federalizing process (Belgium and Spain), and the traditional Western European federal states (Germany and Switzerland). In the second part of the paper the issues of territory, economic relations and collective goals will be assessed in the context of the Canadian and comparative settings.

The first difficulty that must be dispelled is the formal or legal bias of many traditional typologies, especially those based on the distribution of constitutional power. Based on formal constitutional arrangements there were in the 1970s eighteen federal states: Argentina, Australia, Austria, Brazil, Canada, Czechoslovakia, the Federal Republic of Germany, India, Malaysia, Mexico, Pakistan, Switzerland, Tanzania, the United Arab Emirates, the United States,

The research assistance of Scott Evans (Ph.D. candidate, Carleton University) is gladly acknowledged. This paper has been enriched by many of his intellectual insights.

the Union of Soviet Socialist Republics, Venezuela, and Yugoslavia.[1] Few of
these models suggest new options for Canada. While federal in the formal sense,
many of the Third and Second World states are either highly centralized in a
practical sense (e.g., India, Pakistan, Malaysia and Mexico) or involve a
political context that is difficult to apply in Canada (e.g., USSR, Czechoslovakia, Argentina, and Brazil). In the context of this study it was decided to limit
the comparisons to countries that approximate the political tradition of Canada,
but also involve the politics of a multicommunal society.

The conventional wisdom frequently fails to account for the "practical" politics
inherent in both the community and regional conflicts in states that are not
formally federal, or the absence of viable instruments for mediating such
conflicts in federal states that are highly centralized. Such a perspective excludes devolution and decentralizing models currently being developed in
unitary states such as Belgium, Spain, and France. The institutional approach
facilitates an understanding of divergent constitutional developments in federal
states when the focus is on formal institutions (i.e., parliament, courts, constitution) rather than political practice (i.e., negotiations). Without a careful
balance between the informal politics of regions, groups, and communities and
legal-formal politics, it is difficult to evaluate what different federal and
"nonfederal" arrangements have to offer our current understanding of the
Canadian situation.

The sociological approach to federalism, pioneered by scholars such as W.S.
Livingston, suggests the importance of understanding the cleavages existing
within society. However, the necessity of examining possible options for
Canada requires a careful focus on the process whereby compromises and deals
are "worked out" between the dominant groups and the institutional nature of
these arrangements. This demands a combination of the sociological and
institutional approaches which permits a method of rejecting federal models
with little to recommend concerning linguistic cleavages (e.g., the United States
and Australia) and, instead invites a closer examination of features from
nonfederal systems that are currently in the process of resolving intercommunity conflicts (e.g., Belgium and Spain). This also applies to federal states that
either lack the same cleavage types as Canada but have commendable institutional arrangements (e.g., Germany) or multicommunal federal countries such
as Switzerland which have developed political conventions and practices, as
well as institutions that have mitigated regional and cultural conflict.

The following discussion will move between two levels of analysis: *institutional* and *sociological*. At the institutional level the analysis focuses on
arrangements that structure community or regional relations either within

---

1   Henc van Maarseveen and Ger van der Tang, *Written Constitutions: A Computerized
    Comparative Study* (Dobbs Ferry, NY: Oceana, 1978), p. 54.

central institutions (e.g., the U.S. Senate or the German Bundesrat) or between orders of government (e.g., the interlocking fiscal and policy arrangements in Swiss and German federalism). Similarly a combination of these developments are beginning to take place in nonfederal states such as the multitiered Belgian state and the "autonomies" of Spain. The sociological level examines the issue of homogenization or diversity suggestive of varying federal practices and the reaction of groups and communities who feel threatened or who see greater potential in alternative arrangements that give broader expression to community or regional interests.

A BALANCED APPROACH: INTERSTATE-INTRASTATE STRATEGIES

The process of negotiating or the renegotiation of relationships between communities or governments suggests that federalism may be conceived as a strategy for establishing viable and changing institutions capable of facilitating intercommunity or interstate cooperation. This orientation views federalism as politics not law, but accepts the necessity of finding appropriate formal institutions that will legitimize and ensure an adequately functional federal existence. Nevertheless, where institutional practices are called into question or renegotiated, the options are likely to be either "interstate" (e.g., division of powers between orders of government) or "intrastate" relations (e.g., provincial representation at a national level). In other words, new arrangements in a federal state are limited to two broad categories: (a) the distribution of authority such that provinces or regions preserve their distinctiveness; and (b) mechanisms whereby the interests of regional or provincial governments, or people living in these areas, are channelled through and protected by institutions forming part of the central government.[2]

An emphasis on process does not preclude the institutional component, but rather views institutions as following from politics. The genesis of institutions results from the conventions and compromises derived from the conflicts and power struggles of societal and political actors. The following comparisons underscore both the problems and solutions associated with the process of institutional reforms. First, in the Canadian case, we will examine briefly suggestions for restructuring federalism proposed in the late 1970s and in the early 1980s. This is followed by a discussion of comparisons that attempts to contrast Third-World federal options, federalizing options in nonfederal Western European states, and the examples of relevant European federal states.

---

2   Donald V. Smiley and Ronald L. Watts, *Intrastate Federalism and the Development of Canadian Federalism* (Toronto: University of Toronto Press, 1985), p. 4.

Canada

In the Canadian case, temporary compromises (subject to future renegotiations) have in the past been reached between Ottawa and Quebec. This has been possible, in large measure, because of the political weight of the francophone community. However, francophone leaders anticipate a future shift in the balance of power resulting from changing demographic patterns, the politicization of new sectors of Canadian society such as native and immigrant groups, and the impact of increasing integration in a continental economy. A decline in the position of the francophone community endangers the contemporary gains accrued by Quebec. This has forced Quebec's provincial leaders to seek entrenched guarantees that cannot be removed or renegotiated at a later date when the francophone community is in a more vulnerable position.

In periods of flux or conflict between state actors, the list of viable options and historical alternatives influences both the terms of the debate as well as the positions of the various actors participating in the negotiations. For most of the last 30 years, Ottawa has controlled the political agenda by refusing to consider a substantive redivision of powers. Ottawa's lack of sensitivity to Quebec's claims culminated in 1981 in the patriation of the constitution along with an entrenched Charter of Rights and Freedoms that would apply indiscriminately to all provinces. This became known as the renewed federalism or the status quo option of the Trudeau Liberals, as the governing party refused to consider the entrenchment of a distinct status for Quebec.

The amendments negotiated in 1980-81 were not as wide-ranging as those originally proposed by the Trudeau government in the 1978-81 period. The proposed modifications included intrastate changes that would have enhanced provincial representation at the federal level. The transformation would also have involved replacing the Senate with a House of the Federation with half its proposed 118 members selected by provincial assemblies and the other half selected by the House of Commons. This would have been accompanied by an entrenched Supreme Court with more firm representation for Quebec. The House of the Federation could have imposed a 60-day suspensive veto for language legislation following which the support of two-thirds of the House of Commons could nullify the veto.[3] This renewed federalism option constituted

---

3   Douglas Verney, *Three Civilizations, Two Cultures, One State: Canada's Political Traditions* (Durham: Duke University Press, 1986), p. 367. The 1978 proposals were blocked in 1979 by the Supreme Court that ruled in a reference decision that the Parliament was not competent to transform itself in a manner that may affect the provinces. It was argued by the court that despite the power of amendment in section 91(1), the House of the Federation, in replacing the Senate, was affecting an institution that was of interest to the provinces. According to Douglas Verney, the Supreme Court based part of its decision on a 1965 federal White Paper recognizing

an admission that better representation was necessary if Canada was to respond to the sovereignty movement in Quebec following the election of the Parti Québécois in 1976. The solution proposed by Ottawa was aimed at providing the provinces with representation at the federal level.

Alternatives to the proposals by the Trudeau Liberals were provided in the recommendations for new institutions proposed in the Pepin-Robarts Task Force, the Claude Ryan Beige Paper, and the Parti Québécois's White Paper on a new agreement between Quebec and Canada. The 1979 report of the Pepin-Robarts Task Force on Canadian Unity was based on three principles: (a) the existence of different regions, (b) predominance of two cultures, and (c) two equal orders of government. The principal thrust of the proposed changes was the institutionalization of asymmetrical federalism, involving the formal recognition that all provinces are not the same. While avoiding a *de jure* special status for Quebec, the particular relationship of Quebec to the rest-of-Canada would be recognized *de facto* in special arrangements that would be offered to all the provinces but in which Quebec would probably become the only participant (e.g., the earlier Quebec Pension Plan in 1964). This approach was extended to language where it was recognized that each province had the right to determine provincial language policy. Major institutional innovations included proposals for transforming the Senate, a partial introduction of proportional representation, an expanded Supreme Court, and modifications to certain federal powers. The Council of the Federation (80 members) would replace the Senate with an assembly entirely composed of delegates nominated by the provinces. Seats would be added to the House of Commons based on proportional representation in order to redress the imbalances of the political parties. Expanding and dividing the Supreme Court into specialized "benches" attempted to address various deficiencies in the ability of the courts to rule in various jurisdictions. It was proposed that the powers of the federal government to reserve and disallow would be abolished; and concurrency would be required for federal declaratory, spending, and emergency powers. In an effort to reconcile western alienation and Quebec nationalism, the Pepin-Robarts Report attempted to address the issue of provincial autonomy, provincial control over language policy, an upper house responsive to provincial interests, and recognition of Quebec's special position in Canada.[4]

In 1980 the Quebec Liberal Party proposed a decentralist alternative where more powers would be allocated to the provinces, a recognition of two sovereign jurisdictions, and more direct provincial influence on federal activities

---

a "provincial role in amendments to the BNA Act beyond those matters exclusively assigned to the provinces." Ibid., p. 367.

4   Ibid., p. 373.

through a provincially appointed intergovernmental body called the Federal Council (in contrast to the Pepin-Robarts' upper house proposal). This was an effort to meet the legitimate aspirations of Quebec in the context of a Canadian federalism where the equality of the two founding peoples would be affirmed, and popular approval of change would take place in the context of an explicit agreement between the communities comprising Canada.[5] Institutional changes involved the abolition of the Monarchy and the Senate, proportional representation in the House of Commons, and a provincially appointed council capable of curbing federal powers. The Federal Council (an intergovernmental body) would link the provinces, and having its own source of funds, would be free from federal manipulation. Its role would include the approval of federal appointments, ratification of treaties affecting provinces, a veto on federal emergency and spending powers, and advising in matters of fiscal, monetary, and transportation policy. In legislation regarding language it would operate on a double majority principle, with similar mechanisms for cultural issues. Finally, the Federal Council would be responsible for federal-provincial relations, thereby, the authors of the Report hoped, rendering federal-provincial conferences obsolete.

The sovereignty-association proposal of the Parti Québécois in the late 1970s argued for the formation of a community where nine provinces would form Canada and the tenth (Quebec) would exist as a separate state. Quebec would have political sovereignty but would not be totally free in its economic decisions. Economic association included a "common market with free mobility for goods, people, and capital ..." and a monetary union.[6] Community organizations would involve a Council of Ministers, Commission of Experts (secretariat), Court of Justice (Canada and Quebec equally represented), and a Central Monetary Authority (with Canada being paramount). There would be a negotiated settlement regarding Labrador, the country's assets, the St. Lawrence Seaway, membership in NATO and NORAD, and allowances for minority rights.

Some of the most recent attempts to elaborate new federal arrangements, while less developed than the previous models, are suggestive of the wide array of ideas currently in circulation. This ranges from Ontario Premier Bob Rae's vague notion of a government of regions to Robert Bourassa's "Confederal Superstructure," and of late what he terms his "new structure" (the Allaire Committee Report). As we enter into a new phase, there is no doubt that the current Spicer Citizens' Forum and Bélanger-Campeau Commission will be

---

5   Ibid., p. 378.
6   Ibid., p. 374.

influencing the agenda surrounding the renegotiation of the Canadian federal union. They will no doubt take into consideration the issue of duality that has been so fundamental to past debates emerging from previous soul-searching, such as the Tremblay and the Laurendeau-Dunton Commissions.

It is important to turn our attention to a comparative perspective that will infuse the current debate with the added experience of other countries who likewise, have undergone, or are in the process of renegotiating a union of competing governments and communities.

India and Malaysia

Federalism in both India and Malaysia is more centralized than that which currently exists in Canada. The development of Indian federalism involved a transition from a colonial "imposed unity" into one that is a "unity of free choice."[7] However, this unity was never accompanied by significant mechanisms whereby regions or communities could find effective political expression and challenge centralizing tendencies. This is evident in the way in which the central government has been willing to utilize its constitutional entitlements: residual powers, the ability to intrude in areas of state jurisdiction under given circumstances, central paramountcy in concurrent fields, and the power to alter unilaterally territorial boundaries and appoint state governors.[8] It has been argued that these centralizing powers are necessary to curb civil unrest in dissident communities such as the Punjab and West Bengal and to undertake the enormous task of economic development. The centre-dominated hegemony of the Congress party helped foster opposition governments in the states and promoted the emergence of centre-state conflict and the coalescing of regional blocs such as the "rimland states" (Assam, Bengal, Jammu and Kashmir, Tamilnadu and Kerala). These developments suggest a weak bargaining position for the states, which is underscored by the historical tendency of the central government to use its constitutional powers to coerce "erring" states (e.g., the use of Article 356, the "failure of constitutional machinery," 64 times in 30 years).[9]

In India, the juxtapositioning of multiethnic and religious cleavages and the local or provincial focus of much economic activity has created limited

---

7 Ramesh D. Dikshit, *The Political Geography of Federalism* (New Delhi: Macmillan, 1975), p. 123.

8 S.A.H. Haqqi, "Towards Praetorian Federalism in India: A Processual Study," in C. Lloyd Brown-John (ed.), *Centralizing and Decentralizing Trends in Federal States*, (Lanham, MD: University Press of America, 1988), p. 283.

9 Ibid., p. 290.

incentives for regional cooperation. The abortive formation of "Zonal Councils" in the late 1950s was an attempt to challenge separatist forces and foster regional cooperation through a middle tier of government that grouped state representatives on a regional basis. However, while R. D. Dikshit suggests that the failure of the Zonal Councils may have been due to a lack of leadership, it could also be argued that the centralized practice of Indian federalism gave limited scope for the expression of regional interests and few mechanisms for resolving conflict in a conciliatory manner.[10] This suggests that fundamental problems cannot be resolved by minor institutional tinkering.

The centralized orientation of the Malaysian federalism is evident in its upper house where the central government nominates the majority of seats and where the division of powers effectively constrains the states to areas of religion, land tenure and local government (while giving the states residual powers). Even in these latter matters the central government has extensive powers to "procure uniformity of law and policy."[11] Moreover, the Malaysian states have few independent sources of revenue and are not even allowed to borrow money without prior consent from the central government or its central bank.

Another complication in Malaysia is ethnic composition. While the Malay community predominates at the federal level, the Chinese have on occasion challenged the dominant status of Malay political leaders in a number of states. Nevertheless, the centralizing nature of Malaysian federalism has meant that historically the Chinese community has never been able to assert effectively its interests within the federal order. Ethnic tension is exacerbated by the historical tendency of the federal government to utilize its superior taxing and spending powers to interfere effectively in state politics and support profederal coalitions.[12] The continued ability of the Malays to dominate Malaysian politics was a major concern at the time of the initial acceptance of Singapore into the federation. This necessitated the incorporation of the Borneo states with their majority Malay populations to offset Singapore's majority Chinese population. Singapore was expelled from the federation in 1965 amid mounting tension and the threat that its Chinese political base would offset the political dominance of Malaysians at the federal level by mobilizing the ethnic Chinese in other states.[13]

---

10 Dikshit, *The Political Geography of Federalism*, p.127.
11 Ibid., p. 133.
12 Gordon P. Means, "Federalism in Malaya and Malaysia," in Roman Serbyn (ed.), *Fédéralisme et Nations* (Montréal: Presses de l'Université du Québec, 1971), p. 235.
13 Ursula K. Hicks, *Federalism: Failure and Success* (New York: Oxford University Press, 1978), p. 72. For a list of the different configurations of state and concurrent powers accorded to Singapore and the Borneo states (Sabah and Sarawak) see Means, "Federalism in Malaya and Malaysia," p. 230.

Spain and Belgium

Nonfederal states that are in the process of federalizing, such as Belgium and Spain, provide some insights for Canada. In the case of Spain there has been a steady development of constitutionally entrenched regional autonomy since the mid-1970s. In Belgium multiple levels of government have been formed and gradually empowered since the 1980s, corresponding to the dominant linguistic communities and their territorial bases. For Belgium the development has been steadily incremental in nature compared to the major constitutional revisions witnessed in Spain. The Spanish case is instructive for Canada because of the willingness of main actors involved in the formulation of the 1977-78 Constitution (i.e., party and community leaders) to begin anew. Moreover, in addition to rewriting the Constitution, there was a willingness to build a consensus politics that necessitated a constitutional document "rich in ambiguities."

Despite this positive ambiguity, it should be noted that the division of powers places important restrictions on the bargaining position of the Autonomous Communities. While some concessions have been made in "intrastate" mechanisms for minority or regional representation in the Spanish Senate (25 percent of Senate seats are appointed by the Autonomous Communities), the regions or communities do not have the power to extend themselves beyond their legislated mandate. This means that the norms governing the enabling statutes for each community originate in the central government and are approved by the Spanish Parliament. From the legal perspective the Autonomous Communities are at a disadvantage, but this has not stalled developments brought on through political action and negotiation between political forces.

The basis of the Spanish transformation is exemplified in the phrase, "On s'engage et puis on voit."[14] In such a context sufficient room for politics and process are imbedded within the legal matrix of the country's guiding document, the 1977-78 Constitution. The Canadian constitutional deadlock following the failure of the Meech Lake Accord and the developments currently taking place in Quebec suggest the need for a similar approach, one that stresses political viability over formal legalism. Such an approach also limits the role of the courts by placing the onus for defining relationships and the acceptable degree of ambiguity with those participating in the political process. Such ambiguity may also nurture and encourage differences instead of drowning them.

Belgium's development has been incremental with the developments ranging from language legislation in the 1960s to constitutional revisions restructuring

---

14 Audrey Brassloff, "Spain: the state of the autonomies," in Murray Forsyth (ed.), *Federalism and Nationalism* (London: Leicester University Press, 1989), p. 39. For a good outline of Spain's constitution and transformation, see pp. 30-38.

government in the 1970s and 1980s. In the early 1960s laws governing the use of languages in administrative matters were instituted. This created unilingualism in designated regions and involved a number of important changes: abolition of the language census permitting changes in the language statute in communes; the creation of definitive language boundaries and their congruence with those of the provinces; and finally, the required implementation of bilingualism in the communal administration of Greater Brussels and linguistic parity among officials in the national administration.[15] This has resulted in stricter language measures than those currently found in Quebec, which is due to the sense that without the proper balance between linguistic groups or the maintenance of strict guidelines for official language within specified territories, the integrity or health of their respective communities will fail. For some groups such a failure implies economic hardship as well as a cultural loss.

In the 1970s constitutional revisions established fixed territorial boundaries for cultural communities and language regions and areas. Changes in the central institutions, such as the Belgian Parliament (the Chamber of Representatives and the Senate), resulted in the formation of cultural councils that were the vehicles whereby the two dominant linguistic groups would be able to promote cultural autonomy. Members of Parliament were organized into French and Dutch language groups (cultural councils) upon which power was conferred through the constitution (or through laws passed under the constitution). The cultural councils were given the authority to determine legislative measures for their respective linguistic communities on matters of cultural affairs and cooperation, most areas of education, and certain aspects of language use.

The constitutional determination of fixed territorial boundaries for cultural and linguistic groups provided an important precedent which eventually opened the way for a more significant devolution of powers and mechanisms for the promotion and maintenance of different communities at the cultural and economic level. This instituted a mechanism for simultaneous cultural autonomy and socio-economic regionalization.[16] The multiple orders of administrative responsibility correspond to cultural communities (regulated via cultural councils) for the language areas (Dutch, bilingual Brussels, French, and German), and separate regional orders of government and administration for the economic regions (Flanders, Wallonia, and Brussels). The constitutional revision of the

---

15 Robert Senelle, "Constitutional Reform in Belgium: from unitarism towards federalism," in Forsyth (ed.), *Federalism and Nationalism*, p. 57.

16 Frank Delmartino, "Decentralization of Belgium: Federalism, Reform or Decentralization Operation," in C. Lloyd Brown-John (ed.), *Centralizing and Decentralizing Trends in Federal States*, p. 240

1970s modified some features of the Belgium state by assigning authority to cultural councils and regional orders of government.[17]

The lesson for Canada regarding Belgium's experience with federalizing its government arises from the role of political parties in the amending process which requires a formal declaration of the proposed amendments, the dissolution of both legislative houses, and the election of a new parliament with constituent powers (i.e., constituent assembly). The requirement for passing amendments necessitates the attendance of at least two-thirds of the members of each house and a two-thirds majority vote. This means that parties and coalitions play an important role in constitutional transformation within the framework of a constituent assembly.[18]

The 1980 constituent assembly, formed to revise the constitution, began phase one and two by transforming "cultural communities" to "communities" and expanding their areas of jurisdiction beyond cultural matters to those described as "personalized matters" such as medical care, social services, and education (although actual powers in this latter area remain limited due to the "delicate equilibrium" negotiated between the private and public school systems). Subsequently, a mechanism for resolving jurisdictional disputes was established (the Court of Arbitration) to augment and replace the mediating role of the Council of States, and a system was designed to provide financial resources for the new administrative and policy tasks of the Flemish and French communities and the Brussels region. Exceptions to this development are the German community which was excluded from institutional reform until 1983 because of its limited size, and the Brussels region that has yet to receive an entrenched constitutional position similar to its regional counterparts. It continues to be governed by provisional community and regional institutions established under the 1979 "coordinated law."

The final phase of the transition began in 1987 and has involved efforts to give clear recognition of the regions in the constitution, clarifying the division of powers between the central government and regional and community

---

17 With the cultural groups still lacking what they considered sufficient institutions and fields of jurisdiction, Belgium once again embarked on a course of constitutional revision in the early 1980s. This resulted in a three-phase development that called for: (a) the creation of special executives of the communities and regions; (b) the provisional, but irreversible, assignment of legislative jurisdiction to the communities and regions; and (c) the definitive reform of the state involving the government and Parliament (Senelle, "Constitutional Reform in Belgium," pp. 60-61. In many respects this formalized and legitimized the particular practices already taking place and provided a mechanism for democratic accountability (Delmartino, "Decenetralization of Belgium," p. 242).

18 Kenneth McRae, *Conflict and Compromise in Multilingual Societies: Belgium* (Waterloo: Wilfrid Laurier University Press, 1986), pp. 160-161.

authorities. This involves the elaboration of the exclusive powers of the central government and residual and concurrent powers. In addition to these developments, the effort to transform the Senate into an institution representing communities and regions has created a mechanism whereby linguistic and regional territories can have their interests represented within a central institution without diminishing their own responsibilities.[19]

Switzerland and Germany

In Switzerland, the notion of minority status is rejected in favour of a formal equality of national languages and language groups. This is accompanied by a recognition of resource disparities between groups and the concomitant need for compensatory measures that are either representational (e.g., participation in multiparty executives) or financial in nature.[20] The institutional component of this development takes root in a decentralized system where the concentration of language groups by cantons and administrative districts effectively removes the politics of language and culture from the federal sphere.[21]

The underlying constitutional principles are territorial in nature. First, there is cantonal sovereignty in linguistic matters, except where limited by the constitution, but including residual powers and the right to enforce cantonal rules against anyone residing in or passing through the territory. Second, cantons or linguistic areas have the right to preserve and defend their respective linguistic community against any internal or external force, with the implied obligation of the federation to aid in this endeavour (e.g., the case of public signs and federal funding for cultural programs in Ticino). Third, there is the obligation of citizens to adjust to the linguistic milieu of the canton.[22] The territorial orientation is facilitated in the less homogeneous bilingual cantons

---

19 The functional and territorial nature of the new Belgium orders of government have created a complicated network of institutions with separate decision-making processes and regulatory functions. The regional institutions have jurisdiction over 12 enumerated powers: territorial development, environment, rural redevelopment and nature conservation, housing, water, economy, energy, subordinate authorities, employment, applied research, international cooperation, and territorial application of decisions by regional authorities. See Senelle, "Constitutional Reform in Belgium" p. 71. Community institutions have control over cultural matters that promote or defend the dominance of the appropriate language, its use in administration and educational institutions, and the language of social relations between employers and employees and their respective method of communication with the state.

20 Kenneth D. McRae, *Conflict and Compromise in Multilingual Societies: Switzerland* (Waterloo: Wilfrid Laurier University Press, 1983), p. 105.

21 Ibid., p. 107.

22 Ibid., p. 122.

by directing linguistic and cultural issues to smaller homogeneous units such as regional and local government.

The Swiss political and constitutional tradition denotes a series of "checks and balances" that not only protect diversity but provide mechanisms for resolving conflicting interests of cantons and the federation. This can be found in the collegiality of the Federal Council, the federal Council of States, the use of the referendum, limited reliance on simple majority decisions, as well as a concerted effort to include parties and interest groups in the decision-making process. However, because of the demands for coordination and the detailed division of powers between the federal and cantonal governments, constitutional changes are frequently required in order to change policy.[23] This is exceedingly difficult where constitutional changes affect the cantonal powers. The amending process involves a referendum where ratification requires a double majority: an absolute majority of total votes and a majority of cantons.

The development of the modern Swiss state has required an increasing interdependence of the cantons and the federal government. The constitutional division of powers has remained intact with the Swiss federal government playing an increasing role in regulation while the cantonal governments refuse to relinquish any power. This has required cooperation with cantonal governments and has led to the development of an "elaborate system of federal-cantonal committees," which have no formal power but provide a crucial forum for intergovernmental consultation.[24]

The German's version of the committee system differs from that employed by the Swiss in that the institutionalization of the federal-state bargaining process has a longer formal history (e.g., the legal power of the joint committee on regional economic expansion) and is more extensive because of the respective legislative and administrative roles of the various orders of government. According to Lehner, there are approximately two hundred different committees in the German system that participated in the "planning, decision-making and implementation of joint programs, and in the coordination of investment activities."[25]

In the case of West German federalism, one has an example of a unilingual country that offers an important method of organizing territorial relationships regardless of the absence of dominating cultural or linguistic cleavages. The West German division of powers and the "intrastate" politics promoted by the Bundesrat suggest mechanisms whereby territorial concerns can be protected

---

23 Franz Lehner, "The Political Economy of Interlocked Federalism: A Comparative View of Germany and Switzerland," in C. Lloyd Brown-John (ed.), *Centralizing and Decentralizing Trends in Federal States*, p. 211
24 Ibid.
25 Ibid., pp. 208-209.

and channelled into the principal policy process. This balances the centralizing tendencies often associated with federal countries where there are few cultural or linguistic cleavages (e.g., the more homogeneous societies of Australia and the United States.)

In Germany, the administrative character of the division of powers and "intrastate" territorial representation of the Länder in the Bundesrat suggests an institutional solution to "interstate" conflict often associated with executive federalism.[26] The distinction between legislative powers and administrative powers creates interlocking federal arrangements that facilitate cooperation between different orders of government. It is estimated that in Germany sixty percent of the federal government's legislation is constitutionally assigned to the Länder to be administered.[27] This arrangement not only maintains territorial distinction but produces a climate for cooperation rather than the conflict often associated in states where the division of powers is legislative (e.g., Canada, Australia, India, and the United States).

It should be noted that the Länder have never been considered simply administrative units in post-World War II Germany. The declaration in the Basic Law (the German constitution) that the Federal Republic of Germany is a federal state is interpreted to mean an arrangement where governments of the Länder are considered "equal members of the Bund [federation] which voluntarily surrender certain powers to the Bund in their common interest."[28] Similar to the Swiss cantons, the Länder have residual powers. However, unlike Switzerland, the German federal government has considerably greater scope in its sphere of exclusive jurisdiction, and this is combined with federal paramountcy in the list of concurrent fields. Federal legislative prerogative is tempered, nevertheless, by its limited power to administer legislation. This responsibility is generally assigned in the Basic Law to the Länder which in turn is overseen by the Bundesrat, the "intrastate" mechanism that provides an important vehicle for representation of the Länder within the institutions of the national government.

The Bundesrat is an essential institution ensuring the protection and promotion of territorial interests within the federation. It is composed of members of Länd governments who vote in state blocs and who as individual members have the right to attend or speak at all committee and full sessions of the Bundestag (the lower house). Bundestag deputies do not enjoy a similar right. In addition, the Bundesrat has an absolute veto in all legislative matters affecting interests

---

26 See Ronald L. Watts, *Executive Federalism: A Comparative Analysis* (Kingston: Institute of Intergovernmental Relations, Queen's University, 1990).

27 Ibid.

28 David Childs and Jeffrey Johnson, *West Germany: Politics and Society* (New York: St. Martin's Press, 1981), p. 40.

of the Länder. These interests are determined by the constitutional enumeration of legislative fields requiring the consent of the Bundesrat (e.g., amendments to the Basic Law, laws affecting state finances, and legislation affecting the administrative sovereignty of the Länder.) In legislative fields not requiring Bundesrat approval, an objection bill can be tabled. This requires that the Bundestag subjects the piece of legislation in question to another reading. Overriding the Bundesrat objection requires a majority of comparable magnitude in the Bundestag as that which passed the objection bill.

The institutional effectiveness of the Bundesrat in protecting the regional interests of the Länder can be contrasted with the limited success of institutional tinkering in other relatively homogeneous federal states. The experience of the Australian Triple E Senate suggests that centralist "intrastate" reforms have little efficacy in moderating the conflictual dimensions of the territorial or regionally defined interests within a country.[29] This, however, may be due in large measure to the symmetrical structuring of Australian federalism (e.g., the constitutional prohibition against policies that do not apply equally to all states and their equal representation in the Senate), the congruent composition of the parliament through direct election to both houses, and a tradition of judicial review favouring federal laws over those of the state.[30] Despite the symmetrical nature of the Australian Senate, and the legitimacy of its directly elected representatives, Senators have shown no more inclination to act as the conduits of regional interests than their counterparts in the House of Representatives.

THE POLITICS OF DIVERSITY

Following from the survey of comparative experience in other federal and transitional systems, three principal issues can be identified that relate to the Canadian situation: *territory, economic relations*, and *collective goals*. The comparative analysis provides a series of lessons that help in formulating or understanding the possible terms of a renegotiated Canadian federation. At the outset it is necessary to identify a number of interrelated factors affecting the debate over Canadian federalism. The primary factor involves the historic conflict between French Canadian interests mostly articulated by the Quebec government, and English Canadian interests represented by the federal government during the Trudeau period and, occasionally, the other provinces. At a more general level, this constitutes a prevailing tension between the proponents of homogenization and those who wish to promote or safeguard Canadian diversity. While this certainly entails issues of territory and economic union,

---

29 Ibid., p. 454.
30 Cf. Christopher D. Gilbert, *Australia and Canadian Federalism 1867-1984* (Carlton: Melbourne University Press, 1986), p. 152.

since 1982 the tension has been complicated by the demands of what Cairns describes as a Charter culture.[31] This culture utilizes the discourse of diversity, but demands in practice a policy of national uniformity. Its concept of diversity differs from that espoused by Quebec nationalists in that it underscores the rights of individuals or groups on a nonterritorial basis, and fails to account for the collective goals of the Québécois.

While Quebec nationalists are not opposed per se to the individual rights articulated in the Charter, they view the Charter of Rights and its court-driven federal orientation as fragmenting the French-speaking Quebec community. This, they argue, would limit the ability of collectivities to maintain a protective infrastructure that would be systematically eroded by the centrifugal demands for equal status or national uniformity by all groups within Canadian society. Such an endeavour risks levelling all cultural activity or collective autonomy to that of the individual, which in turn erodes ethnolinguistic infrastructures and encourages assimilation into the dominant cultural or linguistic group (e.g., English-speaking Canada). However, given the historical prominence of Quebec in Canadian politics, few French-speaking Québécois would be willing to have their current status diminished in any form.

While the cultural factor remains important, particularly with respect to Quebec, the current discourse of many political actors suggests that the economic question has become paramount. As Parizeau notes, the negotiation of a new union would be based on the primacy of economic issues.[32] This complicates and simplifies the issue. It complicates it in the sense that it adds another dimension, but simplifies it also as it invites the formation of new economic solidarities as we are entering a changing global economic system. Groups and communities are not only formed around a cultural affinity, but their economic interests are equally integral to collective survival and collective goals.

Formal constitutional studies often fail to understand the politics of change, and in particular the political and economic challenges confronted by groups who question institutions that they feel do not provide the greatest possible benefits. The federalizing process in multicommunal countries often continues even under circumstances where constitutions constrain the negotiation of new relationships. In the case of Switzerland, Belgium, and Spain, cultural groups within each of these states have challenged what can be construed as homogenizing institutions. This is not to argue that the concerns of these groups or the resources they drew upon were not connected to economic concerns and

---

31 Alan Cairns and Cynthia Williams, "Constitutionalism, Citizenship and Society in Canada: An Overview," in Alan Cairns and Cynthia Williams (eds.), *Constitutionalism, Citizenship and Society in Canada*, (Toronto: University of Toronto Press, 1985), p. 34.

32 *Le Devoir*, 3 December 1990.

interests. Rather, defined in linguistic and territorial terms, these groups frequently precipitated popular reactions and constitutional negotiations resulting in new intercommunity arrangements affecting political and economic issues.

In Switzerland, the relatively recent case of Jura and its bid for cantonal status involved a complicated process of multiple referenda and federal mediation between the Jura provisional government and the Bern cantonal government. This represented an important development whereby the separatist designs of French-speaking Jurassians eventually precipitated a constitutionally based process that permitted a legitimate break with the German-speaking Bernese, and the subsequent negotiation of a French-speaking canton with complete cantonal powers.

The economic demands of Wallonia and the cultural concerns of Flanders in Belgium also created a situation where new institutions are being formed and intercommunity relations negotiated. The attempt to experiment with new mechanisms promoting territorially defined cultural autonomy and economic decentralization ensures that the federalizing process in Belgium will not stand still. This has been moderated, however, by the unitary structure of the Belgian state and the extent to which the Senate has blocked efforts to have itself replaced by another governmental order capable of producing legislation. The federalizing trend has also been delayed by disagreement over the types of institutional arrangements that will govern the bilingual Brussels region.

The development of autonomous communities in Spain is another example underscoring the process of negotiation demanded by groups objecting to the homogenizing tendencies of a centralist state. In what has been described as the peripheral challenge, the historic nationalities in Catalonia and Basque provinces and in Galicia pushed for a new method of power sharing, resulting in the entrenchment of Autonomous Communities in the 1977-78 constitution.[33] Recently, the central government has attempted to erode the special status of the historic communities that developed out of their negotiated agreement in the late 1970s.

While the highest court in Spain has upheld the exclusive powers accorded the autonomous communities and ruled that the harmonization process instituted by the central government was unconstitutional, both the Catalans and Basque feel that the effort of the central state to provide similar status for other regions or communities undermines their original claims to self-government.[34] Currently, only the regions affiliated with the historic communities are entitled to have powers that include key services such as education and health. Other

---

33 Alistair Hennessy, "The renaissance of federal ideas in contemporary Spain," in Forsyth (ed.), *Federalism and Nationalism.*
34 Brassloff, "Spain: the state of the autonomies," p. 35.

regions or communities have critical ceilings upon their autonomy written into their enabling statutes. Despite this trend, efforts to generalize the autonomies suggest that future central governments may continue to attempt to brake or hamper the demands of the historic communities.

The examples of Switzerland, Belgium and Spain suggest the importance of politics in determining new political institutions that either minimize the homogenization of groups within a centralist structure or promote a more self-governing and autonomous collective existence. Likewise, the Quebec question in Canada has underscored the issue of *la survivance*. This is not to suggest that groups such as the Catalans or French-speaking and Dutch-speaking Belgians have procured a better deal than their Québécois counterparts. However, the failure of renewed federalism, and the subsequent patriation of the constitution with a Charter of Rights and Freedoms, has continued to raise the question of a more critical restructuring of the Canadian federal system compared to the centralist reforms suggested by the Trudeau government in the late 1970s.

The issue of whether or not Quebec will survive or flourish as a French-speaking, economically viable community continues to challenge the status quo. Thus far, Canadian federalism has rejected asymmetrical models providing Quebec with special status. The federal heritage of Sir John A. Macdonald rejects such an asymmetrical model because its centralist vision took for granted the capacity of national institutions to embody or articulate a national interest. At another level, the trend of countering Quebec's special demands by extending Quebec-federal agreements to the other provinces corresponds to a symmetrical notion where all provinces are equal.[35] The minority position of Quebec in Canada means that the federal-provincial agreements of today may be dismantled at a later date when the will of the parliamentary majority changes.

The Canadian federal government has been unwilling to limit any further erosion of the principle of parliamentary supremacy by constitutionally entrenching what has become conventional practice. This was less valid with the Mulroney government's efforts to reach some form of accommodation with Quebec in the failed Meech Lake Accord, but the significant protest from English-speaking Canadians and three provinces, of course, ended that particular attempt. Moreover, with the inclusion of the Charter of Rights in the constitution, the federal government is viewed as more willing to relinquish its powers to the courts rather than to the provinces. Given this tendency, it is argued that the failure to give Quebec special status (e.g., Meech's "distinct

---

35 Alain-G. Gagnon and Joseph Garcea, "Quebec and the Pursuit of Special Status," in R.D. Olling and M.W. Westmacott (eds.), *Perspectives on Canadian Federalism* (Scarborough: Prentice-Hall, 1988), pp. 304-325.

society" clause) means that the threat of future assimilation remains a constant menace influencing political negotiations with the federal government and other provinces. This is not to exclude altogether a symmetrical version of federalism, but rather, it suggests the necessity of taking the French question into consideration in the evaluation of reforms of central institutions (e.g., a veto by Quebec Senators on matters of language, education or culture.)

Against these above factors, then, one may now examine three principle issues where comparative experience may shed light on the Canadian situation. These are the issues of territory, collective goals and economic and fiscal relations.

Territory: Communities and Institutions

Questions of diversity involve more than the survival or promotion of regionally based communities with distinct identities. It can mean, as in the case of Germany, the promotion and maintenance of state identities (e.g., the Länder). Or, as in the United States, where diversity means that identities are protected or promoted at the individual level, is the emphasis on individual rights. However, multicommunal politics frequently embody a territorial component. In countries where a minority or economically subordinate ethnolinguistic group is capable of dominating the politics of a particular region the question of territory predominates. In cases where groups are spread throughout a number of territories and remain unable to dominate in any one region, the alliances and shifting terrain of community or group politics often precipitates serious conflict that is not easily resolved through a system of federal institutions. The following comparisons present a range of situations that provide a broader perspective on the issue of territory and the multiple factors influencing federal politics.

Based on the preceding comparisons the establishment of a territorial base with a governmental structure appears essential to the maintenance of diversity. The intrastate mechanisms suggested in the Canadian options outlined earlier in this paper, with the exception of sovereignty-association, provide some instrument for representing provincial interests within central institutions. However, it is the decentralist, asymmetrical, and renewed federalist options that strengthen provincial powers and could secure provinces control over their territory. Given the centrality of Quebec in this process, any option that fails to establish both a credible augmentation in provincial powers, with the possible addition of intrastate mechanisms for influencing federal policy, would fail to attract the support of Quebec.

Options that attempt, for instance, to avoid the territorial issue by suggesting national bilingualism programs risk alienating a community that views its survival as being integrally tied to its community infrastructure and the political gains that have been acquired either at the regional level or for a region via a national institution. Such is the case of French-speaking Quebecers in Canada, the Dutch and the Walloons in Belgium, French Jurasians in Switzerland, and Basques and Catalans in Spain. All of these countries are confronted with the problem of territorial minority communities and their community survival.

Collective Goals and the "Charter" Culture

The question of promoting diversity extends beyond issues of territory. Collective goals constitute a second key element in understanding the present constitutional conflict. In Canada, the Charter culture has also had an important impact on how Canadians view intergroup relations. The issue of rights is framed in the context of individuals, and despite being applicable to groups, their application can work against the collective interests of those who predominate in a given region or province. In other words, the Charter of Rights has the potential of effectively undermining territorial diversity, not only in Quebec, but in other provinces as well.[36] A renegotiated federalism, if it is still possible, must take into account the legitimating power of the Charter culture, but be willing to build institutions that are still capable of ensuring a greater degree of territorial autonomy.

The tension between group and individual rights in an increasingly rights fixated society means that this becomes a critical issue when formulating a new federal arrangement.[37] The debate over the "distinct society" clause in the Meech Lake Accord and Quebec sign legislation (Bill 178) demonstrates the potential cleavages that such an issue is capable of generating. Alan Cairns and Cynthia Williams provide a convincing argument concerning the impact the Charter has on both political culture and citizen-state relationships.[38] If they are correct in their assessment, the discourse of rights, either collective or individual, must be confronted in a renegotiated federalism if it is to be perceived by the public as legitimate.

In the comparative context, Canada is confronting a relatively unique situation. Its proximity to the United States means that English-speaking Canada is inundated with the discourse of individual rights, while Quebec and its Catholic tradition has been a proponent of collective pursuits. This particular tension

---

36 Peter W. Hogg, "Federalism Fights the Charter of Rights," in David P. Shugarman and Reg Whitaker (eds.), *Federalism and Political Community* (Peterborough: Broadview Press, 1989), pp. 249-266.

37 While the proponents of individual rights recognize the group character of many of the enumerated rights in the Charter they frequently take issue when these group or collective rights are tied to the question of territory.

38 Cairns and Williams, *Constitutionalism, Citizenship and Society in Canada*, pp. 1-50.

between individual and collective rights does not have similar expressions in countries such as Belgium, Spain, Switzerland, or Germany. While the debate in Canada has polarized to some extent, the European examples suggest the possibility of arriving at some sort of balance.

A large measure of the balance achieved by countries such as Belgium and Switzerland has to do with the territorial question and collective goals. While Belgium, in particular, protects basic individual freedoms in its constitution, it has resolved some of its intercommunity problems by forming orders of government with territorial jurisdictions. Article 23 of the Belgian constitution states that while language use is optional it can be regulated by law, but only in the "case of acts by the public authorities and of legal matters." The formalizing of territorial jurisdiction has diminished some individual rights such as the convention of "droit du père de famille" for choosing the language in which a child will be educated. Currently, the language of a region determines the language used in the public education system.

In Switzerland there is even less reliance on constitutionally entrenched "fundamental guarantees of rights or freedoms" for its various communities. Rather, it relies on the consensus style politics which carefully provides representation for all groups. The emphasis in this case is on group rights operating within prescribed territories. As mentioned earlier, this is bolstered by the general acceptance of the canton as guardian of cultural identity and the importance of individuals conforming to cantonal norms. Even when this prerogative has been challenged, as in the case of Ticino and the issue of public signs being in Italian, the collective goals expressed by the canton have been sustained in the courts.

In the Canadian options which address the territorial question there can be a balance between collective goals and individual rights. While the sovereignty-association option certainly eliminates the historic tension based on founding nations and a charter culture by separating the two nations, both decentralist and renewed federal options attempt to address the issue of collective goals. While varying in the formulation of their respective options, both recommend a new power-sharing arrangement and mechanisms capable of protecting both the cultural and territorial integrity of Quebec. Given Quebec's willingness to entrench in the constitution its own provincial charter of rights, it might be expected that once its autonomy and powers to advance collective goals are secured the emphasis on collective rights would diminish and individual rights will increasingly dominate political discourse within the province or new state.

Economic and Fiscal Relations

The third issue (after territory and collective goals) that must be taken into consideration is the economic factor. Despite the perceived demand for greater political autonomy based on territorial criteria (e.g., provincial) there is a general recognition that barriers to economic transactions or the flow of goods and services must be avoided. This necessitates, at the very least, terms for an economic union. In a broader context, economic relations are an integral aspect of all dynamic and healthy federal or federalizing states. While some of these factors have been alluded to in earlier discussions they need further elaboration.

In Canada, the Rowell-Sirois report was the first attempt to propose seriously a restructuring of the fiscal arrangements between the two orders of government. It suggested a coordinated collection of progressive taxes that would become the foundation of the federal government's revenues. The idea of an equitable method of redistributing fiscal resources was likewise promoted, with the express purpose of creating an environment where all Canadians would have access to comparable government services with comparable levels of taxation.[39] The ideas suggested in the Rowell-Sirois report were gradually implemented, in varying degrees and with modifications, in the years following its tabling in 1940.

By 1941 the federal government had implemented the first tax rental arrangement by taking over personal and corporate taxes, and transferring to the provinces the net amount that they obtained in 1941. Failing to withdraw from this field of taxation meant that the provinces would be imposing a double tax on their population. By the late 1940s the federal government actively directed its spending power towards areas under provincial jurisdiction in an effort to apply Keynesian policies and establish uniform social programs (e.g., old age pensions, unemployment insurance, public health care, and later post-secondary education).

Quebec provided the most consistent challenge to the centralist course taken by the federal government. The threat of federal intrusion and its relationship to fiscal relations and territorial basis of the francophone community was explicitly articulated in the Quebec government's response in the Tremblay report. On the question of taxation it was argued that "if Quebec was a sovereign government within its spheres of jurisdiction, dealing with the federal government as an equal, it could not be dependent on the federal transfers for the revenues needed to meet its responsibilities."[40] It is in this context that future Quebec politicians have argued that independent access to an important revenue base is necessary for the protection of a cultural identity and its collective goals. This culminated in the 1970s in Robert Bourassa's efforts to reform the federal system in a manner that would give Quebec the special powers and resources

---

39 Richard Simeon and Ian Robinson, *State, Society, and the Development of Canadian Federalism* (Toronto: University of Toronto Press, 1990), p. 106.
40 Ibid., p. 144.

required to preserve and develop the bicultural character of the Canadian federation.[41] And the subsequent failure of this approach led to the "beau risque" proposed by the Parti Québécois and the possibility of combining political autonomy (e.g., with its concomitant fiscal independence) and economic association (e.g., common market.)

While detailed discussions of these developments are beyond the scope of this paper, they underscore the extent to which fiscal negotiations must be part of any new option, and point to the critical role of fiscal politics and the survival of a territorially based community. The developments in Spain and Belgium indicate the limits to a devolution of powers or the decentralization of the economy when it is not accompanied by corresponding control over the necessary sources of revenue.

In Spain the conflict between different orders of government has been over taxing jurisdiction that until the late 1980s was controlled by the central government. While some taxing power was delegated to the dominant Autonomous Communities, the other communities had only minimal revenues comprised of tax-sharing grants from the central government's budget. These were to cover the costs of the services that had been transferred to the Autonomous Communities, and created a situation where "Communities are reluctant to be seen to add to the fiscal burdens in their regions and so revenues from their own taxes are insignificant: less that 2 percent [sic] of total income derives from them and none at all in 13 of the Communities."[42] After a period of intense bilateral and multilateral negotiations, the revenue base of the communities was revised. Based upon the objectives of autonomy, regional solidarity (e.g., Interterritorial Compensation Fund), and guaranteed financial equilibrium, a new arrangement was instituted which geared fiscal grants to a formula based on factors such as population, territorial size, levels of services, relative poverty, and specific regional conditions. According to Brassloff, the basis of the negotiated arrangements is related to the trade-offs between regional autonomy and interregional solidarity.[43]

In Belgium, the 1980 constitutional changes brought about important changes in the revenue base of the newly formed regional and cultural orders of government. The changes included access to nonfiscal resources, credits chargeable to the national budget, rebates on the yield of taxes and levies imposed by law, the formulation of their respective fiscal systems, and loans.[44] Despite these changes, it is argued that the revenue base of the regional and

---

41 Alain-G. Gagnon and Mary Beth Montcalm, *Quebec: Beyond the Quiet Revolution* (Toronto: Nelson Canada, 1990), p. 157.
42 Brassloff, "Spain: the state of the autonomies," p. 36.
43 Ibid., pp. 36-37.
44 Senelle, "Constitutional Reform in Belgium," p. 63.

cultural bodies remains in essence an "endowment" and only incidentally a "so-called shared taxation revenue."[45] Furthermore, it is argued that the current financing system lacks a direct correspondence between policy responsibilities and revenues. This inhibits an active role for the new orders of government in policy decisions and thereby circumscribes their autonomy.[46]

The complex interlocking relationship and committee system in both Switzerland and Germany offsets, in part, disparities in revenue generating powers by different orders of government. In West Germany the inadequacies of the original revenue-sharing guidelines contained in the Basic Law eventually led to important amendments in 1969. While there has been a concerted effort to accord each order of government exclusive rights to a large number of less important taxes (e.g., consumer and road transport taxes to the Bund and wealth and motor vehicle taxes for the Länder) the most productive taxes are shared: 50 percent each for the Länder and Bund for income and corporation taxes and an estimated 70 percent yield for the Bund of an annually reviewed value-added-tax.[47] However, even in this context the number of joint-programs and federal grants-in-aid tends to undermine or at least restrict the policy-making autonomy of the Länder. Nevertheless, the necessity of obtaining Länder consent in joint programs frequently necessitates far-reaching compromises on policy initiatives.[48]

In Switzerland the weak fiscal base of the federal government has circumscribed its ability to intrude in areas of cantonal jurisdiction. According to Lehner, the federal government only has a temporary right to raise revenue by direct taxation.[49] Unlike the German case, the ability of cantons to invoke a referendum on the financial decisions of the federal Parliament means that the federal government must ensure the cooperation of the cantons in its fiscal arrangements. This not only ensures incentives for federal-cantonal cooperation, but also provides the cantons with considerable influence on federal policies.[50] In addition, cooperation is further reinforced by the growing dependence of cantons on federal transfers.

The examples of the European countries suggests that the incorporation of fiscal relations (e.g., tax sharing) must be an integral part of new federal options for Canada. With the exception of Switzerland, this is based primarily on the

---

45 Ibid., p. 72.
46 In a recent article in *Les Affaires* (21 avril 1990), Michel de Smet states that the Belgium government eventually intends to set aside 40 percent of its budget for transfers to community and regional governments. If this in fact occurs it may have a considerable impact on the autonomy of these governments.
47 Childs and Johnson, *West Germany: Politics and Society*, p. 47.
48 Lehner, "The Political Economy of Interlocked Federalism," p. 209.
49 Ibid., p. 210.
50 Ibid., p. 211.

extent to which the central government recognizes the interdependence of the various orders of government, and the principle that national means should only be applied in cases where local measures are insufficient.

In Canada, the sovereignty-association option presumes either the unwillingness or inability of the federal government to negotiate a suitable arrangement for Quebec. However, recognition of the advantages of economic association requires a level of negotiations unprecedented in contemporary Canadian history. If the experience of the European Community is any indication, even substantial progress similar to the interprovincial arrangements already existing in Canada would be difficult to achieve.[51] A new Quebec-Canada relationship should not restrict itself to a singular association with Canada, but should explore special bilateral arrangements at the economic level with other provinces such as Alberta or Ontario. This may develop within the federal context more easily than pursuing such arrangements after Quebec has unilaterally declared itself independent, particularly if the separation is acrimonious.

CONCLUSION

Several lessons can be drawn for Canada from the preceding comparative analysis. From the Third-World multicommunal federal states (India and Malaysia), we learned that the accommodation of fundamental regional interests is rarely achieved through minor institutional tinkering, and that centralization is often inappropriate in cases where communities are territorially-organized. In such occasions distrust between communities often undermines political change. In the cases of Malaysia and India, regions have

---

51 Each of these countries still aggressively guard the control over fiscal policies. Moreover, modelling a new Quebec-Canada relationship on the EC risks introducing a new array of interstate problems. If Quebec and the rest-of-Canada are to form a new political arrangement we need not copy the EC model. EC institutions are considered "creaky and undemocratic" with their unrepresentative nature augmenting as powers increasingly shift to Brussels. Individual Commissioners form the executive and are appointed by member states. The composition of the Council of Ministers varies according to the issue, with its discussions remaining in camera. Only the Parliament is directly elected, but it still serves primarily as a consultative body despite attempts to give it more power. In addition barriers to further developments have confronted the careful safeguarding of national autonomy and control over fiscal policy. See Michael B. Dolan, "The Single European Act — Origins and Implications," paper presented for the Seminar on the "European Community after 1992: Consequences for Africa," held in Lagos, Nigeria, 13-15 June 1990, p. 16.; cf. Michael Burgess, *Federalism and European Union: Political Ideas, Influences and Strategies in the European Community, 1972-1987* (New York: Routledge, 1989). See also chapter 11 of this volume by Dan Soberman.

not found acceptable and effective political representation at the centre, and this has led to questioning of the viability of the various initiatives elaborated to manage political crises. Centralization was perceived to be unsuited for the expresssion of political differences.

From the unitary states of Europe undergoing a federalizing process (Belgium and Spain), which are probably the most revealing models for the present analysis, we saw countries willing to accommodate differences between regions and political communities. In those two cases, political leaders and political party coalitions were successful in establishing constituent assemblies with a view to finding solutions to their cultural differences. They demonstrate the need of a political will, as well as the desire to reach a compromise on the part of linguistic or cultural communities. The case of Spain is especially important to the current constitutional debate in Canada as it stresses the need to develop a framework that allows sufficient room for politics and institutional processes to be accommodated simultaneously. In Spain, the understanding is that a country's constitution should not be perceived as a straight-jacket but rather it should be defined as a guiding document. Instructive also for Canada is the case of Belgium where political parties play a crucial part in the creation of political arrangements between linguistic communities. In Belgium, key actors have made good use of the constituent assembly as a legitimate means to achieve constitutional transformation.

The traditional Western European federal states (Germany and Switzerland) are also particularly relevant to the Canadian problem. In the German example, an important distinction is made between administrative and legislative powers in the constitution, allowing for the devolution of greater administrative responsibilities to the Länders. In Germany this resulted in a climate of cooperation on the part of the two orders of government. In addition, one should underscore the effectiveness of the Bundesrat in protecting regional interests at the centre. The Swiss case is also instructive for Canada, as the constitutional process has been somewhat eased by the use of referenda. Such a device is intended to protect the various communities as it calls for a double majority (absolute majority of total votes and majority of cantons) before making any modifications to the constitution. Key also to present discussion is the fact that in Switzerland, very much like in Belgium, constitutional arrangements are territorial in nature. To be more specific, cantons have the right and the obligation to protect and promote their respective linguistic community against any infringements, and in doing so they are supported by the central government. In some respect, this policy could be said to be the equivalent of a charter of rights and freedoms whose application varies according to specific regions.

The months and years ahead will tell us more about the maturity of Canadians as they tackle the most serious constitutional crisis since the creation of this country. What this paper demonstrates, however, is that federal and nonfederal countries alike are experiencing difficulties at different moments, and that there is no panacea if the political will is lacking. Significant changes in Spain and Belgium have occurred because community and political leaders made the solving of their respective constitutional crisis a priority, a must. It remains to be seen, however, if a similar will is present in Canada.

VI

Areas of Adjustment

13

Constitutional Design in a Federation: An Economist's Perspective

Robin Boadway

INTRODUCTION: SOME FUNDAMENTAL CONCEPTUAL ISSUES

This paper is concerned with how economic objectives can contribute to the optimal design of a constitution in a federal state. Constitutions set out what activities a government may engage in. In that sense, they impose *limits or constraints* on government decision-making. They may also impose *obligations* on government; that is, they may stipulate certain types of actions that must be taken. Not all constitutional constraints and obligations are of a primarily economic sort, though most will have some economic dimension. Thus, economics alone cannot be the sole determinant of constitutional design; it may not even be the main one. Furthermore, the economic provisions may be less consequential quantitatively than many others (judicial, sociological, political, etc.). They may also be practically unenforceable since it is a well-known property of economic behaviour that the intent of rules and regulations can often be subverted by ingenious and indirect means. In light of this, I am under no illusion about the significance of the role that economic arguments should play in deciding a constitution.

The economic arguments may themselves be somewhat tenuous as well. There is no objective (scientific) basis for establishing the correct economic role of government, even in principle. Roughly speaking, there are those who believe that a minimal amount of state intervention is desirable, and there are those who believe in an activist state. Their disagreements may be based at least partly on value judgment. A minimalist may dislike the coercive use of the state

I would like to thank Paul Hobson and Martin Prachowny for constructive comments on an earlier version of this paper.

for redistributive purposes, while the interventionist may prefer it. Besides this difference in ethical perspective, there may also be disagreement on the objective question as to the efficacy of government intervention to achieve agreed-upon objectives. The literature on regulation is replete with examples of this. The implications of these disagreements for the constitution is not altogether clear either. The minimalists may wish to put a maximum number of constraints on government activity via constitutional provisions, and impose a minimal number of obligations. Other minimalists may, however, view this as an abrogation of minimalists principles themselves (e.g., freedom from regulation). Similarly, interventionists may prefer not to constrain governments at all, but may also wish to impose several obligations on them.

Whichever camp one falls into, there is a fundamental incompleteness in the theory of economic policy that plagues government decision-making and renders the much-vaunted role of the scientific methods of economic analysis to be of limited use. It arises because the evaluation of economic policy *necessarily* involves making a value judgement. Economists are prone not to emphasize this, and to conduct much of their analysis in positive terms. However, it cannot be ignored in designing the constitutional rules that are to govern governments. This is especially true in light of the observation I make below that much of what the government actually does is redistributive in nature.

The necessity for value judgement arises for the following reason. Normative economic analysis (i.e., the evaluation of alternative economic outcomes) has largely embraced the so-called *individualistic* criterion. According to this criterion, policies are beneficial to the extent that they improve the well-being of individuals as judged by the individuals themselves. However, different policies affect the well-being of different individuals differently, some being gainers and some losers from any given policy. To choose among alternative policies, one needs some way of aggregating individual changes in well-being. As the economist Kenneth Arrow observed in his famous Nobel-prize winning work,[1] there is no reasonable political procedure for aggregating individual preferences for policies if the only information used in the procedure is the preferences of individuals (and if the preferences of individuals must count). The difficulty can only be avoided by having some method for making interpersonal equity comparisons, that is, by having an ethical observer who will trade off in a just way one person's well-being for another's (including the unborn). Unfortunately, there is no readily available ethical observer, and it is not at all clear that the political process (or the economist) is a suitable substitute. The best we may be able to do is to bind as much as possible the

---

1   Kenneth J. Arrow, *Social Choice and Individual Values* (New Haven: Yale University Press, 1951).

political process by putting some ethical imperatives into the constitution. To put the point in more familiar terms, economic policy typically involves both efficiency and redistributive (equity) effects. Choosing among different economic policies involves trading off equity versus efficiency and that requires a value judgement.

I raise these fundamental issues of agnosticism about the criteria for choosing economic policies in order to put the discussion of the economic principles of constitution-making into context. It will serve both to inform the reader of where some of my arguments are coming from, and to stress the substantial judgemental content of my arguments. The consequences of Arrow's unfortunate observations will have two sorts of implications for what follows. First, it will clarify our discussion of the nature of economic policy-making and assist in prescribing the preferred assignment of economic functions to levels of government. Second, it will help to demarcate the limits and obligations of economic policy that should be put into the constitution.

The reader can be guaranteed at the outset that many economists will not agree with my point of view. Indeed, I am not sure how strongly I hold the views I am about to present. Much of what I have to say is speculative in nature and intended to get some fundamental economic issues into the debate on the future of the country — something that has been curiously lacking to date.

THE ECONOMIC ROLE OF GOVERNMENT

It is useful for putting the discussion in perspective to begin with some discussion of the role of government in the economy, federal or otherwise, before turning to how this role is to be embodied in the constitution. I take as my perspective a normative one drawn from the welfare-economics literature. According to this view, the competitive market with its decentralized decision-making is recognized as an efficient resource allocation mechanism to be relied on wherever possible. However, there are various ways in which the market may fail to achieve beneficial outcomes. The government is a relatively benevolent institution whose role in a capitalist market economy is to correct for market failure while at the same time facilitating the use of the market itself. This role stresses the potential for government to do good, while recognizing its limitation of government as an economic decision-maker. The rationale for government intervention requires an understanding of the benefits and costs of decentralized decision-making as well as the importance of private property rights for the functioning of the market economy.

This view of government is not shared by all economists. Some economists of the "public choice" school view government as essentially a self-interested

institution, albeit one that is constrained by democratic processes. They often
also abhor the use of government as a redistributive vehicle, viewing these
activities as akin to theft. They would prefer a minimal state. Partial recognition
of this view of government as an imperfect institution is given below in
suggesting that certain obligations may have to be written into the constitution,
such as the pursuit of equity.

Since the role of government depends upon compensating for shortcomings
of the market it is worth summarizing the sources of *market failure* that have
been emphasized in the literature. Space precludes a careful examination of
them; further detail can be found in many standard public finance texts. They
are as follows.

- *Public goods and externalities.* Some types of expenditures simultaneously provide benefits for several users. Private provision would
  either be impossible, or, if possible, would be inefficient because
  private decisions would fail to account for the benefits (or costs)
  imposed on third parties.

- *Increasing returns to scale.* Some goods can be produced in the least
  cost way at a scale of operations that is a significant proportion of the
  market it is intended to serve, perhaps even the entire market. In such
  a situation, competition cannot be sustained and government intervention in some form may improve efficiency (public provision, regulation,
  etc.).

- *Unemployment, inflation.* There may be aggregate coordination problems on the market which implies that some resources go unemployed.
  Government may be able to reduce the unemployment by macroeconomic policies (fiscal and monetary policies), taking into account the
  trade-off that may exist between unemployment and inflation. Labour
  markets may also be made to function more smoothly by microeco-
  nomic policies directed specifically at the labour market.

- *Redistribution.* The market outcome will work to the advantage of some
  persons and against others depending upon their ownership of resources
  and their abilities. Governments may attempt to redistribute from the
  better off to the less well-off using various devices (progressive taxes,
  transfers and expenditures).

- *Social insurance.* Related to the point above, is the fact that some
  persons may be unlucky in their economic status for a variety of reasons
  including location of residence, date of birth, health status, and the like.
  In a market economy, persons can often insure against many types of
  risks. However, private insurance may not be possible for these types
  of risks, and there may be a role for government. Indeed, much of the

redistributive activity that governments undertake may be viewed as being for social insurance reasons.

It is important to recognize that some of these things involve increasing the size of the "economic pie" and some involve redistributing the pie. Although the two are rarely separable, it is convenient to think conceptually of the former as being the *efficiency* role of government and the latter the *equity* role.[2] The former involves exploiting those gains from trade that, for one reason or another, the private sector has not been able to exhaust; the latter involves the dividing up of the gains. Minimalists, including many public choice theorists (e.g., another Nobel Prize winner, James Buchanan), lay almost complete emphasis on the efficiency role of government.[3] That is, they view government as an instrument by which gains from trade can be achieved collectively which the market is not able fully to exploit (e.g., because of public goods and externalities). How the gains obtained from collective action are to be distributed is not discussed, even though they may be sizable. Even in a minimalist state where the only function of government is to protect private property, the collective gains may be substantial. The issue of how to divide them cannot be avoided.

A fundamental characteristic of the pursuit of efficiency and equity, and this reflects their interdependence, is the inherent trade-off between the two objectives. The process of redistributing from the rich to the poor can only be accompanied by some loss in output, the loss being greater the more the redistribution. This is because of the adverse effects that the redistribution has on incentives (of both the donors and recipients). The issue of how redistributive the tax system ought to be, given this trade-off, has been the subject of considerable economic research. The analysis can be technically very complicated. At the risk of some simplification, one of the important qualitative lessons that has been learned from the literature is that the ideal amount of progressivity of the tax-transfer system is surprisingly limited.[4] Constitutions

---

2 One might also distinguish a third role of government, the *stabilization* role, from the efficiency and equity roles, although again the three roles will be interdependent. Much of our discussion will focus on the efficiency and equity aspects of government, they being the more controversial ones for constitutional issues.

3 Buchanan has written widely on these issues. The basic methodology may be found in James Buchanan and Gordon Tullock, *The Calculus of Consent* (Ann Arbor: University of Michigan Press, 1962).

4 In a very famous study, James Mirrlees computed the structure of the ideal redistributive income tax under a set of reasonable assumptions about taxpayer behaviour. He found, much to his surprise, that the "optimal income tax" structure did not differ much from a flat rate with a fixed exemption level. See James Mirrlees, "An Exploration in the Theory of Optimum Income Taxation," *Review of Economic Studies*, vol. 38, 1971, pp. 175-208. This work has spawned an enormous literature,

should recognize this in the sense that it would be unwise to impose absolute equity or equality obligations on the government.

At the same time, it should also be realized that equity objectives can be pursued by other means, some of which are as effective as taxes and transfers. Many components of the expenditure side of the budget have a redistributive element to them, whether or not that is their primary function. Examples include education, health care and insurance, welfare services, unemployment insurance, workmen's compensation, and the like. Indeed, given the limited extent to which taxes can, or do, redistribute, one could argue that government expenditures are first and foremost instruments for massive redistribution. Recognition of the extent of the redistribution inherent in what governments do is critical for designing a federal constitution, and we will come back to it below.

One final conceptual clarification of the use of equity as a policy criterion is useful for constitutional purposes and that is the conceptual distinction between horizontal and vertical equity. Applying the equity criterion involves evaluating the effects of policy on persons at different levels of well-being. Economists have suggested that persons who are equally well-off should be treated equally by policy. This is the principle of *horizontal equity*. Identifying equally well-off persons is not a simple matter. The tax system tries to correct for differences in individuals' ability to generate well-being from a given amount of income by allowing deductions for such things as medical expenses, employment expenses and dependents. These are essentially for horizontal equity reasons. For our purposes, the equal treatment of equals rule has two sorts of implications. One is that it may be used as a justification for nondiscrimination provisions in a charter of rights. The other is critical for a federal economy. It is that the public sector (federal and provincial combined) must treat equally persons who reside in different provinces. This is referred to in the literature as the principle of *fiscal equity*. It forms the basis for the position we take below that the federal government be primarily responsible for equity matters in a federal state. It is also the main principle behind section 36(2) of the *Constitution Act, 1982* and behind the use of the federal spending power in areas of health, education and welfare. In view of the importance of section 36 for my analysis, it is worth quoting explicitly for future reference:

> 36. (1) Without altering the legislative authority of Parliament or of the provincial legislatures, or the rights of any of them with respect to the exercise of their legislative authority, Parliament and the legislatures, together with the government of Canada and the provincial governments, are committed to
> (a) promoting equal opportunities for the well-being of Canadians;
> (b) furthering economic development to reduce disparity in opportunities; and
> (c) providing essential public services of reasonable quality to all Canadians

none of which has cast doubt on the qualitative results of Mirrlees.

(2) Parliament and the Government of Canada are committed to the principle of making equalization payments to ensure that provincial governments have sufficient revenues to provide reasonably comparable levels of public services at reasonably comparable levels of taxation.

While horizontal equity involves the equal treatment of equals, vertical equity involves the appropriate treatment of persons of different levels of well-being. That is, it involves how much redistribution the public sector should undertake. It essentially involves a value judgement. Making such judgements is unavoidable since virtually all policy choices involve different degrees of redistribution.

CONSEQUENCES FOR CONSTITUTIONAL DESIGN

The above discussion stressed that defining the desired extent of government participation in a market economy and evaluating government policy cannot be based solely on objective scientific reasoning. Some value judgement is necessarily involved. That naturally makes the task of deciding which constraints and obligations should be put into the constitution rather than being left as a matter of decision-making for the government of the day a difficult one. One extreme way to put the constitutional design question is to follow the contractarian logic where one asks oneself what kind of measures should be incorporated into the constitution if we could eliminate self-interest. Eliminating self-interest from such a mental exercise is probably impossible. My own attempt leads me to the following reasonable requirements that the constitution should satisfy: it should preserve the best properties of the decentralized market economy, while at the same time admitting an appropriate allocative and stabilization role for government; and it should oblige governments to fulfil certain modest equity obligations. Postponing until the next section the special features of a constitution for a federal (as opposed to a unitary) state, these objectives might suggest that the constitution have the following general characteristics:

- The need to define and protect private property rights (security, the rights of private contracts, the right to engage in trade);
- The need to define public (common) property, such as the natural resources of the country;
- The ability to regulate trading in markets for both goods and services and for factors of production (i.e., labour and capital), including dealings with nonresidents, for the common good;
- The rights of governments to tax and engage in trade for the common good, as judged by the good of individuals in society (both present and

future); since this involves the violation of private property rights it
needs to be carefully specified; some property might be inviolable (e.g.,
the rights of person);

- Control of the currency via control of the central bank, which might be
largely independent of the government of the day; and

- An expression of the equity obligations of the government to include
the promotion of equal opportunities (the analog of section 36(1) stated
above), the elimination of poverty and nondiscrimination; ideally, the
wording of this part should be such as to oblige governments to pursue
some minimal degree of equity while at the same time recognizing the
constraints imposed by efficiency. This might be thought of as part of
a charter of economic rights along with the first point.

In a unitary state it is not necessary to be more explicit than that. In other words,
it is not necessary to specify the instruments of government along the lines of
sections 91 and 92. Indeed, many economists would dispute the need for all the
above parts, especially the last point. One could, for example, leave all economic matters out of the constitution entirely and let the parliament be supreme.
For matters that involve purely efficiency considerations, that may be sensible
since one might argue that governments should always have an incentive to
improve the efficiency of the economy. On the other hand, where equity is
concerned, it may be useful to provide some inducement to the promotion of
fairness or economic justice for government, since, as is well-known, majority
rule might not always be compatible with one's abstract notion of equity.

Some economists have suggested that specific constraints should be placed
on the ability of the government to tax and to borrow.[5] Essentially what they
have in mind is some limit on the size of government and on the ability of
present generations to impose costs on future generations. I am not fully
convinced by these arguments, though there is some merit in them. In principle,
restricting government interference in a market economy to that which pro-
motes the common good is some constraint, though a rather vague one. The
issue of future generations is a rather more difficult one. Equity would seem to
require that some weight be given to it. Perhaps the best way to do so is to
include the rights of future generations in the equity statement.

---

5   See, for example, Geoffrey Brennan and James Buchanan, *The Power to Tax:
    Analytical Foundations of a Fiscal Constitution* (New York: Cambridge University
    Press, 1980). This book stresses both the purely efficiency role of government, and
    its potential for malevolent behaviour. As stated above, I find this to be an unduly
    restrictive view of government.

ECONOMIC PRINCIPLES OF FEDERAL CONSTITUTIONS

Almost all countries have at least two levels of government. But, they have widely differing degrees of decentralization of powers, and different nations choose to devolve different types of responsibilities to lower levels. The purpose of this section is to outline some of the economic principles of determining the division of powers between levels of government. I take the view that these principles must be consistent with the underlying economic roles of government which are to preserve and foster efficiency in the allocation of the nation's resources and to achieve some degree of equity within the nation, both horizontal and vertical. Given that these objectives are not straightforward to put into operation in a unitary state, they are even less so in a federal state. The decentralization of responsibilities can itself have effects on national efficiency and equity. In fact, one might think of there being a trade-off between the benefits of decentralization, which we examine below, and national efficiency and equity objectives. In a federal context, efficiency includes the full efficiencies of a common market encompassing various regions, including those obtained from the unrestricted and undistorted mobility of labour, capital, goods and services among all regions. Equity requires that like persons be treated in a like manner across the country. Both of these can be compromised by the decentralization of economic responsibilities.

As with the resolution of the efficiency-equity trade-off, the ideal amount of decentralization will not be fully agreed upon. One reason is that it is virtually impossible to know the quantitative magnitude of the effects on efficiency from the decentralization of powers. Another is that decentralization typically has both efficiency and equity effects. In particular, the main argument for decentralization is that it improves efficiency. However, it also induces inequities among persons residing in different regions (provinces). Thus, one's view of the desired amount of decentralization depends upon the weight attached to equity as opposed to efficiency considerations. As above, I will present a set of views that incorporates to some extent my own judgements. At the least, that should serve to highlight the sorts of judgements that have to be taken.

The arguments for decentralizing economic responsibilities are well-documented in the fiscal federalism literature. The main ones are as follows. First, some goods that provide collective benefits do so largely in a local or regional manner (so-called *local public goods*). As the preferred amount and type of them depends upon the tastes and needs of those who benefit, different provinces will want to provide different amounts of them. The provinces are in a better position to match their provision with local preferences.

Second, as mentioned earlier, a good proportion of public expenditures is on goods or services that, though essentially private in nature, are nevertheless provided through the public sector. This may be for reasons of equity, of social insurance or of economies of scale. Here again, decentralization may allow the services to be provided in a way that best caters to local tastes. Since these services are largely of a private nature, their main beneficiaries are residents in the jurisdiction involved. Furthermore, delivery itself may be more efficient at the provincial level since at a higher level administrative costs may rise rapidly. It has also been suggested that efficient provision and innovation is encouraged because of an element of competition induced among provincial levels of government.

Third, there may be purely local preferences for redistribution as well, both as regards the type of redistribution (cash, in-kind, etc.) and the extent. This would also argue in favour of the decentralization of the design and delivery of the public provision of those goods and services that serve a redistributive goal.

Fourth, it has been argued that the decentralization of responsibilities may itself induce fiscal responsibility since the provision is at a level of government that is "closer" to the people served, and the government faces the discipline of persons leaving a jurisdiction that behaves irresponsibly. The argument for fiscal responsibility may be especially valid to the extent that provinces must finance their expenditures out of own-source revenues.

Given the decentralization of expenditure responsibilities, some taxing responsibilities should also be decentralized. The question is which ones and how much. This is a difficult question and depends critically on one's view of the extent to which one wants to promote national equity and efficiency. The decentralization of virtually any tax can give rise to inefficiencies and inequities within a federation. Inefficiencies can arise for two reasons. First, if provinces levy different tax rates on factors of production that are highly mobile, this will induce an inefficient allocation of those factors across provinces. Since capital is highly mobile, this would suggest that provincial taxes on capital within their jurisdictions (e.g., corporation income taxes) are potentially highly distortionary. Such a tax might well be retained at the centre. Taxes on less mobile factors such as real capital and even labour will cause less distortion. The latter includes residence-based taxation such as personal income and payroll taxes, destination-based sales taxes, and user fees and licences. Second, and related to the first point, fiscal inefficiency is unavoidable as long as tax capacities differ across provinces. Different tax capacities will result in higher tax levels in poorer provinces and this will provide an incentive for factors to prefer to locate in better-off provinces when on efficiency grounds they should remain in the poor province.

Inequities can also occur for two main reasons. For one, different provinces may have different degrees of progression in their tax systems perhaps due to different local preferences for redistribution. This would imply that otherwise identical persons would face different tax rates in different provinces, thus violating national horizontal equity norms. This would be true even if the tax capacities of the provinces were the same. The fact that they will differ leads to the second source of inequity, one that is closely related to fiscal inefficiency. With different tax capacities, different provinces could provide similar levels of public services with different tax rates. This implies a violation of horizontal equity within the federation since it implies that like persons would be treated differently by the public sector. This fiscal inequity has played an important role in the literature on federal-provincial grants, and we return to it below.[6]

The upshot is that while there may be good reasons for decentralizing some taxing powers to the provinces with which to finance their own expenditures, inefficiencies and inequities are greater the more decentralized the tax system, especially in a nation of heterogeneous provinces. However, in a federal state it is not necessary for provincial taxes to match exactly their expenditures. A shortfall, known as the *fiscal gap*, can be met by federal grants. We return to the important role of federal grants below which, in my view, play an essential role in achieving efficiency and equity in a federal state.

Against the various benefits of decentralization must be set those of centralization. On the expenditure side, central provision of public services has the following advantages. First, if the service is a public good that simultaneously benefits persons in more than one province, efficiency may be improved by central provision (e.g., defence, environment, etc.). Related to this is the fact that provincial provision, though mainly for the benefit of local residents, may spill over to other provinces. At least some type of federal intervention may be important here. Examples include higher education, welfare, and unemployment insurance. Second, there may be economies of scale in providing certain services centrally. Third, there may be efficiency advantages to having some degree of uniformity or harmonization of some types of services, especially those that may be associated with mobile factors of production. Provincial diversity may interfere with the efficient allocation of resources across provinces. Furthermore, provinces may be induced to engage in "beggar-thy-neighbour" policies by using expenditures selectively to attract desirable types of factors. Fourth, and perhaps most important, many public services are essentially redistributive in nature, and derive their ultimate justification for being publicly provided from that fact. National equity, therefore, requires some minimum of uniformity, at least in the level of provision. In the end, one has to weigh the benefits of catering to local tastes, the diversity and perhaps the efficiency of provincial provision against the possible advantages of scale,

---

6   This is discussed fully in Robin Boadway and Frank Flatters, *Equalization in a Federal State: An Economic Analysis* (Ottawa: Economic Council of Canada, 1982); and Economic Council of Canada, *Financing Confederation Today and Tomorrow* (Ottawa: Economic Council of Canada, 1982).

avoidance of wasteful interprovincial competition and spill-overs, and the pursuit of national equity standards from central provision.

On the tax side, similar conflicts apply. The decentralization of taxing responsibilities contributes to provincial accountability for financing their own activities and allows provincial preferences to be taken into account in the choice of the tax structure. At the same time, it can lead to the use of the tax system (particularly as it applies to capital) for interprovincial competitive purposes, and, as mentioned above, to inefficiencies and inequities within the federation. Equally important, central dominance in a tax field has two possible advantages. One is that it may induce greater harmonization of the tax among federal and provincial governments thereby contributing to the efficiency of the common market and reducing the costs of compliance and administration. The other is that central dominance in a tax field will facilitate its use for redistributive purposes to the extent that it leads to a common base and rate structure. As has been argued elsewhere, these arguments suggest a dominant federal presence in the direct (income) tax fields.[7]

The design of the constitution must take these conflicts between the benefits and costs of decentralization into account and try to devise a compromise that balances the benefits of decentralization with the achievement of national equity and efficiency. Different observers will come to different views about the optimal terms of the compromise. What follows are mine; they may serve at least as a basis for discussion. I begin by stating broadly how economic responsibilities should be allocated between the federal and provincial levels of government. It is not altogether obvious which of these can or should be written into the constitution. The above discussion of the economic aspects of constitutional design applies here as well. What remains to be done is to elaborate how economic responsibilities should be assigned to the two levels. For the purposes of this section, the federation is taken to be a symmetric one. In applying these principles to the Canadian case in the next section, we will wish to consider the desirability and feasibility of the asymmetric treatment of a province such as Quebec.

The guiding principles that I use in assigning functions to levels of government are as follows. The federal government should be largely responsible for stabilization, for national equity, for the provision of public goods and services

---

7 This argument is developed more fully in Robin Boadway, "Federal-Provincial Fiscal Relations in the Wake of Deficit Reduction," in Ronald L. Watts and Douglas M. Brown (eds.), *Canada: The State of the Federation 1989* (Kingston: Institute of Intergovernmental Relations, Queen's University, 1989), pp. 107-135; and Robin Boadway and Neil Bruce, "Pressures for the Harmonization of Income Taxation Between Canada and the United States," in John Shoven and John Whalley (eds.), *Canada-U.S. Tax Harmonization* (Cambridge: National Bureau of Economic Research, forthcoming).

whose benefits transcend borders, and for the maintenance of an efficient and smoothly-functioning internal common market in goods and services, labour and capital. There is something to be said for enshrining some of these principles in the constitution. The provinces should be responsible for the provision of services of a local or provincial nature. They should also exercise some shared responsibility for equity with the federal government. The reason for this is partly because provinces might have differing views about the ideal amount of redistribution within their jurisdictions, but also because many of the fiscal actions of the provinces will have unavoidable effects on equity. Giving the federal government primary responsibility for nationwide equity is likely to be controversial since it will imply somewhat more centralization than many observers will like. Nevertheless, I am led to this position by the view that a fundamental defining characteristic of a nation is that otherwise identical persons ought to be treated the same no matter where they happen to reside.

These principles would suggest the following assignment of expenditure responsibilities. The provinces would be responsible for the delivery of public services that are of a quasi-private nature including health care and insurance, education in all forms (including post-secondary and manpower training), welfare services, family and child-support services, provincial transportation and communication services, municipal services, and resource management (including local environmental issues). The federal government, on the other hand, would be responsible for expenditures of a clearly national nature including defence, foreign affairs, international trade, immigration, etc. To ensure a smoothly-functioning common market, those regulatory functions that have effects crossing provincial borders should reside with the federal government. These include the regulation of international and interprovincial trade (in both goods and services, including such things as communications and transportation), of environmental issues involving more than one province, agriculture markets, and capital markets. (The assignment of labour market regulation is problematic. Provincial regulation can cause restrictions in the ability of certain types of workers to migrate from one province to another, or even to cross borders to work. At the same time, there are presumably some advantages from decentralizing labour market regulations so they can be designed to suit provincial circumstances. If one puts great stress on removing barriers to mobility, centralization of labour market regulation would be favoured.) To be effective in the stabilization function, the federal government should assume responsibility for the central bank and the currency. The consequence of this assignment is that responsibilities for expenditures on goods and services would remain fairly decentralized as they are now. However, regulatory functions would be somewhat more centralized, reflecting the fact that many of them involve the regulation of markets for goods, services and factors that extend beyond provincial borders.

The tax assignment can be determined somewhat independently of the expenditure assignment, but it would follow the same objectives as outlined above. To fulfil the objectives of national equity, the federal government must have a commanding presence in the direct tax system, especially the personal tax. This will also assist in maintaining a system of income tax harmonization, much as we have in place now. From the point of view of economic logic, transfer payments to individuals, unlike government expenditures on goods and services, should be thought of as negative tax liabilities and treated symmetrically with direct taxes. This means they too should be available to the federal government. This includes unemployment insurance, public pensions, family allowances, and welfare payments. The delivery of some of these things could be delegated to the provinces by agreement, provided the federal government retains some ability to ensure national standards of equity. The federal government could have access to payroll taxes as well since they are complementary with income taxes. More controversially, economic arguments would suggest centralization of corporate taxes and wealth taxes. These are essentially taxes on mobile factors of production whose decentralized use ultimately leads to tax competition and interprovincial barriers to capital mobility. On the other hand, there is no need for federal presence in the indirect tax fields (apart from tariffs, of course), as the Carter Commission noted 25 years ago. They contribute neither to equity nor to tax harmonization, and in my view, can detract from both.[8]

The provinces would assume sole occupancy of indirect (sales) taxes, licences and fees, property taxes, and would have some access to direct taxes on residents (personal income and payroll taxes). Assuming that the provincial ownership of resources is an immutable fact of life, provinces would also be responsible for resource taxation. Presumably, the provinces will continue to participate in some formal system of direct tax harmonization along the lines of the Income Tax Collection Agreements.

From an economic point of view, it would also be desirable for tax rates to be such that the federal government collects more tax revenues than it needs for its own expenditure purposes. This is partly a consequence of the fact that the desired amount of centralization of taxes exceeds that of expenditures. For example, the federal government needs a large enough presence in the tax field to be able to pursue effective fiscal policy. As well, we have argued that the

---

8   This argument is discussed more fully in Robin Boadway, "The Budget and the Evolution of Federal-Provincial Relations," in Martin F. J. Prachowny (ed.), *Policy Forum on the February 1990 Federal Budget* (Kingston: John Deutsch Institute, Queen's University, 1990), pp. 1-11. There it is argued that from a federal-provincial fiscal relations point of view, the federal Goods and Services Tax and the reduction in transfers to the provinces will have adverse effects.

federal government should maintain enough dominance in direct taxes to be able to achieve tax harmonization and national equity goals. However, the excess of federal tax collections over expenditure responsibilities implies transfers to the provinces, and such transfers have their own independent rationale in a federal economy.

The role of federal-provincial transfers in a decentralized federal system is well-known from the literature.[9] The need for such transfers arises from the fact that the fiscal actions of the provinces inevitably give rise to inefficiencies and inequities in the national economy, and some of these can be best addressed via intergovernmental transfers. There are two general types that the transfers can take. One is transfers for equalization purposes, the object of which is to compensate for the differences in the fiscal ability of different provinces to provide comparable services to their residents. These differences arise primarily because of differing tax capacities, which in turn are a result of differing income levels across provinces as well as resource endowments. If uncorrected, they can lead to both the inefficient allocation of factors of production across provinces as well as fiscal inequities in which otherwise identical persons are treated differently by the public sector. The remedy is an equalization system in rough accordance with the prescription in section 36(2) as stated above.[10] In the Canadian context, this is achieved jointly by all the main transfers — Equalization, Established Programs Financing and the Canada Assistance Plan.

The second role transfers can assume is the more controversial one, and that involves the use of conditional grants (the spending power) to influence provincial behaviour in areas of exclusive provincial jurisdiction. The traditional economic case for conditional grants has stressed their role as corrective devices for interprovincial spill-overs. That could hardly account for their extensive use in health, education and welfare. Two sorts of arguments can be used in support of the spending power for these purposes. One is that they can enforce standardization in the provision of certain services so as to prevent provinces from using these services as competitive devices. The other, more important, argument is that the spending power is used to induce provinces to provide services in accordance with national standards of equity. For example, the conditions of the *Canada Health Act* can probably only be justified from an

---

9 See Economic Council of Canada, *Financing Confederation*; and Robin Boadway, "Federal-Provincial Transfers in Canada," in M. Krasnick (ed.), *Fiscal Federalism* Research Studies of the Royal Commission on the Economic Union and Development Prospects for Canada, vol. 65 (Toronto: University of Toronto Press, 1986), pp. 1-47.

10 In the ideal form, the use of equalization transfers has been said to accomplish the fiscal advantages of a unitary state while at the same time achieving the advantages of decentralized decision-making. See Boadway and Flatters, *Equalization in a Federal State*.

economic point of view on equity grounds. If the federal government is seen as having a responsibility for national equity, and if some of the important instruments for the pursuit of equity are in areas of provincial responsibility, the spending power represents the only recourse the federal government has to fulfil its mandate for equity. This view is quite consistent with how an economist would interpret section 36(1) of the *Constitution Act, 1982.* That section effectively recognizes the joint responsibility of the two levels of government for the pursuit of equity, and thus provides implicit support for the use of the spending power. Furthermore, the spending power clause of the Meech Lake Accord could be interpreted as a natural consequence of that point of view since it explicitly recognized the right of the federal government to use that power in areas of exclusive provincial jurisdiction when the national interest was involved. By section 36(1), equity matters are in the national interest. Thus, to me, the use of the federal spending power is a natural consequence of recognizing the interest of the federal government in the pursuit of equity. That is not to say that it has been exercised perfectly in the past.

For these reasons, the existence of a fiscal imbalance between tax and expenditure responsibilities of the provincial governments is necessary, and the role of federal grants in achieving national equity and efficiency objectives in a decentralized federation is a critical one.

THE APPLICATION TO CANADA: SOME SPECIAL CONSIDERATIONS

The above prescription for a constitution is devised purely from an economic point of view. It differs in some significant ways from the existing constitution, and from those that are likely to be proposed in the near future. Many of the differences arise from the value judgement I have used as a basis for economic policy, which is that the federal government should have a prominent role in equity matters, and in national efficiency. This, in turn, is based on the premise that one of the defining points of a nation is that citizens should be treated alike no matter where they happen to reside. In this final section, two matters are addressed. First, setting aside the special position of Quebec, I examine in some more detail how my ideal federal economy differs from the existing one. This seems to me to be a necessary first step towards evaluating what sorts of constitutional arrangements with Quebec are desirable. It should also serve to define what should be retained in a constitution applying to the rest-of-Canada. Second, we consider the more thorny question of the constitutional relationship of Quebec to the rest-of-Canada, again from a mainly economic point of view.

The Existing System of Fiscal Federalism Versus the Ideal

The main differences between my ideal constitution and existing practices are as follows:

- The free flow of goods and services, labour and capital across provinces would be guaranteed. To that end, the federal government would assume responsibility for regulating such things as capital markets and items entering interprovincial trade.

- The federal government would assume major responsibility for national equity. As in the existing section 36, this would involve two aspects — interpersonal redistribution and interprovincial redistribution. To facilitate the former, the federal government should be responsible for all major transfers to individuals. For the latter, the federal government should have enough tax room relative to its own expenditure responsibilities to be able to finance a scheme of interprovincial redistribution to satisfy the objectives of section 36(2).

- The provinces could be made responsible for the delivery of services affecting mainly the citizens of their own provinces. This would include health, education and welfare services. However, since these services have a major equity component, the federal government will have to retain the right to use the spending power to maintain national standards. This could be made explicit as in the Meech Lake Accord. (It might also be recognized that significant economies might be achieved by centralizing the delivery of some of these services among, say, the three Maritime provinces.)

- The tax assignment would differ from the present one as well. The federal government would vacate the indirect tax field altogether, leaving that to the provinces. The provinces could use the personal income tax, but the federal government would retain a large enough share to be able to maintain a harmonized tax system and to pursue equity through this tax. The federal government would be the sole occupant of the corporate tax field thereby avoiding the distortions on interprovincial capital movements imposed by provincial corporate taxes. The federal government would regain control of personal wealth taxation. The tax structure should be ample to maintain enough of a fiscal gap to finance federal-provincial transfers both for equalizing purposes and for the use of the spending power to achieve national objectives. Provinces would retain the ownership of natural resources, though the income from this wealth would give rise to equalization payments along the lines suggested by the Economic Council of Canada.[11]

Some of these differences are presumably unchangeable. However, others are not so great. In fact, putting teeth into existing provisions would go a long way towards them. Furthermore, some are more a matter of day-to-day political choice rather than constitutional matters. For example, the assignment of taxes to the two levels of government might be difficult to write into the constitution. The tax assignment issue is, however, of fundamental importance both to the maintenance of an efficient common market and to achieving national equity standards. It has been my view that the introduction of the Goods and Services Tax (GST) by the federal government constitutes a significant step backward in federal-provincial fiscal relations. It makes it more difficult for the federal government to fulfil its equity obligations, and it increases the likelihood of a loss of harmonization of the income tax system.

The Place of Quebec in the Constitution

It seems likely that Quebec cannot accept anything approaching the above prescription for fiscal federalism. That prescription is considerably more centralized in the assignment of taxes, in regulatory functions of transactions crossing provincial borders, and in the provision of transfers to both individuals and provinces than Quebec would like. Recall that centralization in these areas is a consequence of two working principles — the assignment to the federal government of responsibility for national equity and the federal government role as regulator of the internal common market to ensure the free flow of goods, services, labour and capital among provinces. In the absence of federal responsibility in these areas, the decentralization of financial responsibilities would entail fiscal inefficiency and inequity across provinces as well as the balkanization of the common market. But ultimately, Quebec would almost certainly balk at turning over to the federal government such large responsibilities for equity, which is the source of much of the financial centralization of power. Quebec may also prefer to retain regulatory powers over such things as capital and labour markets, communications, environment and agriculture, even though these are essentially matters of common market efficiency rather than equity.

The issue is whether Quebec's aspirations can be met in the framework of a federation. There are two possible responses to this. One would be to maintain a symmetric federation and decentralize to all provinces the same areas of

---

11 Economic Council of Canada, *Financing Confederation.*

responsibility as to Quebec. The other would be to attempt to construct an asymmetric federation that gives Quebec greater economic responsibilities than the other provinces. Consider these briefly in turn.

Decentralizing to all provinces the responsibilities desired by Quebec would have fairly dramatic consequences for the efficiency and equity of the Canadian common market. On the tax side, it is unlikely that a harmonized tax system could be retained as different provinces would prefer to raise their taxes in different ways. Beggar-thy-neighbour tax policies would be the rule, and factors of production would be inefficiently allocated across provinces. Giving the federal government some responsibility for enforcing the precepts of a common market would be of little use. The principle of national horizontal equity could not be fulfilled. Similarly, if provinces were fully responsible for all instruments of redistribution on the expenditure side, there would be an enormous divergence among provinces in the services provided. Both on efficiency and equity grounds, this would seem to me to be undesirable. Those who have opted for this solution seem to have as part of their objective a view of government as both leaner and less obtrusive, as well as one that has a much smaller role in pursuing equity objectives.[12] In my view, such an outcome as a result of decentralizing power to the provinces is highly unlikely.

The other alternative is to allow Quebec and Quebec alone to become selectively disengaged from certain federal programs. From a purely economic point of view, this would be feasible, given the tax assignment I outlined above. Purely regulatory functions can be selectively decentralized to Quebec, though with the obvious cost in terms of efficiency of the common market.[13] Decentralizing these regulatory functions need not entail much decentralization of financial power. On the other hand, since these measures entail costs for other provinces, they should be subject to negotiation.

The extrication of Quebec from federal programs of transfers to individuals and provinces is a bit more complicated, but still feasible. Given that the federal government maintains control over the income taxes, and that the system

---

12 See, for example, the following submissions to the Bélanger-Campeau Commission: Quebec Chamber of Commerce, "Quebec's Political and Constitutional Future: Its Economic Dimension"; Thomas Courchene, "The Community of the Canadas"; Jean-Luc Migué, "Institutionalizing Competition Between Governments: A Return to True Federalism," (mimeos, 1990).

13 I cannot resist the observation that, despite lip service being paid to the notion of an economic union with the rest-of-Canada, many Quebec observers propose the decentralization of regulatory functions which would have as their effect a balkanization of the common market, manpower, communications, agriculture, energy, etc., all of which involve interference with the free flow of labour, capital or goods and services. A good example of this is the Allaire Committee report for the Liberal Party of Quebec.

remains harmonized, it is possible to devise an opting-out type of arrangement according to which tax points are turned over to the province of Quebec in rough accordance with the funds that otherwise would have been transferred to the province and its residents. This is not an ideal solution for a number of reasons. First, it will be difficult to determine the precise tax point transfer that will compensate Quebec residents for their withdrawal from federal transfer programs, given that many of these programs are redistributive in nature. Presumably some compromise can be reached on that. Second, it is not ideal because it necessarily implies that persons living in Quebec will be treated differently by the fiscal system than those living outside. That is, fiscal equity will be sacrificed. Third, by the same token, fiscal efficiency will be compromised. There will inevitably be incentives for labour and capital to locate in one part of the country rather than the other. Being a resident in Quebec will be distinctly different than being a resident in the rest of the country. No common market provision or guarantee will be able to avoid this. Still, it may be regarded by those in Quebec and outside as a cost worth bearing. Finally, there is the obvious political difficulty of making such a mechanism acceptable to the rest-of-Canada. This issue is addressed in other chapters in this volume by persons in a better position to make that judgement.

Thus, from a purely economic point of view, an asymmetric federation is viable, though not particularly desirable. From the point of view of dealing with the desires of Quebec, it has a number of advantages. It allows the rest of the country to maintain the advantages of centralization while at the same time meeting at least some of the aspirations of Quebec. It also leaves enough flexibility in the system to allow Quebec to change its financial relationship with the rest-of-Canada in the future. On the other hand, it is very difficult to see how it can prevent the federal fiscal system in the rest-of-Canada from unraveling, that is, how it can survive other provinces or regions from seeking the same powers. If that were the case, a cleaner separation of Quebec would be the only alternative.

CONCLUDING REMARKS

The main thesis of this paper is that, like it or not, a substantial part of what governments do is of a redistributive nature. Economists have been loathe to recognize this, devoting their attention instead solely to efficiency matters. In a federal state, the assignment of efficiency responsibilities to the two levels of government would be relatively noncontroversial. The federal government might assume responsibility for ensuring the free flow of goods, services and factors of production, and for expenditures that simultaneously benefit persons from different provinces. They would also be responsible for stabilization. The provinces would be responsible for those expenditures that benefit mainly residents of their own jurisdictions. These would include the major areas of health, education and welfare (although the public provision of these would not amount to much if efficiency were the only criterion). The system might be fairly decentralized, though the federal government would have to assume additional regulatory functions to ensure the efficient operation of the internal common market.

Once equity considerations are taken into account, both the role of government itself and the responsibilities of the federal and provincial levels change substantially. I have taken the view that the federal government should assume a primary role for equity on the grounds that horizontal equity should apply nationwide. That being the case, the federal government must have the levers for redistributing among residents of different provinces. This implies a relatively centralized system of taxes and transfers, combined with much more decentralized expenditure responsibilities.

In the current setting of uncertainty about the place of Quebec in the federation, this can be looked at largely as a prescription for constitutional design for the rest-of-Canada. Should it be decided that Quebec will assume considerably more regulatory and financial power and yet remain part of the federation, ways would have to be found to do so that do not involve decentralizing further responsibilities to the remaining provinces. Extricating Quebec from the full federal fiscal system could be done by decentralizing some regulatory functions and using the tax point transfer mechanism to decentralize some financial powers. However, this will inevitably involve fiscal inefficiencies and inequities, even if a commitment to a full common market is maintained. That is the inevitable price to be paid for an asymmetric system.

14

Distribution of Functions and Jurisdiction: A Political Scientist's Analysis

J. Peter Meekison

The division of powers is central to the operation of federal systems. More than anything else it is the hallmark of federalism. There is no single method for dividing legislative authority, nor is there universal agreement as to which particular responsibilities should be assigned to federal governments or to provincial governments. Each formula is dependent upon the circumstances of the particular federation. What is best for one may not be acceptable to others.

In examining the division of powers, one must also take into consideration that the Canadian constitution was written in the mid-1860s and reflects the realities of that period. While the original bargain or consensus underlying the division may not have changed, it is equally evident that change has occurred. Thus, the division of powers is not static but dynamic or, to be more poetic, kaleidoscopic.

Since the *Constitution Act, 1982*, less attention has been given to the division of powers. Instead, the spotlight has shifted to the Charter of Rights and Freedoms and on the limits of legislative authority as opposed to which order of government possesses that authority. This new emphasis is understandable given the tremendous importance that Canadians have attached to the Charter and how they have identified with it. Of even greater significance is the effect of the Charter on the Supreme Court of Canada. Most of the Court's time is now devoted to the Charter leaving less time for other matters, notably the division of powers.

Before proceeding with the analysis of the Canadian system, three general points need to be understood.

First, the term division of powers is a phrase that conjures up a split that can be measured with a certain degree of mathematical precision, comparable to dividing a pie or a piece of land according to a predetermined mathematical ratio. Indeed, one can draw a pie chart as a shorthand way of depicting the division of powers (Figure 14.1).

Figure 14.1
The Responsibilities of Government

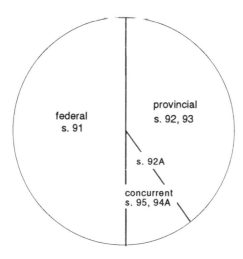

The diagram gives one a quick appreciation of what is involved and some understanding of the relative importance of each order. However, one should begin with the notion of watertight compartments, or a recognition of the concept of exclusive jurisdiction when approaching the division of powers. From this starting point one can go to the next stage, the interdependence of governments.

A second point to be considered is the minimum division of powers necessary to characterize the polity as a federal system as opposed to a confederal or unitary state. Again, there is no agreed-upon formulation. If the centre is so dominant or all-pervasive, or if the states are predominant, then the political system will not be a federation but a hybrid of either a unitary or confederal state. A short list of federal powers that are, in my opinion, an irreducible minimum includes foreign affairs, defence, currency, international and inter-provincial trade, taxation, enforcement of federal laws, postal service, customs and citizenship. This short list does not preclude a provincial role in any or all of these matters. A national government must possess sufficient authority to manage the economy, to protect the public from external threats and to maintain internal order.

There are certain subject matters where the federating units will usually claim primacy of place including; education, taxation (local), municipal activities, roads, law and order, sanitation, economic development and cultural matters. Again, any or all of these may have a national dimension. Nevertheless, it is difficult to see how a provincial government would not continue to exercise legislative jurisdiction on some or all of these subject matters.

Everything else, in my view, is subject to negotiation and will vary from federation to federation and from time to time.

Third, when dividing the governing function, two decisions are made. The first is what level or order will provide what services or regulate which activities. The second is the fiscal means by which governments can finance these services and activities. There is little point in giving a government responsibility without at the same time ensuring that they have the means to finance these services.

Just how "the means" is determined varies from federation to federation. What is important is that the problem be recognized when the federation is established. Recognition of fiscal capacity is critical to the division of powers and to the long-run stability of the federation. Provinces cannot be totally dependent on federal largesse nor can a central government be dependent upon the whim of a province to transfer funds.

THE CASE OF CANADA

One can learn a great deal from the division of powers at Confederation. During the Confederation debates Sir John A. Macdonald said:

> We have given the General Legislature all the great subjects of legislation.... [W]e have expressly declared that all subjects of general interest not distinctly and exclusively conferred upon the local governments and local legislatures, shall be conferred upon the General Government and Legislatures.... We have avoided all conflict of jurisdiction and authority....[1]

Central to his argument is the notion of "great subjects" of government. By way of contrast the provinces were considered to be no more than "local governments." However, the legislative jurisdiction given to these local governments was exclusive, a point of considerable importance in later court battles. By "great" one must conclude that these were the important matters of the day. By local, one must interpret the term as having both a geographical meaning, i.e., confined to a limited area, and also matters that were not of national significance. The reality, of course, is that what was or was not important in 1867 may be different today. That reality is the dilemma one encounters when dividing the governing function and trying to anticipate the future.

---

1   P.B. Waite (ed.), *The Confederation Debates in the Province of Canada, 1865* (Toronto: McClelland and Stewart, 1979), p. 44.

In his study for the Rowell-Sirois Commission, Donald Creighton stated:

> Any theory designed to account for the division of these powers into the two categories of general and local matters, must admittedly be tentative in character; but it is suggested here that the Fathers of Confederation attempted to separate the affairs and interests associated with commerce from certain rights and customs dependent upon land. The former, which covered the great bulk of the economic activities of British North America as they knew it, they gave to the control of the Dominion; the latter, which included matters of minor economic, or of largely *cultural*, importance, they entrusted to the provinces.[2]

The federal government was given the responsibility to chart the course of the nation. It was given authority over the "great subjects," and an unlimited taxing power. The provinces were to be subordinate when the federal powers of disallowance, reservation and the declaratory power are considered. However, things did not work out the way the Fathers intended. While today the division of powers, on paper, remains remarkably similar to what it was in 1867, we know that significant changes have occurred.

THE DIVISION OF POWERS TODAY

Why have changes to the division of powers taken place and how have these changes occurred? First of all Canada has changed from a rural to an urban society. Second, the economy has evolved from mercantilism to industrialism to post-industrialism. Third, cataclysmic events such as wars, depression and inflation have also shaped the federal system.

> [E]conomic depression and wars have ever been known as the great enemies of true federalism.[3]

This quotation from a mid-1950s Quebec Royal Commission reflects the sentiment that certain events tended to shift powers from the provinces to the federal government, or put another way, have been the cause of centralization. Fourth, governments do more today than they did in 1867. As governments expand their spheres of legislative activity they are more likely to come in conflict either through competition or through overlapping jurisdiction. Fifth, there are new areas of public concern which require government action. An obvious example today is the environment; another is the whole area of social

---

2 D.G. Creighton, *British North America at Confederation: A Study Prepared for the Royal Commission on Dominion Provincial Relations* (Ottawa: King's Printer, 1939), p. 50.

3 *Report of the Royal Commission of Inquiry on Constitutional Problems*, vol. I (Quebec: The Commission, 1956), p. 127.

services which led to constitutional change in the form of an amendment concerning pensions.

It was during the Depression that the federal government established the Rowell-Sirois Commission to, among other things, "provide for a reexamination...of the distribution of legislative powers in the light of the economic and social developments of the last seventy years."[4] This Royal Commission was the first of a series of studies spanning a period of over 50 years, all basically asking the same question — should there be a change to the division of powers. In this instance, the pressure was to add to federal responsibilities.

The division of powers has been transformed through a number of different ways. Given the current discussion of (and apparent dissatisfaction with) the amending formula, one would imagine this mechanism has been pivotal to our constitutional evolution. There have been, however, only four changes to the division of powers as a result of formal constitutional amendments since 1867. They are:

- unemployment insurance 1940 — transfer from the provinces to the federal parliament;
- old age pensions 1951 — establishing a new sphere of concurrent jurisdiction;
- supplementary benefits 1964 — an expansion of the 1951 amendment;
- section 92A on natural resource jurisdiction in 1982 which both outlines an area of exclusive provincial jurisdiction and establishes a new area of concurrency in interprovincial trade.

Of the four amendments, three expanded federal jurisdiction while the fourth expanded provincial. With respect to both unemployment insurance and old age pensions, this was a direct result of the development of national programs in two areas of social policy, which to some were beyond the fiscal capacity of provinces to resolve, and which required national action and standards. Natural resources became important constitutionally after the 1973 energy crisis when federal policies were perceived to challenge or undermine provincial ownership. Two of the amendments, unemployment insurance and natural resources, have something in common. Both were issues that had been the subject of constitutional challenge before the courts. The amendments came afterwards as a means of finally resolving the jurisdictional question. Four amendments in 123 years does not constitute an avalanche of change.

The most important forum for change has been the courts and their interpretation of the constitution resulting from challenges to both federal and provincial legislation. From Confederation through to today both federal and

---

4 *Report of the Royal Commission on Dominion-Provincial Relations*, Reprinted (Ottawa: Queen's Printer, 1954), p. 9.

provincial governments have used their legislative capacities to the fullest. It is not surprising therefore that clashes would take place as federal and provincial laws collided. As government became more complex, the areas of conflict increased.

What is important to realize is that these decisions gave flesh to the bones of sections 91 and 92 of the *Constitution Act, 1867.* Courts were required to deal with matters such as aeronautics, communications, unemployment assistance, war powers, treaty-making, inflation, agricultural marketing and offshore resources. Each time a question was answered either the federal or provincial list was expanded or made more explicit. The courts have been the brokers of the division of powers.

A third way the division of powers has been modified or influenced is through the exercise of the federal spending power. The principal manifestation of the spending power is the shared-cost or conditional-grant program. The most well-known programs are hospital care, medicare, post-secondary education and the Canada Assistance Plan. A basic characteristic of these programs is that they are a result of federal-provincial negotiation or the processes of executive federalism. Whatever one's views are of executive federalism, an understanding of the process of dialogue and discussion which has forged these agreements is essential if one is to understand the complexity of the division of powers today. With shared-cost programs, one can see the high degree of interdependence between the two orders of government.

The fourth way the division of powers has been influenced is by what I would call the new reality or the new politics. Four examples are: environment, energy, consumer protection and economic development. In all four instances large government bureaucracies have been established "to regulate" or "to manage" these areas. Each term is so vague or extensive that one can only conclude that both orders of government will have an interest in and a jurisdictional claim to the subject. Thus there has evolved over the last 20 or so years a vast constitutional tangle where programs, services and regulations are duplicated with an ever-expanding sphere of concurrent or overlapping jurisdiction.

The difficulty is that these subject areas are so all-encompassing that it is difficult to link one of them to a particular heading under either section 91 or 92. To facilitate policy-making in such areas, one also finds an increasing number of intergovernmental agreements. While jurisdiction may be important, it may not be in anybody's interest to seek a clarification of where the boundaries lie. Thus, it may be better to cooperate than to risk losing jurisdiction.

Part of the new reality is the significance of technology in modifying the division of powers. Technology influences how governments operate and pushes the governing function to new limits and therefore into new areas of conflict and competition. It should be evident that the potential for conflict in any case among the four examples increases as jurisdictional questions are pushed to their limit. For example, in the case of the energy dispute between Alberta and Canada the conflict was over both ownership and jurisdiction.

A final word of caution when reflecting on the division of powers relates to the cost of providing programs. In 1867 health and education expenditures costs were negligible. Today they are not. Indeed, they are increasing at a rate that causes some to believe they are out of control. Without getting into a debate on the importance of these expenditures what must be recognized is that the cost alone of these program areas makes them important. Moreover, the importance threshhold, once crossed, intensifies pressure for federal intervention to establish national standards, a situation comparable to the development of the health-care program in the 1960s.

As a result of the blurring of jurisdictional boundaries, the imbalance of fiscal means to fiscal responsibilities, the emergence of new policy areas, the growing strength of regions, the Quiet Revolution in Quebec and the changing nature of what are the "great subjects," constitutional reform has become a national past-time in Canada. The balance of this paper will examine reform proposals as they relate to the division of powers and recommend some solutions.

CONSTITUTIONAL REFORM IN CANADA

In one way or another the question of constitutional reform has dominated the federal-provincial agenda since the mid-1960s. Beginning with the February 1968 Constitutional Conference tremendous effort and energy have been expended on this subject. With the search for an amending formula in the early sixties one can trace the evolution and development of constitutional reform through to the collapse of the Meech Lake Accord and the current discussion in Canada of our constitutional future. Central to the discussion has been the division of powers. Despite the prominence given to this subject, the results of discussions have been singularly unproductive and agreement elusive.

The term "division of powers" is of limited assistance. Once having agreed to discuss what is generally acknowledged to be at the very centre of the federal system, experience shows that attention soon focuses on particular topics that are currently contentious or topical for some other reason. Despite efforts to design a model or theoretical approach to the division of powers, most individuals will generally (and usually very quickly) gravitate towards specifics because they are easier to understand and, it is believed, easier to resolve. Once a particular subject has been identified for scrutiny it is then subject to microscopic examination, including its linkages to other areas of jurisdiction and its component parts.

Take as an example "education." Under this heading one runs into various subcategories such as post-secondary education, research activities of universities, standardization and harmonization of curriculum, training of immigrants, relationship of education to manpower training, literacy, denominational schools, language of instruction, certification of teachers, mobility rights, and educational communications, to mention but a few of the facets that must be considered. Agreement will need to be reached as to whether or not education is a social objective or an economic necessity. Clearly they are both important but they also contain the seeds of conflict as a review of the various manpower training programs will demonstrate.

The second difficulty is securing agreement on the existing division of powers. It has changed considerably since 1867 and while certain specific changes can be documented there is not universal agreement or, for that matter, understanding, on what an annotated section 91 and 92 would, in fact, look like or should include. Refer again to the four examples used earlier. How does one define or refine the various components of say, environment policy? Would there be agreement as to where responsibility rests? The fact of the matter is that too detailed a list would inevitably lead to conflicting jurisdictional claims or attempts to put fresh interpretations on previous court decisions.

A third problem is that the division of powers, while considered important was usually set aside until other matters were resolved. For example, until governments reached agreement on "regional disparities," or for that matter, the Charter, it was seen to be premature to discuss the division of powers. Agreements in these areas would influence discussions on jurisdiction and it was therefore best to wait. Thus a comprehensive review never materialized.

The fourth problem is the question of specificity. For example, during the negotiations on a proposed section 92A to be added to the *Constitution Act, 1867* on natural resources, the question of "too much" or "too little" was constantly raised. While the federal government was prepared to see a limited expansion of provincial legislative jurisdiction in this area, they were not prepared to do so without first determining precisely what was being transferred and the possible consequences of the transfer. Conversely, the oil and natural gas producing provinces wanted to ensure that any transfer was in fact meaningful. Hours were spent on "what ifs" and attempting to identify all possible consequences of the transfer. To take the example of tree farming, is it forestry (a natural resource) or agriculture (a subject of concurrent jurisdiction)? The sixth schedule to the *Constitution Act, 1982*, which provides detail on the scope of section 92A, illustrates clearly the requirements of precision. To secure agreement, a very detailed definition of "primary production" from natural resources was necessary. It reads in part:

> Production from a forestry resource is primary production therefrom if it consists of sawlogs, poles, lumber, wood chips, sawdust or any other primary wood product or wood pulp, and is not a product manufactured from wood.

This example should be kept in mind when one goes about rewriting the division of powers. It is not as easy and simple as one initially believes.

Federalism for the Future (1968)

In *Federalism for the Future*, the federal government outlined its approach to the division of powers. It suggested that, "Discussions on the division of powers should take place... *after* the constitutional conferences have considered the other principal elements of the Constitution." Having said that it outlined four principles to guide those future discussions.

> First, ...Canada requires both a strong federal government and strong provincial governments.
>
> ...[t]he Parliament of Canada must have responsibility for the major ... instruments of economic policy if it is to stimulate employment and control inflation....
>
> The Government of Canada must have the power to redistribute income between persons and between provinces....
>
> The Government of Canada believes it must be able to speak for Canada, internationally, and that it must be able to act for Canada in strengthening the bonds of nationhood....
>
> The third principle...in discussions concerning the division of powers is that most services involving the most immediate contact between the citizen and the government, and those which contribute most directly to the traditions and heritages which are uniquely provincial, should generally be provided by Canada's provincial governments....
>
> The fourth generalization we would advance concerning the division of powers has to do with the effect each government's activities inevitably will have upon the activities of the others.... We question whether it is any longer realistic to expect that some neat compartmentalization of powers can be found to avoid this. Instead we suspect that the answer is to be found in the processes by which governments consult one another and by which they seek to influence each other before decisions are formally taken.[5]

In addition to the four principles the paper gave a number of specific examples. Under the federal list were included monetary and credit policy, fiscal policy, tariff policy, balance-of-payments policy, economic growth, old age security pensions, unemployment insurance, family allowances, equalization payments, foreign policy, representation abroad, cultural and technological development. Under the provincial list were included education, technological and cultural

---

5   Lester B. Pearson, *Federalism for the Future* (Ottawa: Queen's Printer, 1968), pp. 35-42.

development, health and welfare services, hospitals, regional economic development programs and taxing powers commensurate with their responsibilities.[6]

The discussion on the division of powers was not deferred until the other agenda items had been addressed. Rather than discuss general principles such as the meaning of a strong federal and strong provincial governments, attention quickly focused on a few specific policy areas. Six subjects were given detailed consideration under the general heading "distribution of powers." They were:

- the spending power
- the taxing power
  (a) sales taxes
  (b) death duties
- income security and social services
- economic growth
- capital markets and financial institutions
- the environment

There is a telling comment in the Secretary's Report on this agenda item:

> Despite the prominence of the subject in the overall scope of the constitutional discussions very few propositions, apart from those submitted by Quebec, dealt specifically with the details of an actual distribution of powers.[7]

The 1972 Parliamentary Committee Report

A Special Joint Committee of the Senate and the House of Commons released a comprehensive proposal on constitutional reform in early 1972.

The Report was produced after the Committee held public hearings across Canada. The Committee acknowledged the constantly changing nature of the federal system and recommended that a new constitution be drafted. The Committee also concluded that "there is a consensus among Canadians in favour of a *more functional federalism.*"[8]

The guiding principle for the division of powers is contained in the Committee's second recommendation:

---

6 These examples are referred to in *Federalism for the Future*, pp. 36-42. The references to the international arena are found in a section on international relations in the same paper, pp. 30-32.

7 Canadian Intergovernmental Conference Secretariat, *The Constitutional Review, 1968-71, Secretary's Report* (Ottawa: Information Canada, 1974), p. 72.

8 The Special Joint Committee of the Senate and the House of Commons on the Constitution of Canada, *Final Report* (Ottawa: Queen's Printer, 1972), p.1. It should be noted that the Committee began its deliberations well before the 1971 Victoria Conference and reported after the quest for reform had been slowed down.

> A new Canadian Constitution should be based on functional considerations, which would lead to greater decentralization of governmental powers in areas touching culture and social policy and a greater centralization of powers which have important economic effects at the national level.[9]

Leaving aside the centralization-decentralization dichotomy, the Committee recommended that the federal government's powers should relate to the economy while provincial powers should relate to social and cultural considerations.

In the chapter devoted to "the division of powers" there are three recommendations that relate to the structural aspects of the division of powers but not to the substance. The Committee recommended that there continue to be two exclusive lists, one federal and one provincial, greater use of concurrent powers, and a provision allowing delegation of executive and administrative powers, but not delegation of legislative powers.[10]

The Committee made a number of specific recommendations with respect to how the governing function should be divided. Once the theoretical framework had been established one could assign individual powers to either government. One quickly runs into difficulty, however, when one considers a policy area such as unemployment insurance which has both an economic and a social dimension.

What is of interest today is an examination of the list of matters discussed and those that are omitted. For example, one finds a recommendation giving the federal government extensive powers to regulate foreign ownership, an issue of some concern at that time, whereas there is no reference to energy or natural resources other than offshore resources. The natural resource question would dominate later constitutional discussions. Instead of the word "environment," one finds references to air and water pollution. Once again the dynamic nature of the division of powers is clearly demonstrated.

The Task Force on Canadian Unity (1979)

Seven years after the Parliamentary Committee Report, a second comprehensive report on the constitution was produced, this time by the Task Force on Canadian Unity, otherwise known as the Pepin-Robarts Commission. This Task Force was established after the Parti Québécois election victory in 1976. The new reality of Quebec politics was the focal point of its cross-Canada odyssey.

The Pepin-Robarts Commission called for clarification of the division of powers, the continuation of two exclusive lists and established some important guidelines by which the division of powers might be reviewed. There are strong

---

9   Ibid.
10 Ibid., p. 43.

parallels in the approach found in *Federalism for the Future*, the Parliamentary Committee Report and the Pepin-Robarts report.

To Pepin-Robarts, "the principal roles and responsibilities of the central government should be:

- the strengthening of Canadian identity;
- the preservation and enhancement of the integrity of the Canadian state;
- the overriding responsibility for the conduct of international relations;
- the management of Canada-wide economic policy (including monetary policy) and participation in the stimulation of regional economic activity;
- the establishment of Canada-wide standards where appropriate; and
- the redistribution of income.

The principal roles and responsibilities of the provincial governments should be:

- the social and cultural well-being and development of their communities;
- provincial economic development, including the exploitation of their natural resources;
- property and civil rights; and
- the management of their territory.[11]

Having defined the roles and responsibilities, the Commission then went on to give certain guidelines as to how the distribution should be designed. They recommended that the distribution should take account of the five following considerations: general and particular concern; effectiveness, efficiency and responsiveness; common agreement; continuity; and overall balance.

As a means of clarifying the division of powers, they also recommended that responsibilities be divided into generally acknowledged subject headings such as health, welfare, defence and each one in turn, subdivided into readily identifiable subcategories.

One other point requires further mention. The Pepin-Robarts Commission recommended that concurrent powers should be "avoided wherever possible."[12] This recommendation is very different from the one found in the Parliamentary Committee Report which felt that Canada had too few areas of concurrent jurisdiction. On the other hand, the Pepin-Robarts Commission

---

11 The Task Force on Canadian Unity, *A Future Together* (Ottawa: Minister of Supply and Services Canada, 1979), p. 125.

12 Ibid., p. 126.

recommended that legislative authority be delegated whereas the Parliamentary Committee Report recommended against this approach.

A Time for Action (1978)

In the spring of 1978 the federal government responded to the Parti Québécois electoral success and the promised referendum by calling for a completely new Canadian constitution. In *A Time for Action* it was recognized that discussions on the division of legislative powers were critical to the outcome. The provinces were cautioned that "a solution to Canadian problems will not be found, therefore, in any massive shift of power from the federal government to the provinces."[13] Powers should be transferred in both directions.

> It would be vain, however, to seek to divide these powers into watertight compartments. The complexity of governmental functions is such, nowadays, that even in the case of compartments considered the most "exclusive" to one order of government or the other, both have had to act in concert and will have to do so even more in future.[14]

The document also called for a clarification of the division of powers "so that citizens will know better which order of government is responsible for what, without imprisoning either order in a constitutional straitjacket."[15]

Just as Lester Pearson had suggested ten years earlier, Pierre Trudeau recommended that the discussion on the division of powers be considered in a second phase given the complexity and enormity of the task.

The provincial response to *A Time for Action* was short and to the point and came in the form of a communiqué released at the 1978 Premiers' Conference. To premiers "the division of powers is the key issue in constitutional reform and should be addressed in conjunction with other matters."[16]

The premiers were telling the federal government that discussion on the division of powers would not be deferred until patriation and the amending formula had been resolved. The negotiations had to go on simultaneously. The provinces were insistent on discussing specific areas of jurisdiction and in their communiqué mentioned a number of them such as natural resources, culture, communications, the federal spending power, fisheries, treaties, and immigration.

---

13 Pierre E. Trudeau, *A Time for Action* (Ottawa: Canadian Unity Information Office, 1978), p. 22.

14 Ibid., p. 23.

15 Ibid.

16 Alberta Federal and Intergovernmental Affairs, *Sixth Annual Report to 31 March 1979* (Edmonton: Government of Alberta, 1979), p. 43.

In addition to their comments on constitutional reform, the premiers also raised concerns about the duplication of government services and criticized the federal government for intruding into what they claimed were areas of provincial jurisdiction. They listed the following as "promising areas for early action":

- consumer and corporate affairs
- environmental protection
- agricultural research
- offshore mineral resources
- the regulation of uranium mining and the nuclear industry
- housing and urban affairs
- administration of justice
- correctional services, and
- post-secondary education[17]

Not only did they seek to clarify jurisdictional boundaries, but they also pointed out to the federal government that the clarification of these boundaries might also require the transfer of financial resources from the federal government to the provinces. This would be particularly true, for example, in the case of post-secondary education.

The preceding commentary gives a fairly clear understanding of the two approaches to discussions on the division of powers. One is to set up a general analytical framework and then to identify what powers or responsibilities are appropriate for each order of government. The second is to take specific policy areas and to debate whether or not they should be transferred from the federal to the provincial governments or vice versa.

Linked to the second approach were efforts to protect provincial powers or federal powers from intrusion by the other level of government. The question of duplication became much more pervasive in the 1970s as both orders of government endeavoured to respond to new issues of public policy. Duplication is both inefficient and leads to conflicting policies and standards of service. For example, while the provinces were concerned about federal encroachment into the area of natural resources, the federal government was equally concerned about provincial encroachment into the area of international relations.

What did all of these position papers and studies produce with respect to reforms to the division of powers? In the final analysis, very little. The only proposed change to the division of powers in the 1971 Victoria Charter was the addition of "family, youth and occupational training allowances" to section 94A of the *Constitution Act, 1867*. This matter was not considered during the early years of the review. It was added in 1971 to the agenda at the insistence of

---

17 Ibid., p. 42.

Quebec. At Victoria, Quebec achieved a partial victory, namely the proposed expansion of the subject areas contained in section 94A, but they were unsuccessful in securing a guarantee of financial compensation, the rock on which the Victoria Charter foundered.

Perhaps the difficulties associated with considering the division of powers in its entirety was best illustrated in the fall of 1978. Rather than undertaking a comprehensive review Prime Minister Trudeau suggested establishing a priority list. The items he included on the short list were drawn from provincial proposals developed at the 1976 and 1978 Premiers' Conferences. The list consisted of federal spending power, taxation, natural resources, family law, communications, the declaratory power, equalization and regional disparaties. To this list the provinces added fisheries and offshore resources.

The federal government gave the provinces the opportunity to discuss those areas of the division of powers that were of great concern to them and were willing to defer consideration of the federal wish list to future meetings. This strategy, of course, assumed there would be future meetings. The federal wish list was tabled at the February 1979 meeting of first ministers. It contained the following:

- Powers in the economic field to fight inflation, unemployment and regional disparaties, and to protect the dollar.
- The question of nontariff barriers to interprovincial and international trade and investment.
- The question of interprovincial and international movement of goods and services including the right of passage of electricity and oil, gas and other minerals.
- The question of barriers to the movement of persons for employment.
- The regulation of competition.
- Regulation of the Canadian securities market.
- The question of marketing boards.
- The problem of jurisdiction over minimum wages.
- Foreign relations and the role of provinces.
- The question of the appointment of Superior Court judges, and of the setting up of federal courts for the administration of federal laws.
- Canada's native peoples and the constitution.

While a useful reference, the federal wish list was never given serious consideration. "Powers over the Economy" was considered during the marathon discussions of the summer of 1980 after the Quebec referendum. Mobility rights were eventually included in the constitution via the Charter.

Although those items identified in the fall of 1978 dominated the discussions on the division of powers throughout the 1978-80 period, the results were again disappointing if one looks at either the areas of agreement or the changes that were subsequently included in the *Constitution Act, 1982.* The only change was in the area of natural resources, to create section 92A of the *Constitution Act, 1867.* In every other instance agreement was elusive. In part this was due to the complexity of particular areas and in part to an unwillingness to transfer jurisdiction in either direction. It became clear, for example, during the discussions in 1980 that in order for the provinces to gain additional jurisdiction in the area of natural resources, they would have to reciprocate by giving to the federal government additional responsibilities over the economy. The provinces were not prepared to do so, therefore little progress was made.

The Macdonald Commission (1985)

The Royal Commission on the Economic Union and Development Prospects for Canada (The Macdonald Commission) gave short shrift to the idea of rewriting or codifying the division of powers. The final report concluded that: "Another reason for hesitation about comprehensive constitutional revision is that any reallocation of the full range of constitutional powers to accord with current concepts of government would probably become obsolete almost the day it was put in writing."[18] The Commission did "not find...any compelling reason either for significantly increasing centralization or for promoting decentralization. We see no merits in efforts to restore the classic model of watertight compartments."[19]

Concluding Assessment

The foregoing commentary covering the period 1968-85 has led me to conclude that it is almost virtually impossible to give a complete overhaul to the division of powers found in the Canadian constitution. Moreover if one accepts the findings of the Macdonald Commission, there is no need to do so. It is not so much that the participants lack the political will, but rather the subject matters are so complex and constantly changing that it would be futile to embark on a complete rewrite of the division of powers. Moreover, while agreement may be reached on a framework for the discussion, I am not convinced that there would be universal agreement on, for example, the economic and social dimensions of particular subject areas. While a laudable objective, the fact of the matter is that a total rewrite is unlikely to take place. Another consideration is that the Government of Quebec is unlikely to transfer any part of its legislative juris-

---

18 Royal Commission on the Economic Union and Development Prospects for Canada, *Report,* vol. 3 (Ottawa: Minister of Supply and Services, Canada, 1985), p. 255.
19 Ibid., p. 256.

diction to the federal government. This reality has been patently clear in every constitutional conference since 1968. If this is so, and there is really little evidence to contradict it, then in reality, a revision to the division of powers means transfers of specific responsibilities from the federal government to Quebec and the other provinces.

An expansion of provincial legislative jurisdiction is the position adopted by the Allaire report released on 28 January 1991, entitled *A Québec Free to Choose*.[20] A good part of the paper is devoted to the division of powers. The proposed breakdown contains few surprises. The areas of exclusive provincial jurisdiction include existing areas. Additions include those that are part of what I have referred to earlier as the new reality where policy areas are so broad that both governments have jurisdictional claims. Part of the rationale for the list is the elimination of duplication of effort. Again this approach can be found in the position developed by the ten provinces in 1978.

In my view, a massive transfer is an unrealistic proposition, if the reactions to the Meech Lake Accord are indicative of public opinion. A standard criticism of the Accord was that the federal government gave away everything and got nothing in return. If something as modest as the Meech Lake Accord could generate such concern over the future efficacy of the national government, it is highly unlikely that a wholesale transfer of responsibilities would be acceptable to the vast majority of Canadians outside Quebec. Nor does the controversy over the "distinct society" clause auger well for a special arrangement with Quebec although it or something like it must be reconsidered. Such difficulty casts doubt on the efficacy of proposals for asymmetrical federalism where one province's authority is fundamentally different than that of the others. If these assumptions are correct and if it is further assumed that the status quo is not acceptable then one must look elsewhere for solutions.

FUTURE ALTERNATIVES

Two come to mind. The first is to continue what we have done in the past, namely identify certain policy areas and seek solutions to those particular problems. For example, while section 92A on natural resources, which includes generation of electricity, may not have resolved all the difficulties, it certainly dampened some of the provincial criticisms that existed at that time. While probably not satisfactory to those who prefer a comprehensive approach, an incremental approach is more likely to lead to the successful resolution of issues that divide us. For one thing there is not time to initiate a total rewrite because

---

20 The Constitutional Committee of the Québec Liberal Party, *A Québec Free to Choose: Report of the Constitutional Committee*. (Montreal: Québec Liberal Party, 1991). The report has been named for the chairman of the committee, Jean Allaire.

Quebec has run out of patience and is now pressing for immediate action. The Allaire report recommends a final make or break referendum by the fall of 1992, which has served to dramatize the urgent need to resolve this question.

Over the past 25 years certain specific issues have tended to dominate discussions on the division of powers. I would recommend we begin with these, if for no other reason than that much of the work has already been done. In some instances draft constitutional texts are available. At the outset I would recommend the following as an initial list for consideration; taxation, federal spending power, immigration, communications, foreign relations and the role of provinces, fisheries, interprovincial trade barriers, family allowances, youth and occupational training allowances, the declaratory power, natural resources including offshore resources, environment and income security. Each of these issues has been discussed, each is of interest to both the federal and provincial governments. Finally, this approach will provide individuals and groups with a specific list of issue areas for debate. The constitutional debate will therefore move from the abstract to the specific.

Of the different items I have identified for negotiation most of them are included in the Allaire report's recommendations on the division of powers. To achieve the degree of autonomy proposed by the report will require limits to the federal spending power, and I would expect to the declaratory power. At the same time the Allaire report recognizes that interprovincial trade barriers need to be eliminated. Issues such as energy have been encompassed in the past by the discussions on natural resources. In short, a review of only those matters that have been on the agenda since 1968 incorporates most of the matters Quebec has now placed on the agenda. For example, agreement on a provincial role in international affairs was nearly reached at the 1971 Victoria Conference. Agreement was reached on a provincial role in the area of family, youth and occupational training allowances. What future negotiations will produce is, of course, unknown. For the purposes of this paper I have assumed the matters previously identified can be examined once again and that Quebec's opening position is flexible to some extent.

The second approach, which is the one I believe would be most fruitful in the future, is to design and develop devices or mechanisms for the transfer of jurisdiction either temporarily or permanently without attempting the wholesale reform of the division of powers under section 91 and section 92. In my opinion, not only is this approach more low-key, but also it has a much greater opportunity of being successful. Moreover, it has the advantage of not conferring special status on any particular province and it can be combined with, or adapted to, consideration of the specific subject areas already mentioned. What devices are, therefore, available?

Concurrent Powers

Most studies and commissions have recommended the continuation of two lists of exclusive powers. I agree with this approach, but in order to clarify the constitution these lists would have to become exceedingly detailed. The greater the specificity, the greater the possibility of intergovernmental conflict and rivalry. The reality of the federal system is interdependence which is best recognized through the establishment of more areas of concurrent jurisdiction with one or the other order of government having paramountcy in the event of a conflict. For example, any area of federal jurisdiction that becomes concurrent would be subject to federal paramountcy while areas of provincial jurisdiction that become concurrent would be subject to provincial paramountcy. The negotiations would then focus on what should be the areas of concurrent jurisdiction.

In those areas, it should also be made clear that federal or provincial legislation would stand unless it contravened a specific piece of legislation. In other words, if either order of government wandered (intentionally or unintentionally) into the other's sphere of jurisdiction, unless there was a specific statutory conflict, then the offending law would remain valid, something that is not possible in Canada today.

A classic example of what is possible is found in section 94A of the *Constitution Act, 1867* which reads:

> 94A. The Parliament of Canada may make laws in relation to old age pensions and supplementary benefits, including survivor and disability benefits irrespective of age, but no such law shall affect the operation of any law present or future of a provincial legislature in relation to any such matter.

When this amendment was approved in 1951, one could not have anticipated that the Canada and Quebec Pensions Plans could coexist without serious consequences for the country. As noted, the Victoria Charter would have expanded the list of matters referred to in section 94A to include family, youth and occupational training allowances. Under this model jurisdictional boundaries can be clarified (or expanded) but it is left open as to whether or not individual provinces will choose to exercise their authority. It is probable that few, if any, provinces other than Quebec will exercise this authority, but there is nothing preventing them from doing so. One word of caution. The question of financial compensation may need to be addressed, just as it was under the spending power provisions contained in the Meech Lake Constitutional Accord and just as it was proposed in 1971 with a revised section 94A.

Why concurrent legislative authority? First of all it reflects reality. Second, it permits governments to vacate an area of jurisdiction temporarily depending upon circumstances. The genius of section 94A is that the federal government can establish national programs and the provinces, by virtue of paramountcy, have a strong say in their development because they have the opportunity to reoccupy the field. The provision has its own built-in checks and balances and avoids duplication. To me, this approach has considerable merit because it avoids jurisdictional battles and provides a framework for intergovernmental negotiation. Concurrent powers would be negotiated on a piecemeal basis and are most likely to emerge in new areas of public policy such as environment. It is more prudent to attempt to write a clause covering a specific area such as environment just as it was to write something on natural resources. Section 92A confirms areas of exclusive provincial jurisdiction and includes a new area of concurrent jurisdiction. The advantage of this approach is that it is both necessary, given the complexity of the subject matters, and desirable given the importance which the public attaches to the issue. Concurrent jurisdiction clarifies issues and lays the constitutional foundation for intergovernmental cooperation rather than for intergovernmental conflict.

The Allaire report appears to favour greater use of concurrent jurisdiction in identifying areas of shared jurisdiction. In some instances the report makes very specific recommendations. For example, under justice they propose that Quebec be responsible for civil law, administration of justice and courts, whereas Canada would be responsible for criminal law. Since Quebec is the only civil law province, there can be a strong case made to limit appeals in this area to the Quebec court of appeal.

In areas such as environment, energy and regional development, a detailed provision might identify areas of federal paramountcy and other areas where the provinces are paramount. For example, the interprovincial and international dimension of environmental protection cannot be ignored. The authors of the report also recognize the need for harmonization of government policy. In drafting areas of concurrency, more attention to incorporating this objective may reduce the reluctance for governments to share jurisdiction.

Delegation of Powers

Provision should be made in the constitution to make it possible to delegate legislative authority from one or more provinces to the federal government and from the federal government to one or more provinces. In instances where delegation is used, it should be for a specific period of time and subject to review. This would not prevent it from being renewed but rather would ensure that the delegation is not seen as being permanent. In other words, to be effective there should be a system of checks and balances.

When the Fulton-Favreau amending formula was drafted in 1964, there was a second part to the proposed constitutional amendment that provided for the delegation of legislative authority. The wording was really very straightforward. It allowed for either the Parliament of Canada or the legislature of a province to legislate in each other's legislative jurisdiction provided the other order of government approved. One limiting factor was that before delegation could take effect at least four provinces had to agree. In other words, it was insufficient to have delegation from or to a single province. In later discussions, the threshold of four provinces was seen to be a limiting factor. Any future discussions should probably confine themselves to the principle of delegation and not the number of provinces that need to be involved in any such transfers.

If a delegation clause is included in the constitution some of the proposals for change in the Allaire report are likely candidates for serious consideration. The one that comes to mind is unemployment insurance, which was transferred from the provinces to the federal government in 1940. As federal policy in this area continues to evolve there are certain aspects that can be assumed by provinces.

Federal-provincial Agreements

In the mid-1970s when the federal and provincial governments engaged in a mini-series of constitutional discussions, the federal government proposed that there be a constitutional provision that would authorize the federal government and the provinces to enter into agreements in certain specified areas. The proposed wording in 1975 was as follows:

> In order to ensure a greater harmony of action by governments, and especially in order to reduce the possibility of action that could adversely affect the preservation and development in Canada of the French language and the culture based on it, the Government of Canada and governments of the provinces or of any one or more of the provinces may, within the limits of the powers otherwise accorded to each of them respectively by law, enter into agreements with one another concerning the manner of exercise of such powers, particularly in the fields of immigration, communications and social policy.

It should be noted that the subject matter of the agreements was confined to the preservation and development of the French language and culture, but there is no reason why such a restriction would be necessary in any future discussions. The proposal was a direct result of concerns expressed by Premier Bourassa to the federal government. He was looking for constitutional protection of Quebec's language and culture. The immigration agreement between Canada and Quebec, signed on 5 February 1991, is an example of this approach, although it does not carry the mantle of being sanctioned by the constitution. The agreement satisfies Quebec's jurisdictional claims. The importance of the agreement is that it demonstrates that solutions are possible without constitutional amendment even though immigration was included in the Meech Lake agreement.

Premier Wells of Newfoundland was quick to criticize the idea of a special immigration agreement between Quebec and Canada and insisted that the same opportunities be given to each province.[21] This reaction is understandable and can be avoided in the future if provisions permitting flexibility are either introduced into the constitution or if the federal government offers similar arrangements to the other provinces.

Opting-out

To some extent the principle of opting-out is already found in the constitution in section 94A. While the section establishes an area of concurrent jurisdiction, it also allows a province to continue or to initiate its own programs. The principle is also contained in the amending formula with respect to constitutional amendments that would have the effect of derogating from existing provincial legislative powers. It is also found in the notwithstanding clause of the Charter, section 33 of the *Constitution Act, 1982*.

More recently, the same principle was found in the spending power provisions contained in the Meech Lake Constitutional Accord. That provision read as follows:

> The Government of Canada shall provide reasonable compensation to the government of a province that chooses not to participate in a national shared-cost program that is established by the Government of Canada after the coming into force of this section in an area of exclusive provincial jurisdiction, if the province carries on a program or initiative that is compatible with the national objectives.

Without getting into too much detail, this provision would have legitimized the exercise of the federal spending power in areas of exclusive provincial jurisdiction but also recognized that certain provinces may choose to establish or operate a parallel program. While it is possible that national standards, as a result, may not be universal, at the same time new federal programs could be established. This particular provision was the subject of a great deal of criticism from those who felt it would erode the Government of Canada's ability to establish national standards, but it must be remembered that these standards are in areas of exclusive provincial jurisdiction. That helps to bring the matter into perspective.

A recent event that underlines Quebec's continuing concern over the federal spending power is the insistence by Mr. Rémillard, Quebec's Intergovernmental Affairs Minister, that the federal government get out of the health field.[22] It is

---

21 "Immigration deal transfers powers," *The Globe and Mail*, 24 December 1990, p. A1.
22 "Scrap Canada Health Act, Quebec Minister urges," *The Globe and Mail*, 12 December 1990, p. A5.

no coincidence that this statement was made simultaneously with the province announcing it will charge fees for individuals using the emergency wards. The federal government rejected Quebec's request to get out of the health field and reaffirmed its commitment to medicare.[23] What is significant about this exchange is that it demonstrates that the issues associated with the spending power and exclusive areas of provincial jurisdiction such as health have not really changed. At the same time, the Quebec government has asked the federal government to get out of the area of manpower training.[24] In both instances, namely health and manpower, Quebec would expect to receive fiscal compensation. There is nothing to prevent an agreement being reached in either of these areas similar to what was negotiated in the area of immigration. What must be remembered is that each province must be given the same opportunities.

Opting-in

The principle of opting-in to policies or programs is also something that has been provided for in the past. One example is section 94 of the *Constitution Act, 1867* which provides for the Parliament of Canada to pass uniform laws governing property and civil rights, provided the Provinces of Ontario, Nova Scotia and New Brunswick agreed to have these laws apply to their respective jurisdictions. Another proposal for opting-in is found in Bill C-60, which was the draft constitution tabled by the federal government in June 1978. In the draft legislation the proposed Charter of Rights was applicable to the Parliament and Government of Canada only. If provinces opted-in to the Charter then the federal powers of reservation and disallowance would no longer apply to those provinces. Another example is found in section 59 of the *Constitution Act, 1982*. Also, section 23(1)(a) of the Charter of Rights does not apply in Quebec until the legislature or government gives its consent.

Interprovincial Agreements

The United States Constitution recognizes interstate compacts or agreements that require Congressional assent before they become effective. There is no reason why the Canadian constitution could not provide for or give sanction to interprovincial agreements. Through this type of arrangement national standards could be established in areas such as securities legislation, certification of teachers, water quality, and interprovincial trade barriers to mention a few examples. To me, there are compelling reasons for the federal government to

---

23 "Beatty rejects Quebec's proposal," *The Globe and Mail*, 13 December 1990, p. A7.
24 "Quebec steps up demand for powers," *The Globe and Mail*, 14 December 1990, p. A1.

encourage this approach to problem solving. It removes the appearance of a federal power grab and accomplishes the same objective, a pan-Canadian solution. What must be recognized here is that a national consensus does not necessarily always require participation by the federal government.

In mid-December Prime Minister Mulroney gave a speech suggesting that he was amenable to a review of the division of powers.[25] He emphasized in his remarks, however, that he remained concerned with interprovincial trade barriers and that these had to be eliminated. This position is similar to the one adopted by the Pepin-Robarts Commission and in the position paper tabled by the Government of Canada during the 1980 constitutional discussions which was entitled "Securing the Canadian Economic Union in the Constitution." The elimination of trade barriers is extremely difficult and is something that provinces have tackled in the area of provincial purchasing, but it is possible to achieve results without amending the constitution.

Federal-provincial "Accords"

This is one of two proposals suggested by the Macdonald Commission, and differs from the device of the "federal-provincial agreement" reviewed above. To the Commission, an accord has "some of the characteristics of a treaty."[26] The example they give is the 1985 Atlantic Accord between the federal government and Newfoundland covering offshore resources. This accord is also of interest because it anticipates or provides for its eventual constitutionalization. Another example is the agreement in 1985 to hold annual First Ministers's Conferences for a five-year period.

Assessment

These seven techniques, devices or mechanisms are all ways in which flexibility can be achieved within the federal system without significant amendments to the division of powers. Each approach referred to makes it possible to accommodate the diverse interests that make up our polity. What must be appreciated is that in every instance the provinces are treated alike in law, and therefore, we get around the problems associated with conferring special status or giving preferential treatment to one particular province.

To me, special recognition of Quebec can be achieved in other ways than preferential treatment under the division of powers. Some have proposed that

---

25 "PM suggests power shuffle with provinces," *The Globe and Mail*, 17 December 1990, p. A1.
26 Royal Commission on the Economic Union and Development Prospects for Canada, *Report*, vol. 3, p. 257.

recognition of this fact be included in the preamble to the constitution. Another approach is to draft a clause similar to the "distinct society" clause contained in the Meech Lake Accord. The reality is that Quebec could end up with a *de facto* special status if the mechanisms referred to earlier are fully utilized.

Since it is impossible to know the future shape of the division of powers, it is far more prudent to design techniques that will accommodate change. In each instance one could put in conditions such as federal-provincial consultation, equal opportunity to the other provinces within a fixed period of time, provisions for dispute resolution and time limits. The advantage to this approach is that it is less emotionally charged since each individual provision is neutral in that it does not have too great an impact on the status quo. Since one cannot foretell the future, one cannot anticipate how any or all these devices will develop. That can be left to future generations. To me, incrementalism is better than separatism.

CONCLUSION

This paper started out with a general discussion of the division of powers and the difficulties associated with securing agreement on which powers should be assigned to which order of government. At the same time it has been recognized that change is inevitable and that what is agreed to today may be out of date tomorrow. Another observation is that while major studies on the constitution have argued for a systematic and coherent approach to the division of powers, this has proven to be unsuccessful. In all probability governments and the public will focus on specific policy areas such as health, the environment, interprovincial trade, and economic development to mention some issues that are currently under discussion. In my view it is better to try and resolve these policy differences on an individual basis or with an agenda based on matters previously discussed since it is unlikely that there will be agreement on a general approach to the division of powers.

The more prudent approach is to design techniques that will allow for more flexible arrangements on the division of powers to be developed, including constitutional recognition of more areas of concurrent powers and the delegation of powers. This does not mean that intergovernmental disputes over jurisdiction will disappear. Far from it, but at least mechanisms for their subsequent resolution will have been previously identified. In other words, if a provision already existed in the constitution to recognize federal-provincial agreements over the exercise of power, it would not be necessary to resort to formal constitutional amendments to constitutionalize, for example, the recently concluded Canada-Quebec immigration agreement. Whatever mechanisms are established, the principle of provincial equality must be respected. While it is probable that most other provinces will not avail themselves of these opportunities, the fact that they have that right will, in most instances, be sufficient.

Finally, we should not delude ourselves about the difficult discussions that lie ahead. It is highly improbable that Quebec will agree to any transfer of powers from that province to the federal government. There is also the persistent belief that Quebec's position on the constitution is an impediment to centralization which is thought to be desired by the other provinces.[27] This is one myth that should be put to rest.

Nor is it clear that Canada is prepared for a massive decentralization of powers if our experience with Meech Lake serves as an example. If these two assertions are correct and it is further assumed that the status quo is unacceptable then other approaches are needed. Any attempt to rewrite the constitution with the expectation that there will be a major rewrite to the division of powers, is simply not going to be successful. What is possible are the two approaches to a more flexible federal system, namely dealing with specific issues such as the environment and identifying mechanisms to promote change while recognizing the interdependence of governments.

Will this approach be acceptable to Quebec? That is hard to say, but the Allaire report gives some indication that greater use of concurrent powers and delegation of powers are worthy of consideration. What must be realized is that the negotiations will not be confined to the division of powers, but will include among other things: amendments to the Charter; reform of the Senate, House of Commons and Supreme Court; constitutional principles such as self determination, distinct society and provincial equality; the role of the monarchy; the amending procedure; and the constitutional position of aboriginal peoples. If the desired (or assumed) result is an entirely new constitution, then negotiations on the division of powers must be placed in this perspective, i.e., it is only one of a number of agenda items. When considered in isolation the recommendations in this paper may not by themselves be sufficient for Quebec's purposes, but in the context of a global review they are certainly a reasonable and realistic alternative.

---

27 "Quebec independence would help 'crumbling' country, panel told," *The Globe and Mail*, 19 December 1990, p. A1.

15

Equality or Asymmetry: Why Choose?

David Milne

Whatever the reasons for the invention of fancy new language such as "asymmetrical federalism" — I will leave the politics of that question aside for the moment — there is no doubt that Canadians are familiar with the basic idea. The concept asks Canadians to consider a federalism that would not only recognize natural differences (such as size, population, history, etc.) among the units of a federation, but also formal differences in law among the units either with respect to jurisdictional powers and duties, the shape of central institutions, or the application of national laws and programs. In part, this view of federalism seeks to know whether a federation can tolerate one or more forms of "special status" without the federation falling apart on the shoals of provincial equality. It need hardly be said that "asymmetry" sounds a lot less offensive to Canadian ears than does the hoary old language of "special status," rights to "diversity" more appealing than rights to preferential treatment.

Now this kind of question would be delicate for any federation since it challenges a people's sense of national political community on the one hand, and their notions of equality and inequality among state or provincial communities on the other. Probably no people are more acutely sensitized to these issues than are Canadians. They have long been participants in these kinds of debates, for example, when deciding the nature and powers of the French-speaking state of Quebec historically, or the legal status of newly emerging provincial communities in the Canadian west and elsewhere. At all of these times, Canadians have not hesitated to make special arrangements where

I wish to thank Professor Ronald Watts for his generous contribution to this essay, particularly his sharing with me his own notes on asymmetry and his thoughts on Canada's asymmetrical options cited later in Table 15.5. I am also indebted to the meticulous work on the tables in this essay by Patrick Fafard, a Queen's University Ph.D. student, and by Phillip MacLellan, a graduate of the University of Prince Edward Island and the University of Western Ontario.

necessary — asymmetrical elements in law and policy — but these have had to be balanced against the claims and logic of equality. At times, when unequal arrangements have been made, they have sown a later harvest of bitterness and regret. The federal decision, for example, to withhold provincial control over public lands in the prairie provinces, while in part defensible, proved to be a costly departure from the logic of provincial equality.

In recent years in Canada, the demand for asymmetry has come from Quebec and not from the centre and, in response, it was Pierre Trudeau, *not* Peter Lougheed or any other provincialist leader, who stoutly expounded the inviolable principle of provincial equality. It was Trudeau who insisted, at least with respect to the division of powers, on that standard of legal symmetry in our federation.[1] His argument was also extended to the notion of equality of Canadian citizenship, with his proposal for a national Charter of Rights and Freedoms. It is that legacy that challenged the mildly asymmetrical features of the Meech Lake Accord and prevented its ratification, although the chief spokesmen for that vision are now provincial leaders like Clyde Wells and Gary Filmon.

It is worth underlining, therefore, the profound ideological debate that is often engendered in Canada, even by well-meaning and carefully tailored proposals for asymmetry. That is surely a lesson we can draw from the Meech Lake debacle. Although some would simply attribute that outcome to Trudeau's well-publicized denunciation of special status, that surely underrates the deeper psychological and political dimensions of the issue. It is only because such departures from the equality principle cause such soul-searching that Trudeau was effective in his appeal. Ironically, it is worth remembering that after 1971 the language of equality was turned against Trudeau too in his attempts to provide for asymmetrical arrangements in Canada's amending formula. Indeed, it will be the thesis of this paper that, though formalized asymmetry may be defensible from any number of perspectives, it will most often be trumped by the equality principle in constitutional politics. Indeed, Canada's history shows the gradual struggle and triumph of the equality principle against different forms of asymmetry in Canadian life. If that is so, any future constitutional designers may want to think very carefully before playing directly with this option.

So much for the warning. But if, as frequently claimed, federalism means that one can have one's cake and eat it too, you would be right to suspect that there must be some way out of this dilemma. The good news is that there are a

---

1   It is important to recognize that Trudeau was by no means hostile to asymmetry in other respects. On the contrary, he advocated asymmetry in provincial representation in a reformed Senate, and in amending formulas. Moreover, he accepted a variety of asymmetrical administrative arrangements with the provinces.

variety of ingenious devices that might be considered to provide for asymmetry while respecting the equality principle. These will be taken up later in this paper. For now, however, a brief detour into the history and politics of equality's struggle with asymmetry is in order.

THE LOGIC OF ASYMMETRY

It would seem that asymmetry is a fact of nature. In no federation are the units symmetrical — they vary in size, shape, economy, geography, population, wealth — if not in culture and history. In Canada, the asymmetries are sharp indeed. As the tables on the following pages show, there are vast differences among the provinces in some of these key indicators. These substantive inequalities — with indicators often reinforcing each other — breed asymmetrical attitudes too. The figures on population, wealth and size support and sustain our continuing imagery of Canada as a centre (consisting of Ontario and Quebec) and peripheries (consisting of all the rest). They are taken as surrogates for a real inequality of power and dignity among provinces. This is the resentful food upon which provincial politicians feed. Canadians do not need to be reminded of the strains to national unity contained here.

Quebec too stands out by virtue of its distinct linguistic composition as the home of the only majority francophone province in Canada — or indeed the only independent majority francophone jurisdiction in all of North America. With that kind of asymmetry, it is scarcely likely that Quebec will ever regard itself as a province like the others. Indeed, its distinctiveness as a province was already evident at Confederation in many formal ways: it alone made French an official language in the legislature, adopted the civil code system, and assumed the protection of the Protestant minority's separate school rights.

That was yet another telling indication of asymmetry in Canadian federalism: the unique constitutional provisions that applied either to Quebec or to other provinces. As Table 15.2 indicates, there is a host of such special features that belie the contention of symmetry in provincial constitutions. Among the most important of these are the omission of western provinces' control over their public lands (until 1930), bilingual constitutional requirements in the legislatures of Manitoba and Quebec, the extension of denominational school rights in Ontario to Quebec in section 93 (2), and the exemption of Quebec from the provision to unify property and civil rights under section 94.

Other constitutional provisions outlined in Table 15.3, while respecting equality of provinces in a formal sense, nonetheless make asymmetry inescapable by providing each province with rights to opt out of national standards or programs. One of these is in section 94A where provinces can, in effect, establish their own pension plans outside the terms of the federal government's Canada Pension Plan and thereby achieve *de facto* asymmetry. Another is to be found in the charter where under section 6(4) the mobility rights of Canadian citizens can be abridged in any province with above-average unemployment rates. Opting-out of constitutional amendments transferring provincial powers to Ottawa under sections 38 and 40 with compensation is another such feature, as is the notwithstanding clause permitting provinces to insulate themselves from the scope of certain sections of the Charter under section 33. While such clauses are extended equally to all provinces, they provide the basis for asymmetrical constitutional outcomes.

Table 15.1
Provincial Comparisons (1988)
Size, Population, Wealth, Dependency

	Area (000 km²)	Population (000's)	Provincial GDP Per Capita ($000's)	Federal Dependency Ratio*
Newfoundland	405.7	567.4	13.86	46.5%
Prince Edward Island	5.7	128.0	13.77	45.4
Nova Scotia	55.5	879.8	16.84	39.4
New Brunswick	73.4	713.1	16.44	39.8
Quebec	1540.7	6618.8	21.76	19.5
Ontario	1068.6	9371.4	26.46	13.3
Manitoba	650.0	1081.1	19.87	29.2
Saskatchewan	652.3	1013.9	18.32	22.8
Alberta	661.2	2377.0	26.71	14.7
British Columbia	947.8	2958.9	23.05	16.7
Yukon	483.5	24.7	31.26	70.6
Northwest Territories	3426.3	51.8	35.79	83.8

*Federal dependency ratio is the proportion of the provincial government total revenues that consists of transfers from the federal government.

Sources: Geographic Area: *Canada Yearbook*, 1990, Table 1.1
               Population: Statistics Canada 91-209E, 46-52
               GDP: Statistics Canada 13-213
               Federal Dependency: Statistics Canada 13-213

Table 15.2

Constitutional Asymmetry in Law: Selected Examples

Subject of Provision	Section	Notes
Constitution Act, 1867		
denominational education	93(2)	extends minority education rights in Ontario to Quebec
language and civil law	133 129	bilingual legislative regime and civil law system only in province of Quebec
uniformity of laws in certain provinces (opting-in)	94	Ontario, New Brunswick, and Nova Scotia (but *not* Quebec) are invited to unify laws on property and civil rights and court procedure by opting for federal control
Senate representation	22, 23	unequal representation of provinces, different qualifications for senators from Quebec
Judges' qualifications	97, 98	section 98 applies only to Quebec; different system of appointment of judges from other provinces if section 94 is activated
Provincial Constitutions		
natural resources	109	Alberta, Saskatchewan, and Manitoba are not given this jurisdiction until 1930
language	23 (Manitoba)	Manitoba joins Quebec with bilingual regime in its legislature
subsidies	118, 119	differential direct grants
denominational education rights	various	different denominational rights (some in section 93, others in provincial constitutions)
Terms of Union (British Columbia, Prince Edward Island, Newfoundland)	various	different constitutional commitments to provinces (e.g., P.E.I. steamship & telegraph service)

David Milne

Table 15.3
Constitutional Asymmetry in Practice: Selected Examples

Subject of Provision	Section (Act)	Form of Asymmetry
pensions	94A (1964)	concurrency with provincial paramountcy permits QPP and CPP asymmetry
amending procedure	38(3), 40 (1982)	opting-out of constitutional amendments increases asymmetry
	38(1)(b) (1982)	population provision of 7/50 rule is asymmetric
notwithstanding clause	33 Charter (1982)	provincial overrides permit unequal applications of the Charter
mobility rights	6(4) Charter (1982)	limit to mobility rights of Canadians in provinces with high unemployment

There are other examples of asymmetry, too, in federal fiscal programs and arrangements. These, too, have the same egalitarian character as the constitutional provisions above, but knowingly provide, through opting-out, for asymmetrical outcomes. As Table 15.4 shows, there have been a variety of programs, policies, and arrangements that reflect asymmetry.

In central institutions, too, much of the formal pattern is asymmetrical. Much to the distress of Alberta, Newfoundland and other provinces, the Senate does not enshrine a neat symmetrical pattern of provincial equality. On the contrary, the only approximation of equality is regional and, even here, the definitions are arguably arbitrary. Quebec and Ontario can parade as regions, while the other eight provinces must merge their provincial identities within two highly dubious regional categories. Nova Scotia and New Brunswick enjoy ten senators each, while Newfoundland and the western provinces get six only. The Atlantic region, with the lowest population figures, enjoys more seats than any other region, including the west. The anomalies abound.

Even at the level of theory and of international experience, the case for asymmetry is not a retiring one. After all, even Kenneth Wheare, the classic writer on federalism, who had preferred the principle of equality among the units of a federation, had not *required* it as a necessary condition in every federation.[2] And while Canada's closest English-speaking federations, Australia and the United States, have adopted equality in state representation in the

---

2 See, Kenneth C. Wheare, *Federal Government*, 3d ed. (London: Oxford University Press, 1953), p. 93.

Senate, other federal countries such as Germany and Switzerland have not. Even the principle of equality in jurisdiction among the units in the federation has been abridged, most strikingly in Malaysia where *different* powers were conferred upon the units in its federation. This variation at the level of jurisdiction led in the case of Singapore to a compensating reduction in its representation in central institutions. The consequent alienation of the people of Singapore from the federation ultimately led to the secession of Singapore. While the political experience of Malaysia with asymmetrical jurisdiction for Singapore in its federation has not been a happy one and is hardly an encouraging model for an enduring solution to Quebec-Canada relations, at least the evidence of asymmetry in Canadian and other federations can hardly be denied.

Table 15.4
Asymmetry in Federal Programs and Policies: Selected Examples

Asymmetry by Design: Not Available to All Provinces	
Program Area	*Notes*
regional development	regionally specific programs allow only certain provinces to benefit (ACOA, WDO)
foreign policy	only New Brunswick and Quebec are represented in *la francophonie*
variable cost-sharing formulae	uneven distribution of costs for shared-cost programs (e.g., forestry 90/10 Newfoundland, 60/40 British Columbia)
Atlantic Accord	unique model shielding equalization for Newfoundland and providing for shifting paramountcy on offshore decision-making

Asymmetry in Practice: Available but not Used by All Provinces	
Program Area	*Notes*
immigration	special federal-provincial agreement (e.g., Cullen-Couture Agreement) with Quebec in this concurrent area
tax collection	Quebec, Ontario and Alberta collect corporate tax; Quebec alone collects corporate and individual tax
opting-out/tax abatement	available to all, only Quebec has opted out of various programs (special welfare, youth allowance, etc.) and received tax abatements
program delivery	provincial variations in per child rates in family allowances, Quebec opted-out of student loans plan

THE EQUALITY PRINCIPLE CONFRONTS ASYMMETRY

It is testament to the power and tenacity of the equality principle, however, that despite an unpromising beginning with the presence of real and substantive differences among provinces, the Canadian federation has seen a steady and growing movement towards that idea. Given the early evidence of substantial legal asymmetry among provinces, we might well ask how that is plausible. After all, do not the asymmetrical features of provincial constitutions, outlined earlier, contradict the notion of a juridical equality among provinces? Is not this *level* of constitutional asymmetry fatal to provincial equality? If uniformity is thought to be the only test that will pass muster, then clearly this is so. Not only are there distinct constitutional provisions reflecting the varying terms upon which provinces entered the union, but even the authorizing instruments bringing provinces into being differed: some joined Canada by imperial statute, others by imperial order-in-council, yet others by federal statute. The picture is hardly comparable to the American portrait of sovereign states freely covenanting to form a federal union.

But the logic of uniformity might be flawed in thinking that, if provincial constitutions are not uniform, they are then by definition unequal. This would be so if, as Peter Hogg has argued, the "differences are not so marked as to justify special status for any province."[3] Certainly, according to this standard, it would be quite possible to contend that, following the return of control over western public lands in 1930, the provinces enjoyed a basic juridical equality despite the presence of minor legal differences. Hence, all provinces share a fundamental equality with respect to the basic grant of legislative powers under section 92 and elsewhere in the *Constitution Act, 1867*. That juridical equality is underlined, too, in the insistence on a formal equality among provinces in exercising opting-out rights, whether over certain amendments under sections 38 and 40, over fiscal matters and shared-cost programs, or over exercises of the notwithstanding clause under section 33 of the Charter.

A glance over the tables would reaffirm that view since virtually all of the constitutional asymmetry relates to special obligations, duties, or arrangements to reflect distinct provincial needs. They do not show, except for the anomalous and temporary removal of provincial control over crown lands in the prairie provinces, a genuinely asymmetrical distribution of legislative powers. No one would be inclined to find here obnoxious "tier 1, tier 2, or tier 3" status provinces.[4] Even the distinct Quebec civil code reflects a *choice* of an

---

3   Peter Hogg, *Constitutional Law of Canada*, 2d edition (Toronto: Carswell, 1985), p. 84.
4   This slogan is, of course, familiar to Canadians. It reflects established ways of denigrating constitutional asymmetry among provinces. The same idea has been

alternative legal system to the common law, a choice that might be made by other provinces, and even here the last word on its interpretation rests with the Supreme Court of Canada. None of the asymmetrical provisions, in short, appear to undermine the basic juridical equality of the provinces.

This view of the matter would now appear to have received standing in law with the 1982 ruling by the Quebec Court of Appeal on the Quebec government's reference respecting a special right of veto for that province. Discarding Quebec's arguments for recognition of a special status flowing out of its unique civil law tradition in the constitution and its distinct language and religion, the court concluded that "ces distinctions ... ne confèrent pas à la législature du Québec des pouvoirs plus étendus que ceux qui sont conférés aux autres." At law, all of the provinces are fundamentally equal. The court went on to say:

> Il est reconnu que certaines provinces sont supérieures à d'autres en superficie, population et richesses, mais légalement parlant elles ont toutes été placées sur un même pied. Les articles 91 and 92 de l'A.A.N.B. donnent aux plus petites des provinces les mêmes pouvoirs qu'aux plus grandes.[5]

Oddly enough, during the historical struggle for provincial equality, it was Ontario and Quebec, not the provinces in the periphery, who first championed provincial equality. As the leaders of the nineteenth-century struggle over provincial rights, they unwittingly authored the later provincialist doctrines of a Peter Lougheed or a Clyde Wells. For the battle over equality began first *not* as an interprovincial struggle at all. What we see in the provincial rights movement is a common effort of large provinces and small to resist the imposition of a centralized quasi-imperial form of federalism from Ottawa. After all, John A. Macdonald's federalism that dismissed both large and small provinces as "quasi-municipalities" and freely disallowed any provincial laws, constituted a threat to all; if this model were to be resisted, the status of provincehood as such would have to be enlarged and defended. It was in this curious fashion that Oliver Mowat of Ontario and Honoré Mercier of Quebec were compelled to articulate a provincial rights rhetoric from which *all* provinces would necessarily draw benefit. These sentiments were confirmed in an interprovincial conference in Quebec city attended by five premiers in 1887.

Similar encouragement came too with federal Liberal support for the sanctity of provincial status and that party's championing of classical federalism against Macdonald's centralized version. Ultimately, these ideas prevailed in law when the Judicial Committee of the Privy Council in Britain under the leadership of

---

conveyed in recent constitutional rhetoric by "class a, class b, and class c" provinces.
5   [1982] C.A. 38

Lord Watson and Lord Haldane declared that all provinces enjoyed a "quasi-sovereign" authority in no way inferior to that of Ottawa.[6]

It was not long before these principles, first expressed in federal-provincial terms, began to be expressed interprovincially. If each province is "quasi-sovereign," what could possibly justify formal and substantive inequalities among provinces? The anomaly of federal control over provincial lands in western Canada could not long be tolerated according to that standard. The federal government ultimately retreated in 1930 and placed Manitoba, Saskatchewan and Alberta on equal terms with all the other provinces. The preamble of the *Alberta Natural Resources Act* of 1930 proudly declared that by that amendment Alberta was to be "placed in a position of equality with the other provinces of Confederation with respect to the administration and control of its natural resources as from its entrance into Confederation in 1905."

There was no avoiding the question of provincial equality too when Canada began the long trek in 1927 to get an agreement on a domestic amending formula. Equality of provinces was set out clearly then in terms that would remain constant for over half a century (except for the Victoria formula championed by Trudeau) and that would later become entrenched in Canada's amending formula in 1982. What were these principles precisely and how did they reflect equality?

- first, there would be no veto for any province over amendments on most subjects either by virtue of a province's population or of its linguistic character (therefore no special status);

- second, *all* provinces would equally enjoy a veto over a certain limited number of subjects of extraordinary importance requiring unanimous consent for change.

This consensus over equality of provincial status over amendments — vigorously supported by Quebec and Ontario — proved to be enduring. Its importance can hardly be exaggerated in the light of the Meech Lake Accord and the struggle over its ratification. Under these rules, on most subjects neither Quebec nor Ontario could be assured of always being a party to an amendment (though

---

6   Following the earlier logic of *Hodge v Queen* (1883), probably the most decisive case in this legal underpinning of classical federalism was *Liquidators of the Maritime Bank of Canada and Receiver-General of New Brunswick* (1892) where Lord Watson spoke of the "supreme" and "autonomous" status of the provinces with the "same authority as the Imperial Parliament and the Parliament of the Dominion" in its subject areas — "in no way analogous to that of a municipal institution." Richard A. Olmsted (ed.), *Decisions of the Judicial Committee of the Privy Council*, (Ottawa: Queen's Printer, 1954) v.1, pp. 269-270. The same spirit continued in the *Local Prohibition Case* (1896), and in several subsequent landmark decisions.

the consent of at least one would be needed to fulfil the 50 percent population requirement under the formula); moreover, *both* might be blocked in their ambitions over securing desired amendments touching on certain delicate subjects by the veto of a single small province! Doubtless, the latter possibility was considered improbable by the larger provinces at the centre as each sought to fortify its own defence with the veto.

Quebec has normally tolerated equality of provinces under the general amending formula only in return for a right to opt out of amendments transferring provincial powers to Ottawa. That was evident as early as 1936 when the idea of opting-out was first raised; it subsequently was built into the amending formula of the Gang of Eight that Premier Lévesque signed in 1981, although this time the question of full financial compensation was added. This formula became the law of Canada when Trudeau eventually accepted it in a compromise with all premiers but Lévesque, although compensation was limited to matters concerning education and culture. It is worth noting that here, too, equality prevailed: there would be no special status since *all* provinces were accorded the same right to opt out.

But the signs of a genuine movement towards provincial equality in the federation were more than merely formal. When the Great Depression made a mockery of the old provincial rights rhetoric by pushing many provinces to virtual bankruptcy, the Rowell-Sirois report recommended that national adjustment grants be provided by Ottawa so that each province would enjoy approximately equal practical capacity to deliver services without imposing undue levels of taxation. It was accepted as an implied obligation of Confederation that all provinces be provided with the requisite financial means to carry out their responsibilities under the constitution. In due course, this recommendation led to our modern system of equalization grants, their very name betraying the trend towards equality among provinces. No mere lip service, this commitment to equalizing so that all provinces enjoy "sufficient revenues to provide reasonably comparable levels of public services at reasonably comparable levels of taxation" is now enshrined in section 36 of the *Constitution Act, 1982*. The concept of equalization is a pillar of modern Canadian federalism, influencing the design of many other federal programs.[7] Indeed, the idea has been extended

---

7   See Robin Boadway "Federal-Provincial Transfers in Canada: A Critical Review of the Existing Arrangements" in Mark Krasnick, *Fiscal Federalism*, vol. 65, Research Studies of the Royal Commission on the Economic Union and Development Prospects for Canada (Toronto: University of Toronto, 1986) for a treatment of the equalizing features of other transfer programs. Note, too, the clear rejection of a Canada consisting of "cart areas and cadillac areas" under Lester Pearson, and the development of regional economic development programs aimed at reducing the gap between prosperous and poor provinces.

interprovincially with proposals in some contemporary studies to involve the provinces in revenue-sharing schemes.[8]

The language of provincial equality was also a powerful element in the 1985 Atlantic Accord where Newfoundland and subsequently other coastal provinces succeeded in winning federal approval to treat offshore lands, for purposes of royalties and taxes, as "if these resources were on land, within the province." That provision and others in the agreement, *despite* the constitutional law that dictated asymmetrical treatment of land and sea-based resources, helped to equalize the land ownership rights of land-based and coastal provinces in keeping with the federation's developing notions of symmetry.

Of course, with the arrival of executive federalism, the old idea of the quasi-sovereign status of provincehood has been given an enormous boost. The First Ministers' Conference as the centrepiece of the system legitimizes provincial equality. Just as in international gatherings, the symbolism of state actors sitting equally about the conference table, backed by their own flags and officialdom is not lost on the public. Though real and substantive inequalities exist among the actors at both international and intergovernmental conferences, the formal image is powerfully egalitarian nonetheless.

Provincial equality has become a virtual diplomatic norm of modern executive federalism. Moreover, horizontally extended, provincial equality is now being vigorously pressed as a principle in reform of central institutions, particularly with Alberta's Triple E Senate proposal. As noted earlier, Senate representation by region in Canada is itself a direct attack on provincial equality. This regional system also served as the basis for Trudeau's later Victoria amending formula proposal with its grant of a constitutional veto to Quebec and Ontario and its provision for regional vetoes elsewhere. It is instructive that Trudeau's proposal was not successful in the end, and that the current system of representation in the Senate is regarded as unsatisfactory and under attack. The only question is not *whether* but how far to move Senate representation from a regional towards an equal or a weighted provincial basis.

In the negotiations for a companion resolution to the Meech Lake Accord in June of 1990, Canadians learned how far the provincial equality principle had fractured the old notion of regional symmetry. Under the terms of that deal, first ministers had ensured symmetry in Senate representation for all provinces except Quebec, Ontario, and Prince Edward Island. Only intense political pressure from Quebec not to permit any reduction in its relative proportion of Senate seats prevented a more radical restructuring.[9] This attempted horizontal

---

8   See Peter A. Cumming, "Equitable Fiscal Federalism: A Problem in Respect of
      Resources Revenue Sharing" in Mark Krasnick, *Fiscal Federalism*, pp. 49-95.
9   See, for example, Andrew Cohen, *A Deal Undone: The Making and Breaking of the
      Meech Lake Accord* (Vancouver/Toronto: Douglas & McIntyre, 1990), pp. 238-240.

transfer of provincial equality from the diplomatic world of executive federalism to central institutions is an important step, demonstrating the kind of qualified symmetry that may ultimately prevail in Senate reform. Certainly, given the wide popularity of the Triple E Senate proposal, the pressures for equalizing are not likely to go away.

In fact, any realistic look at the Meech Lake Accord itself would surely show that, with the single exception of the "distinct society" clause, the equality principle trumped on every element of the package in the so-called Quebec round. Despite the fact that Quebec had tabled proposals providing for asymmetry over the veto in the amending formula and some other subjects, first ministers reasserted equality at every turn:

- in the Meech Lake discussions the actors expressly rejected the idea of returning to a veto for larger provinces and reaffirmed equality of provinces in the general amending formula;
- the defensive veto for all provinces was extended to a wider list of subjects in order to give Quebec the protection it sought, while still respecting the equality principle;
- compensation for opting-out of transfers of provincial powers was extended to all provinces;
- all transfers of federal powers in the agreement were extended to all provinces equally (no special status);
- most important of all, the principle of equality of the provinces was expressly declared in the Accord.

There was only one significant contradiction in the Accord that did not sit well with the idea of provincial equality. That was, of course, the recognition of Quebec as a "distinct society." The meaning of the clause both in law and politics was at best uncertain: supporters and critics alike argued from the outset that it might provide the basis for claims to special status for the province. There was also the exclusive role of Quebec in nominating candidates for three positions on the Supreme Court of Canada. This status grew out of the need to provide justices from Quebec's distinctive civil law system, but it nonetheless provided additional support for the unique position of the province of Quebec.

First ministers themselves were sensitive to the possible contradictions in these parts of the Meech Lake Accord. Aware of the undoubted support in English-speaking public opinion for Trudeau's or Clyde Well's denunciations of inequality and special status, some English-speaking premiers, both before the final legal draft was announced in June of 1987 and again during the eleventh-hour negotiations to save it three years later, sought to contain and circumscribe this asymmetry. There was the addition of subsection 4 ensuring that the "distinct society" clause would not derogate from the legislative powers

of Ottawa or other provinces. There was the long discussion at the outset of the
Meech Lake negotiations about whether other provinces might be specifically
guaranteed places on the Supreme Court too. There was the ceaseless effort to
prevent an asymmetrical subversion of the national Charter of Rights and
Freedoms. For its part, Quebec was not only busy in seeking to protect the
"distinct society" clause as a ground for its own special status, but it was worried
lest the express declaration of the equality of provinces put a shadow on the
victory of the "distinct society" clause itself.

Of course, it was in the battle for ratification of the Meech Lake Accord that
the tensions over provincial equality and inequality became the most pronounced. Because the dissenting provinces of Manitoba and Newfoundland
were small with negligible proportions of the Canadian population and the
supporting provinces accounted for the vast majority of the population, Canada
faced in 1990 the kind of split between big provinces and small feared by the
founding fathers of all federations.[10] The apparent conflict between majority
will and the federalism vetoes of smaller provinces was exposed. As expected,
the more powerful provinces such as Ontario and Quebec showed marked
impatience when their ambitions were blocked by the actual exercise of equal
powers granted to all provinces in 1982. The decision to require unanimity on
certain subjects in the amending formula permitted this kind of outcome, but it
surely put the principle of equality to a more severe test than anyone could have
anticipated when the rules were set in 1982.

The anti-egalitarian rhetoric in the Meech debate was unusually vicious. On
the one hand, there was ceaseless trumpeting of majoritarian democracy against
vetoes from small, poor provinces; on the other, open questioning, by then
Environment Minister Lucien Bouchard, whether Quebec as a larger and richer
province was more central to the union than Newfoundland. Oblivious to the
irony, those who denounced the blocking power of smaller provinces over
Meech Lake were precisely those who proposed to *add* to those blocking powers
by extending the subjects over which every province could exercise a veto.
Symmetry again, not asymmetry. Such was the remarkable victory of the
equality principle at the Quebec round.

IS THERE A WAY OUT?

While Canada must certainly examine all of the range of options that may
somehow allow us to reconcile Quebec's desire for special recognition and
special powers with equality of provinces, that examination must be realistic.

---

10 It should be noted, however, that much of this argument presupposes that the
   premiers of these provinces actually represent the people in their provinces on this
   question. This is, of course, a very questionable assumption.

Even in a crisis atmosphere, there are clear limits to the compromises that Canadians are likely to make with the formal principle of equality. That is true whether the issue concerns provincial powers themselves, reform of central institutions, or asymmetrical applications of the Charter. Nor is it likely that Canadians can resolve the crisis simply by decentralizing down equally to Quebec's negotiated bottom line. As the critics correctly say, if Meech was too much for English-speaking Canada, what likelihood is there that the grocery list of powers demanded by the Allaire report or the Bélanger-Campeau Commission will be acceptable?

At a recent workshop of the C.D. Howe Institute, Ronald Watts outlined an impressive range of options that might be considered, either singly or in combination, to provide for some asymmetrical resolutions to Canada's constitutional crisis. These are summarized in Table 15.5. These choices indicate, at least abstractly, the smorgasbord of policy choices that might be made to accommodate Quebec and English-speaking Canada. The table suggests that the problem is neither inflexibility in federalism nor lack of technical means to give effect to asymmetry. They do indicate, however, the radical nature of the changes that might well be required if the federation is to accommodate Quebec in the post-Meech climate. Needless to say, they also indirectly test the political will of Canadians, including Quebecers, to consider these options.

From the perspective of this author, the special status option is likely to be a nonstarter in English-speaking Canada. Not only does it offend deeply entrenched equality norms in the federation, but there is currently scant support for this kind of accommodation in English-speaking Canada. Moreover, as is plainly evident from the Liberal party's Allaire report, it is becoming increasingly difficult to distinguish the older option of special status for Quebec within the federation from the Parti Québécois' sovereignty-association model. As Alan Cairns' essay in this collection also indicates, special status always occupies an ambiguous constitutional zone, constantly drawn towards the ultimate logic of independence. Hence, special status advocates cannot promise the country stability with this option. Moreover, they know that if special status were adopted, it would quickly lead to demands that voting by Quebec representatives in central institutions be reduced or circumscribed on subjects where it has autonomy. This is a prescription for Quebec's increasing alienation from the centre and rising resentment elsewhere.

On the matter of recasting provincial units, though that might well even out the more glaring disparities, it is difficult to see how it could seriously address the national question in Quebec. Nor will schemes for merging provinces into regional units or breaking up existing provinces be easy: they fly in the face of Canadian history, politics and experience. In any event, despite frequent arguments to the contrary in the Senate reform literature, there is nothing exceptional about Canada's asymmetrical population distribution among provinces.

Table 15.5
Organizing for Symmetry and Asymmetry

I. UNITS

Restructuring Options	*Proposals and Examples*
Reorganize units	reduce natural asymmetries by amalgamating provinces (Maritime Union?) and/or splitting up larger provinces
Federation within a federation	possible federation of Quebec with federation of provinces of rest-of-Canada (e.g., Russia within USSR)
Bipolar federation	possible dual federation of Quebec and rest-of-Canada (e.g., Belgium, Pakistan)

II. JURISDICTION

Adaptations	*Range of Some Existing Alternatives*
Asymmetrical jurisdiction	confer different constitutional powers on provinces, hence enshrining special status for Quebec (e.g., Borneo states in Malaysia)
Formal equality but asymmetrical adaptations	opting-in (section 94) to permit some provinces to pass powers to Ottawa, while others may retain them
	opting-out (sections 38 and 40): permit all provinces to opt out knowing probably only one will regularly do so
	delegation: permit transfer of powers between Ottawa and provinces knowing that it will be used asymmetrically
	increase concurrency (sections 94A and 95): add to powers where both provinces and Ottawa may legislate with differing patterns of paramountcy
	increase adjustable fiscal transfer programs to permit more asymmetry
	increase use of special federal-provincial agreements, such as Cullen-Couture
	employ more interprovincial agreements permitting asymmetry

Table 15.5 (continued)

III. REPRESENTATION IN CENTRAL INSTITUTIONS

Rules/Representation	*Patterns and Complexities*
Equality/inequality in Senate representation	different examples abroad for equality/symmetry (U.S., Australia) and inequality/asymmetry in Senate (Germany)
General representation in central institutions	if asymmetrical jurisdiction exists among units, it may cause asymmetrical representation or restricted voting rights for certain provinces in central institutions (e.g., Malaysia)
Voting rules in central institutions, especially second house	may provide for special voting rules conferring asymmetry on certain subjects (e.g., Quebec veto over federal laws on education or culture); suspensive or absolute vetoes for different subjects in Senate (e.g., Germany)
	such rules might complicate responsible government but not necessarily unworkable

IV. CHARTER AND ASYMMETRY

Notwithstanding Clause (s. 33)	allows for asymmetry but under attack for creating asymmetrical citizenship
Citizenship/federalism	Charter must not be so uniform that it obstructs federalism (Canadian Charter as basic minimum above which diversity can be tolerated: Quebec charter additional to Canadian?)
	Original U.S. Bill of Rights directed to federal level, applied to states only after civil war in 14th amendment

Source: Comments by R.L. Watts in forthcoming Proceedings of C.D. Howe Conference, "Imagining Constitutional Futures," 17-18 November 1990.

On the contrary, Canada's pattern with two provinces overwhelmingly dominating the rest conforms closely to Australia's experience among its states both
at the time of union and since.[11]

The usual way that federations resolve "natural" asymmetries is through
second chamber design. As indicated earlier, the pressures to move closer
towards provincial equality in representation are growing in English-speaking
Canada, though it is unlikely that failure to achieve perfect symmetry here
would be fatal. Most Canadians are aware that the case of Quebec as the
principal home of francophone Canada is unique: that reality must be reflected
both in representation in the second chamber and possibly in special voting
rules over decisions affecting cultural questions and the like.

RESOLVING THE PUZZLE: THE CONCURRENCY SOLUTION?

We still have not addressed the heart of the problem: How to provide for
sufficient asymmetry in practice so that Quebec may consider staying in the
federation, while not offending the resistance of English Canadians to formalizing inequality? The answer lies in some mix of those sets of devices set out
in Section II of Table 15.5. In my view, the approach that is likely to be most
productive is an increase in the option of concurrency with provincial paramountcy (henceforth, CPP). As the acronym ironically indicates, it is the
side-by-side pattern of the Canadian and Quebec pension plans that may suggest
a possible way out of the equality-asymmetry dilemma.

The beauty of using concurrency in this form is that it does not *force* Canada
into a radically decentralizing direction against the wishes of most English-
speaking Canadians, nor does it formally raise the spectre of special status. Yet,
in principle, CPP could provide Quebec with very extensive additional
jurisdictional powers which that province could use to express and define its
de facto distinctness within Canada. We can see the embryo of the idea now in
section 94A where Quebec has been able to proceed with its own Quebec
Pension Plan (QPP), while all other provinces have been content to leave
Ottawa's Canada Pension Plan (CPP) in place, provided they have a say in

---

11 For example, the states of New South Wales (38 percent) and Victoria (35 percent)
    were fully as dominant as Ontario and Quebec at the time of their political union.
    Either state had a population exceeding the *total* of all four other states in the
    federation at the time. Even today, the population dominance of these two Australian
    states conforms closely to that of Quebec and Ontario in Canada. For a breakdown
    of population by state in Australia in 1897, see B.R. Wise, *The Making of the
    Australian Commonwealth, 1889-1900* (London: Longman, 1913), p. 240. For a full
    range of population ratios among states to the present in Australia, see Ian Castles,
    Year Book Australia 1986 (Canberra: Australian Bureau of Statistics, 1986), p. 98.

setting its terms. It takes very little imagination to realize how well section 94A has already served Quebec: over the last two decades, it has opened up the vast pension funds of the province for investment by the *caisse de dépôt.* The deployment of this capital fund has been critical to Quebec's modern economic growth, even if other provinces have been content with less exciting and innovative results under the terms of the Canada Pension Plan. Such an apparently modest constitutional mechanism, enshrining formal equality not special status, has nonetheless led to rather startling practical asymmetry. This is the sort of "live and let live" option that Canadians can use in other areas to resolve the clashing aspirations of Quebec and Canada without the necessity for breakup.

It is easiest to see this device extended in a field such as unemployment insurance, for example, since the system is self-financing and the subject matter had been provincial in any case prior to the 1940 amendment that transferred it to Ottawa. In cases such as these where the subject matter is very discrete and clear and where no tax complications arise, Ottawa would simply withdraw its program in a province that had in effect "occupied" the area with its own plan while maintaining its national program elsewhere. In cases where a program is not self-financing but the same clear transference of a program takes place, Ottawa could compensate a province that chooses to assume the program through tax abatement — hence, leaving room for the province to increase its own taxes and face its own electorate for the program it chooses to mount. In cases where there is no such discreteness to the legislative program, the financing system would operate in much the same way that agriculture, a field of concurrent jurisdiction with federal paramountcy under section 95, does now: each level of government would continue to tax and spend for its programs in the joint area and account to their electors in the usual way. In this fashion and subject to certain overriding national constraints, it should be possible to consider adding in whole or in part many jurisdictions, sought by Quebec such as communications and manpower policy without dismantling Ottawa.

It is worth underlining that the courts have generally interpreted the paramountcy rule as it applies to federal paramountcy very strictly: only if there is a direct conflict between federal and provincial laws have the courts declared provincial laws inoperative to the extent of the inconsistency. In this way, the courts have ensured that the provinces' powers are not reduced unduly by too expansive a reading of the paramountcy rule. There has been no ruling on section 94A with its implied notion of provincial paramountcy and scholars are divided over precisely how the courts might interpret its meaning at law.[12] But,

---

12 Bora Laskin's argument that the section implies a provincial paramountcy rule has been argued by William Lederman (Book Review, 43 C.B.R., 1965, 229 at 671) though many authorities remain skeptical. See, for example, Neil Finkelstein (ed.),

politically there can be little doubt that 94A is meant to assure for the first time the primacy of the provincial over the federal law in the event of a conflict. While concurrent jurisdiction is widely used in other contemporary federal constitutions such as those of the United States, Australia and Germany, the principle of provincial paramountcy is a departure from the normal practice. Nevertheless, there is no reason why Canada cannot tilt its rules in this way. Indeed, the country has already done so and the only question is whether there is the will to employ this device more extensively at this time. If this course of action is chosen, the ambiguity in the language of section 94A will need to be faced and a clear paramountcy rule established. There is no guarantee of course that the courts would interpret the provincial paramountcy rule under section 94A as narrowly as they have federal paramountcy, but if so, the federal government could count on protecting its role in the joint fields in all circumstances except those where a direct inconsistency arises.

There is a tactical advantage in proceeding with concurrency in this fashion as well. Any restructuring would be accomplished *gradually*, and incrementally. There would be no immediate statutory discontinuity or administrative distress, since Ottawa's laws and programs would continue in place under CPP jurisdictions unless and until a province creates a law that directly contradicts them. Even then, the conflicting federal law would not become invalid but would be merely put in abeyance, as it were, free to be restored if circumstances change and the sentiment for a national approach returns in the province previously asserting paramountcy. Of course, there is no way of knowing in advance precisely which provinces might exercise which concurrent powers, how extensively they might use them, or how distinctive the provincial policies might be. But if the pension plan arrangements are any indication, most provinces will choose not to disturb functional national arrangements, while Quebec for its part would be free to take its own distinctive approach within an equal community of provinces.

CPP, unlike the opting-in feature, does not require that provinces take the uncharacteristic decision to cede power to Ottawa. As we all know, section 94 has been a dead letter; there is little likelihood that other opting-in provisions would enjoy a better fate. For that reason, Canadians would be wise not to accept the Quebec Liberal Party Allaire report in its suggestion that other provinces assume with Quebec certain federal powers and then be left free to delegate them back according to their centralist inclinations. Concurrency is certainly a preferable route to take. Because it is available to all provinces CPP would not expose Ottawa politically for favouring one province over another as the device of negotiated special agreements. (Note the attack on bilateral

---

Laskin's Canadian Constitutional Law (Toronto: Carswell, 1986), pp. 263-264. Hogg, *Constitutional Law of Canada*, p. 354, is equally reserved and noncommittal.

federalism in the post-Meech period). Of course, to the extent that special agreements, including interprovincial agreements, can be worked out, these can complement the policy of concurrency by removing some elements that might better not be constitutionally extended to all provinces in this way.

It is worth underlining, therefore, that concurrency will not always be the standard remedy for settling Canada's jurisdictional puzzle. There will continue to be a need for exclusive areas of jurisdiction in certain areas and perhaps, as at present, for a federal paramountcy rule in certain joint fields. There will also be room for consideration of other flexible devices for accommodating asymmetry as spelled out in Section II of Table 15.5, particularly in fiscal and adminstrative matters. It is, however, the unique strength of CPP as a strategic approach to the division of powers that it can so easily work in concert with these other existing modalities of change, promoting diversity without at the same time doing violence to essential principles of the federation.

There is another major advantage to this approach. Unlike special status arrangements, there need be no reduction in the representation or voting rights of Quebec MPs in Ottawa with CPP. This is true for several reasons. First, because equality at law is maintained, there is little ground for demanding asymmetrical treatment for Quebec representatives or those of any other province in central institutions. All provinces enjoy the same powers of concurrency; the fact that one or more provinces choose to exercise these powers differently cannot be a basis for unequal federal treatment. Historically, the evidence suggests that this view is correct: we have not encountered any difficulties in the past when Quebec MPs have debated and voted on the Canada Pension Plan despite the fact that Quebec operates its own plan. It could be argued, however, that if the list of CPP powers is long and Quebec alone chooses to legislate distinctively in all of these fields, then matters would be viewed differently. Perhaps so, but such a long list of CPP jurisdiction would undoubtedly increase the likelihood of other provinces exercising some of these powers too, hence hastening the breaking up of any dangerously solitary pattern of *de facto* special status for Quebec. If that outcome did not follow naturally and difficulties in the status of Quebec MPs did arise, it would certainly not be beyond the wit of other provinces to head off trouble by themselves legislating over some CPP subjects. Finally, so long as Parliament in its program designs in concurrent jurisdictional areas continues to influence those mounted separately by Quebec or by other opting-out provinces, there will be practical reasons for encouraging the full participation of the elected federal members from those provinces. Hence, with CPP, we have every reason to expect that the thorny question of differential representation in central institutions can be avoided.

CPP can be used to augment the relative autonomy of the province of Quebec *within* the Canadian federation without violating English-Canadian desires and sensibilities. In an age where the idea of complete independence is irrelevant in any case, this route should have attractions for practically minded Quebecers. Moreover, this process can proceed without all of the uncertainty and risks associated with more radical options. CPP is not revolutionary; it is already present in our constitution. Additions to the CPP list can be made with the consent of Parliament and seven provinces representing 50 percent of the Canadian population: the easiest and most flexible of our amending formulas. Hence, we may be able to extend CPP further without undue difficulty. It is worth remembering too that Canada has now fewer areas of concurrency than that of any other federation. The norm in most other federal constitutions (for example, United States, Australia and Germany) is for much longer lists of concurrent powers, as compared to exclusive powers.

Movement towards more CPP does not, of course, address the awkward politics of provincial equality versus the distinct society nor does it directly answer the clash between individual liberal Charter values and collective rights. The experience with Meech Lake would seem to suggest, however, that issues of special constitutional recognition, including aboriginal rights, will need to be tackled comprehensively, preferably in a new preamble to the Canadian constitution, or alternatively, in several carefully tailored sections. One thing is certain: no one in this exercise will be willing to wait trustingly and patiently in line according to governments' lists of priority and precedence. Nor will anyone again ignore the Charter and its notion of equality of citizenship when drafting special sections on constitutional recognition. It may well be, however, that *significant* grants of power to Canada's distinct communities through CPP and aboriginal self-government may compensate for a more cautious movement in this symbolic and more dangerous part of constitutional restructuring.

For those worried about the balance of powers in the Canadian federation with this proposal, it is worth underlining that CPP allows for considerable decentralization but does not require it. To ensure that CPP is widely endorsed by the people of a province, and not merely by the governing provincial elite, use of CPP powers over discrete subjects such as unemployment insurance could be made subject to a provincial referendum or to a higher-than-normal majority vote of the provincial legislature. Which federal powers might be added to the formal CPP list (and which handled in other ways) — unemployment insurance, manpower policy, or certain parts of communications jurisdiction — will be a delicate question of planning and negotiation, but it is obvious that in the end, if the central government is not to be rendered completely irrelevant to the citizens in the more autonomy-seeking unit or units, there must remain important powers and functions vested at the centre. Without agreement on that, there really is no point in Quebec continuing within the federal model at all.

CPP permits Quebecers to answer that fateful question — to decide whether reformed federalism (with more powers for Quebec within Canada) is really what most have wanted for this past quarter century, or whether the agenda has always really been about sovereignty. Canadians will finally learn the answer to that question first as the Quebec government indicates its negotiating flexibility over the next 18 months and more conclusively, after Quebecers express themselves as a people in subsequent referenda. In that fight for the hearts and minds of Quebecers, CPP may play an important role. Although essentially a flexible and pragmatic tool lacking the emotional symbolism of special status and sovereignty, concurrency with its notion of Quebec "trumps" against countervailing federal laws may yet rhetorically capture enough of the sovereigntist symbolism in Quebec to permit federalists a stronger fight against the *indépendantistes*. As for English-speaking Canadians, CPP will doubtless challenge their sense of country and ultimately test what things they would like to do separately and what things they would like to do in common. The virtue of CPP is that it might just give Canada, in an unhurried way, the time and opportunity to work through these choices.

16

The Federative Superstructure

Ronald L. Watts

INTRODUCTION: THE ISSUES

Federative Superstructures and the Current Canadian Impasse

The term "federative superstructure" is used in this paper to encompass the central institutions that are responsible for the areas of common jurisdiction and also the institutions that affect relations between the central government and the governments of the constituent units.

In considering Canada's constitutional options, the shape of the federative institutional structures is a particularly important issue for two reasons. First, the character of the federative superstructure needs to be related to the functions and powers assigned to it. The current constitutional debate has focused upon the desires for a major revision in the jurisdiction to be assigned to the provinces and to the central superstructure. These issues will be significant regardless of whether the final form is one of a revised federalism, a looser confederation or sovereignty-association. Such proposals raise the further issue, however, of the form the common institutional superstructure should take if it is to manage its powers most effectively.

Second, if there is to be mutual agreement upon a resolution to the current constitutional impasse, account will have to be taken of the concerns not only of Quebec but of the provinces elsewhere. These other sources of dissatisfaction with the status quo, arise largely because of the perception in the western and Atlantic provinces that they have lacked influence in the operations of central government. Indeed, for the past decade and a half the major thrust of western sentiment has been for constitutional reforms that would provide for greater participation in and recognition by the national government. This has expressed itself in various proposals since 1976 for improved "intrastate federalism" (a

I would like to express my appreciation to Dwight Herperger, Research Assistant at the Institute of Intergovernmental Relations, for his role in the research for this paper.

term used by Canadian political scientists to refer to the provisions for regional representation in central institutions). The most recent example has been the advocacy of a Triple-E Senate in which the members would be elected, provinces would be represented equally, and the Senate would possess effective powers. Indeed the tentative but ill-fated agreement reached in support of the Meech Lake Accord in Ottawa on 9 June 1990 included as a major element a commitment to a process of significant Senate reform.

The solution is not a simple one, however. There is a problem in attempting to meet the concerns of the western and Atlantic provinces about their perceived insufficient input into policy-making within the central institutions. That is, that any increase in their representation, for instance by treating all provinces equally, means a commensurate reduction in the representation not only of Ontario but also of Quebec. In the latter province, the federal union tends to be regarded as primarily binational, uniting one province with its French-speaking majority with nine English-speaking provinces. Representation of Quebec as just one of ten equal provinces is feared as leading to a permanent under-representation of a major and historic Canadian minority that constitutes a quarter of the federal population. Indeed, some advocates of sovereignty-association or of a confederal system have argued for equality of status for Quebec and "English Canada" within a binational federative superstructure. Here there is a clash between equality of provinces and adequate representation of major minority communities as principles of representation in central institutions. Thus, the issue of the representation of the constituent units within the federative superstructure has to be resolved as part of any resolution to the current constitutional difficulties.

The Role of Federative Superstructures

In the organization of all federal or confederal unions there are two fundamental sets of issues. The first set relates to the form and scope of the distribution of jurisdiction (legislative and executive powers and financial resources) between the governments of the constituent units and of the federative superstructure. The economic and political implications of possible revisions to the distribution of jurisdiction in Canada have been analyzed in the preceding chapters by Robin Boadway, Peter Meekison and David Milne.

A second and equally important set of issues arising in the design of any federal or confederal system relates to the organization and character of the shared superstructure that manages the common areas of jurisdiction. That is the aspect upon which this paper focuses. There are two basic considerations here. The first concerns the form of institutions that will enable them to manage those shared powers and responsibilities most effectively. The second concerns the arrangements required to ensure that the interests of the constituent units

— of either the governments or the residents of these units — are channelled through and protected by the structures and operations of the common institutions. Significantly, in the original negotiations for the founding of the Canadian and also the American and Australian federations, it was not the constitutional distribution of powers that proved to be the most intractable issue in each of these federations, but rather conflicts among the constituent units about the composition, powers and structure of the central institutions, particularly the Senate. Because control of the common institutions and particularly the legislature is a major element in central power, the organization of those common institutions has proved a contentious issue during the creation of every federal or confederal union.

FEDERAL VERSUS CONFEDERAL SUPERSTRUCTURES

The Relationship of Federative Institutions to the Form of Polity

Among the nine basic structural options that have been identified in Chapter 2 were five federal variants, three confederal variants (of which sovereignty-association was one), and complete separation. The appropriate form for the common institutions will vary according to the choice made from among these basic options.

To begin with, the basic distinction between federal and confederal systems has implications for the type of federative institutions that are appropriate. The basic distinction between federal and confederal systems is that the former are communities of both individuals and constituent polities, while the latter are primarily communities of the constituent political units. In *federal* systems sovereignty is divided between two orders of government—strong constituent governments and a strong general government—each assigned specific sovereign powers by the constitution and each empowered to deal directly with the citizenry in the exercise of their powers. Consequently, the common government in parallel with the constituent governments is elected by and acts directly on the people. In *confederal* systems, which are primarily communities of political units, it is those units themselves that provide the basis for the representation in the federative institutions. Consequently confederal institutions are usually composed of delegates from the constituent governments and relate to the citizenry only indirectly through these constituent governments.

In federations the federative institutions have as a rule been structured to express their compound character as a community of both individuals and of constituent governments. Thus common to virtually all federal systems has been the adoption of a bicameral central legislature. These have usually involved representation according to population in one house, and the weighted or equal representation of constituent units in the other house. Members of the second house are either directly elected by the citizens, indirectly elected by the state legislatures, or appointed by the state governments. Most federations have paid particular attention, therefore, to facilitating the representation and accommodation of distinctive regional, interests, both of smaller constituent territories and of significant linguistic or religious minorities, not only within the central legislature but also in the executive and other institutions.

In confederal systems, representation within the confederal superstructure has typically taken the form of indirectly elected representatives, selected by the legislatures or governments of the constituent units, with each of the constituent units equally represented. Sometimes, although not invariably, the representatives of each constituent unit are granted a veto in the most important matters. For example, under the American Articles of Confederation (written in 1777 and fully ratified in 1781), delegates to Congress were appointed annually, each state had one vote in Congress and each state could veto any constitutional amendment to the Articles. A majority of 9 out of 13 states was required for most decisions. Only minor matters were dealt with by majority rule. In the Swiss Confederation of 1815-47 each canton had one vote in the Diet, but the requirement of unanimity on important questions which had existed in previous Swiss confederations was replaced by the requirement of a three-quarters majority. Thus, in a confederal system, the operation of the central institutions is normally controlled to a large extent by the views of the constituent governments. This means that there is usually a heavy reliance as well upon a multitude of other collaborative institutions involving representatives of the constituent governments. Where each constituent government plays such an important role in the development of common policies, agreement has often been difficult to reach, particularly where any redistribution of resources has been involved.

There are also examples of hybrid political unions that involve elements of both federal and confederal unions. The European Community until recently has represented to a large extent an example of confederal central institutions, although the development of a directly elected European Parliament and the introduction of majority voting in some areas in the Council of Ministers represents a movement towards more typically federal institutions.

While one may identify in broad terms these basic alternative forms of union and the character of the federative superstructures appropriate to them, many variations are possible within each type of political union. These variations will themselves have implications for the appropriate design of the federative superstructure. For instance, in federations where there is asymmetry in the powers assigned to the constituent governments there will be implications for the number of representatives or the voting powers in the central institutions of representatives from those constituent units having greater jurisdictional autonomy. (This is discussed further in the section on the reform of the parliamentary federal institutions). Federations composed of only two constituent units, for example, Pakistan and Czechoslovakia, have invariably been marked by contention over the appropriate representation of the two units where there is a significant difference in their populations. Representation according to population would result in the larger unit dominating permanently. But parity of representation has in practice usually produced permanent deadlocks, an experience not unknown in Canadian history, as exemplified by the problems of the Province of Canada under the Act of Union, 1840-67. Even where there are more than two units the number and size of the constituent units can be a complicating factor in balancing the representation of citizens and of constituent units in the common institutions. Disparity of population and wealth raises problems of the appropriate weight that should be given to the representation of provinces as provinces within the federal institutions and raises questions as to whether some provinces should be grouped together or others divided. Canada provides one of the more extreme examples of the problem with provinces ranging from Ontario with 36.5 percent of the population and 41.4 percent of the Gross Domestic Product (GDP) to Prince Edward Island with 0.5 percent of the population and 0.3 percent of the GDP.[1] Furthermore, the 3 to 1 population imbalance in any proposal for a binational two-unit structure composed of Quebec and the rest-of-Canada would clearly create problems for the design of the federative superstructure.

There are variations among confederal systems as well. The complexity and range of common collaborative institutions has varied with the extensiveness of the common functions. These range from the complex array of the almost-federal common institutions and the judicial arm in the European Community to one rudimentary governing Council with no formal dispute settling mechanisms in the European Free Trade Area.

The Effectiveness of Confederal and Federal Superstructures

Up to the eighteenth century, most political unions that were not unitary were confederal. Among examples were the Holy Roman Empire, the medieval city leagues of Germany, Belgium and Italy, and the United Provinces of the Netherlands, all of which either disintegrated or were subsequently reconstituted as consolidated nation-states. In both the United States in 1789 and Switzerland in 1848 previously ineffective and troubled confederal institutions were replaced by federal institutions that since their establishment have proved more effective and stable. The German Confederation established in the nine-

---

1   *1990 Corpus Almanac and Canadian Source Book* (Toronto: Corpus Information Services, 1990), pp. 17-237, 17-305.

teenth century eventually evolved by way of the quasi-federal Empire, the Weimar Republic and the Third Reich into the current Federal Republic of Germany. Thus, the historical record seems to suggest that confederal, by comparison with federal, superstructures have been less effective and ultimately prone to instability, either dissolving or evolving into federal or even unitary systems.

In the late twentieth century, there have been indications that the European Community with its functional arrangements presages a revival of confederal unions.[2] Unlike earlier confederations that focused particularly upon common action relating to foreign affairs and defence, the European Community has proceeded through creating common institutions for specific economic functions rather than through a general act of confederation. Thus the construction of common institutions has proceeded stage by stage in a way that has minimized the threat to the existing states who wish to retain independence in the areas not assigned to the common institutions. How far these confederal arrangements of the European Community represent permanent ones or merely way stations along the way to more fully federal ones, is difficult to assert conclusively. Pressures to change voting patterns in the Council, to make the Commission more accountable, and to reduce the "democratic deficit" in common policy-making by increasing the powers of the European Parliament all indicate efforts to modify the federative superstructure of the European Community in a direction that would be closer to those normally found in federations.

On the basis of historical and comparative experience, one would have to conclude that the prospects for effective and cohesive common policies are likely to be greater in a federal rather than a confederal form of federative superstructure. But even within the category of federal superstructures there is room for considerable variation, and it is to a consideration of such variations that the balance of this paper turns.

PARLIAMENTARY AND NONPARLIAMENTARY FEDERAL SUPERSTRUCTURES

The Current Canadian Form

The Canadian political structure created in 1867 was a hybrid combining the institutions of parliamentary responsible government following the British model with those of federalism derived from the American model. Canadians

---

2   Daniel Elazar, *Exploring Federalism* (Tuscaloosa: The University of Alabama Press, 1987), pp. 50-54.

have attempted to combine a British inheritance with an American model, each based on fundamentally different premises and apparently contradictory to each other. The tradition of British parliamentary institutions is based on the notion that power should be tamed by concentrating it under the control of a majority of the electorate's representatives in a parliament where executive and legislative power is fused. The United States Constitution was based on a very different premise: that power is to be tamed by dispersing it among multiple separated decision-making centres, no one of which should dominate. The federal division of power between national and state governments and the separation within each government of executive, legislative and judicial power were seen as different expressions of the same fundamental principle of dispersed power and therefore inherently interrelated.

Until the past decade, the efficacy of the combination of parliamentary and federal institutions in Canada went largely unchallenged. In recent years, however, it has come increasingly into question. There have been three sets of concerns. The first has been the dominance of the cabinet and of party discipline constraining the expression of regional concerns within Parliament. The second has been the difficulty of creating an effective Senate as a house for the expression of regional views in a parliamentary system where the cabinet is responsible to the House of Commons. The third has been the inevitable corollary of "executive federalism" as the predominant mode of intergovernmental relations when the executive dominates within each level of government. These three concerns have led to the expression of increasing dissatisfaction with the operation of the present form of Canadian parliamentary institutions.

Three Alternative Models for the Form of Executive

Broadly speaking, executives in federations have followed one of three forms: the presidential, collegial and the parliamentary.

The classical example of the presidential system in a federation is that of the United States. There, in both the national and state governments the chief executive (i.e., the president or the governor) is directly elected for a fixed term and selects his or her own ministers without restriction.[3] Within the federal government authoritative decision-making power is dispersed among the President, the House of Representatives, the Senate and the Supreme Court. In this presidential-congressional system, the various institutions have been assigned powers that check and balance each other, and central decision-making requires

---

3 Strictly speaking, the president is indirectly elected by an electoral college, but to all intents and purposes the system is now in practice one of direct election.

compromises that take into account the variety of regional, local, and minority views.

Switzerland has incorporated into its federal system a collegial form of executive. It is based on the same fundamental principle of dispersed but interacting multiple centres of power as in the United States. Its adoption involved a conscious departure from the American example, however, in making the federal executive a collective one composed of a group of seven members rather than a single individual. The members of the Federal Council, while elected by the two houses in joint session from their membership, are then excluded from membership in either chamber and hold office for a fixed term of four years. The chairmanship rotates annually. The Swiss collegial executive with its fixed term and nonmembership in the legislative houses contrasts with the parliamentary form found in Canada. The collegial executive is not responsible to the legislature for its continuance in office and, as in the United States, the principle of the separation of powers between the various branches of government operates generally. This creates plural centres of political power interacting to balance and check each other in order to facilitate the resolution of conflicts through the emergence of widely accepted compromises.

Canada was the first, but a number of federations, notably Australia, Germany and a host of successful and unsuccessful new federations established in former British colonies since World War II, have attempted to incorporate parliamentary executives. By contrast with the United States and Switzerland the executives in the parliamentary systems are responsible to the legislature and stay in office only as long as they have the support of the legislature. This means that unless there is a stable majority in the legislature, an unstable executive is likely to result, a problem that does not arise in the American or Swiss arrangements. The requirement in a parliamentary system of a stable majority and the power of dissolution placed in the hands of the prime minister has invariably induced a pattern of strong party discipline and cabinet dominance not found in the American and Swiss legislatures.

Implications for Federal Cohesion

The form of the common institutions has an important bearing upon the ability to encourage cohesion among the diverse groups within a federation. On the whole, the presidential system of the United States has in the past been relatively successful in resolving conflicts within the central institutions. The one significant exception was during the period leading up to the Civil War in the nineteenth century. Generally, however, the need to capture a single presidential post has induced political parties to seek compromises in order to win maximum electoral support through aggregating a wide range of political demands. Furthermore, the separation of powers and the multiple checks and balances have usually provided a strong inducement for compromises among the various elements involved in central policy-making. But this beneficial influence has been achieved at a price. The various checks and balances have often meant that a solution has taken a long time to emerge or that sometimes there have been serious deadlocks, especially when the President and Congress have been controlled by different political parties. The result is that some fundamental problems have remained unresolved, and this lack of resolution has in certain periods contributed to considerable stress.

The Swiss federal system, created in 1848 after the previous confederacy had disintegrated into civil war, has been renowned for the manner in which since then it has reconciled unity with religious and linguistic diversity. The Swiss collegial form of executive combines the stability of the fixed-term executive and the checks and balances found within the American system with the further benefits of explicit representation of different regional and minority groups in the federal executive.[4] There has also been a pattern of broad multiparty governing coalitions encompassing not just a bare majority but the support of virtually all the major parties and interest groups. The incentive for these broad governing coalitions has been the existence of the arrangement whereby any federal legislation challenged by a specified number of citizens must be put to a referendum. To forestall such challenges, the tendency has been to ensure widespread support by all major parties of any major legislation before it is enacted. This system would appear to have maximized the inducements for reconciling political conflicts and cleavages and to have minimized adversarial politics. But it too has its price. As in the United States, decision-making is protracted and there are sometimes difficulties in achieving urgent action, or even any action at all, in areas where diverse groups are disagreed. Nevertheless, the Swiss system has ensured the avoidance of action that would sharpen political cleavages.

The parliamentary federations, by contrast to those employing the other two forms of federal executive, have been able, by concentrating political power in cabinets possessing majority legislative support, to undertake more rapid and coherent decision-making and action. But this arrangement has exacted its own price. Within the central institutions, it has in effect placed complete political control over those functions assigned to the federal government in the party and government enjoying majority support in the lower house. This is exemplified by the resulting typical relative weakness of the second chambers in most parliamentary systems, contrasting with the relative strength of the American and Swiss federal second chambers. It is also exemplified by the dominance in

---

4   For example, the Federal Council is constitutionally limited to no more than one
     representative from any canton and the Roman Catholic and French minorities have
     always been represented in it.

parliamentary federations of cabinet initiative in legislation and of party discipline within both federal houses. The lack of institutional checks upon the majority in parliamentary federations has usually put the responsibility for reconciling regional and minority interests directly upon the internal organization and processes of the federal political parties themselves. Where the political parties have failed in this task, and particularly where a fragmented multiparty system or a primarily regional differentiation of federal parties has developed, parliamentary federations have been prone to instability. The clearest examples of this are Pakistan before 1958, Nigeria before 1966, and the current situation in India.

Implications for Intergovernmental Relations

The form of executive established within a federal system has also had a fundamental impact upon the character of intergovernmental relations. The American and Swiss forms of presidential or collegial executive, incorporating within both levels of government the separation of powers and multiple centres of decision-making, have meant that not just the executive but all the various branches of both levels of government have been heavily involved in intergovernmental relations. By contrast, in parliamentary federations the central role of the cabinet within each level of government has made the cabinets the dominant focus for intergovernmental relations. This has resulted in what has come to be known as "executive federalism," a pattern of intergovernmental relations that is not unique to Canada but rather is typical of all parliamentary federations.[5] In these federations the major instrument for intergovernmental relations has been consultation and negotiation between the executives (and their officials) of the different governments. As a result, intergovernmental relations in parliamentary federations have often taken on a character similar to international diplomacy, serving as a place for public confrontation as much as a place for resolving differences, and as a place where agreements are more likely to be possible only behind closed doors.

Conclusion: The Choice Among Alternatives

Given the current conditions and pressures for radical change what should be the preferred form of federal superstructure for Canada?

To most Canadians, the American presidential-congressional system is the best known alternative form for structuring federal institutions. But while that example has some advantages, it is for a number of reasons a dubious solution

---

5 Ronald L. Watts, *Executive Federalism: A Comparative Analysis*, Research Paper no.26, (Kingston: Institute of Intergovernmental Relations, Queen's University, 1989).

for Canada. As noted above it has some serious disadvantages with respect to effective decision-making. It lacks the advantages possessed by the Swiss federal institutions for providing regional and minority representation within the collegial executive and for reducing adversarial relations between parties. Furthermore, since parliamentary institutions are one of the major features distinguishing Canada from the United States, the removal of this distinctiveness would probably contribute significantly to a reduction in the sense that Canadians have of their own distinct identity in relation to the republic to the south. Finally, while there is increasing grumbling among Canadians about cabinet dominance, overly rigid party discipline and "executive federalism," there is no clear evidence that a majority of Canadians are at present clamouring for an American-style presidential-congressional system.

What then about conversion to a collegial form of fixed-term executive? The conversion itself would not be difficult to achieve. All that would be required is to institute in the constitution a fixed term for parliament and the cabinet. Since the life of the House of Commons would no longer depend upon the discretion of the prime minister or the continued cohesion of party support for the cabinet, party discipline and confrontation in Parliament would be substantially weakened. Furthermore, were the Canadian party system to evolve, as it may, into a multiparty system with no party having a majority, a fixed-term collegial executive would ensure governmental stability. It is noteworthy that in Australia after the constitutional crisis of 1975 there was for a time considerable pressure to move towards a fixed-term federal Parliament, although in the end that has not come to pass.[6] But so far, there has been little discussion in Canada about the advantages or disadvantages. In many respects a fixed-term Parliament and executive might best meet longer-run Canadian needs. Should public debate and education eventually make a fixed-term Parliament publicly acceptable, it could be adopted at that point simply by introducing a constitutional amendment specifying a fixed term between elections.

Nevertheless, at the present time Canadians do not appear to be prepared for a radical alteration of federal institutions towards a fixed-term federal legislature and collegial executive. Therefore, the more promising direction may be to consider modifications to the existing parliamentary institutions that would enable them to overcome some of their present difficulties and to work more effectively. It is worth noting that among the many proposals for constitutional reform that have been advanced in the past decade none have advocated abandoning parliamentary institutions. The proposals of the Quebec Liberal Party for a renewed Canadian federalism in the 1980 Beige Paper, for example, expressly called for preserving the parliamentary system and responsible

---

6 George Winterton, *Parliament, the Executive and the Governor-General* (Melbourne, Melbourne University Press, 1983), pp. 158-160.

government although some modifications were suggested.[7] The recent report of the Constitutional Committee of the Quebec Liberal Party (Allaire), of 28 January 1991, also envisages the continuation of Parliament, although it advocates abolition of the Senate. Nor have the proposals for reform of federal institutions emanating from western Canada envisaged abandoning parliamentary responsible government as such. They have focused instead upon reforms, particularly relating to the Senate. Since modification to the existing parliamentary institutions appears to be the preferable path, the next section will deal with such reforms.

REFORM OF THE PARLIAMENTARY FEDERAL INSTITUTIONS

The Working Executive

In the past two decades or so there have been two contradictory forces at work in the structure and operations of the Canadian federal executive.

First, there has been the movement towards organizational rationalization expressed in a variety of forms such as the "Program Planning and Budgeting System," "Management by Objectives," long-term budgetary projections, the vastly extended role of cabinet committees, the increased size and power of the Prime Minister's Office and of other central agencies, ministries of state, and the increased reliance on research.

Second, there has been a continued effort to ensure regional representativeness. At the time of Confederation it was recognized that, given the importance of the cabinet, the representation of regional interests in the cabinet would be more important than representation in the Senate. Every cabinet has been formed with a careful eye to the representation of regions as well as of other interests. Nevertheless from the point of view of less populous provinces, the cabinet as a device for accommodating regional concerns and demands is perceived to suffer from the same basic limitations as the House of Commons since both reflect majoritarian tendencies and decisions in caucus or the cabinet are made behind closed doors. Furthermore, it is often argued that the organizational rationalization of the cabinet that has occurred in recent decades has further limited the ability of the cabinet to accommodate and reconcile regional claims and demands. Nevertheless, some studies indicate that regional ministers have continued to play a significant role in the making of policy.[8] This has

---

7   Constitutional Committee of the Québec Liberal Party, *A New Canadian Federation* (Montreal, 1980), recommendations 5 and 7, pp. 39-40, 45-47.
8   Herman Bakvis, "Regional Politics and Policy in the Mulroney Cabinet 1984-88: Towards a Theory of the Regional Minister System in Canada," *Canadian Public Policy*, vol. 15, no. 2, June 1989, pp. 121-134.

been a natural response to the regional pressures exerted upon the federal government in any federation.

The tension between the two impulses — the technocratic and the regional — will continue, and any effective federal executive will have to achieve a balance between the two. If that balance is to be attained, conscious efforts will need to be made to overcome the actual and perceived unresponsiveness of federal officialdom to the provinces and regions, and to ensure a more effective input of regional concerns into central executive and administrative decision-making. A number of steps might be considered for countering the general disposition of the structure and operation of the federal government to downplay values and interests that are spatially delimited. These include the structuring of central agencies so as to provide more regional information upon which the cabinet and the prime minister can base policy decisions, the decentralization of federal departments and agencies incorporating a regional dimension into departmental planning and policy development, and arrangements for ensuring that those reaching senior executive positions in the public service have served both in the field and in the national capital region.[9] Most such reforms would not require formal constitutional amendments to be achieved.

The Symbolic Executive

Canada from its inception as a federation has been a constitutional monarchy, a feature that distinguishes it from the republic to the south. The question of the monarchy's continued utility as a unifying symbol at a time when Canadians of British stock have become a minority needs to be considered. The meaningfulness of the symbolic executive would seem to be limited not only for those in Quebec but for the many Canadians elsewhere whose roots lie in continental Europe, Asia or Africa. Is the monarchy as a symbol of unity now more divisive than unifying?

Raising the issue of abolishing the monarchy, however, is itself likely to stir considerable controversy, especially among the minority who find in it significant symbolic value. Such opposition might well be counter-productive to the effort to find grounds for more common agreement. Since the issue of the monarchy is not at the moment one of explicit contention, it may be more fruitful to concentrate upon those features of the federal institutions where there is overt contention rather than to create yet another.

---

9   See, for instance, Royal Commission on the Economic Union and Development Prospects for Canada, *Report*, vol. 3, (Ottawa: Minister of Supply and Services, Canada, 1985), pp. 92-95, 464-5.

The House of Commons

Calls for reform of the House of Commons to improve its representativeness have generally proceeded from two main perspectives. The first asserts that the influence of the political parties is too strong and that members of Parliament (MPs) unduly subordinate the interests of the regions, provinces and localities from which they come to party interests. Consequently, there have been numerous suggestions that party cohesion should be weakened. The second perspective argues that there is a need to ensure that representation of the parties in the House of Commons reflects more accurately the degree of support for them in each province. In certain periods major parties have been shut out of major regions of the country, even though they draw a significant proportion of the popular vote in those regions. The deficiency can be remedied, it is claimed, by changes to the electoral system. The following sections deal with these two issues.

Pervasiveness of party. Many Canadian exponents of the enhanced independence of MPs are explicitly or implicitly thinking in terms of the independence from party enjoyed by American legislators. Such independence of legislators is possible within the American and Swiss systems of the separation of powers in which the tenure of the executive does not depend on the continuing support of legislative majorities. However, these models have little relevance so long as we maintain the parliamentary system. All parliamentary systems with responsible cabinets have been marked by strong party discipline and cohesion.

Nevertheless, the degree of party cohesion in the contemporary Canadian House of Commons is high even by comparison with other parliamentary systems such as Britain. Studies have suggested that this is attributable more to self-imposed norms than to the sanctions at the disposal of the party leaders and also to the active role that party caucuses have assumed since the late 1960s. While it was hoped that the major overhaul of the committee system in 1968-69 would give MPs increased opportunity to act independently of their respective parties, in practice partisanship has permeated the committees just as it has the other dimensions of parliamentary life. As long as the cabinet is responsible to the House of Commons, the Commons will continue to act in a relatively cohesive way, despite the wishes of many outside the House that backbench MPs should act otherwise. Moreover, it should not be overlooked that the requirement of party cohesion is one of the processes for reconciling differences and finding implementing solutions where there is a diversity of opinion represented within the party. One of the problems, however, is that in parliamentary systems these compromises are worked out in party caucuses behind closed doors. In the age of heightened television and media attention a key problem with caucus secrecy and party discipline is that opportunity is not provided for federal parliamentarians to be seen to be representing regional or other diverse interests. Nevertheless, the degree of overt party voting might be moderated if it were more generally recognized by the House of Commons and by the public that only defeats on a specific vote of confidence would require the government to resign or the prime minister to request a dissolution. The posturing and media attention that accompanies every case where a private MP of the governing party fails to vote with the government might then be reduced.

Changes in the electoral system. The second major set of possible reforms involving the House of Commons relates to the electoral system. Compared to many other countries Canadians have been remarkably conservative about their federal electoral system. During the 1970s and 1980s, elections to the House of Commons which over-represented regional majority votes and returned virtually no Liberals from the west and almost no Progressive Conservatives from Quebec led many students of Canadian politics to see the electoral system itself as a cause of disunity. As a result in recent years a number of specific proposals for electoral reform have been advanced. Their major impulse has been to bring the distribution of seats won by each party in the various provinces more in line with the proportion of the popular vote cast for each. Many of them would involve some form or element of proportional representation.

Electoral reformers have tended to overestimate the extent to which the electoral system explains the behaviour of federal parties towards the provinces and regions. Nevertheless, there is good reason to attempt to reduce the distorting effect of the current electoral system and its impact upon party behaviour. The major objectives of electoral reform should be to make the House of Commons more effectively representative and give political parties more incentives than they now have to build support in areas where they are weak. Such reforms might be expected also to enhance representation of women and other groups now relatively under-represented in the Commons. Some variant of proportional representation such as the use of the single transferable vote in multimember urban ridings and the alternative vote procedure in other areas may be worth considering.[10] While electoral reform is no panacea, it may contribute towards a more representative House of Commons and hence improve its legitimacy as a focal point for federal policy-making. Under existing constitutional provisions electoral reform could be achieved by ordinary legislation and would not require a formal constitutional amendment.

---

10 For an elaboration of such a proposal see Donald Smiley and Ronald L. Watts, *Intrastate Federalism in Canada* (Toronto: University of Toronto Press, 1985), pp. 113-115.

The Senate

The federal institution that has received the most attention during the past two decades as a candidate for reform has been the Senate.[11] This is hardly surprising since among federations Canada does less than any other to use the second chamber as a body for ensuring effective participation for distinctive regional and minority interests in the formation of federal policies and decisions. Nearly all other federations have found a bicameral central legislature (i.e., with two houses) essential. The few rare exceptions have been cases where the constituent units have been given equal representation in a unicameral legislature. While from time to time, and most recently in the Allaire report of the Quebec Liberal Party, abolition of the Senate without any replacement has been advocated in Canada, and that would seem to fly in the face of federal experience elsewhere.

Federal second chambers elsewhere. These have taken a variety of forms. In terms of method of appointment members may be: (1) directly elected, as is now the case in the United States, Switzerland and Australia; (2) indirectly elected (i.e., chosen by state legislatures), as was originally the case in the United States and Switzerland and is now the case for most second chamber members in India and Malaysia (a small proportion in the former and a substantial number in the latter are appointed by the central government to represent particular minorities or interests); or (3) appointed as delegates of the state governments as in the German Bundesrat. In Switzerland the method of selection is left to each canton to decide.

In terms of composition, constituent units may be: (1) equally represented, as in the United States, Australia and Malaysia; (2) represented by categories, as in Switzerland (where 20 cantons classed as full cantons have two seats each and six cantons classed as half cantons have one seat each); or (3) based on some formula related to population, but giving additional weighting to smaller states, as in Germany and India.

In terms of formal powers relative to the first chambers, those in the United States and Switzerland have formally equal powers, but those in all the parliamentary federations, where the cabinet is responsible to the first house, have more limited formal powers. Nevertheless, the powers of the Australian Senate and the German Bundesrat are not inconsiderable. The Australian Senate can in some circumstances force a government to face the electorate through a "double dissolution" (i.e., calling an election for both the Senate and the lower house, the House of Representatives). The German Bundesrat possesses an

---

11 For a summary of many of the proposals, see, Attorney General of Ontario, *Rethinking the Senate: A Discussion Paper* (Toronto, 1990), pp. 51-101.

absolute veto over all federal legislation in the extensive areas of concurrent jurisdiction.

Canadian proposals for a "house of the provinces. " In Canada the late 1970s saw many proposals for establishing a body composed of persons appointed by and taking their instructions from the provincial governments on the lines of the German Bundesrat.[12] Canadian critics of these proposals have feared that such a "house of the provinces" might operate as a "house of obstruction" preventing effective and cohesive federal action. Such critics have overlooked the integrative dynamics that in practice have been induced by the Bundesrat. This occurs in intergovernmental relations because Bundesrat decisions do not require unanimity, thus reducing the leverage of hold-out states. The Bundesrat also has an integrative influence on federal-state party relations because state election results affect the ability of a governing federal party to achieve its legislative objectives in the Bundesrat. This has made the governing parties more sensitive to state interests. A more valid criticism is to point out that the significant role of the Bundesrat derives from the particular form which the distribution of jurisdiction between the federal and state governments takes in Germany. The constitution requires administration by the states for a large area of federal legislation. This makes the consent of a majority of the states (through the Bundesrat) for such legislation a necessary vehicle for coordination. In Canada where most executive powers are assigned to the same government as that having legislative jurisdiction the context is different.

Canadian proposals for an elected Senate. More recently, during the past decade, attention has shifted to proposals for a Senate whose members would be directly elected by the Canadian people.[13] The overwhelming popular preference for this alternative derives from its clearly democratic appearance. A major focus of interest in western Canada, arising out of a continued sense of lack of influence in Ottawa, has been the advocacy of a Triple E Senate,

---

12 Among such proposals were those of British Columbia (1978), the Ontario Advisory Committee on Confederation (1978), the Progressive Conservative Party of Canada (1978), the Canada West Foundation (1978), the Canadian Bar Association (1978), the Task Force on Canadian Unity (Pepin-Robarts) (1979), the Quebec Liberal Party (Beige Paper) (1980), and the Government of Alberta (1982).

13 Among such proposals have been those of the Canada West Foundation (1981), the Minister of Justice of the Government of Canada (1983), the Special Joint Committee of the Senate and the House of Commons on Senate Reform (1984), the Royal Commission on the Economic Union and Development Prospects for Canada (Macdonald) (1985), the Alberta Special Select Committee on Upper House Reform (1985), the Government of Newfoundland and Labrador (1989), Gordon Robertson in *A House Divided* (1989), and the First Ministers' Meeting on the Constitution, Final Communiqué, 9 June 1990.

elected directly, equal in representation from every province, and effective in power. While some have questioned the appropriateness of such a Senate for Canada because of its parliamentary institutions, the Australian Senate which is in every respect a Triple-E Senate shows that such a body is not incompatible with a system of parliamentary responsible government. The tentative June 1990 constitutional agreement arrived at by the first ministers in Ottawa when they were attempting to save the Meech Lake Accord set out a process involving a commission of federal, provincial and territorial representatives to prepare specific proposals for Senate reform. The commission was to give effect to the following objectives:

- The Senate should be elected.
- The Senate should provide for more equitable representation of the less populous provinces and territories.
- The Senate should have effective powers to ensure the interests of residents of the less populous provinces and territories figure more prominently in national decision-making, reflect Canadian duality and strengthen the Government of Canada's capacity to govern on behalf of all citizens, while preserving the principle of responsibility of the Government to the House of Commons.

That agreement died with the demise of the Meech Lake Accord, but it indicates the direction in which agreement upon Senate reform might be possible to achieve.

The general principle of a Senate directly elected by the people appears to be popular among the general public. It has two particular attractions. First, it suggests a way of specifically representing the interests of the provincial electorates within the federal institutions while bypassing the provincial governments. Second, a directly elected Senate employing a method of proportional representation (as occurs in Australia) would provide another way of correcting electoral distortions in Ottawa.

Equal representation of all provinces has been a major element in western Canadian proposals for Senate reform. This is understandable given the present representation by under-representation of the four western provinces. Not only do each of them have fewer senators than the less populous provinces of Nova Scotia and New Brunswick, but the two largest provinces (Ontario and Quebec) are actually somewhat more favourably represented in relation to their population than British Columbia and Alberta. This is clearly a ridiculous anomaly with no justification. But the proposal for equal representation of provinces, often advocated as the solution, in turn raises particular difficulties in the Canadian context. The function of federal second chambers as a check on majoritarian interests is not simply to favour the representation of smaller provinces but also of nonmajoritarian minority interests in general. In the

Canadian case this presents a particular problem: equal representation for all provincial units would require reducing the representation of the one province whose majority is French-speaking from its current 23 percent to 10 percent. This clearly violates the principle of reinforcing the representation of significant federal minorities.

To balance these two pressures the distribution of seats in the Senate will have to be a pragmatic one, weighted to favour the less populous provinces and territories, but also taking account of the special needs for both adequate francophone and aboriginal representation while at the same time correcting the present anomalies. This requirement was recognized in the communiqué of the First Ministers' Meeting on 9 June 1990 identifying the objectives of a "more equitable" representation of the less populous provinces and territories and of the need to "reflect Canadian duality." A number of proposals have attempted to make major corrections in regional representation along these lines (See Table 16.1). An alternative or supplementary approach would be to adopt rules of procedure requiring special majorities or the concurrence of Quebec representatives or of francophone representatives on legislation identified as being in areas of their special interest.

A number of other federations, notably India and Malaysia, have reserved a number of places in the federal second chamber for members nominated to represent special minority interests. Such an approach might be incorporated in a reformed Canadian Senate to guarantee a minimum number of seats to representatives of the aboriginal peoples. A system of election rather than nomination for these reserved seats would be preferable, however.

A persuasive case can be made that a popularly elected Senate should have effective powers to influence and even to obstruct governments backed by House of Commons majorities. Some of the hesitation about establishing a strong elected Senate appears to have arisen from a fear that such a Senate would undermine the principle of responsible cabinet government and from Canadian interpretations of the Australian constitutional crisis of 1975. Closer analysis of Australian experience suggests, however, that while an effective Senate at the federal level will inevitably operate in tension with cabinet government, the existence of a powerful and autonomous upper house in the federal institutions helps in practice to ensure that the values implicit in federalism are pervasive in the system.[14]

Senate reform would be an important element in improving the effectiveness of our federal institutions. At the same time Canadians should be wary of expecting too much from Senate reform by itself. It will be no panacea. It is

---

14 Campbell Sharman, "Second Chambers," in H. Bakvis and W.H. Chandler (eds.), *Federalism and the Role of the State* (Toronto: University of Toronto Press, 1987), p. 96.

Table 16.1
Senate Composition Schemes

Prov	Current by province	Current by region	Joint Committee, 1972 by province	Joint Committee, 1972 by region	Bill C-60, 1978 by province	Bill C-60, 1978 by region	British Columbia, 1978 by province	British Columbia, 1978 by region	Task Force, 1979 by province	Task Force, 1979 by region	Ont. Adv. Comm., 1978-9 by province	Ont. Adv. Comm., 1978-9 by region	Quebec Beige Paper, 1980 by province	Quebec Beige Paper, 1980 by region
Nfld	6 (5.8)	30 (28.8)	6 (4.6)	30 (23)	8 (6.8)	32 (27.1)	3 (5)	12 (20)	4 (6.7)	14 (23.3)	2 (6.7)	7 (23.3)	3 (3.8)	13 (16.3)
PEI	4 (3.8)		4 (3.0)		4 (3.4)		3 (5)		2 (3.3)		1 (3.3)		2 (2.5)	
NS	10 (9.6)		10 (7.7)		10 (8.5)		3 (5)		4 (6.7)		2 (6.7)		4 (5.0)	
NB	10 (9.6)		10 (7.7)		10 (8.5)		3 (5)		4 (6.7)		2 (6.7)		4 (5.0)	
Que	24 (23)	24 (23)	24 (18.5)	24 (18.5)	24 (20.3)	24 (20.3)	12 (20)	12 (20)	12 (20)	12 (20)	6 (20)	6 (20)	20 (25)	20 (25)
Ont	24 (23)	24 (23)	24 (18.5)	24 (18.5)	24 (20.3)	24 (20.3)	12 (20)	12 (20)	12 (20)	12 (20)	6 (20)	6 (20)	20 (25)	20 (25)
Man	6 (5.8)	24 (23)	12 (9.2)	48 (37)	8 (6.8)	36 (30.5)	4 (6.7)	12 (20)	4 (6.7)	22 (36.7)	2 (6.7)	11 (36.7)	5 (6.3)	27 (33.8)
Sask	6 (5.8)		12 (9.2)		8 (6.8)		4 (6.7)		4 (6.7)		2 (6.7)		5 (6.3)	
Alta	6 (5.8)		12 (9.2)		10 (8.5)		4 (6.7)		6 (10)		3 (10)		8 (10)	
BC	6 (5.8)		12 (9.2)		10 (8.5)		12 (20)		8 (13.3)		4 (13.3)		9 (11.3)	
Ykn	1 (1.0)	2 (1.9)	2 (1.5)	4 (3.0)	1 (0.8)	2 (1.7)	-	-	-	-	-	-	-	-
NWT	1 (1.0)		2 (1.5)		1 (0.8)		-		-		-		-	
Total	104 (100)	104 (100)	130 (100)	130 (100)	118 (100)	118 (100)	60 (100)	60 (100)	60 (100)	60 (100)	30 (100)	30 (100)	80 (100)	80 (100)

Prov	Canada West, 1981 by province	Canada West, 1981 by region	Joint Committee, 1984 by province	Joint Committee, 1984 by region	Alberta Comm., 1985 by province	Alberta Comm., 1985 by region	Macdonald Comm., 1985 by province	Macdonald Comm., 1985 by region	Newfoundland, 1989 by province	Newfoundland, 1989 by region	Ghiz Proposal, 1990 by province	Ghiz Proposal, 1990 by region	Ottawa, June 1990 by province	Ottawa, June 1990 by region
Nfld	6 (9.7)	24 (38.7)	12 (8.3)	42 (29.2)	6 (9.4)	24 (37.5)	12 (8.3)	42 (29.2)	10 (9.6)	40 (38.5)	10 (8.0)	35 (28.0)	8 (7.7)	28 (26.9)
PEI	6 (9.7)		6 (4.2)		6 (9.4)		6 (4.2)		10 (9.6)		5 (4.0)		4 (3.8)	
NS	6 (9.7)		12 (8.3)		6 (9.4)		12 (8.3)		10 (9.6)		10 (8.0)		8 (7.7)	
NB	6 (9.7)		12 (8.3)		6 (9.4)		12 (8.3)		10 (9.6)		10 (8.0)		8 (7.7)	
Que	6 (9.7)	6 (9.7)	24 (16.7)	24 (16.7)	6 (9.4)	6 (9.4)	24 (16.7)	24 (16.7)	10 (9.6)	10 (9.6)	24 (19.2)	24 (19.2)	24 (23.1)	24 (23.1)
Ont	6 (9.7)	6 (9.7)	24 (16.7)	24 (16.7)	6 (9.4)	6 (9.4)	24 (16.7)	24 (16.7)	10 (9.6)	10 (9.6)	24 (19.2)	24 (19.2)	18 (17.3)	18 (17.3)
Man	6 (9.7)	24 (38.7)	12 (8.3)	48 (33.3)	6 (9.4)	24 (37.5)	12 (8.3)	48 (33.3)	10 (9.6)	40 (38.5)	10 (8.0)	40 (32.0)	8 (7.7)	32 (30.8)
Sask	6 (9.7)		12 (8.3)		6 (9.4)		12 (8.3)		10 (9.6)		10 (8.0)		8 (7.7)	
Alta	6 (9.7)		12 (8.3)		6 (9.4)		12 (8.3)		10 (9.6)		10 (8.0)		8 (7.7)	
BC	6 (9.7)		12 (8.3)		6 (9.4)		12 (8.3)		10 (9.6)		10 (8.0)		8 (7.7)	
Ykn	1 (1.6)	2 (3.2)	2 (1.3)	6 (4.2)	2 (3.1)	4 (6.3)	3 (2.0)	6 (4.2)	2 (1.9)	4 (3.8)	1 (0.8)	2 (1.6)	1 (1.0)	2 (1.9)
NWT	1 (1.6)		4 (2.8)		2 (3.1)		3 (2.0)		2 (1.9)		1 (0.8)		1 (1.0)	
Total	62 (100)	62 (100)	144 (100)	144 (100)	64 (100)	64 (100)	144 (100)	144 (100)	104 (100)	104 (100)	125 (100)	125 (100)	104 (100)	104 (100)

* percentages may not add up to exactly 100 due to rounding.

Source: prepared by the Institute of Intergovernmental Relations, Queen's University (June 1990)

only one element in a total solution. As long as a Senate operates within a system of parliamentary responsible government, there will be limits to its impact. The Australian example shows that an effective elected Senate can operate within a system of parliamentary institutions. But that experience also indicates that it will not diminish the tendency to "executive federalism" as the primary mode of intergovernmental relations within parliamentary federations, nor diminish the predominance of party coherence. To press for a Senate isolated from party ties is to confine the Senate to virtual irrelevance in a parliamentary system where parties are a fundamental part of the political process. The primary contribution of an effective elected Senate would be to sensitize the federal parties to the need to accommodate provincial and minority concerns. As Campbell Sharman has put it: effective bicameralism "is the ally of federalism; both imply preference for incremental rather than radical change, for negotiated rather than coerced solutions, and for responsiveness to a range of political preferences rather than the artificial simplicity of dichotomous choice."[15]

Federal Institutions in an Asymmetrical Federation

There remains the issue of the arrangements and procedures within the federal institutions that might be required in a federation with a significant asymmetry in the distribution of powers — i.e., one providing substantially greater legislative and executive autonomy for one or more provinces. Since an element of asymmetry is one of the possible options for a revised Canadian federation, the implications for the operation of the federal institutions must be considered. The basic issue raised in the earlier chapters by Alan Cairns and David Milne is whether representatives from provinces with more autonomy should vote in federal institutions on those subjects where their province has autonomy.

In other federations where asymmetry in the distribution of powers has not been substantial or has resulted from incremental delegations of authority over time, no such adjustments have been made. Indeed, while the *Constitution Act, 1867*, included some asymmetrical features, no corresponding adjustment of provincial representation in federal institutions was envisaged. Nor did the asymmetry relating to the separation of the Canada and Quebec Pension Plans in the 1960s lead to any change in the role of Quebec MPs. The issue appears to come to the fore only where the degree of asymmetry is substantial.

Reduction of representation in federal institutions. Other federations such as India, Pakistan, and Germany (in the arrangements for German reunification) have involved a considerable measure of jurisdictional asymmetry without limiting the participation of the representatives of the more autonomous units

---

15 Ibid., p. 96.

in deliberations within the federal institutions. However, the Federation of Malaysia after the accession of the Borneo states and Singapore in 1963, and the Federation of Rhodesia and Nyasaland 1953-63, provide significant examples of federations where some states with more autonomy were given reduced representation in the central legislature.[16] In the case of Singapore, to balance its greater autonomy, the proportion of its representation in the central legislature was reduced (to 9 percent although its population was 17 percent of the federal total) and the federal franchise of Singapore citizens outside Singapore was restricted. The consequent resentment in Singapore, and the annoyance of the federal governing party at the failure of the different governing party in Singapore to confine its activities to its own state, resulted in mounting tension that culminated in the complete separation of Singapore only two years after it joined the federation. By contrast, when the two Borneo states, Sarawak and Sabah, joined the Malaysian Federation at the same time as Singapore, and were also granted substantially greater autonomy than the other states in the federation, they did not have the same disabilities in terms of representation applied to them. They have continued to the present as member states of the Malaysian Federation. The experience of Singapore and also of the Federation of Rhodesia and Nyasaland which lasted for only a decade suggests that the reduction in the number of representatives in the federal legislature for a more autonomous province does not work well as a solution. It is likely to foster an increased sense that the citizens of that province are second-class citizens in the federation and lead to federal instability and perhaps disintegration in the long run.

Special voting rules and procedures. An alternative adjustment to reducing the representation of the more autonomous provinces in the federal legislature, is to adopt voting rules and procedures whereby these representatives would abstain in votes on matters over which their province has autonomous jurisdiction. This might involve some complexity and difficulties in deciding when these representatives should not vote, but procedural rules should not be impossible to devise. The German Bundesrat has an absolute veto over matters that are under concurrent jurisdiction and only a suspensive veto over matters that are under exclusive federal jurisdiction. The line between the two has not always been easy to draw, but it has been workable. Given that experience, it should be no more difficult to define procedures for when representatives of a more autonomous province should abstain in voting within the federal legislature. Such an arrangement would certainly be a more logical solution than reducing the proportionate representation of the more autonomous provinces

---

16 Ronald L. Watts, *Multicultural Societies and Federalism*, Study no. 8 for the Royal Commission on Bilingualism and Biculturalism (Ottawa: Information Canada, 1970), pp. 47-50.

within the federal institutions, thereby also reducing their weight in federal policy-making in those areas that do affect them.

OTHER FEDERATIVE INSTITUTIONS

Regulatory Agencies

While it is appropriate to avoid as far as possible unnecessary and costly duplication in the jurisdiction of federal and provincial governments, in practice no federal system has been able to avoid overlaps. One area where this situation has a particular significance is in the operation of major regulatory agencies. Concern is often expressed that such bodies established by the federal government are insensitive to the needs and concerns of the constituent governments and the different groups and regions of Canada. Consequently, it has been argued that "the constitution should state the principle that federal bodies charged with the responsibilities in key sectors of Canadian affairs and those of a political nature must reflect the duality and regional character of Canada."[17] One approach to realizing this objective is to provide provincial governments with a role in appointments to major regulatory agencies including the Bank of Canada. Indeed, the Constitutional Committee of the Quebec Liberal Party (Allaire) has argued for reform of the Bank of Canada to ensure regional representation, citing the Federal Reserve of the United States as an example.[18]

The Macdonald Commission recommended that regional representation should receive consideration in nominations to the boards of crown corporations and regulatory agencies in order to enhance their political legitimacy and improve their sensitivity to regional concerns. It went on to suggest that a reformed elected Senate with strengthened regional representation would be the appropriate body to scrutinize through a committee all appointments of the heads of crown corporations and all the members of major regulatory agencies.[19] Such a public process of appointment would both promote greater public confidence in the representative character of such bodies and encourage these bodies to be more sensitive to regional considerations in conducting their operations and coming to decisions.

---

17 *A New Canadian Federation*, recommendation 8.2, p. 50.
18 Constitutional Committee of the Québec Liberal Party, *A Québec Free to Choose: Report of the Constitutional Committee*: (Montreal: Québec Liberal Party, 1991), pp. 42 and 62.
19 *Report*, vol. 3, pp. 464-465.

Collaborative Institutions

In confederal systems, the common institutions of the federative superstructure tend to be primarily collaborative in form, being composed of delegates of the constituent governments and dealing primarily with areas for collaborative action.

But even in federations, where common federal institutions directly representing and acting upon the citizens are established, there is a need for institutions facilitating collaboration between the federal and provincial and among the provincial governments. The notion of a strictly dual federal polity of two tiers of government operating independently of each other has in all federations proved both impossible and undesirable in practice. While it is appropriate to avoid as far as possible unnecessary and costly duplication in the responsibilities of governments within a federation, overlaps can never be completely avoided. All federations have found it necessary, therefore, to establish institutions and processes to facilitate consultation, cooperation, coordination and harmonization, and to moderate intergovernmental conflict in those areas where the activities of their governments interpenetrate.

While greater intergovernmental harmonization is desirable, the diversity of action inherent in a federal system also makes a positive contribution to society. A balance must be found, therefore, between encouraging institutional diversity or competition and establishing institutions and procedures producing federal-provincial coordination. Furthermore, in parliamentary federations, where "executive federalism" is a logical dynamic resulting from the marriage of federal and parliamentary institutions and is, therefore, unavoidable, there is a need to harness "executive federalism" in order to make it more effective and accountable.

Informal and formal collaborative institutions. Most often in federations the intergovernmental collaborative bodies and procedures have not been specified in the constitutions, but have been established simply by agreement as the need arose. This has the advantage of enabling flexible and pragmatic arrangements. Nevertheless, in some federations intergovernmental institutions have actually been specified in the constitutions. In some of these cases there are special voting rules that do not necessarily require unanimity, and in some these bodies have powers to make decisions binding upon the participating governments. Among such examples are the Australian Loans Council, the German Bundesrat which shapes the character of intergovernmental relations in that federation, and a variety of councils and commissions established in the newer parliamentary federations in the Commonwealth.

Canadian proposals. In Canada, by contrast with the examples referred to above, there has been some resistance to constitutionalizing such arrangements for fear that they might encroach upon the sovereignty of Parliament and of the provincial legislatures. Nevertheless, there is a need to improve the operation of our intergovernmental collaborative institutions. The Quebec Liberal Party's Beige Paper of 1980 advanced an interesting proposal in this respect for an "intergovernmental institution which will frame the interdependence of the two orders of government." [20] The proposed Federal Council would have involved weighted representation of different provincial governments and territories and a voting procedure not requiring unanimity. The Federal Council would have had advisory powers in certain areas, and powers of ratification in others. There would have been a "Dualist Committee" with advisory or ratification powers in some other specified areas relating to the maintenance of cultural duality. While envisaged as a body supplementing a unicameral federal parliament, a revised adaptation of this proposal could serve as a supplement to a bicameral federal parliament even with a reformed Senate.

A less radical approach directed at making "executive federalism" more effective was that of the Macdonald Commission in 1985.[21] While emphasizing the value of intergovernmental diversity and competition, it proposed (1) that the First Ministers' Conference be formally established in the constitution with the requirement that it meet at least once a year; (2) that the First Ministers' Conference appoint a network of Councils of Ministers to serve in major functional policy areas and particularly in the fields of finance, economic development and social policy, and (3) that to ensure that governments are held accountable for their conduct of intergovernmental affairs, Parliament and the provincial legislatures should establish permanent standing committees responsible for intergovernmental relations. These proposals could all be implemented without having to resort to formal constitutional amendments.

The Allaire report of the Quebec Liberal Party, after defining a restricted list in which Parliament would share authority with Quebec and other provinces, suggests that "as far as the coordinating functions are concerned, the decisions of Parliament will have to be ratified by the Quebec National Assembly and the assemblies of all the other legislatures (provincial or regional) that have adopted the same approach as Quebec."[22] It goes on to suggest that specific targets would be set to limit severely the power of central institutions to contract debts. These proposals are only sketched out and, therefore, the full implications are not clear. They do seem to imply that any coordination in areas of shared jurisdiction would require the formal consent of the legislatures of the provinces involved rather than mere intergovernmental agreement implying a primarily confederal rather than a federal arrangement. The reference to limits on the

---

20 *A New Canadian Federation*, recommendation 9, pp. 51-56.
21 *Report*, vol. 3, pp. 473-475.
22 Constitutional Committee of the Québec Liberal Party, *A Québec Free to Choose*, p. 41.

contracting of debts might require a body like the Australian Loans Council. That body coordinates public borrowing but makes decisions binding on both federal and state governments.

Adjudicative Bodies: The Supreme Court

Adjudicative institutions for resolving jurisdictional disputes between governments in federations have most often taken the form of a Supreme Court. Examples elsewhere are the United States, Australia, India, and Malaysia. An alternative is the establishment of a specialized constitutional court dealing only with constitutional matters, as in Germany. In Switzerland, cantonal legislation is subject to judicial review by the Federal Tribunal, but adjudication of the validity of federal legislation involves the process of the legislative referendum.

In the past there have been few proposals for Canada to abandon employing the Supreme Court as the ultimate constitutional adjudicative body. But if the Supreme Court is to be the ultimate umpire in disputes between governments, it is anomalous that its status is not entrenched in the constitution and that appointments to it are solely in the hands of only one of the governments: the federal government.

Arrangements in other federations. In most federations the status of the Supreme Court, Constitutional Court or Federal Tribunal is entrenched in the constitution. Furthermore, appointments are not made simply by the federal executive but involve the states (or their representatives) through one of the following: (a) the requirement of Senate ratification, as in the United States; (b) appointment of half the members by the state governments, as in effect occurs in Germany through the Bundesrat; or (c) the requirement of prior consultation either with state governments or chief justices of the state high courts as occurs in Australia, Malaysia, and India.

Canadian proposals. Various proposals relating to the procedure for appointments to the Supreme Court have been advanced in Canada such as the constitutional requirement of mandatory consultation with the provinces, ratification by a reformed Senate, ratification of federal appointments by provinces, nomination by federal-provincial nominating commissions, or selection by an Appointing Council composed of both federal and provincial appointees. The Meech Lake Accord proposed a system of federal government appointments from lists of provincial nominations. If the Supreme Court is to continue as the ultimate constitutional adjudicator, there still remains, as a result of the demise of the Meech Lake Accord, the need to entrench in the constitution the status of the Supreme Court as the ultimate adjudicative body. This should include a procedure for appointments that does not leave them solely at the discretion of one level of government. Of the various appointment procedures that have been advocated, two would seem to recommend themselves most for consideration. One would be mandatory consultation of the provinces by the federal government prior to it making nominations that would have to be ratified by a reformed Senate. The other would be appointments by an independent Appointing Council, half of whose members would be appointed by the federal government and half by the provincial governments.[23]

The Allaire report of the Quebec Liberal Party proposes a special "common tribunal to ensure compliance with the Constitution and enforcement of laws under the new central state."[24] It would not act as a court of appeal for Quebec courts and decisions of Quebec superior courts would no longer be subject to appeal to the Supreme Court of Canada. Under this proposal the Supreme Court of Canada would no longer be the ultimate constitutional adjudicative body, that function being performed by the new common tribunal. The details are not spelled out and so it is not clear whether this tribunal would be limited to ruling on the constitutionality of central and not provincial actions, or whether it would be a specialized constitutional court ruling on all constitutional matters along the lines of that in Germany. In any case the elimination of appeals from the Quebec courts would contrast with the stronger judicial authority of the European Court. The proposal will clearly need clarification.

CONCLUSIONS

The effectiveness and stability of any future federal or confederal union in Canada will depend not only upon the way in which jurisdiction is distributed between the common and constituent governments but also upon the federative superstructure that is established. Historically the predominantly collaborative form of federative superstructure that typifies confederal systems has been less effective than those normally associated with federal systems. But even among federations there is considerable variety in the form that the central institutions may take. While a fixed-term collegial executive and legislature has much to recommend it, there appears to be continued general support in Canada for parliamentary institutions. Consequently, the appropriate path would seem to be to retain those parliamentary institutions, but to reform them substantially to improve their effectiveness in managing the responsibilities assigned to the

---

23 For the latter proposal see C.F. Beckton and A.W. MacKay, *Recurring Issues in Canadian Federalism*, Research Studies of the Royal Commission on the Economic Union and Development Prospects for Canada, vol. 57 (Toronto: University of Toronto Press, 1986), pp. 60-61.

24 Constitutional Committee of the Québec Liberal Party, *A Québec Free to Choose*, pp. 42 and 62.

federal government and to provide greater confidence in their representativeness in terms of provincial interests, of Canadian duality and of significant minorities including the aboriginal peoples.

A number of reforms that do not require formal constitutional amendment could be made to achieve a better balance between the technocratic and regional impulses within the executive and administration. In the case of the House of Commons there is a need to reduce the pervasiveness of party cohesion. This could be done through a more general recognition by the House of Commons and the public that only defeats on a specific vote of confidence would require the government to resign or the prime minister to request a dissolution. To improve the representativeness of the House of Commons electoral reform involving some variant of proportional representation may be worth considering.

While it should not be considered a panacea, Senate reform would be an important element in improving both the effectiveness and representativeness of our federal institutions. An elected and effective Senate can be compatible with parliamentary institutions. The need for more equitable representation of the less populous provinces and territories will need to be balanced against the need to reflect adequately Canadian duality and the need to provide reserved representation for representatives of the aboriginal peoples.

Should constitutional revision involve a substantial measure of asymmetry in the allocation of jurisdiction to the provinces, voting rules and procedures will need to be developed for both Houses of Parliament limiting the votes of the representatives of a province on those matters where their province has autonomous jurisdiction.

Steps should also be taken to improve the legitimacy and effectiveness of federal and regulatory agencies, the intergovernmental collaborative institutions, and the ultimate constitutional adjudicative body. Regional representation on the major federal regulatory agencies would enhance their political legitimacy and improve their sensitivity to regional concerns. Executive federalism is an inevitable feature of any parliamentary federation, but it could be better harnessed by the establishment of standing legislative committees for intergovernmental relations to ensure greater accountability of governments for their conduct of intergovernmental affairs. The operation of the First Ministers' Conference might also be made more systematic. The status of the ultimate constitutional adjudicative body, the Supreme Court or possibly a separate specialized Constitutional Court, and the procedure for appointments to that body involving a role for both the federal and provincial governments, should be constitutionalized.

Such reforms to Canadian federal institutions could assist in restoring confidence in their representativeness and effectiveness. This in turn would make a major contribution to restoring a sense of legitimacy and loyalty to the Canadian federation.

17

Areas of Adjustment:
A Lawyer's Perspective

Katherine Swinton

The four papers in this volume dealing with areas of adjustment complement each other well. Professor Boadway suggests a design for the reallocation of powers in the Canadian federal system from an economist's perspective, while Professor Meekison, pessimistic about the political viability of efforts towards a major redesign of the distribution of powers, suggests an incremental approach to the reallocation of powers and, more importantly, an emphasis on the design and use of mechanisms that allow for less formal transfers of jurisdiction between governments, either temporarily or permanently. Professor Milne advocates the device of concurrent jurisdiction with provincial paramountcy as a way of enabling variations in the exercise of provincial autonomy within a framework of formal equality of status among the provinces. Professor Watts concentrates on the difficult issue of designing central institutions to deal with the pressures of regionalism.

The one area that did not receive mention, and that will undoubtedly be a part of future constitutional reform discussions, is the treatment of rights in the Canadian constitution, most specifically whether rights can be defined in a way that allows Quebec to protect her distinct nature, whether the override on Charter rights found in section 33 should continue in its present form, and whether language rights should continue to be pan-Canadian, rather than geographically determined. These are important issues, and ones that have divided us in the past, most recently in the Meech Lake Accord round. While they will not occupy as much time as the issues discussed in these papers, they cannot be ignored.

Turning to the content of the papers on which I have been asked to comment, I find it useful to start with Professor Meekison's. While he feels that it is impossible to obtain agreement on a complete overhaul of the distribution of powers, I doubt that we can escape a major debate about redesign. This is in part because Quebec will not proceed with incrementalism in the discussion of powers. There will undoubtedly be a large number of issues on the negotiating list, which will be supplemented by other actors.

But even Professor Meekison's suggested course of action immediately sets such a debate in train, since one of his proposals is an expanded notion of concurrency in selected areas. As a constitutional lawyer, I might note that the Canadian constitution now allows a very significant degree of concurrency (albeit that this is couched in the language of "double aspects"). However, he would expand these areas of overlap, as would an earlier contributor in these proceedings, Professor Milne, who also suggests greater concurrency. The difference between them is in the rules of paramountcy, with Meekison leaving primacy in the case of conflicting laws with the government that had jurisdiction before the move towards concurrency, and Milne advocating provincial primacy. The increase in concurrency, especially along Milne's lines, changes the distribution of powers in important ways, although not so obviously as an explicit transfer of jurisdiction between governments. For example, to make communications (now federal) a concurrent field, especially with provincial paramountcy, creates important changes in this policy area, allowing a diversity that many would find unattractive. Even Meekison's proposals for concurrency, with paramountcy remaining with the government that originally had the power, should give cause for serious debate, since the judiciary has given a very narrow definition to the doctrine of paramountcy.[1] This leaves much room for duplication and interference with policies of the other level of government that many would argue is unacceptable. Think of the limited value of concurrency in the area of securities regulation for the federal government if the provinces remain paramount. Moreover, think of the difficulties of protecting a policy based on the market, rather than government intervention, when conflict only arises if there are two conflicting statutes. In such a case, a federal communications policy emphasizing the market can be undercut by the provinces through regulation.

The legitimacy of future constitutional arrangements requires that concurrency not be put forth as a simple "mechanism" as if it does not change much. Depending on the chosen rules of paramountcy, there are important policy issues that accompany this change, and it would be foolhardy to try to obscure that fact.

Moreover, I doubt that Quebec would be satisfied with Meekison's proposal to emphasize mechanisms, at least as a first best response to its demands. Constitutions serve two major purposes in a society like Canada's: they create governmental institutions and allocate and circumscribe government powers; they also serve a symbolic function, as a statement of the principles and

---

1   *Multiple Access Ltd. v. McCutcheon* (1982), 138 *Dominion Law Reports* (3d) 1 at 23-24.

aspirations of a nation. Both these functions will lead to demands for clear constitutional changes in the distribution of powers. Quebec will be concerned about the adequacy of many of the devices suggested to protect its interests, especially if used in their present form. In particular, there is uncertainty about the enforceability of intergovernmental agreements, as demonstrated in recent litigation involving the Canada Assistance Plan.[2] As well, many of these mechanisms, in their present form, are subject to unilateral change by one government — for example, delegation. Therefore, Quebec, interested in protecting its interests in the best way possible in fields such as communications or financial instruments, should press for constitutional language that explicitly allocates these powers and provincial primacy to the province, since the special formulae for amendment of the constitution provide some protection through the ensuing rigidity.

Quebec will also have symbolic concerns about the Meekison proposal, since such flexibility (often found outside the formal constitutional document) fails to satisfy the demand for recognition of Quebec's distinct position in Canada. After the failure of the Meech Lake Accord, it will be important to Quebec nationalists to have a constitutional recognition and affirmation, in stronger language than that of the Accord, of Quebec's distinctness.

Thus, we cannot escape a major debate about the redistribution of powers that will be more than incremental. That brings me to Professor Boadway's paper. He rightly suggests that the debate should be guided by concerns of equity as well as efficiency, and he is well aware that those terms are not uncontroversial. While he advocates a theory of formal equality, there are many who would suggest that equality often requires that people be treated differently, not in the same way, in order to meet their specific needs and aspirations. Moreover, part of the debate must also involve concepts of community, for Canadians in all parts of the country will have to decide the community across which to measure efficiency or distributional objectives — and for many it will not be the nation as we know it today.

Professor Boadway has suggested a reallocation that lists different powers for the two levels of government. This suggests a concern that will be omnipresent in the debate, as it has been in past debates. That is the degree of overlap allowed between federal heads of power and, a related issue, the degree of detail we shall seek in the constitutional allocation. Those who see the problems of the present federal system as in some degree caused by duplication of effort and competition between levels of government often call for exclusivity in the allocation of powers. This suggests the need for more detail, rather than less,

---

2 *Reference re Canada Assistance Plan (B.C.)* (1990), 71 *Dominion Law Reports* (4th) 99 (B.C.C.A.), under appeal to the Supreme Court of Canada.

in the allocation of powers in order to make clear who is responsible for a certain policy area.

Yet there are problems with this search for detail in constitutions, as Meekison notes. Our imaginations are limited, and we cannot anticipate all the policy areas that may emerge over time. Thus, there must be a decision about the locus of the residuary power to deal with new matters. Indeed, the search for detail may be inconsistent with the nature of a constitution, which is a document meant to last. Thus, it should enshrine general concepts about governmental responsibilities, rather than particular conceptions of policy grounded in time.

Inevitably, constitutional language will be ambiguous, to some degree, to allow for change. Moreover, even if we try to spell out exclusive powers with minimal overlap, we must remember that language is inherently ambiguous and in need of interpretation. This has important political ramifications. Creative ambiguity can be important as a way of promoting agreement, as we saw in the early Meech Lake discussions among first ministers or as we see in most collective bargaining scenarios. Unfortunately, the ambiguity of language can also generate political opposition, as we saw in the opposition to Meech Lake by those who insisted on a degree of precision of meaning that could not be accepted at the political level in Quebec.

A second important ramification of the ambiguity of language is the role that it leaves to the courts, and especially the Supreme Court of Canada. No matter how precise we shall try to be in the language chosen for the new constitution, the courts will play an important interpretive and adaptive role, as we have seen with both the 1867 and 1982 *Constitution Acts*. A good example of the scope for judicial creativity is presented by one of Professor Boadway's suggestions that the environment should be a federal matter but municipal law should be provincial. Who then can regulate garbage disposal — one or both? And if both can do so (and should if many of the suggestions in this volume are followed and concurrency is to be sought), what constitutes "conflict" for purposes of paramountcy — inability to satisfy both laws? duplication? economic inefficiency? interference with the other government's policy? These are difficult questions that the courts will face, and while guided by the words of the constitution, the judges will also bring to the process the kinds of values that Boadway mentioned in his paper — concerns about efficiency, equity, community, individual rights, and political accountability.

This brings me to a final point about the design of our national institutions that extends beyond the Supreme Court to the other institutions discussed in Professor Watts' paper. He does an excellent job of considering alternative ways to incorporate regional interests in national institutions, including the Supreme Court. But it is absolutely vital that we remember that those are not the only interests that legitimately lay claim to participation in those bodies. We must also be vigilant to design institutions that make us attentive to the perspectives of women, aboriginal people, ethnic groups, the poor — all groups who have not dominated our political and social institutions, but who are important members of the society and who are no longer willing to be ignored in the policy process.

I do not mean to suggest that these groups are homogeneous, nor that they speak with one voice, nor that they see their gender, ethnicity, race or class as their primary defining characteristic at all times. Indeed, we all have multiple identities, and we may put more emphasis on one characteristic than another, depending on the issue, as we saw with the different approaches to the "distinct society" clause during the Meech Lake round by some English Canadian and Quebec women's groups. I do argue, though, that members of these groups have had different experiences from the white males who have dominated our decision-making institutions, and we must design our institutions to allow those experiences to be heard.

This is not to say that we need necessarily provide constitutional guarantees for women's seats in the House of Commons or on the Supreme Court, but we do need to think of ways to design institutions that are sensitive to the richness and diversity of Canadian society and that ensure regionalism is not the only measure of our diversity.

The redesign of institutions to bring in new perspectives may well change the agenda and the product of those bodies. Members from ethnic groups other than French and English might well question the policy of pan-Canadian bilingualism; representatives of certain women's groups were critical of any threat to Charter rights in the last round. These perspectives are important to the next round of constitutional negotiations. They may well influence the product of discussions in institutions like Peter Russell's constituent assembly. Their involvement, as well, can only help to increase the legitimacy of the product, both by educating them to the importance of regional forces and by allowing them to be heard by those with other perspectives.

DATE DUE